THE JOHN HARVARD LIBRARY

Bernard Bailyn
Editor-in-Chief

THE WORKS OF JAMES WILSON

Edited by Robert Green McCloskey

IN TWO VOLUMES

VOLUME II

THE BELKNAP PRESS OF
HARVARD UNIVERSITY PRESS
CAMBRIDGE, MASSACHUSETTS

1967

Distributed in Great Britain by Oxford University Press, London

John Harvard Library books are edited
at the Charles Warren Center for Studies
in American History, Harvard University.

Library of Congress Catalog Card Number 67-14344

Printed in the United States of America

CONTENTS

MISCELLANEOUS PAPERS

LECTURES ON LAW

PART TWO, *continued*

II

—OF THE EXECUTIVE DEPARTMENT
(*continued*)

The observations which I have delivered concerning the appointment of officers, apply likewise to treaties; the making of which is another power, that the president has, with the advice and consent of the senate.

The president has power to fill up all vacancies that may happen, in offices, during the recess of the senate, by granting commissions, which shall expire at the end of their next session.

He has no stated counsellors appointed for him by the constitution. Their inutility, and the dangers arising from them, were before[t] fully shown. He may, however, when he thinks proper, require the opinion, in writing, of the principal officer in each of the executive departments, upon any subject relating to the duties of their offices.

On extraordinary occasions, he may convene both houses of the legislature, or either of them: and, in case of disagreement between them, with respect to the time of adjournment, he may adjourn them to such time as he shall think proper.

It is his duty, from time to time, to lay before congress information of the state of the Union; and to recommend to their consideration such measures, as he shall judge necessary and expedient.

He has power to grant reprieves and pardons for offences against the United States, except in cases of impeachment.

To prevent crimes, is the noblest end and aim of criminal jurisprudence. To punish them, is one of the means necessary for the accomplishment of this noble end and aim.

The certainty of punishments is of the greatest importance, in order to constitute them fit preventives of crimes. This certainty is best obtained by accuracy in the publick police, by vigilance and activity in the executive officers of justice, by a prompt and certain communication of intelligence, by a proper distribution of rewards for the discovery and apprehension of criminals, and, when they are apprehended, by an undeviating and inflexible strictness in carrying the laws against them into sure and full execution.

[t] Ante. pp. 318–319.

All this will be readily allowed. What should we then think of a power, given by the constitution or the laws, to dispense with accuracy in the publick police, and with vigilance, vigour, and activity in the search and seizure of offenders? Such a power, it must be admitted, would seem somewhat extraordinary.

What, it will next be asked, should we think of a power, given by the constitution or the laws, to dispense with their execution upon criminals, after they have been apprehended, tried, convicted, and condemned? In other words — can the power to pardon be admissible into any well regulated government? Shall a power be given to insult the laws, to protect crimes, to indemnify, and, by indemnifying, to encourage criminals?

From this, or from a similar view of things, many writers, and some of them very respectable as well as humane, have been induced to conclude, that, in a government of laws, the power of pardoning should be altogether unknown.

Would you prevent crimes? says the Marquis of Beccaria: let the laws be clear and simple: let the entire force of the nation be united in their defence: let them, and them only, be feared. The fear of the laws is salutary: but the fear of man is a fruitful and a fatal source of crimes. Happy the nation, in which pardons will be considered as dangerous! Clemency is a virtue which belongs to the legislator, and not to the executor of the laws; a virtue, which should shine in the code, and not in private judgment. The prince, in pardoning, gives up the publick security in favour of an individual: and, by his ill judged benevolence, proclaims an act of impunity.[u]

With regard, says Rousseau, to the prerogative of granting pardon to criminals, condemned by the laws of their country, and sentenced by the judges, it belongs only to that power, which is superiour both to the judges and the laws — the sovereign authority. Not that it is very clear, that even the supreme power is vested with such a right, or that the circumstances, in which it might be exerted, are frequent or determinate. In a well governed state, there are but few executions; not because many are pardoned; but because there are few criminals. Under the Roman republick, neither the senate nor the consuls ever attempted to grant pardons: even the people never did this, although they sometimes recalled their own sentence.[v]

In Persia, when the king has condemned a person, it is no longer lawful to mention his name, or to intercede in his favour. Though his majesty were drunk and beside himself; yet the decree must be executed; otherwise he would contradict himself; and the law admits of no contradiction.[w]

[u] Bec. c. 41. 46.   [v] Rous. Or. Com. 54. l. 2. c. 5.   [w] Mont. Sp. L. b. 3. c. 10.

"Extremes, in nature, equal ends produce;" so in politicks, as it would seem.

The more general opinion, however, is, that in a state, there ought to be a power of pardoning offences. The exclusion of pardons, says Sir William Blackstone, must necessarily introduce a very dangerous power in the judge or jury, that of construing the criminal law by the spirit instead of the letter; or else it must be holden, what no man will seriously avow, that the situation and circumstances of the offender (though they alter not the essence of the crime) ought to make no distinction in the punishment.[x]

I cannot, upon this occasion, enter into the discussion of the great point suggested and decided, in a very few words, by the learned Author of the Commentaries — that judges and juries have no power of construing the criminal law by the spirit instead of the letter. But I cannot, upon any occasion, suffer it to pass under my notice, without entering my caveat against implicit submission to this decision. I well know the humane rule, that, in the construction of a penal law, neither judge nor jury can extend it to facts equally criminal to those specified in the letter, if they are not contained in the letter. But I profess myself totally ignorant of any rule — I think it would be an inhuman one — that the letter of a penal law may be carried beyond the spirit of it; and it may certainly be carried by the letter beyond the spirit, if judges and juries are prohibited, in construing it, from considering the spirit as well as the letter. But to return to our present subject.

The most general opinion, as we have already observed, and, we may add, the best opinion, is, that, in every state, there ought to be a power to pardon offences. In the mildest systems, of which human societies are capable, there will still exist a necessity of this discretionary power, the proper exercise of which may arise from the possible circumstances of every conviction. Citizens, even condemned citizens, may be unfortunate in a higher degree, than that, in which they are criminal. When the cry of the nation rises in their favour; when the judges themselves, descending from their seats, and laying aside the formidable sword of justice, come to supplicate in behalf of the person, whom they have been obliged to condemn; in such a situation, clemency is a virtue; it becomes a duty.

But where ought this most amiable prerogative to be placed? Is it compatible with the nature of every species of government? With regard to both these questions, different opinions are entertained.

With regard to the last, the learned Author of the Commentaries on the laws of England declares his unqualified sentiment — "In democracies, this power of pardon can never subsist; for there nothing higher

---

[x] 4. Bl. Com. 390.

is acknowledged than the magistrate, who administers the laws: and it would be impolitick for the power of judging and of pardoning to centre in one and the same person. This would oblige him (as the President Montesquieu observes) very often to contradict himself, to make and unmake his decisions: it would tend to confound all ideas of right among the mass of the people; as they would find it difficult to tell, whether a prisoner were discharged by his innocence, or obtained a pardon through favour. In Holland, therefore, if there be no stadtholder, there is no power of pardoning lodged in any other member of the state.

"But in monarchies, the king acts in a superior sphere; and though he regulates the whole government as the first mover, yet he does not appear in any of the disagreeable or invidious parts of it. Whenever the nation see him personally engaged, it is only in works of legislature, magnificence, or compassion." [y]

Let us observe, by the way, the mighty difference between the person described by Selden, as the first magistrate among the Saxons, and him described by Sir William Blackstone, as the monarch of England since that period. The former was set in regular motion by the laws: the latter is the first mover, who regulates the whole government.

Let me also repeat here, what has been mentioned in another place. One of the most enlightened writers on English jurisprudence imagines, that the power of pardoning is a power incommunicable to the democratical species of government. For the western world new and rich discoveries in jurisprudence have been reserved. We have found, that this species of government — the best and the purest of all — that, in which the supreme power remains with the people — is capable of being formed, arranged, proportioned, and organized in such a manner, as to exclude the inconveniences, and to secure the advantages of all the others.

Why, according to Sir William Blackstone, can the power to pardon never subsist in a democracy? Because, says he, there, nothing higher is acknowledged, than the magistrate, who administers the laws. By pursuing the principle of democracy to its true source, we have discovered, that the law is higher than the magistrate, who administers it; that the constitution is higher than both; and that the supreme power, remaining with the people, is higher than all the three. With perfect consistency, therefore, the power of pardoning may subsist in our democratical governments: with perfect propriety, we think, it is vested in the president of the United States.

The constitution, too, of Pennsylvania, animated by the wise and powerful recommendation, conveyed, by innumerable channels, to the con-

[y] 4. Bl. Com. 390. 391.

vention, which proposed and framed it, "that they should imitate, as far as it applies, the excellent model exhibited in the constitution of the United States" — the constitution of Pennsylvania[z] vests the power of pardoning in the governour of the commonwealth.

It is by no means, however, a unanimous sentiment, if we collect the publick sentiment from the constitutions of the different states of the Union, that the power of pardoning criminals should be vested *solely* in the supreme executive authority of the state.

By the constitution of New York,[a] the governour, in cases of treason or murder, can only suspend the execution of the sentence, until it shall be reported to the legislature, at their subsequent meeting; and they shall either pardon, or direct the execution of the criminal, or grant a further reprieve.

In the state of Delaware the governour possesses the power of granting pardons, except where the law shall otherwise direct.[b] A similar legislative control is imposed on the governours of Maryland, Virginia, and North Carolina, by the constitutions[c] of those states.[d]

In the states of New Hampshire, Massachusetts and South Carolina, pardons can be granted only after a conviction.[e]

The president and vice president hold their offices during the term of four years.

The president shall, at stated times, receive, for his services, a compensation, which shall neither be increased nor diminished during the period, for which he is elected; and he shall not receive, within that period, any other emolument from the United States, or any of them.

I here finish what I propose to say concerning the second great division of the national government — its executive authority.

[z] Art. 2. s. 9.   [a] S. 18.   [b] Cons. Del. s. 7.

[c] Cons. Mar. s. 33. Cons. Vir. p. 127. Cons. N. C. s. 19.

[d] By the present constitution of Delaware, this legislative control over the power of the governour to grant pardons is destroyed — Art. 3. s. 9. In Vermont, the power of the executive to grant pardons is restrained in cases of treason and murder; in which they have power "to grant reprieves, but not to pardon, until after the end of the next session of assembly." Cons. c. 2. s. 11. By the constitution of Kentucky, the power of pardoning is, in cases of treason, vested in the general assembly, but the governour may grant reprieves until the end of their next session. Art. 3. s. 11. In Tennessee and Ohio, pardons can be granted only after conviction. Cons. Ten. art. 2. s. 6. Cons. Ohio, art. 2. s. 5. In Georgia likewise, according to her present constitution, the governour can grant pardons only after conviction; and in cases of treason and murder, he can only respite the execution, and make report thereof to the next general assembly, by whom a pardon may be granted. Cons. Geor. art. 2. s. 7. *Ed.*

[e] Cons. N. H. p. 18. 19. Cons. Mas. c. 2. s. 1. a. 8. Cons. S. C. art. 2. s. 7.

III

—OF THE JUDICIAL DEPARTMENT

THE judicial power of the United States is vested in one supreme court, and in such inferiour courts as are established by congress.[a]

A court, according to my Lord Coke,[b] is a place where justice is judicially administered.

To Egypt, where much wisdom, we are assured, was to be learned, we trace the first institution of courts of justice. Concerning its administration, the Egyptians were remarkably vigilant and exact; for they believed, that on it depended entirely the support or the dissolution of society. Their highest tribunal was composed of thirty judges.[c] At the head of it was placed the person, who, at once, possessed the greatest share of wisdom, of probity, and of the publick esteem.

The trials, it is said, were carried on in writing; and, to avoid unnecessary delay, the parties were allowed to make only one reply on each side. When the evidence was closed, the judges consulted together concerning the merits of the cause. When they were fully understood and considered, the president gave the signal for proceeding to a judgment, by taking in his hand a small image, adorned with precious stones. When the sentence was pronounced, the president touched, with the image, the party, who had gained his cause. The image was without eyes; and was the symbol, by which the Egyptians were accustomed to represent Truth. It is probably from this circumstance, that Justice has been painted blind.

The judges of this court received from government what was necessary for their support; so that the people paid them nothing for obtaining justice.

We are told, that no advocates were admitted in this tribunal; but that the parties themselves drew up their own processes. This, however, must probably be understood with some limitation; for we cannot reasonably imagine, that all the inhabitants of Egypt were not only taught to write, but were also possessed of a degree of legal skill, sufficient to qualify them for composing their own defences. It is not unlikely, that the regu-

[a] Cons. U. S. art. 3. s. 1.   [b] 1. Ins. 58.   [c] 1. Gog. Or. L. 55.

lation went no farther than one, which we have seen adopted in another state — Every one has a right to be heard by himself and his counsel.

On the model of this high tribunal of Egypt, was formed the celebrated court of the Areopagus at Athens. This court was instituted, one thousand and five hundred years before the Christian era, by Cecrops, who was originally of Sais, a city of the lower Egypt, and to whom Athens, the seat of literature and politeness, of eloquence and patriotism, owed its foundation and first establishments.

This excellent man relinquished the fertile banks of the Nile, in order to avoid the tyranny, under which his native country, at that time, groaned. After a tedious voyage, he reached the shores of Attica: and was received in the most friendly manner by its inhabitants. Placed, after some time, at the head of their affairs, he conceived the noble design of bestowing happiness on his adopted country. For this purpose, he introduced among his new compatriots many valuable and memorable institutions, of which, indeed, he was not strictly the author — if he had, he would have been the first of legislators and the greatest of mortals — but which he brought, probably with his own judicious improvements, from a nation, who had been attentive to carry them to perfection during a long series of ages. Some of his institutions — in all of them wisdom and humanity shone conspicuous — will claim our future attention. At present, it is directed to the court of the Areopagus.

Aristides — well qualified to decide upon this subject; for he was distinguished by the appellation of the just — informs us, that this court was the most sacred and venerable tribunal in all Greece. From its first establishment, it never pronounced a sentence, which gave reasonable cause of complaint. Strangers, even sovereigns, solicited and submitted to its decisions; which contributed, more than any thing else, to disseminate the principles of justice first among the Grecians.[d]

The proceedings in this tribunal were, in some instances, very solemn and striking. In a prosecution for murder, the prosecutor was obliged to swear, that he was related to the person deceased — for none but near relations could prosecute — and that the prisoner was the cause of his death. The prisoner swore, that he was innocent of the crime, of which he was accused. Each confirmed his oath with the most direful imprecations; wishing that, if he swore falsely, himself, his family, and his houses might be utterly destroyed and extirpated by the divine vengeance.[e]

In early times, it is said, the parties were obliged to plead their causes themselves. But this severity was afterwards relaxed. Those, who were accused, might avail themselves of the assistance of counsel. The counsel, however, were never permitted, in pleading, to wander from the merits

[d] 2. Gog. Or. L. 16. 21. 1. Anac. 11.   [e] 1. Pot. Ant. 106.

of the cause. This close and pertinent manner of speaking gave the tone to the bar of Athens, and extended itself to the speeches, which were delivered in other assemblies.[f] In this manner, we may naturally account for the condensed vehemence so remarkable in the orations of Demosthenes.

Let me conclude this account of the Areopagus by mentioning an incident, seemingly of slight importance, but which will not be related without producing, in my hearers, fealings in proper unison with those, which the incident occasioned. A little bird, pursued by its enemy, took refuge in the bosom of one of the judges. Instead of protecting, he stifled it. For this instance of cruelty he received punishment; and was thus taught that he, whose heart is callous to compassion, should not be suffered to have the lives of the citizens at his mercy.

You will not, after this, be surprised, when you are told, that the decisions of the Areopagus were deemed the standards of humanity, as well as of wisdom.[g]

In order to understand, fully and in their true spirit, the juridical institutions of the United States and of Pennsylvania, it will be of the greatest use to take a minute and historical view of the judicial establishments of England; especially those which were formed under the government of the Saxons.

Civil governments, in their first institutions, are nothing more than voluntary associations for the purposes of society. When the Saxons first settled in Britain, they found themselves obliged, by the disorders of the times, to associate, in their different settlements, for their mutual security and protection. Families, connected by consanguinity or other ties, found it agreeable, as well as necessary, to live together in the same neighbourhood, in order to enjoy the social pleasures of peace, as well as to give and receive assistance in the time of war. These societies were known by the appellation of vills or towns.[h] On some occasions, an association of the same kind was necessary, and it was therefore gradually introduced, between the inhabitants of a larger district. Those larger districts were distinguished by the name of hundreds.[i] The connexions and the exigencies of society becoming, on great emergencies, still more important and extensive, the members of different hundreds also associated together, and formed districts larger still, which were denominated shires. The officer who presided over them was called alderman or earl. Hundreders and tythingmen, as their names import, presided over the lesser associations.[j]

This establishment of tythings, and hundreds, and shires, though, at first, intended chiefly for the mutual defence of the inhabitants, was soon

---

[f] 2. Gog. Or. L. 23.   [g] 2. Anac. 290.   [h] Millar. 113   [i] Millar. 117.
[j] Id. 117. 114.

rendered subservient to other purposes, salutary and important.[k] The same motives which induced them to associate for their security against foreign danger, induced them also to take measures for preventing or composing internal differences or animosities. In this manner, a judicial authority was gradually assumed by every tything over the members, of which it was formed. In the same manner and upon the same principles, the hundred exercised the power of determining the controversies, which arose within the bounds of its larger district. In the same manner and upon the same principles still, the shire established a similar jurisdiction over the different hundreds comprehended within its still more extensive territory.[l]

These courts took cognizance of every cause, civil and criminal; and as, in the first instance, they enjoyed respectively the sole jurisdiction within the boundaries of each, they soon and naturally became subordinate, one to another: from the sentence of the tything, an appeal lay to the hundred, and from the sentence of the hundred, an appeal lay to the shire.

It deserves also to be known — for it is important to know — that, besides the defence of the country and the decision of law suits, the Saxon tythings, hundreds, and shires were accustomed to deliberate upon matters of still greater consequence. They received complaints concerning the grievances or abuses in administration, which happened within their respective districts, and applied a remedy by introducing new regulations. Thus the heads of families in every tything exercised a legislative power, within their own limits: but were liable to be controlled by the meetings of the hundred, which enjoyed the same power in a larger district: both of these were subordinate to the assemblies of the shire, which possessed a legislative authority over all the hundreds in that extensive division.[m] Unto the county court, says Selden,[n] all the freemen of the county assembled, to learn the law, to administer justice, and to provide remedy for publick inconvenience.[o]

As the freemen of a tything, of a hundred, and of a shire determined the common affairs of their several districts: so the union of people belonging to different shires produced a greater assembly, consisting of all

[k] Id. 121.　　[l] Id. 122.　　[m] Millar. 130.　　[n] Bac. on Gov. 42.
[o] A striking analogy will sometimes be found where it is least to be expected. The empire of Peru was divided into small districts, each consisting of ten families: five of these constituted a higher class: two of these composed a third class, called a hundred; ten hundreds formed the great class of a thousand. Over each of these a superintending officer was appointed to administer justice, and to provide, that those committed to his care should be furnished with the means of industry and the necessaries of life.
Between two governments, so remote from each other in time and place, this analogy could not have been the effect of imitation: it must have been the native result of similar states and circumstances of society. Bever. 7, 8.

the freemen of a kingdom. This national council was called the wit-tenagemote. The king presided. During the heptarchy, each of the Saxon kingdoms had a wittenagemote of its own: but when they were all reduced into one, a greater wittenagemote was formed, whose authority extended over the whole English nation.[p] Those who could not attend the wit-tenagemote in person, had always the right of appointing a procurator to represent them in their absence.[q]

The wittenagemote exercised powers of a judiciary, as well as of a legislative kind. They heard complaints concerning great quarrels and enormities, which could not be adjusted or redressed by the ordinary courts; and they endeavoured, by their superiour authority, either to reconcile the parties, or to decide their controversies. By frequent inter-positions of this nature, the great council was formed into a regular court of justice, and became the supreme tribunal of the kingdom. In this tribunal, appeals from the courts of every shire, as well as original suits between the inhabitants of different shires, were finally determined.[r]

The original meetings of the wittenagemote were held regularly at two seasons of the year: but the increase of business, especially of that which regarded the administration of justice, rendered it afterwards necessary that its meetings should be more frequent. Occasional meetings were, therefore, convened by the king. At those occasional meetings, the nobility, who resided at a distance, seldom gave themselves the trouble of appearing. Of consequence, the business devolved on those members who happened to be at court, or who might be said to compose the privy council of the king. For this reason, they seldom undertook matters of general legislation; but confined themselves chiefly to the hearing of appeals. These smaller and occasional meetings of the wittenagemote seem to have suggested the idea of the aula regis.[s]

After the conquests, appeals to parliament multiplied: the members of that assembly became daily less disposed to execute this part of their duty: a regular tribunal was, therefore, formed, in order to discharge it. Of this tribunal, the great officers of the crown became the constituent members. To these were added such as, from their knowledge of the law, were thought qualified to give the best assistance.[t] This court re-ceived, from the place in which it was commonly held, the appellation of the *aula regis*. In its constitution, it corresponded exactly with the *cour de roy*, which, after the accession of Hugh Capet, was gradually formed out of the ancient parliament of France; and with the aulick council, which, after the time of Otho the Great, arose, in the same manner, out of the diet of the German empire.[u]

[p] Millar. 132.   [q] Id. 143. 144.   [r] Id. 150.   [s] Millar. 242. 243.
[t] Id. 316.   [u] Id. 317.

For some time after its first formation, the king, whenever he thought proper to sit as a judge, presided in the aula regis: but he, at length, ceased to discharge the ordinary functions of a judge; and the grand justiciary became, in a manner, the sole magistrate of the court.[v]

The institution of this court was a great improvement in the system of judicial policy. It was always in readiness to determine every controversy, criminal and civil. The reparation of injuries was secured; the expenses of litigation were diminished; and justice pervaded the remotest parts of the kingdom. It had the power of reviewing the sentences of inferiour jurisdictions; and, by that means, produced a consistency and even a uniformity of decision, in the judiciary system of the nation.[w]

From circumstances, however, which were the natural consequences of the introduction and progress of the feudal system in England, this court began and continued to make ambitious and unnecessary encroachments on the inferiour jurisdictions. Soon after the conquest, too, a complete separation of the ecclesiastical from the temporal courts took place. The bishop no longer sat as a judge in the court of the county; nor the arch-deacon in that of the hundred. From the moment of this separation, the clergy were zealous, and they were successful, in extending their own jurisdiction, and invading that of the subordinate temporal tribunals.[x] By the gradual and strong operation of these causes and circumstances, the county courts, in particular, dwindled into a state of insignificance, their power was, at length, exercised only on matters of an inconsiderable value; and the greatest part of causes, civil, criminal, and fiscal, were drawn into the vortex of the aula regis, or into that of the ecclesiastical courts.[y]

So far as these changes related to the aula regis, the consequence of them was, that this court, at first admirably accommodated to the arrangements of the juridical system then existing in vigour, became, afterwards, defective, unwieldy, and inconvenient. It followed the king, wherever the political state of the kingdom required his presence. A court, thus ambulatory, was inconsistent with the leisure and deliberation, which are necessary for judges in forming their decisions; and it was still more incompatible with the interest of the parties, who, with their witnesses, were obliged to travel about from place to place, before they could obtain a final determination of their suits.[z] Besides, the great increase of judicial business, which now crowded into the aula regis, rendered the proper despatch of that business an object altogether unattainable: from this cause, therefore, as well as from the other, the administration of justice became tedious, burthensome, and expensive.

[v] Millar. 318.   [w] Id. 324. 325.   [x] Id. 331.   [y] Millar. 326. 331.
[z] Id. 421. 422.

The remedies for these grievances seem to have been natural and easy — to establish the aula regis as a stationary court — and to remand a great proportion of the original causes to those tribunals, which were best fitted, in the first instance, to decide them. These remedies, however, though easy and natural, were not applied. The county jurisdictions had ceased to be objects of favour at court: and the splendour of a retinue, composed of the officers of the judicial as well as the executive department, was a gratification too fascinating to be easily relinquished.

One of the remedies, indeed, it was found necessary to adopt in part; and the remedy, even in that part, was obtained with difficulty, and was soon abridged by ingenious and favourite fictions of law. When magna charta was demanded of King John, one of the articles inserted in the important instrument was — "that common pleas should no longer follow the court of the king, but should be held in some certain and appropriated place." When we see this regulation forming a part of that great transaction between the king and the nation, we may be fully satisfied, that it was much wished for, but could not be easily obtained. In consequence of this regulation, a court of common pleas, detached from the aula regis, was erected, and was appointed, for the future, to have a fixed and permanent residence. But though the court of common pleas obtained, in this manner, a separate establishment, and was held by separate judges, yet it was deemed inferiour in rank to the aula regis held by the grand justiciary, and in which the king still continued to sit sometimes in person; and, for this reason, was considered as subject to its decisions of review.[a]

There is much reason to believe, that the other remedy, so natural and easy, for lessening or removing the inconveniences, which arose from the crowd of business in the aula regis — that of reinstating the inferiour jurisdictions in their original degree of respectability — was, by no means, suffered to escape the attention of those, who obtained the great charter. One of the articles of their demand was — "that the king should promise to appoint justiciaries, constables, sheriffs, and bailiffs of such as knew the law of the land, and were well disposed to observe it."[b] With this demand the king literally complied, and engaged to appoint men only of such characters.[c] Had this engagement continued and been fulfilled, the subordinate, and, in particular, the county establishments for the administration of justice — for to the county establishments I wish to direct your particular attention — would have gradually regained, as they gradually lost, their original dignity and importance. The uniform and uninterrupted appointment of judges, intelligent, upright, and independent — men, who, in the language of magna charta, "knew and

---

[a] Millar. 424.   [b] Bl. 8. art. 42.   [c] Id. 18. art. 45.

would observe the law of the land" — would, without any farther or more explicit provision, have been amply sufficient to have attracted and secured the confidence of suitors, and, by a necessary consequence, to recover and retain the usefulness and the respectability of the courts. This engagement, however, was neither continued nor fulfilled. In the instrument confirmed by Henry the third, this, among many other important regulations of the magna charta of John, was unfortunately omitted. The county establishments, from that period to the present moment, have been despised or disregarded in England; and other establishments, less natural and less convenient to the nation, have been substituted in their place. To the view of those other establishments we now proceed.

When we consider the administration of justice in theory, it seems very susceptible of an arrangement in three great divisions. Prosecutions for crimes are easily distinguished from suits concerning property: and, in suits concerning property, the demands of government are as easily distinguished from demands of individuals. On the foundation of this specious theory, a triple division was made, in England, of the unwieldy jurisdiction accumulated in the aula regis. We have already seen, that "common pleas," or demands of property made by individuals, were detached from that court by an article of the great charter. In the reign of Edward the first, a farther division was made of its powers; the court of exchequer was erected to decide in matters regarding the publick revenue. The cognizance of crimes was the only division now remaining to the original court. To an alteration, so material, in its jurisdiction and power, an alteration, equally material, in its establishment and name was added, and the aula regis now subsided into the court of king's bench. This court is still, in its constitution, ambulatory; and may attend the person of the king in whatever part of the kingdom he shall be. The process of this court is in the king's name, and must be returned before him "ubicunque fuerimus in Anglia." [d]

We now see, clearly and fully, the origin of the three great courts of common law, which, during a series of centuries, have been the ornaments of Westminster hall; and we now see, clearly and fully, the distinct principles, on which those three courts were separately erected. To the king's bench was allotted the jurisdiction of offences and crimes: decisions concerning the property of individuals — meum and tuum, as our books express it — were committed to the court of common pleas: the enforced collection of the publick revenue was intrusted to the court of exchequer.

I conclude my inquiries respecting the juridical history of England, at a period, at which others generally begin theirs.

[d] 3. Bl. Com. 41. [Wherever we shall have been in England.]

To the jurists of Pennsylvania, this investigation, though minute, concerning the distribution of the powers and the jurisdiction of the aula regis, is deeply interesting; nay, it is of indispensable necessity; for, by the constitution and laws of Pennsylvania, a jurisdiction, similar to the combined jurisdiction of that court, is reunited in the supreme court of this commonwealth. But along with that reunion, the measures proper for avoiding its inconveniences have been adopted. The supreme court is stationary; and juridical establishments, highly respectable, are formed in every county. These, in due course, will become the objects of particular attention.

By the historical deduction which we have made, we are now properly prepared to examine, by a particular survey, the judicial departments of the United States and this commonwealth; and to estimate, with correctness, the numerous jurisdictions, supreme and subordinate, of which those departments are composed, and upon the qualities and proportions of which, the declining or the flourishing state of those departments, and of every thing connected with those departments, must ultimately depend.

The judicial power of the national government extends — to all cases, in law or equity, arising under the constitution, the laws, or the treaties of the United States; to all cases affecting publick ministers and consuls; to all cases of admiralty and maritime jurisdiction; to controversies, to which the United States shall be a party; to controversies between two or more states; between a state and citizens of another state; between citizens of different states; between citizens of the same state, claiming lands under grants of different states; and between a state, or the citizens thereof, and foreign states, citizens, or[e] subjects.[f]

Besides the supreme court established by the constitution, the judicial power of the United States is, at present, vested in circuit and in district courts.

The supreme court has original jurisdiction in all cases, to which a state shall be party, and in all cases affecting publick ministers and consuls. In all the other cases before mentioned, it has appellate jurisdiction, both as to law and fact; but with such exceptions, and under such regulations, as are made by congress.[g] It consists of a chief justice and five associate

---

[e] Cons. U. S. art. 3. s. 2.

[f] The supreme court of the United States, in the case of Chisholm v. the state of Georgia (2 Dall. 419.) decided, that under the clause of the constitution which extends the judicial power of the United States to controversies "between a state and citizens of another state," a state was liable, as defendant, to a suit commenced by such citizens. But by the eleventh article of the amendments to the constitution, it is declared that "the judicial power of the United States shall not be construed to extend to any suit in law or equity, commenced or prosecuted against one of the United States by citizens of another state, or by citizens or subjects of any foreign state." Vide post. ch. 4. Ed.

[g] Cons. U. S. Art. 3. s. 2.

justices; and holds annually two sessions at the seat of the national government. One session commences on the first Monday of February; the other, on the first Monday of August. Four judges are a[h] quorum.[i]

The judges, both of the supreme and inferiour courts, hold their offices during good behaviour; and, at stated times, receive, for their services, a compensation, which cannot be diminished during their continuance in office.[j]

The supreme court has power to issue writs of prohibition to the district courts, when they proceed as courts of admiralty and maritime jurisdiction; and writs of mandamus, in cases warranted by the principles and usages of law, to any courts appointed, or persons holding office, under the authority of the United States.[k]

Final judgments and decrees of a circuit court, where the matter in dispute exceeds two thousand dollars, may be reexamined and reversed or affirmed in the supreme court,[l] upon a writ of errour.[m]

If the validity of a statute or treaty of the United States, or of an authority exercised under them, be drawn in question, in any suit in the highest court of law or equity of a state, in which a decision of the suit could be had; and a decision is against their validity — if the validity of a statute of any state, or of an authority exercised under that state, is, in any suit in such court, drawn in question, as repugnant to the constitu-

---

[h] Laws. U. S. 1. con. 1. sess. c. 20. s. 1.

[i] By an act of congress passed 29th April, 1802, the supreme court is to hold but one session annually, commencing on the first Monday in February. Four of the justices form a quorum. If four shall not attend within ten days after the time appointed for the commencement of the session, the business shall be continued to the next stated session; but any one or more of the justices may make all necessary orders preparatory to the hearing, trial, or decision of any case returned to or depending in the court. The August session is abolished; but one of the justices is directed to attend at the seat of government on the first Monday of August annually, and has power to make all necessary orders in any case returned to or depending in the court, preparatory to the hearing, trial, or decision. Writs and process may be returnable on the first Monday in August, in the same manner as to the February session, and may also bear *teste* on that day, as though a session of the court was holden. Laws. U. S. 7. con. 1. sess. c. 31. s. 1. 2. *Ed.*

[j] Cons. U. S. art. 3. s. 1.   [k] Laws. U. S. 1. con. 1. sess. c. 20. s. 13.

[l] Laws. U. S. 1. con. 1. sess. c. 20. s. 22.

[m] See the case of Wiscart et al. *v.* Dauchy, (3. Dall. 321. 327) in which the supreme court of the United States decided, that causes of admiralty and maritime jurisdiction and suits in equity, as well as other civil actions, could be removed from the circuit into the supreme court by writ of errour only, and not by appeal; and that therefore nothing was removed for reexamination but the law. By an act of congress since passed (7. con. 2. sess. c. 93. s. 2.) it is provided that an appeal shall be allowed to the supreme court of the United States from final judgments or decrees rendered in the circuit court in cases of equity, of admiralty and maritime jurisdiction, and of prize or no prize; where the matter in dispute, exclusive of costs, shall exceed the value of two thousand dollars. No new evidence, however, can be received in the supreme court on the hearing of the appeal, except in admiralty and prize causes. *Ed.*

tion, treaties, or laws of the United States; and a decision is in favour
of their validity — if the construction of any clause of the constitution,
of a treaty, of a statute of the United States, or of a commission held
under under them, is, in any suit in such court, drawn in question; and a
decision is against the title, right, privilege, or exemption, specially set up
or claimed by either party under such clause — a final judgment or
decree, in all these cases, may, upon a writ of errour, be reexamined and
affirmed or reversed in the supreme court of the United States.[n]

The United States are divided into circuits and districts.

The districts are, in number, sixteen: one consists of that part of the
state of Massachusetts, which lies easterly of the state of New Hampshire,
and is called Maine district: one consists of the state of New Hampshire,
and is called New Hampshire district: one consists of the remaining part
of the state of Massachusetts, and is called Massachusetts district: one
consists of the state of Rhode Island and Providence Plantations, and is
called Rhode Island district: one consists of the state of Connecticut, and
is called Connecticut district: one consists of the state of New York, and
is called New York district: one consists of the state of New Jersey, and
is called New Jersey district: one consists of the state of Pennsylvania,
and is called Pennsylvania district: one consists of the state of Delaware,
and is called Delaware district: one consists of the state of Maryland,
and is called Maryland district: one consists of the state of Virginia, and
is called Virginia district: one consists of the state of North Carolina, and
is called North Carolina district: one consists of the state of South Carolina, and is called South Carolina district: one consists of the State of
Georgia, and is called Georgia district:[o] one consists of the state of Vermont, and is called Vermont district:[p] one consists of Kentucky, and is
called Kentucky district.

These districts, except Maine and Kentucky, are divided into three
circuits, the eastern, the middle, and the southern. The eastern circuit
consists of the districts of New Hampshire, Massachusetts, Rhode Island,
Connecticut, New York, and Vermont: the middle circuit consists of the
districts of New Jersey, Pennsylvania, Delaware, Maryland, and Virginia:
the southern circuit consists of the districts of North Carolina, South
Carolina, and Georgia.[q]

In each district, there is a district court, consisting of one judge,[r] who
resides in the district, and holds four sessions annually.[s]

---

[n] Laws. U. S. 1. con. 1. sess. c. 20. s. 25.   [o] Id. 1. con. 1. sess. c. 20. s. 2.
[p] Laws U. S. 1. con. 3. sess. c. 12. s. 2.   [q] Id. 1. con. 1. sess. c. 20. s. 4.
[r] Id. s. 3.
[s] For the alterations which have been made in the distribution of the United States
into districts and circuits, and in the sessions of the district courts, the number of
which now varies in different districts, see Laws U. S. 3. cong. 1. sess. c. 54. 7. cong.
1. sess. c. 31. 7. cong. 2. sess. c. 60. *Ed.*

In each district of the three circuits, two courts, called circuit courts, are annually held. These courts consist of any two justices of the supreme court, and of the district judge of the district, any two of whom constitute a quorum.[t][u]

Over crimes and offences, committed upon the high seas, or within the respective districts, and cognizable under the authority of the United States, the district courts have jurisdiction; provided the punishment exceed not whipping with thirty stripes, a fine of one hundred dollars, or imprisonment for six months. From jurisdiction over such crimes or offences, the courts of the several states are excluded.[v]

The district courts have, in the first instance, exclusive cognizance of all causes of admiralty and maritime jurisdiction,[w] and of seizures under laws of impost, navigation, or trade; provided the seizures be made on the high seas, or within their respective districts, on waters navigable from the sea by vessels of ten or more tons burthen. But the right of a common law remedy is saved to suitors in all cases, in which the common law is competent to give it.[x] Of seizures on land, or on waters, other than as above described, and of all suits for penalties and forfeitures incurred under the laws of the United States, the district courts have, likewise, in the first instance, exclusive cognizance.

Of all causes, in which an alien sues for a tort only in violation of the law of nations or of a treaty of the United States, the district courts have cognizance, concurrent, as the case may be, with the circuit courts, or with the courts of the several states. They have a similar concurrent cognizance of all suits at common law, in which the United States sue, and the matter in dispute, exclusive of costs, amounts to the value of one hundred dollars. They have, exclusively of the courts of the several states, jurisdiction of all suits against consuls or vice consuls, except for offences above the description before mentioned.[y]

[t] Laws U. S. 1. con. 1. sess. c. 20. s. 4.
[u] The circuit courts now consist of one of the judges of the supreme court and the judge of the district; either of whom may hold the court. In cases removed from a district to a circuit court by appeal or writ of errour, judgment shall be rendered in conformity to the opinion of the judge of the supreme court. In other cases, if the opinions of the judges shall be opposed, the question respecting which they disagree shall, during the same term, at the request of either party or their counsel, be stated under the direction of the judges, and certified to the supreme court, by whom it shall be finally decided; and their decision and order shall be remitted to the circuit court, and be then entered of record, and shall have effect according to the nature of the decision or order. No punishment shall, in any case, be inflicted, when the judges are divided in opinion on the question respecting it — Laws U. S. 7. cong. 1. sess. c. 31. s. 4. 5. 6. *Ed.*
[v] Laws U. S. 1. con. 1. sess. c. 20. s. 9.
[w] Every district court in the United States possesses all the powers of a court of admiralty, whether considered as an instance or as a prize court. 3. Dall. 16. *Ed.*
[x] Laws U. S. 1. con. 1. sess. c. 20. s. 9.   [y] Id. **ibid.**

The circuit courts have concurrent jurisdiction with the district courts of the crimes and offences cognizable in the latter, and they have exclusive cognizance of all other crimes and offences cognizable under the authority of the United States, except where provision is or shall be otherwise made.

They have, concurrent with the courts of the several states, original cognizance of all civil suits at common law or in equity, where the matter in dispute, exclusive of costs, exceeds the value of five hundred dollars, and where the United States are plaintiffs, or an alien is a party, or a suit is between a citizen of the state, in which it is brought, and a citizen of another state.[z]

The final decrees and judgments of a district court in civil actions, where the matter in dispute, exclusive of costs, exceeds the value of fifty dollars, may, upon a writ of errour, be reexamined, and reversed or affirmed in a circuit court, holden in the same district.[a] [b]

From the foregoing detail, which was necessary, though not entertaining, we find, that as yet, only three species of courts are known to the constitution and laws of the United States; and that even to one of those species no appropriate order of judges is assigned; for the judges of the circuit courts are drawn together, in opposite directions, from the supreme court and the district. This very uncommon establishment may become the subject of some future remarks.

I proceed to take a view of the courts of Pennsylvania.

The first, which attracts our notice, is "the high court of errours and appeals." This court was constituted by a late law. A court of the same name and of much the same kind was known in Pennsylvania, before the present constitution. This court, as at present established, consists of the judges of the supreme court, of the presidents of the courts of common pleas, and of three other persons, appointed during good behaviour, and removable in the same manner as the judges of the supreme court. Five judges form a quorum. It is empowered to decide on writs of errour from the supreme court, and on appeals from the register's courts in the several counties of the commonwealth.[c]

The supreme court has been long known in Pennsylvania, though not always by the same name. By consulting the records of our laws, we

---

[z] Laws U. S. 1. con. 1. sess. c. 20. s. 11.   [a] Id. s. 22.

[b] By the 21st. section of the same act, an *appeal* to the circuit court was allowed from final decrees in a district court *in causes of admiralty and maritime jurisdiction*, where the matter in dispute exceeded the value of three hundred dollars exclusive of costs. By a later act (7. cong. 2. sess. c. 93. s. 2.) it is provided that from *all final judgments or decrees* in any of the district courts of the United States, an appeal, where the matter in dispute, exclusive of costs, shall exceed the value of fifty dollars, shall be allowed to the circuit court for the same district. *Ed.*

[c] 3. Laws Penn. 97. s. 17.

shall find "an act for erecting a provincial court," passed as early as the year one thousand six hundred and eighty four. It had power to try titles of land, to try all causes civil and criminal, both in law and equity, not determinable in the county courts, and to decide appeals from inferiour jurisdictions.[d] This law was continued, according to a general regulation in force at that time, from one session of the general assembly to another, till the year one thousand six hundred and ninety. From that year to the year one thousand seven hundred, there is a chasm in the laws of Pennsylvania. To those, who are conversant in the general history of the province, the reasons of this chasm are well known.

In the year one thousand seven hundred and one, a new act was passed for establishing a provincial court. By this act, the court had jurisdiction in equity by bill and answer, such as is necessary in courts of chancery, and *proper in these parts*.[e] This law was, in the year one thousand seven hundred and five, repealed by the queen in council.

In the year one thousand seven hundred and fifteen, another law was passed "for erecting a supreme or provincial court of law and equity." [f] This experienced the fate of the former — it was repealed by the king in council in the year one thousand seven hundred and nineteen.

I may be permitted to remark, by the way, that such was the fate of many of the most valuable laws, which were passed in the early periods of Pennsylvania. They well deserve the attention of every one, who wishes to become a master of her juridical history. They disclose, in the most striking as well as the most authentick manner, how soon and how strongly a spirit of jealousy began to operate in the administration of the colonies.

Will it be believed, that the benefit of the great palladium of liberty — the writ of habeas corpus — was refused to be imparted to the plantations? Will it be believed, that the name of Somers — a name, in Europe, so dear to liberty — stands first in the list of those, by whom the tyrannick refusal was given? These things ought not to be believed without the most irrefragable testimony: if the most irrefragable testimony of their authenticity can be produced, these things ought to be both believed and published. They show how dangerous it is for freedom to depend upon her best friends for a *foreign* support.

In December one thousand six hundred and ninety five, the committee of plantations wrote, to the governour and council of Massachusetts, a letter on the subject of a variety of laws passed by the legislature of that colony. Many of those laws were favourable to liberty; and, among others of this spirit, there was one concerning the writ of habeas corpus.

[d] R. O. book A. p. 71.   [e] R. O. book A. vol. 1. p. 110.
[f] R. O. book A. vol. 2. p. 109.

With regard to this law, the committee expressed themselves in the following manner, truly remarkable. "Whereas by the act for securing the liberty of the subject, and preventing illegal imprisonments, the writ of habeas corpus is required to be granted, in like manner as is appointed by the statute of 31. Charles II. in England; which privilege has not as yet been granted in any of his majesty's plantations: it was not thought fit in his majesty's absence, that the said act should be continued in force; and, therefore, the same hath been repealed." My Lord Somers signed the letter! [g]

I return to the supreme court of this commonwealth.

By a law, made in the year one thousand seven hundred and twenty two, and which is still in force, a court of record was established, and styled the supreme court of Pennsylvania. To that court power is given to issue writs of habeas corpus, certiorari, and writs of errour, and all remedial and other writs and process, in pursuance of the powers given to it.[h] Its judges are authorized to minister justice to all persons, and exercise the jurisdictions and powers granted by law, as fully and amply as the justices of the court of king's bench, common pleas, and exchequer, at Westminster, or any of them, can do.[i] It was made a doubt, whether, under the authority of this law, the supreme court could exercise original jurisdiction, and take cognizance of causes at their commencement. A law, passed a few years ago, gives it expressly original jurisdiction in enumerated cases.[j]

By the constitution of Pennsylvania,[k] the jurisdiction of the supreme court shall extend over the state; and the judges of it shall, by virtue of their offices, be justices of oyer and terminer and general gaol delivery in the several counties.

Besides the powers formerly and usually exercised by it, it has now the powers of a court of chancery so far as relates to the perpetuating of testimony, the obtaining of evidence from places not within the state, and the care of the persons and estates of those, who are *non compotes mentis.*[l]

The judges of this court hold their offices during good behaviour; but, for any reasonable cause, which shall not be ground of impeachment, the governour may remove any of them, on the address of two thirds of each branch of the legislature.[m] They shall, at stated times, receive, for their services, an adequate compensation, to be fixed by law; which shall not be diminished during their continuance in office.

By a law passed during the present year, the supreme court is established in the same manner, and with the same powers, as it has been here-

[g] Chal. 74.   [h] 1. Laws Penn. 179. s. 11.   [i] Id. 180. s. 13.
[j] 2. Laws Penn. 472. s. 4. 5.   [k] Art. 5. s. 3.   [l] Cons. Penn. art 5. s. 6.
[m] Cons. Penn. art. 5. s. 2.

tofore established by the laws of the state, consistently with the provisions contained in the constitution.[n] It holds three terms in the year; one, on the first Monday in January; another, on the first Monday in April; and the third, on the first Monday in[o] September.[p]

By the constitution of Pennsylvania,[q] a court of common pleas, an orphans' court, a register's court, and a court of quarter sessions of the peace are established for each county. Before I consider these jurisdictions separately, it will be proper to premise some observations, equally applicable to them all.

Among the dispositions and arrangements of judicial power, the institution of counties has long made a conspicuous figure. The division of England into counties is generally ascribed to the legislative genius of the great Alfred. His genius was unquestionably equal to the task; but part of it was performed before his reign. A country so large as some of the kingdoms of the heptarchy could not, according to the policy and the exigencies of the times, enjoy the administration of justice without a division into subordinate districts. Accordingly, in the old laws, before the union of England under Egbert, we find the mention of sheriffs and shires.[r] But though Alfred did not commence, he undoubtedly extended the county establishments of England. Before his reign, the Danes had made extensive settlements in the northern parts of the kingdom. During some years after the commencement of his reign, they confined him within very narrow limits, and ravaged the rest according to their savage pleasure. At last, however, this great man, whom so many embarrassments surrounded, and who surmounted so many embarrassments, obliged those, who had viewed him with supercilious contempt, to acknowledge him as their superiour and lord. After his conquest over the Danes, he then settled the boundaries of the counties through every part of England. In the southern parts of the kingdom, they were, probably, laid out according to the former limits. In the northern parts, which were less fertile and more uncultivated, they were laid out on a larger scale. Hence, to this day, we find the largest counties in the north of England.

In every county, justice was administered to the inhabitants near their places of residence, without the delay and expense of resorting to Westminster.

Each of the counties or shires had, as we are told by Selden, their two chief governours for distributive justice: of these, the sheriff was the more ancient and worthy; being, in certain cases, aided by the power of

---

[n] 3. Laws Penn. 92. s. 1.   [o] Id. ibid.

[p] The terms of the supreme court now commence on the first Mondays in March, September, and December. March term continues three weeks; September term, two weeks; and December term four weeks. The first and last days of each term are return days. 5. Laws Penn. 166. *Ed.*

[q] Art. 5. s. 1.   [r] Sulliv. 245.

the county. His office was partly judicial and partly ministerial. In the last character, he was the king's servant to execute his writs: in the first, he regulated the courts of justice within the county. The other officer was the coroner, whose duty it was to inquire of homicide upon the view, to seize escheats and forfeitures, to receive appeals of felony, and to keep the rolls of criminal proceedings. He was chosen, as was the sheriff, from among the men of the first rank in the county.[s]

In those times, the county court was surrounded with numerous and respectable attendants: it was considered as the great theatre, on which the justice and the power of the county were displayed.[t] In those times, justice was administered principally in the county establishments; and it was only in cases of uncommon magnitude or difficulty, that recourse was had to that judicial tribunal, whose jurisdiction extended over the whole kingdom. In those times, the proceedings and decisions of the courts were simple and unembarrassed — an advantage, as a learned writer says,[u] which always attends the infancy of laws — an advantage, as I will venture to say, which always attends their perfection. Such have been, and such will be the true character and native consequences of county establishments, properly instituted and properly organized.

Let us now trace their origin and their progress in Pennsylvania.

In the second session of her legislature, it was enacted, that "all actions of debt, account, slander, and trespass, shall be first tried by the court of the county, in which the cause of action arises." [v] In a subsequent session, it was constituted a court of equity as well as of law.[w] Soon afterwards the sphere of the county jurisdictions was enlarged. It was enacted, that trials of titles of lands, actions of debt, account, and slander, and all actions civil or criminal whatever (excepting treason, murder, manslaughter, and other enormous crimes) shall be first heard and determined in the proper counties by the respective justices; and that the county courts shall be held quarterly, and oftener, if there be occasion.[x]

These institutions fell at the chasm of legislation, which I have already mentioned; but their spirit was afterwards revived, continued, and invigorated. They received, it is true, some checks, similar to those, which were experienced by the supreme court. In the year one thousand seven hundred and fourteen, an act was passed for establishing the several courts of common pleas within the province.[y] It met its fate at the same time and in the same manner as the law for establishing the supreme court.

---

[s] Bac. on Gov. 40, 41.
[t] Forum plebeiæ justitiæ, et theatrum comitivæ potestatis. Spel. Gloss. v. comitatus.
[u] 4. Bl. Com. 407.   [v] R. O. Book A. p. 32.   [w] Id. p. 70.   [x] Id. p. 84.
[y] Id. vol. 2. p. 112.

By a subsequent law, more fortunate, a court of record, styled the county court of common pleas, was established in every county, with power to hear and determine all pleas and causes, civil, personal, real, and mixed, according to the laws and constitutions of the province.[z] Here appears a plain separation of the civil from the criminal jurisdiction, both of which were, before this time, vested in the county courts. The criminal jurisdiction was, by the same law, transferred to a court instituted at the same time,[a] and styled "the general quarter sessions of the peace and gaol delivery."[b]

By the constitution,[c] the judges of the courts of common pleas shall hold their offices during good behaviour.

I am next to consider the establishment and the jurisdiction of orphans' courts in Pennsylvania. These are institutions of the last importance to the welfare of the commonwealth.

Among the ancients, those who studied and practised the sciences of jurisprudence and government with the greatest success, were convinced, and, by their conduct showed their conviction, that the fate of states depends on the education of youth.

History, experience, and philosophy combine in declaring — that the best and most happy of countries is that country, which is the most enlightened.

"It was a leading principle with our ancestors," says Isocrates in his oration on reforming the government of Athens, "not to limit the education of the citizens to any particular period of life. Great pains were employed upon them during their youth; and, as they advanced to the years of maturity, they were watched with an attention still more sedulous than before. Their manners were an object of such high concern, that the Areopagus seemed instituted with no other view but to preserve them."[d] It was the business of this court to appoint tutors and governours for the youth; and to take care that they were educated in a manner corresponding to their situation and circumstances.[e]

A similar degree of watchfulness and assiduity was bestowed upon education, in other parts of Greece. Epaminondas, we are told, in the last year of his life, said, heard, beheld, and performed the very same things, as at the age in which he received the first principles of his education.[f]

Nothing, indeed, can be of greater importance, than to conduct our children in the same manner, in which we ought to conduct ourselves.

"Custom," says my Lord Bacon, "is the principal magistrate of man's life. But custom is certainly most perfect, when it beginneth in young years. This we call education; which, in effect, is but an early custom.

[z] 1. Laws Penn. 182. s. 21.   [a] See R. O. Book A. vol. 2. p. 90.
[b] 1. Laws Penn. p. 176. s. 3.   [c] Art. 5. s. 2.   [d] Gil. Lys. & Isoc. 487.
[e] 1. Pot. Ant. 104.   [f] Mont. Sp. L. b. 4. c. 4.

But if the force of custom, simple and segregate, be great; the force of custom, copulate and conjoined and collegiate, is far greater. For there, example teacheth, company comforteth, emulation quickeneth, glory raiseth. Certainly the great multiplication of virtues upon human nature resteth upon societies well ordained and disciplined." [g]

Things are sometimes best displayed by the side of their contraries. It has been the benign aim of patriot legislators to disseminate knowledge: it has been the infernal wish of despots and the minions of despots to extinguish it. The political principles of Mr. Hobbes are well known. Such an abhorrence he contracted for popular government, and the principles of freedom, that he was anxious to see both extirpated from the face of the earth. In order to obtain this consummation, in his perverted judgment so devoutly to be wished, he recommends it to princes to destroy the Greek and Latin authors. "By reading them," says he, "men have, under a false show of liberty, acquired a habit of favouring tumults, and of licentiously controlling the conduct of their sovereigns." [h] In France, during a late reign, a minister was heard to say — "I will put an end to all schools;" and another is said to have declared — "I am tired with these publications; if I continue ten years longer in office, I am determined that no books, except the court calender, shall be printed in Paris." [i] But in France, that late reign is now passed.

The same savage and tyrannick maxims have, in former times, been avowed in America. But those times are now also passed. It will not, however, be unuseful to turn our eyes back upon them; and, with the mingled emotions of disdain and conscious joy, to trace the striking contrast between the views of government in a past, and those in the present age.

In the reign of Charles the second, the lords of the committee of plantations transmitted to Virginia a series of inquiries concerning the condition of the colony. Among the answers returned by Sir William Berkeley, who was then its governour, we find the following one, too extraordinary to be passed without particular notice. "I thank God, there are no free schools, nor printing; and, I hope, we shall not have, these hundred years. For learning has brought disobedience, and heresy, and sects into the world; and printing has divulged them and libels against the best government: God keep us from both!" [j] By the court of Charles, this prayer was received most graciously; and, agreeably to its principle, a succeeding governour was ordered "to allow no person to use a printing press on any occasion whatsoever." [k]

Very different were the principles, which animated the genius of the immortal Alfred. He considered learning and the sciences as the glory and the felicity of his reign. He founded and endowed schools: difficult as the

[g] 3. Ld. Bac. 357. 358. [h] Lev. P. 2. c. 21. 1. Shaft. Char. 88. [i] Fr. Rev. 266.
[j] Chal. 328. [k] Id. 345.

task was in that unenlightened age, he provided those schools with proper instructors. Still farther to diffuse a taste for knowledge, and to transmit its blessings to posterity, he made a law, obliging all freeholders, possessing two hides of land or upwards, to send their sons to school, and give them a liberal education. By his own example — for he was the most accomplished scholar of his age — by his powerful recommendations of learning — for he made it the great road to preferment — he introduced among his people the most ardent pursuits after intellectual acquirements. The old bewailed their unhappiness in being ignorant; some, at a very advanced age, applied themselves to study; and all took care to procure proper instruction for their children, and their other young relations.[1]

According to the theory of Plato[m] and the institutions of Lycurgus,[n] the care and education of children were taken entirely out of the hands of their parents. The propriety of this regulation I will not, at present, examine. Suffice it to say, that the laws ought to give every possible encouragement and assistance to the education of children; but particularly of those, who are unfortunately deprived of their parents.

We now see the reasons and the importance of establishing orphans' courts. The first object of their jurisdiction is the education of orphans: their property is the second.

So early as the second session of the legislature of Pennsylvania, orphans' courts were established in every county to inspect the estates, usage, and employment of orphans; "that care," says the law, "may be taken for those, that are not able to take care for themselves." [o] Their education is more immediately the object of a subsequent law, which was made in the same session.[p] "That poor as well as rich may be instructed in commendable learning," it was enacted, "that all persons having children, and the guardians or trustees of orphans, shall cause them to be instructed in reading and writing; and to be taught some useful trade or profession; that the poor may work to live, and the rich, if they become poor, may not want."

By a law still in force, orphans' courts appoint guardians over such orphans as the court shall judge incapable, according to the rules of the common law, of choosing guardians for themselves; admit orphans, of the proper age, to choose their own guardians; and direct the binding of orphans to be apprentices to trades or other employments. But it is provided, that no orphan shall be bound an apprentice to any person, or be placed under the guardianship of any person, whose religious persuasion is different from that of the orphan's parents.[q]

You will probably be surprised, that the regulations known to our laws for the education of orphans here close. You have reason for your sur-

[1] 2. Henry 356. [m] 4. Anac. 341. [n] Id. 163. [o] R. O. Book. A. p. 34.
[p] Id. p. 46. [q] 1. Laws. Penn. 101. s. 7. 102. s. 12.

prise. Those regulations are, indeed, defective. To parental affection the care of education may, in most instances, be safely intrusted. But in no other principle ought the laws to repose an implicit confidence, concerning an object of the greatest magnitude, immediately to orphans, and eventually to the publick. In Sparta, one of the most respectable members of the state was placed at the head of all the children. Would not some similiar institution be eligible with regard to such of them as are deprived of their parents?

The jurisdiction of the orphans' courts, as it respects the property of orphans, will be discussed with more propriety, when we come to the second great division of the law — that, which relates to things.

By the constitution of Pennsylvania,[r] the judges of the court of common pleas of each county compose its orphans' court.

I proceed to the consideration of the register's court.

In England, the probate of wills and the granting of letters of administration belong to the jurisdiction of the ecclesiastical courts. In Pennsylvania, this jurisdiction is turned into a very different channel.

In the first session of the legislature of Pennsylvania, a registry was established for wills, for letters of administration, and for the names of guardians and executors.[s]

A law passed in the year one thousand seventeen hundred and five directed, that an officer, called register general, should be appointed for the probate of wills, and granting letters of administration. He was directed to keep his office at Philadelphia, and to constitute a deputy in each county of the province. The deputies were empowered to take probates and grant letters of administration, as amply as the register general himself could do. A will proved, or letters of administration granted, in any one county, superceded the necessity of another probate or other letters of administration in any other county.[t]

When objections were made, or caveats entered against the proving of any will, or granting letters of administration; and when there was occasion to take the final accounts of executors or administrators, or to make distribution of decedents' estates, the register general and his deputies were respectively obliged to call to their assistance two or more of the justices of the court of common pleas, who were empowered and required to give their assistance, accordingly, to do all judicial acts concerning the matters before mentioned. This was the register's court.[u]

The office of register general is now abolished; and, by the constitution, a register's office for the probate of wills and granting letters of adminstration shall be kept in each county.[v]

[r] Art. 5. s. 7.   [s] R. O. Book. A. p. 18.   [t] 1. Laws. Penn. 56. s. 8.
[u] R. O. book A. vol. 2. p. 43.   [v] Cons. Penn. art. 5. s. 11.

The register of wills, together with the judges of the court of common pleas, or any two of them, compose the register's court.[w]

The court of quarter sessions of the peace is the last of those courts, which, by the constitution of Pennsylvania, form the juridical establishment for every county in the commonwealth.

In England, the general or quarter sessions of the peace is a court of record held, in every county, once in every quarter of the year. It is held before two or more justices of the peace, for the execution of that authority, which is conferred on them by the commission of the peace, and a great variety of acts of parliament.

By the statute of 34 Ed. III. c. 1. the court of general quarter sessions have authority to hear and determine all felonies and trespasses whatever done in the county in which they sit. But they seldom try any greater offences than small felonies; remitting crimes of a heinous nature to the assizes, for a more publick and solemn trial and decision. There are many offences, which ought to be prosecuted in the quarter sessions, as belonging particularly to the jurisdiction of that court. Of this kind are the smaller misdemeanors, not amounting to felony; such as offences relating to the highways, taverns, vagrants, and apprentices. It has cognizance also of controversies relating to the settlement and provision for the poor, and orders for their removal. It cannot try any newly created offence, without an express authority given by the statute, which creates it.[x]

In Pennsylvania, the courts of quarter sessions of the peace are formed upon the model, and exercise jurisdiction according to the practice of the courts of the same denomination in England. In one important particular, however, there is a very material difference between them. The courts of quarter sessions in England are composed of the justices of the peace, who hold their commissions only during the pleasure of the crown: those in Pennsylvania are composed of the judges of the court of common pleas, who hold their commissions during their good behaviour.[y]

Thus much concerning the court of quarter sessions.

In each county, and in such convenient districts as are directed by law, the governour of Pennsylvania appoints a competent number of justices of the peace.[z]

To the common law, the conservation of the peace has always been an object of the most particular attention and regard. Long before the institution of justices of the peace was known, many officers were, ex officio, or by election, or by particular appointment, guardians of the publick tranquility — conservatores pacis.[a]

---

[w] Id. art. 5. s. 7. [x] Wood. Ins. 499. 4. Bl. Com. 268.
[y] Cons. Penn. art. 5. s. 7. 2. [z] Cons. Penn. art. 5. s. 10. [a] Millar, 433.

When quarrels suddenly arise — when violence is committed — when riots and tumults are likely to ensue, it is vain to wait for the interposition of the ordinary courts of justice. That cannot be obtained soon enough for preventing or suppressing the disorders. It is highly important, therefore, that men of character and influence, to whom, upon any emergency, application may be easily made, should be invested with sufficent power to arrest disorderly persons, to confine them, and to preserve or restore the quiet of the country.

The peace, in the most extensive sense of the term, comprehends the whole of the criminal law. "Against the peace," all crimes are laid to be committed. Whoever, therefore, had authority to take cognizance of crimes was, from the nature of his office, considered as a conservator of the peace. The king himself was styled its great conservator through all his dominions. His judges and his ministers of justice were also official conservators of the peace. Others were conservators by tenure or prescription. Others, again, were elected in the full county court, in pursuance of a writ directed to the sheriff. Besides all these, extraordinary conservators of the peace were appointed by commission from the king, as occasion required. They were to continue, says my Lord Bacon, for the term of their lives, or at the king's pleasure. For this service, adds the same great authority, choice was made of the best men of calling in the county, and but few in the shire. They might bind any man to keep the peace, and be of the good behaviour; and they might send for the party, directing their warrant to the sheriff or constable to arrest the party and bring him before them.

This it was usual to do, when complaint was made, upon oath, by any one, that he stood in fear of another; or when the conservator himself saw the disposition of any man inclined to a breach of the peace, or to misbehave himself in some outrageous manner. In such cases, the conservator might, by his own discretion, send for such a fellow, and, as he should see cause, oblige him to find sureties for the peace, or for his good behaviour. If he refused to find them, a commitment to gaol would be the unavoidable consequence.

Those, who were conservators of the peace by virtue of their offices, still retain the character and power: those, who became so by election or appointment, are superseded by the justices of the peace.[b]

Of this institution, says my Lord Coke,[c] it is such a form of subordinate government for the tranquillity and quiet of the realm, as no part of the christian world hath; provided it be duly executed.

The power of the justices of the peace arises from two different

---

[b] 4. Ld. Bac. 59. 99. 1. Bl. Com. 349. 2. Reev. 122.   [c] 4. Ins. 170.

sources — their commission, and acts of parliament, which have created the objects of their jurisdiction.

By his commission, every justice is appointed a conservator of the peace, and is vested with a separate power to suppress riots and affrays, to take securities for the peace or good behaviour; and for defect of sureties may commit to the common gaol or house of correction. For treason, felony, or breach of the peace, he may commit even a fellow-justice.[d]

The powers, which, by acts of parliament, have been conferred, from time to time, upon one, two, or more justices of the peace, are accumulated to such a degree as to form a jurisdiction of immense variety and importance. They are so many and so great that, as Sir William Blackstone observes,[e] the country is greatly obliged to any worthy magistrate, who, without sinister views of his own, will engage in this troublesome service. For this reason, he is protected, by many statutes, in the honest discharge of his office; and, for any unintentional errour in his practice, great indulgence is shown to him in the courts of law. On the other hand, tyrannical abuses of his office are punished with the merited severity; and all persons, who recover a verdict against him, for a wilful or malicious injury, are entitled to double costs.

In England, a justice of the peace holds his office only during the pleasure of the king: by the constitution of Pennsylvania, he holds it during his good behaviour. He may be removed on conviction of misbehaviour in office, or of any infamous crime, or on the address of both houses of the legislature.[f]

The presidents of the courts of common pleas, within their circuits, and the other judges, within their several counties, are justices of the peace, so far as relates to criminal matters.[g]

This distinction, suggested by the constitution, brings into our view a very important branch of the power of a justice of the peace. He possesses civil as well as criminal jurisdiction in Pennsylvania, and decides concerning property as well as concerning offences. This branch of his power deserves a particular consideration.

The easy, the regular, and the expeditious administration of justice has, in every good government, been an object of particular attention and care. To the attainment of an object so interesting, the distribution of the juridical powers among convenient districts is highly conducive. Such distribution, therefore, has, in many states, been made with a degree of precision suited to its importance. Every citizen should be always under the eye and under the protection of the law and of its officers:

[d] Wood. Ins. 80.   [e] 1. Bl. Com. 354.   [f] Cons. Penn. art. 5. s. 10.
[g] Id. art. 5. s. 9.

each part of the juridical system should give and receive reciprocally an impulse in the direction of the whole.

In Athens, there was a grade of magistrates, who, in the several districts, had jurisdiction of suits, when the sum in controversy did not exceed ten drachms. They had cognizance also of actions of assault and battery.[h]

Arbitrators likewise acted a very considerable part on the juridical theatre of Athens. There were two kinds of them. One kind consisted of those, who were drawn by lot to determine controversies, in their own tribe, concerning demands, which exceeded ten drachms in value. Their sentence was not final; for if either of the contending parties thought himself injured by it, he might appeal, for redress, to a superior court of justice.[i] Arbitrators of the other kind were such as the parties themselves chose to determine the controversy between them. From the determination of these arbitrators, the law permitted no appeal. But they took an oath to give their sentence without partiality.[j]

We have seen and traced the importance of the county establishments. But counties are too extensive for their inhabitants to meet on every occasion. Hence the propriety of inferiour divisions.

Among the Saxons, there was a magistrate called the hundredary, who presided over that division of a shire which was called a hundred. This magistrate was known to the ancient Germans, as we find, in Tacitus,[k] an express reference made to his jurisdiction. The hundredary was, in virtue of his office, empowered to appoint the times and places for the meetings of the hundred court; to preside in those meetings, and to carry the sentences of the court into full execution. All the members within the hundred were originally members of the hundred court, and obliged, under severe penalties, to attend. This, however, was discovered, by experience, to be inconvenient; and, therefore, the court was new modelled by a law of the great Alfred. It was reduced to the hundredary or his bailiff, and twelve of the hundred; and these twelve were sworn, neither to condemn the innocent, nor to acquit the guilty. It was a mixed court, possessing both civil and criminal jurisdiction. Many petty causes came before it. Its proceedings were simple and summary: but if any one thought himself aggrieved by its decision, he had the right of appealing to a superiour tribunal. In this court also, sales of land, and other important transactions between members of the same hundred were published and confirmed.[l]

We have seen, that, in Pennsylvania, a very early attention was given to the respectable establishment of county courts. In the same session,

---

[h] Gil. Lys. & Isoc. 489. 1. Pot. Ant. 122.   [i] 1. Pot. Ant. 122.
[j] 1. Pot. Ant. 123.   [k] De mor. Ger. c. 12.
[l] Bac. on. Gov. 42, 43. 2. Henry. 241. 242.

which was the second after the settlement of the province, attention was also given to districts more circumscribed. It was enacted, that, in every precinct, three persons should be chosen yearly as peace makers in that precinct. That arbitrations might be as valid as the judgments of courts, it was directed, that the parties should sign a reference of the matter in controversy to the peace makers so chosen. This reference being ratified by the county court, the award of the peace makers was as conclusive as a judgment; and was registered in court in the same manner as other judgments.[m]

A farther regulation was made, also in the same session, that speedy justice might be administered to the poor, and in matters of small value. Debts under forty shillings were ordered to be heard and determined, upon sufficient evidence, by any two justices of the peace of that county, in which the cause arose. The justices were directed to report their judgment to the next county court. This judgment, if approved by the court, was to be recorded as good and binding.[n] Thus matters stood with regard to small debts, before the chasm of legislation, which has been repeatedly mentioned.

In the year one thousand seven hundred and five, a law was made, empowering any one justice of the peace to take cognizance of debts under the sum of forty shillings. His judgment concerning them is declared to be final and conclusive, and without appeal.[o] This law was repealed, but its principle was confirmed by another, made ten years afterwards.[p] Such is the law still with regard to debts under the sum of forty shillings.

By a law made in the year one thousand seven hundred and forty five, the jurisdiction of a single justice of the peace was extended, from sums under forty shillings, to sums not exceeding five pounds. But with regard to the exercise of the extended jurisdiction, two very salutary precautions are used. At the request of the parties, referees, named by them and approved by the justice, shall hear and examine the cause. Upon their return, the justice shall give judgment. In all cases, except those determined on the return of referees, an appeal lies from the judgment of the justice to the next court of common pleas. Upon an appeal made, the justice shall send a transcript of his judgment to the prothonotary of the court, which has the appellate jurisdiction of the cause.[q]

Since the revolution,[r] the jurisdiction of a single justice is carried as high as debts not exceeding the sum of ten pounds.[s]

[m] R. O. Book A. p. 29.   [n] Id. p. 34.   [o] Id. vol. 1. p. 154.
[p] 1. Laws Penn. 113, 114.   [q] 1. Laws Penn. 305. s. 1. 307. s. 7. 8.
[r] 2. Laws Penn. 304.
[s] By a law passed in the year one thousand seven hundred and ninety four (3. Laws Penn. 536.) the jurisdiction of the justices of the peace was extended to actions

From this historical deduction, it is natural to observe, that the civil jurisdiction of justices of the peace seems to have been a growing favourite with the legislature of Pennsylvania. It was introduced, at first, with apparent hesitation and reserve: it was confined to sums under forty shillings: it was intrusted to two magistrates, not to one: the judgment even of two magistrates was not binding till it was approved by the county court. The same jurisdiction was afterwards intrusted to a single magistrate, conclusively and without appeal. The jurisdiction of a single magistrate has been since extended from two to five, and from five to ten pounds: with the two precautions, indeed, of which I have already taken notice.

It may be observed, and the observation certainly has weight, that experience, the best test of things, must unquestionably have witnessed in favour of this jurisdiction; otherwise it would not, in this gradually progressive manner, have been intrusted and extended. But the weight of this observation ought to be compared with that of another, which is found in the opposite scale.

We have seen who are to exercise this jurisdiction: let us now see upon whom it is to be exercised — "upon the poorer sort of people," says the

---

of debt and other demands not exceeding twenty pounds, under the regulations and exceptions contained in the act of 1745. An appeal from the judgment of the justice to the court of common pleas was allowed only in cases, where the debt or demand exceeded five pounds. Either party might, before judgment given by the justice, elect to have the cause tried in the court of common pleas, if the debt or demand exceeded ten pounds.

By the present constitution of Pennsylvania (art. 9. s. 6.) it is declared, "that trial by jury shall be as heretofore, and the right thereof remain inviolate." This constitution was adopted in the year 1790. At that time, the jurisdiction of justices of the peace, (before whom a trial by jury cannot be had) was confined to cases of debt and contract not exceeding ten pounds; and even of such cases, some, in which unliquidated damages were claimed, were excepted out of their jurisdiction. In cases of torts, they possessed no jurisdiction whatever. The law of 1794 was early opposed, as repugnant to the above mentioned provision of the constitution, which, it declared, "was excepted out of the general powers of government," and should "for ever remain inviolate." (Art. 9. s. 26.) A respectable minority in the house of representatives protested against the act, at the time it was passed in that house, on this, among other grounds. (Jour. H. Rep. 23d. Feb. 1793.) No judicial determination on the subject has taken place. It was once brought before the supreme court of the state; but the law, which was temporary, expiring, the judges declined pronouncing a decision.

The attachment of the legislature, however, to the jurisdiction of the justices of the peace, has continued and increased. By a law passed at their last session (March 1804.) which repeals all the prior laws above mentioned, that jurisdiction has been extended to all cases of debts, and of demands for damages on promises of whatever kind, not exceeding the amount of one hundred dollars. (s. 1.) But it is declared that their jurisdiction shall not be construed to extend to actions of ejectment, of replevin, on real contracts for the sale or conveyance of lands or tenements, or upon promise of marriage. (s. 15.) And in cases of rent not exceeding one hundred dollars, they have power to compel the landlord to defalcate or set off the just account of the tenant out of the same; but the landlord *may* then *wave* farther proceedings law, "who are unable to bear the expenses arising by the common method of prosecution." [t] Let us suppose it possible, that a magistrate, in the exercise of his final and conclusive jurisdiction, may be guilty of gross partiality or wilful injustice; how is redress to be obtained by the unhappy sufferer under his injustice or partiality? Only by a prosecution against him. But the unhappy sufferer appeared or was brought before him, only because he was unable to bear the expense of a common prosecution. Would the prosecution of a magistrate, clothed with authority, and heretofore answering before his associates in office — would such a prosecution be less expensive? Would he, who was unable to bear the former, be strengthened in such a manner as to support the burthen of the latter? That the oppressed have suffered in silence, is no proof that the oppressed have not suffered.

Before the establishment of the present constitution, this was, in Pennsylvania, a subject of well founded alarm. One half, probably, of the personal property, which, in this commonwealth, becomes, during the revolution of a year, the subject of judicial decision, is withdrawn from the

---

before the justice, and pursue the method of distress, in the usual manner, for the balance so settled. (s. 12.)

If the demand does not exceed five dollars and thirty three cents, the justice himself hears the parties, and gives judgment, which is final. If the demand is for a sum exceeding that amount, the case shall, if both parties consent, be submitted to referees, whose award shall be transmitted to the justice, and he shall enter judgment on it, which shall be final and conclusive, if for a sum not exceeding fifty three dollars. (s. 3.) If either of the parties refuse to refer, the justice may hear them and give judgment. (s. 4.)

If the cause is decided by the justice alone, and the demand exceeds the sum of five dollars and thirty three cents, either party, if dissatisfied with the judgment, may appeal to the court of common pleas; as he may likewise do, if judgment is given on the award of referees, and such award exceeds the sum of fifty three dollars. (s. 4.) No appeal lies in the case of rent: but the remedy by replevin is declared to remain as before the act passed. (s. 12.)

This act did not receive the sanction of the governour; not being returned by him, to the house in which it originated, within ten days after it was presented to him, it became a law. Acts of a similar nature passed by the two houses at the two prior sessions, had been negatived by him, on account of their being contrary to the above cited provision of the constitution (which he declared to be his decided opinion, and to be more and more confirmed by reflection) as well as of their dangerous and oppressive tendency.

From these circumstances, and those before stated in this note, the question respecting the constitutionality of the late law must be considered as *at least doubtful*. It is worthy of observation, too, that the objections apply more forcibly to the late law, than to that of 1794. For, by the former, no right is given to either party to elect, before judgment given by the justice, to have the cause tried by a jury in the court of common pleas, as was given by the latter.

The justices of the peace also possess, by an act passed 1st March, 1799, (4. Laws Penn. 351.) which was temporary, but has been revived and made perpetual, jurisdiction over actions brought for the recovery of damages for any trespass done to real or personal property, where they do not exceed twenty dollars. *Ed.*

[t] 1. Laws Penn. 304. 305.

trial by jury, and committed to the summary and solitary determinations of the justices of the peace. Before the establishment of the present constitution, the single magistrates, on whom this jurisdiction was conferred, were not appointed by any respectable and responsible officer, nor chosen by any considerable part of the community, or at stated and well known times: they were elected in a corner, as occasion offered, or contrivance planned. The causes, which came before a justice chosen, and anxious to be again chosen, in this manner, were frequently suits between a party, on one side, who would have a vote at his succeeding election, and a party, on the other side, who would be entitled to no such vote. The poor and friendless part of the community — those, who were soonest ruined by oppression — those, who were least able to struggle against it — were the part selected to be delivered over, bound hand and foot, to magistrates possessing such powers, and possessing them by such means, and in such a manner. Surely, this was a subject of well founded alarm.

The cause of alarm is removed by the salutary provisions, which we find in the present constitution of the commonwealth. The justices of the peace are appointed by the governour, who, by the citizens of the commonwealth, is himself elected, and who, to the citizens of the commonwealth, is himself responsible. The justices of the peace are appointed during good behaviour; and can no longer be seduced, by a dependent situation, to disgrace themselves and their offices by sinister adjudications. Farther; they are habitually controlled by the judges of the court of common pleas. Those judges have, within their respective counties, the like powers with the judges of the supreme court, to issue writs of certiorari to the justices of the peace, and to cause their proceedings to be brought before them, and the like right and justice to be done.[u]

But though the cause of alarm be now removed, the cause of considerate circumspection still subsists: for it is still true, that the property decided by justices of the peace is property withdrawn from a trial by jury. The constitution suggests, indeed, that those magistrates are to exercise a civil jurisdiction; but the terms, on which, and the extent, to which that jurisdiction is to be exercised, are left, as is proper, to be marked and ascertained by the wisdom and the experience of the legislature.

Perhaps the distant view which I have taken of the hundred courts, may not have been altogether impertinent to the present subject. Perhaps it will not be impracticable, after some time, to introduce them into Pennsylvania, modified, indeed, but with modifications not destructive of their principle. Such a tribunal should not be considered as a fanciful

---

[u] Cons. Penn. art. 5. s. 8.

alteration, or a wild experiment; it ought rather to be deemed a close adherence to the wisdom of the ancient plan, concerted by the great Alfred, and to the spirit of his excellent and venerable institutions. To an object of this kind, the legislature is fully competent; for the constitution[v] empowers it to establish courts from time to time.

I have now made a tour through the courts of the United States, and through a number of the courts of Pennsylvania. Perhaps I ought here to make an apology for the degree of minuteness, with which I have surveyed and described them. Let me apologize by reciting an incident, which I remember to have heard in my younger years.

From the castle of Edinburgh, in Scotland, the prospect is uncommonly rich, extensive, and diversified. A young gentleman, born and educated at no very considerable distance from it, set out on his travels through Europe, with a view to notice attentively every thing, which he should find most worthy of his remark. When he was at Rome, the subject of exquisite prospects became, one day, the topick of conversation in a company of literati, to whom he had been introduced. Among others, that from the castle of Edinburgh was mentioned; and to our young traveller a reference was naturally made for a minute description of its different parts and beauties. They expressed themselves happy in so fine an opportunity of learning every particular concerning that, of which vague and general accounts had so much excited their admiration. With blushes, he was obliged to disclose the fact — that though he had resided, from his birth, near an object, which so well deserved to be known, yet he had never bestowed upon it the least share of attention, and was, therefore, totally unqualified to gratify the company by describing it. A profound silence was observed. It was not lost upon the young traveller. He returned immediately to Scotland, and acquired the knowledge of what was worthy to be known at home, before he went farther abroad in search of what was remarkable in foreign countries.

The institutions of other nations and of other times merit, most unquestionably, our perusal and our study. The travels of a young Anacharisis, in which the governments and laws of Sparta and of Athens are so beautifully delineated, richly deserve to be read and admired. But to us, the governments, and laws, and institutions of the United States and of Pennsylvania ought to be the constant standard, with which we compare those of every other country. How can we compare them with a standard, which is unknown?

Trusting, therefore, that the interesting nature of the things which I describe will compensate for my minuteness and for my many imperfections in describing them, I proceed to give an account of some other

[v] Art. 5. s. 1.

jurisdictions known to the constitution and laws of the United States and of this commonwealth.

Circuit courts form a part, and a very valuable part, of our juridical system in Pennsylvania. These are of two kinds — courts of nisi prius, which try issues joined in civil causes — courts of oyer and terminer and general gaol delivery, which hear and determine criminal causes.

The courts of nisi prius are derived from the supreme court; and act as its auxiliaries in the exercise of its very important jurisdiction. They decide, in the several counties, all questions of fact, which arise in civil causes depending in the supreme court. They are called courts of nisi prius from the following circumstance — The causes commenced in the courts of Westminster Hall are, by the course of those courts, appointed to be tried at their bar, by a jury returned from the county, in which the cause of action arises. But in the writ, enjoining the attendance of the jury, there is this proviso — *nisi prius* justitiarii ad assisas capiendas venerint — unless, before the day prefixed, the judges of assize come into the county in question. This they do: the issue joined in the cause is tried in the proper county: the verdict is taken, and returned to the court above, on the day when the jury would otherwise have been obliged to appear and try it at bar.[w] By this means, much trouble and expense are saved to the parties, the jury, and the witnesses.[x] By this wise arrangement, the investigation of the facts — a matter frequently of the greatest consequence even in civil causes, is carried on in the county, sometimes in the very neighbourhood, in which the dispute arose; while questions of law are left to be considered by a court, which, from its permanent situation, is better qualified for deciding points of difficulty and importance.

The courts of nisi prius are held between the terms of the supreme court, at such times as the judges think most convenient for the[y] people.[z]

---

[w] 4. Ld. Bac. 64.   [x] 3. Bl. Com. 59.   [y] 3. Laws Penn. 92. s. 1.

[z] Courts of nisi prius are now held only in the county of Philadelphia. In the other counties of the state, they have been superseded by courts, styled "circuit courts," established by an act of assembly passed in the year one thousand seven hundred and ninety nine. (4. Laws Penn. 362.)

The circuit courts are held by one or more of the justices of the supreme court, at such times and places as the justices of that court appoint, having due regard to the convenience of the people (s. 1.) In most of the countries, they are held once, and sometimes twice in the year, at the discretion of the justices.

They have no original jurisdiction; but have power to issue writs of certiorari, habeas corpus, and all other remedial and other writs and process, grantable by the justices of the supreme court by virtue of their offices (except writs of errour, and certiorari after judgments, orders, or decrees); and the writs and process so issued are returnable in the circuit court. Appeals also lie to the circuit court in each county from the register's and orphans' courts of that county. (s. 3.)

The circuit courts have power to give judgment, pass decrees, and award execution, and generally exercise similar power in any cause before them, and in which jurisdiction is given to them, in as ample a manner as if sitting in bank. They have power, though not sitting as a court of oyer and terminer, to try any capital or

If it is highly expedient and convenient, that civil actions should be tried in the county, in which the causes of action arose; it is much more so, that criminal prosecutions should be tried in the county, in which the crimes were committed. A crime can seldom be proved in any other manner than by oral testimony. But of all the modes of proof, that which requires the attendance of witnesses from a great distance, is necessarily the most burthensome and expensive. In another view, too, it is very important, that every crime should be tried and every criminal should be punished near the place, where the guilt was contracted. One great design of punishment is to deter others from imitating the conduct, for which it is inflicted. This design is most effectually accomplished, when the same persons, who have seen the law violated, are witnesses also of the dismal consequences, by which its violation is unavoidably succeeded.

In England, crimes are generally tried before judges, who sit by virtue of two commissions from the crown. One is a commission of oyer and terminer: the other is a commission of general gaol delivery. The first is directed to the judges of the circuits, and to many others of the best account within the circuits, as we are informed by my Lord Bacon. By this commission, they are authorized to hear and determine all treasons, felonies, and misdemeanors. But this commission gives them no power to proceed upon any other indictments than those found before themselves. The second commission is directed only to the judges themselves, and the clerk of the assize associate. This commission empowers them to try and deliver every prisoner in the gaol, for whatever offence he may have been committed, or before whatever judges he may have been indicted: but, by this commission, they have authority only over those who are prisoners in the gaol.[a]

By the law of the land, says my Lord Coke,[b] this commission was instituted, that men might not be detained a long time in prison; but might receive full and speedy justice.

Commissions of oyer and terminer are either general, or they are particular, in respect of the persons, of the offences, or of the places where the offences are committed.[c] Sometimes, upon urgent occasions, the king issues a special or extraordinary commission of oyer and terminer and gaol delivery, confined to those offences, which demand immediate

---

other criminal case removed into the circuit court, and to pronounce judgment, and award execution, as fully as the supreme court may do. (s. 4.)

If either of the parties to any suit removed from the common pleas, register's court, or orphans' court is dissatisfied with the decision of the circuit court on any demurrer, special verdict, case stated, point reserved on the trial, motion in arrest of judgment or for a new trial, or to set aside a judgment, discontinuance, or non pros, he may appeal to the supreme court. (s. 4.) *Ed.*

[a] 4. Ld. Bac. 61.   [b] 4. Ins. 168.   [c] 4. Ins. 162. 163.

inquiry and punishment. On these, the course of proceeding is the same as on ordinary and general commissions.[d]

The constitution of Pennsylvania declares,[e] that no commission of oyer and terminer or gaol delivery shall be issued. This power is expressly excepted out of the general powers of government. The powers granted, in England, by those commissions, are, in this commonwealth, placed much better for the security and advantage of the citizens. The judges of the supreme court are, by virtue of their offices, justices of oyer and terminer and general gaol delivery in the several counties of the state. The judges of the court of common pleas, in each county, are, in the same manner, justices of oyer and terminer and general gaol delivery for the trial of capital and other offences in such county.[f]

We have already seen that all those judges hold their offices during their good behaviour. The judges, both of the supreme and inferiour courts of the United States, hold their offices by the same tenure. The important nature of this difference between the situation of those, who exercise criminal jurisdiction in England, and that of those, who exercise it in the United States and in Pennsylvania, was fully shown in a former lecture,[g] When I was engaged in drawing a parallel between the government of the United States and that of Great Britain.

You have frequently heard of the distinction between law and equity, of courts of equity, and of equitable jurisdiction and powers.

Though no court of equity subsists separately in the United States or in Pennsylvania, yet this subject demands your closest attention. It occupies an important station in the science of law.

By Aristotle, equity is thus defined — "the correction of that, in which the law is defective, by being too general." [h] In making laws, it is impossible to specify or to foresee every case: it is, therefore, necessary, that, in interpreting them, those cases should be excepted, which the legislator himself, had he foreseen them, would have specified and excepted. Such interpretation, however, ought to be made with the greatest circumspection. By indulging it rashly, the judges would become the arbiters, instead of being the ministers of the laws. It is not to be used, unless where the strongest and most convincing reasons appear for using it. A strong reason for using it is drawn from the spirit of the law, or the motive which prevailed on the legislature to make it. When equity is taken in this sense, every court of law is also a court of equity. When equity is taken in this sense — and, applied to the interpretation of law, this is its genuine meaning — it is an expression synonimous to true and sound construction.[i]

[d] 4. Bl. Com. 267.   [e] Art. 9. s. 15. 26.   [f] Cons. Penn. art. 5. s. 3. 5.
[g] Ante. p. 331.   [h] Gro. 366.   [i] 3. Bl. Com. 429.

Terms, and the relative positions of terms, are frequently too apt to mislead us. When we find a court of law and a court of equity placed in contradistinction to each other, how natural is it to conclude, that the former decides without equity, and that the latter decides without law. Such a conclusion, however, is greatly erroneous.

It has, indeed, been said, concerning a court of equity, that it determines by the spirit, and not by the letter of a rule. But ought not this to be said concerning a court of law likewise? Is not each equally bound — does not each profess itself to be equally bound — to explain the law according to the intention of those, who made it? In the interpretation of laws, whether strictly or liberally, there is not a single maxim, which is not adopted, in the same manner, and with the same force, by both courts. Hitherto, then, we find no difference between a court of law and a court of equity.

It has been supposed, that it is the peculiar and exclusive business of a court of equity to take cognizance of frauds, and accidents, and trusts. One kind of trusts, indeed — a technical, a useless, and a mischievous kind, as I shall show in the proper place — a trust created by the limitation of a second use — has been forced into the courts of equity, by the narrowness of the courts of law. But of other trusts, the courts of law take full and unreserved cognizance; particularly the very important and extensive trust of money received by one to the use of another. An action, founded on this trust, has often been compared to a bill in equity, on account of its useful and salutary influence. For accidents, too, remedy is found in a court of law: for the loss of deeds; for mistakes in payments, receipts, and accounts; for the destruction of records; and for a variety of other contingencies. For relief from other accidents, which might be specified, application to a court of law, we own, is vain; but application to a court of equity is vain also. With regard to frauds, they are as much the objects of cognizance and resentment in the courts of law, as they are in the courts of equity: a fraud in obtaining a devise of lands is always sent out of chancery to be determined at law.[j] Hitherto, again, we find no difference between a court of law and a court of equity.

A court of equity has been represented as bound by no precedents or rules, but as proceeding arbitrarily, according to the sentiments of the chancellor, arising from the circumstances of every particular case. But, in truth, precedents and rules govern as much in chancery as they govern in courts of law. Decrees are often founded on no other principle, than a reverence for a series of former concurring determinations. Hitherto, still, again, we find no difference between a court of equity and a court of law. The rules of property, the rules of interpretation, and the

[j] 3. Bl. Com. 431.

rules of evidence are, in both, the same. The systems of jurisprudence in both are systems equally laboured and artificial, and founded equally on the same principles of justice and positive law.

Let it be observed farther, that the distinction between law and equity, as administered in separate courts, is not known at present, nor seems to have been known at any former period, in any country, excepting England, and those of her colonies, who, in this instance, have imitated the practice of England. Even in England, the aula regis, anciently, as we have seen, a court of supreme jurisdiction over the whole kingdom, administered equal justice, according to the rules of equity as well as of law. In none of our very ancient authors, such as Glanvil, Bracton, Fleta, and Britton, do we find the remotest reference or allusion to the equitable jurisdiction in the court of chancery. When the aula regis, become unwieldy and cumbersome, was divided into a number of distinct courts, a court of equity, existing separately from a court of law, did not, by any means, enter into the original plan of partition.[k]

Whence then the origin and progress of this distinct and independent equitable jurisdiction, which, in England, has become so very extensive and important? In what material or essential points, does it differ from a jurisdiction exercised according to the rules and principles of law? These questions merit full and satisfactory answers.

In very early times, the chancellor of England was nothing more than an officer merely ministerial. He was the king's secretary. In this character, he had the sole charge of writing the king's letters. In the same character, he acquired the sole power of issuing the king's writs.[l] These writs were necessary, not only to bring the defendant into court, but also to give the court jurisdiction over the cause. For, soon after the conquest, it became a general rule, that no plea could be held in the king's court without the king's writ.[m] As causes and the kinds of causes multiplied, the chancellor was more and more employed in issuing writs, and in framing new writs, directed to the courts of common law, in order to empower them to give remedy in cases, in which none could before be obtained.

On this subject we find an early legislative provision.[n] "When, in one case, a writ was found in the chancery; and, in a like case falling under the same right and requiring the like remedy, no precedent of a writ could be produced, the clerks in chancery were directed to form a new one. If they could not agree, it was adjourned to the next parliament, that a writ might be framed by the consent of the learned in the law." This provision was made, "lest it should happen that the court of the king should be deficient in doing justice to the suitors." Here we see the chan-

[k] 3. Bl. Com. 49.   [l] Millar. 469.   [m] 1. Reev. 66.   [n] St. 13. Edw. 1. c. 24.

cery fully established as the great *officina brevium*. These writs, however, were all intended to be returnable in the courts of justice. At this time, the chancery itself was not considered as a court: it is always mentioned as an office merely.[o]

In the reign of Richard the second, the provision, which we have just now read, was applied to a purpose, unforeseen and unexpected. Uses of land — a species, not of property, but of an artificial and mysterious claim to the advantages of property, which I shall hereafter consider minutely — began, about that time, to be introduced. The establishment of them was, to the clergy, a lucrative and a favourite object: for it would have eluded the statutes of mortmain. To accomplish this object, John Waltham, the bishop of Salisbury, and at that time chancellor, by a strained interpretation of the law, devised the writ of subpæna — the powerful instrument of chancery jurisdiction — and made it returnable before himself in chancery, in order to oblige a feoffee to uses to account for the profits of the land.[p] Successful in assuming the jurisdiction of one case, the chancellor afterwards extended it to others; and, in the time of Edward the fourth, the process by subpæna was become the daily practice of the court. Such was the origin of the equitable jurisdiction of chancery.

The description which we have given of courts of equity and courts of law, and of equitable and legal jurisdictions, is conformable to the practice and proceedings of the court of chancery and of the courts of common law in England, at present, and during the last hundred years, or the greatest part of them. But this description cannot, with propriety, be applied to the practice and proceedings of those courts at periods more remote: in those remote periods, a court of equity was considered and acted as possessing a power, altogether discretionary. "Equity," says Mr. Selden,[q] "is a roguish thing. For law we have a measure: know what to trust to. Equity is according to the conscience of him that is chancellor, and as that is larger or narrower, so is equity. It is all one as if they should make the standard of measure a chancellor's foot. What an uncertain measure would this be! One chancellor has a long foot: another, a short foot; a third, an indifferent foot. 'Tis the same thing in the chancellor's conscience." Similar, though not expressed, perhaps, in a similar manner, were the sentiments of the principal lawyers of that age — of Spelman, of Coke, of Lambard, and even of the great Bacon,[r] who himself held the office of chancellor, and who, of all others, appears to have been the best qualified to understand the nature of that office. This, indeed, was in the infancy, as it may be called, of the court of chancery,

---

[o] 1. Reev. 43.   [p] Millar. 475. 3. Bl. Com. 51.   [q] Table talk.
[r] Millar. 477. 3. Bl. Com. 433.

before its jurisdiction was settled, and when the chancellors, partly from their ignorance of law, and partly from ambition and lust of power, had arrogated to themselves such unlimited authority, as has since been totally disclaimed by their successours.

In the remote periods, which we have mentioned, while a court of equity acted and was considered as possessing powers altogether discretionary, the courts of law, on the other hand, acted upon principles, which were both narrow and unjust.[s] If the judges of the courts of common law had been as liberal then as they have been since, the court of chancery would never have swelled to its present enormous bulk. "I have always thought," said the very able and learned Judge,[t] whose opinion I now quote, "that formerly there was too confined a way of thinking in the judges of the courts of common law; and that courts of equity have risen, because the judges have not properly applied the principles of the common law, but, being too narrowly governed by old cases and maxims, have too much prevented the publick from having the benefit of that law." This contracted spirit, prevailing, for a long time, in the courts of common law, necessarily drove a multitude of suitors into a court of equity for relief. The doors of this court were constantly open to receive them.

I adduce an instance, familiar and striking. A double bond — a bond, with a penalty containing the double of the sum really due — is an instrument peculiar, I believe, to England, and those countries which have adopted the laws of England. It was originally contrived to evade those absurd constitutions, which interdicted the receipt or payment of interest for the use of money lent. Since interest could not be allowed by the law, as it then stood, the penalty was, in the courts of law, considered as the real debt, when the debtor did not perform his agreement at the time stipulated; and for the penalty, judgment was accordingly given. In proportion as business and trade became considerable and extended, the necessity and the propriety of paying and receiving interest became daily more apparent, and was allowed by the law; and, in the reign of Henry the eighth, it was declared, by an act of parliament, that the debt or loan itself was, "the just and true intent," for which the obligation was given. One would naturally suppose, that this legislative declaration would have been a sufficient authority for the courts of law to alter the principle, on which their former judgments had been given. The narrow minded judges of those times thought otherwise; and, adhering wilfully and technically to the letter of the settled precedents, refused to consider the payment of principal, interest, and costs as a full satisfaction for the bond. In the courts of equity, where a more liberal spirit prevailed, the

[s] 3. Bl. Com. 433.   [t] Lord Chief Justice Wilmot. 2. Wils. 350.

instrument, according to "its just and true intent," was considered as merely a security for the money really due, and was discharged on its payment. But so pertinaciously, in this instance, did the courts of law cling to their precedents, even so late as the present century, that the parliament was obliged, at length, to interpose, and to direct, that what had long been the practice in the courts of equity, should, in future, be the practice in the courts of law.[u]

We now see the causes of the progress, which a distinct and independent equitable jurisdiction made in England.

In many instances, however, and, indeed, in the general principles of their proceedings and adjudications, the courts of law and equity have, for a century past, gradually approximated to one another. A series of eminent lawyers, who successively filled the chancellor's chair, formed the system of equity into a regular science, which, like the science of law, cannot be acquired without the aids of study and experience. In the courts of law, a series of lawyers, equally eminent, have, by degrees, embraced the enlarged and enlightened principles, by which law as well as equity should be governed and illustrated. In chancery, it is a maxim, that equity follows the law. In the courts of law, a powerful reason for adopting a principle or rule is the consideration, that the principle or rule has been adopted in chancery. Each jurisdiction, as far as possible, follows the other, in the best and most effectual measures for attaining the great ends of certainty, peace, and justice. The suggestion, indeed, of every bill in equity, in order to give jurisdiction to the court, is still, that the complainant has no remedy at the common law. But he who views the variety and extent of the causes determined in chancery, must be satisfied that this suggestion is now a mere fiction, copied, indeed, from the realities of former times.

We are now prepared to give an answer to the second question, which was proposed some time ago — In what material or essential points, does the jurisdiction of chancery differ from a jurisdiction exercised according to the rules and principles of the common law?

They differ not, as we have seen, in the rules of property, of evidence, or of interpretation: they differ not in the principles of justice or of positive law. Still, however, they differ in some points very material, and which ought to be known.

They differ with regard to the mode of proof. By the rules of the common law, as a party cannot be a witness in his own favour, so he cannot be obliged to become a witness, or to furnish evidence, against himself. But the views of equity, with regard to this subject, are more extensive and refined. If the defendant knows the claim made upon him

[u] 3. Bl. Com. 435.

to be well founded, he ought neither to conceal it, nor refuse to satisfy it. If he has done nothing improperly, he can sustain no loss by a candid declaration of what he has done. If his conduct has been fraudulent, the fraud should receive no protection: but it receives protection, if it is suffered to be concealed. For these reasons, when material facts rest only in the knowledge of the party, a court of equity examines him, on oath, with regard to the truth of the transaction.

In mercantile transactions, this mode of discovery is peculiarly reasonable and important. In such transactions, the parties are generally at a distance from one another: their contracts, therefore, cannot be made in the presence of witnesses. Of such transactions, each party keeps or ought to keep a regular diary or account. On the truth and accuracy of this account, the other party may naturally be supposed to place a very considerable degree of dependence.

As this mode of discovery is unknown to the courts of law, equity has acquired a concurrent jurisdiction with those courts in all matters of account. From the same source, it has acquired a jurisdiction in matters of fraud, and judgments at law obtained by fraud or concealment.

In the courts of common law, the trial is by a jury. This trial requires, that the witnesses should give their testimony *viva voce,* and in open court. But in courts of equity, the mode of trial is by administering interrogatories to the witnesses, and taking their depositions in writing, wherever they may happen to reside. For this reason, the chancery alone can take proofs by commission, when the witnesses are abroad, or about to go abroad, or are prevented by age or infirmity from attending.

When a contract has been made and broken, a court of law only awards damages for the breach; but a court of equity will decree a specifick performance. It will likewise set aside deeds, and order sales and conveyances of lands.[v]

These are the principal, though not the only points, in which the jurisdiction of a court of equity differs materially from that of the courts of common law. I speak of those jurisdictions as considered under the aspects, under which they have been hitherto viewed. There is a particular aspect, in which they have never, so far as I know, been viewed; but to which I shall, by and by, direct your minute attention.

In the mean time, it will be proper to consider a question, which has employed the talents of the most eminent writers on jurisprudence. Should the jurisdiction according to equity, and the jurisdiction according to law, be committed to the same court? or should they be divided between different courts?

My Lord Bacon thinks that they should be divided: my Lord Kaims

[v] Millar. 482. 3. Bl. Com. 437.

thinks that they should be united. All this is very natural. My Lord Bacon presided in a divided, my Lord Kaims was a judge in a united jurisdiction. Let us attend to their arguments: the arguments of such consummate masters will suggest abundant matter of instruction, even if we cannot subscribe to them implicitly.

The reason assigned by my Lord Bacon for preferring the division of these jurisdictions between several courts is, that if they are committed to the same court, the distinction between them will soon be lost; for that the discretionary will soon draw along with it the legal power.[w]

My Lord Kaims admits, that, in the science of jurisprudence, it is undoubtedly of great importance, that the boundary between equity and common law be clearly ascertained; because, otherwise, we shall in vain hope for just decisions. A judge, adds he, who is uncertain whether the case belong to equity or to common law, cannot have a clear conception what judgment ought to be pronounced. But, on the other hand, may it not be urged, that to divide, among different courts, things intimately connected bears hard upon every man, who has a claim to prosecute; because, before he bring his action, he must, at his peril, determine a point extremely nice — whether the case is to be governed by equity, or by common law? Nor is the most profound knowledge always sufficient to prevent inconveniences upon this subject: for, though he may be perfectly acquainted with his own demand, he cannot certainly foresee the defence, nor divine whether it will be a defence at law or in equity. Weighing these different arguments, the preponderancy seems, in his opinion, to be on the side of a united jurisdiction. The sole inconvenience of a united jurisdiction — that it tends to blend common law with equity — may admit a remedy by an institute, distinguishing, with accuracy, their boundaries: but the inconvenience of a divided jurisdiction admits not any effectual remedy.[x]

Both these great men agree in one point — that the distinction between common law and equity ought, by all means, to be preserved; and one of them recommends even an institute to distinguish their limits with accuracy. With the becoming deference to such high authority, it may be worth while to examine, whether, in the fluctuating situation of men and business, an attempt to fix permanently the line of division between law and equity would not be fruitless and impracticable. This line, I am apt to believe, will be found to change necessarily according to different circumstances — the state of property — the improvement of the arts — the experience of the judges — the refinement of the people.

In rude ages, the first decisions of judges arose, probably, from their immediate feelings; in other words, from considerations of equity. In the

[w] 1. Ld. Bac. 253. Aph. 45.   [x] Prin. Eq. 49.

course of their business, many similar cases would successively occur: upon these, similar decisions would naturally be given. A number of precedents, thus introduced, would, from the power of custom, acquire authority and respect. General rules would gradually be formed; and the utility of establishing them would become an object of attention. Those rules, however, upon a little further experience, would be found, at some times, too narrow; at other times, too broad. To adhere rigidly to them, at all times, would be to commit injustice under the sanction of law. To avoid an evil so alarming, it would be thought advisable, upon extraordinary occasions, to recede from general maxims, and to decide, as originally, according to the immediate sentiments of justice. In this manner, the distinction between equity and strict law was, probably, introduced: the former comprehended the established rules: the latter comprised their exceptions.

But when the exceptions became numerous, many of them also would be found to be similar, and, consequently, to require a similar decision. Those similar decisions would, in time, produce a new rule; and this new rule would, in its turn, give birth to new exceptions.

If this account of the matter is just — and it seems to be natural — law and equity are in a state of continual progression; one occupying incessantly the ground, which the other, in its advancement, has left. The posts now possessed by strict law were formerly possessed by equity; and the posts now possessed by equity will hereafter be possessed by strict law.

In this view of the subject — and it is an interesting one — equity may be well deemed the conductor of law towards a state of refinement and perfection.

In this view of the subject, we can find no difficulty in pronouncing, that every court of law ought also to be a court of equity; for every institution should contain in it the seeds of its perfection, as well as of its preservation.

In this view of the subject, we shall find as little difficulty in pronouncing, that every court of equity will gradually become a court of law; for its decisions, at first discretionary, will gradually be directed by general principles and rules. Thus, in England, the court of chancery has gradually devested itself of its original and arbitrary character, and has approached to that of the courts of common law. Thus, again, in England, the courts of common law, animated lately with the spirit of improvement inspired by a liberal age, have enlarged their powers of just decision, and have advanced within the precincts of equity.

The particulars, in which they still differ, are, indeed, of importance; but I see no reason why the separate powers of chancery, placed there very properly, indeed, should be thought incommunicable to the courts of common law.

A power to compel discoveries by a party may, without any incongruity, be annexed to a common law jurisdiction. This, to a certain degree, has been already done by a law of the United States. In the trial of actions at law, the courts of the national government are authorized to require the parties to produce books or writings in their power, in cases, in which they might be compelled to produce them by the ordinary rules of proceeding in chancery.[y]

The power of granting commissions to take, upon interrogatories, the depositions of foreign, removing, or infirm witnesses is familiar, in practice, to the courts both of the United States and of Pennsylvania.

The power of compelling a specifick performance is, I apprehend, strictly and originally a power at the common law. In some of its unpropitious eras, indeed, the exercise of this part of its authority has, in most cases, fallen into disuse, and has not been revived, but anciently it subsisted in its full force and vigour; and, in one case, it is supposed to subsist in its full force and vigour to this day. I fortify my opinion by instances of the fact.

Fines, or solemn agreements acknowledged and entered of record, are well known to be of very high antiquity at the common law. It is generally, I believe, supposed, that they took place only in pleas respecting land. But the fact is unquestionably otherwise. Fines were executed in other pleas. If either of the parties violated the agreement, a suit upon it was commenced. When they both appeared in court; if they both acknowledged the writing containing the agreement; or if the agreement was stated to be such by the justices, before whom it was taken, and this was testified by their record; then the party, who had broken it, was in the king's mercy, and was attached till he gave good security to perform the concord in future — either the specifick thing agreed on, if that was possible; or otherwise, in some instances, an equivalent.[z] Can a power to adjudge a specifick performance be expressed more unequivocally or more strongly? This instance is referred to a period so ancient as the reign of Henry the second.

In the reign of Edward the first, we find that, in some cases, land could be recovered in a writ of covenant; and in such cases, it was a real action: in other cases, damages only could be recovered; and in such cases, it was a personal action. The former writ of covenant was generally that, on which fines were levied.[a] Actions of covenant for land occur likewise in the time of Edward the second. It was held, that this action was appropriated for the recovery of a fee simple or of a term.[b]

In tracing this subject down to the reign of Edward the third, we find that a writ of covenant was that, upon which fines were most commonly

[y] Laws U.S. 1. cong. 1. sess. c. 20. s. 15.   [z] 1. Reev. 119.   [a] Id. 477.
[b] 2. Reev. 33. 147.

levied. But, by this time, the writ of covenant was usually brought upon a supposed transaction. The writ of covenant, in this instance, had the effect of actually transferring the land; and thus produced a *specifick* effect.[e] Such, with regard to fines, continues to be the practice to the present day.

I think I have now proved, that the power to adjudge a specifick performance is strictly and originally a power at common law.

The power to set aside deeds, and to order sales and conveyances of land, can be considered only as branches of the power to compel a specifick performance.

In all the views which we have hitherto taken of this important part of jurisprudence, we find no reason to conclude, that a court of chancery would bestow any improvement of essential importance, on the juridical system of the United States, or of this commonwealth.

There is, however, another view, in which this subject ought to be considered. In that other view, if I mistake not, the establishment of a court of chancery will be found a matter of great moment both to the United States and to Pennsylvania.

Military power has too long governed in the affairs of men: influence of a kind more peaceful and benign is, we hope, about to assume its place. We trust that, in future, men, instead of knowing and treating one another as enemies, and as engaged in enterprises mutually destructive, will know and treat one another as friends, and as jointly operating in plans and systems for promoting the prosperity, the virtue, and the felicity of the human race.

Deeds of arms, we fondly anticipate, will not be the themes of future songs. The more delightful subjects of agriculture, of the arts, and of commerce will employ the efforts of genius the most sublime.

Commerce arrests our present attention. Its encouragement is justly a favourite object with every government, which is good and wise. The protection of commerce, and of foreign merchants engaged in commerce, forms an article in the great charter of the liberties of England. A regulation, so salutary and so humane, deserves, as it has obtained, the warmest eulogium of the eloquent Montesquieu. Upon this subject, his powers carried him away like a torrent, rapid and irresistible: my humbler aim is to glide along a smooth and gentle stream.

The law merchant as well as the law maritime forms a branch of the general law of nations. The inference is natural, that mercantile as well as as maritime transactions should be the object of a separate jurisdiction; and that we should see courts of commerce as well as courts of admiralty. Things done upon the sea are deemed worthy of peculiar cognizance: are things done beyond the sea less entitled to peculiar notice?

[e] Id. 173.

In the rude and barbarous times, which are past, and which, we pray, may never return — in those times, above alluded to, when nations were known to nations only by feats of hostility; even their hostile feats were subjected to the cognizance of law, and were dignified with an appropriate jurisdiction. The court of chivalry, held before the lord high constable and earl marshal of England, had cognizance of contracts and deeds of arms and of war out of the realm, and also of things which touched war within the realm.[d] When war was the general trade, this court enjoyed a high degree of consequence and reputation. My Lord Coke calls it "the honourable court." As commerce comes in the place of war, should not commercial come in the place of military institutions?

Even with regard to commerce, we shall find, in former ages, establishments expressly made and calculated for its protection and encouragement, in the manner in which it was then carried on. This was chiefly in markets and publick fairs, at which merchants attended personally with their merchandise. It was not then usual to trust property to a great amount in the hands of foreign correspondents.

So early as the reign of Henry the third, we find the delays, and what were called the solemnities, of proceedings dispensed with, where the plaintiff deserved a particular respect or privilege; as noble persons, or merchants, who were continually leaving the kingdom.[e]

Edward the first has been often and deservedly styled the English Justinian. In his reign we may expect to find a proper attention paid to the interests of commerce. Our expectation will not be disappointed. In his reign the statute of merchants was made.

The pressing demands, which arise in the course of mercantile transactions, rendered the delays and the niceties of the law inconvenient, and sometimes fatal, to the credit and fortunes of the merchants. This, it is said, occasioned many to withdraw from the kingdom. Those, who remained, made application that some speedy course might be appointed for recovering their debts at the stipulated times of payment. In compliance with their application, the following method of securing a ready payment of their debts was provided by parliament. The merchant was to bring his debtor before the magistrates specified in the law, to acknowledge the debt and the time of payment. This recognisance was entered on a roll. If the debtor did not make payment at the time appointed, the magistrate, before whom the recognisance was acknowledged, was, on the application of the creditor, obliged immediately to cause the chattels and devisable lands of the debtor to be sold, to the amount of the debt, by the appraisement of honest men. The money, if the property was sold, was paid instantly to the creditor: if the property could not be sold, it was delivered to him according to the appraisement. If, from partiality to the

[d] 4. Ins. 123.   [e] 1. Reev. 295. 296. 300.

debtor, the appraisers set too high a price upon the goods, they were themselves obliged to take them at the price which they fixed, and to satisfy the creditor for the money due to him.[f]

Commerce continued to be patronised by the kings, and encouraged by the legislature, of England. In the twenty seventh year of Edward the third, was made the famous statute of the staple, containing a most complete code of regulations for commercial transactions at the staple, or great mart, which was then established in certain places of England.

As this mart was intended, in its very institution, for the resort of foreign merchants, a mode, consonant to the ideas of foreigners, and fitted to the nature of mercantile transactions, was adopted for administering justice. That disputes might be decided among them according to their own conceptions, it was provided, that none of the justices of the courts of Westminster Hall, nor any other justices, if they came to the places where the mart was, should interfere with the jurisdiction of the mayor and constables of the staple. Within the town where the mart was, those officers had cognizance of people and of things touching the mart. All merchants coming to it, and their servants, were, in all things concerning it, governed by the law merchant, and not by the common law of the land, nor by the usages of cities, or boroughs, or towns; nor were they, concerning such things, to implead or be impleaded before the magistrates of such cities, boroughs, or towns. That the foreign merchants might have reason to complain of no one, and that no one might have reason to complain of them, speedy justice was administered from day to day, and from hour to hour.

That contracts made within the staple might be strictly observed, and that payments might be punctually made, a course similar to that of the statute merchant was directed. The mayor of the staple was empowered to take similar recognisances of debts; and upon those recognisances, similar proceedings were held. A recognisance of this kind has obtained the name of a statute staple.[g]

It was directed that, in every staple town, the mayor should be one well acquainted with the law merchant, that he might be qualified for the discharge of such an important trust.[h]

If we refer to the institutions of the ancient nations; we shall find that, among them too, tribunals have been established for the decision of mercantile causes. Magistrates, called ναυτοδικαι, had the jurisdiction of them in Athens.[i] The prætor peregrinus determined them in Rome.[j] Even after the fall of the western empire, the institution of courts for the trial of commercial suits subsisted in many places:[k] and fairs and markets

[f] 1. Reev. 405.   [g] 2. Reev. 71.   [h] 2. Reev. 75.   [i] Bouch. The. Com. 134.
[j] Id. 138.   [k] Id. 140.

had their peculiar jurisdictions assigned for the expeditious determination of controversies that might arise in them.

The United States have the most extensive prospects of commerce before them. The variety of their climate, the richness of their soil, the number and value of their productions furnish them with abundant materials to exchange for the manufactures and refined commodities of Europe and of Asia. The genius of their governments is favourable to trade, because it is favourable to equality and industry, the only pillars, on which trade can be supported. The long and cumbrous list of duties and customs, which publick debts, the arts of finance, and the political views of government have introduced into every country of Europe, is, in a great measure, unknown in their ports. They possess not, indeed, the advantages of use and habit to form precedents for their transactions, publick and private, with foreign nations, and with the individuals of whom foreign nations are composed: but to compensate for this, they are disengaged from one inconvenience, with which use and habit are naturally accompanied — I mean that of confining the imagination, and damping the spirit of vigorous and enlarged enterprise. In order to improve the opportunities, with which they are favoured, and to avail themselves, as they ought, of the happy situation, in which they are placed, they should encourage commerce by a liberal system of mercantile jurisprudence.

These observations concerning the situation, the duty, and the interest of the United States, receive an easy and a strong application to the situation, the duty, and the interest of Pennsylvania.

In other countries, as we have seen, where commerce has been regarded as an object worthy of the publick attention, jurisdictions have been established for the trial and determination of commercial causes. In the United States and in Pennsylvania, commercial causes are tried in the same manner, by the same tribunals, at the same expense, and with the same delay, as other controversies relating to property. This must be often productive of the most serious disadvantages.

Before the revolution, we were strangers, in a great measure, to what is properly called foreign commerce. The same system of commercial law pervaded Great Britain and her colonies. The rules, therefore, of admitting foreign testimony, and of authenticating foreign transactions, have been but lately the objects of much consideration. They have not been fixed with the clearness and precision, which are now become requisite. But they should, as soon as possible, be ascertained, particularized, and rendered as easy as the precautions necessary to avoid fraud will admit.

Great innovations should not be made: a wise and well tempered system must owe much to experience. But the foundations should be laid betimes. They should be broad, and deep, and well compacted, that they may be sufficient to support the magnificent structure, which the present and future ages will build upon them.

The important ends, which may be attained by a court of chancery formed and organized for commercial purposes, now begin to appear in prospect before us. In this view, the establishment of courts of chancery appears to be of high importance to the United States in general, and to the commonwealth of Pennsylvania in particular.

It will not, I am sure, be supposed, that I am unfriendly to the trial by jury. I love — I admire it: but my love and my admiration spring from proper principles: I love and I admire with reason on my side. Sacrilege would be offered to the venerable institution, by profaning it to purposes, for which it was never intended. Let it be maintained in purity — let it be maintained in vigour: but if it be so maintained, it must be maintained in that spirit, and in that application, for which it was formed, and to which it is so exquisitely adjusted. Its genius should be encouraged and concentred: if it be applied to foreign and unnatural objects, its strength will soon dissolve and evaporate.

Let us attend to the nature of mercantile transactions. Accounts never were, by the course of the common law, brought to trial before a jury. To a jury, indeed, the general question — ought the party to account — was submitted for its determination. But the adjustment of the accounts was submitted to auditors, instead of being tried by a jury. If, upon any article in account, the auditors cannot agree; or, if agreeing, the parties are not satisfied; then, upon each point, so litigated, a separate and distinct issue may be taken, and that issue must be tried by a jury. In this manner, a hundred issues may be joined in the same cause, and tried separately by as many juries; but the general statement of the disputed accounts still remains before the auditors, and by them the general result from the whole must be formed and ascertained. This mode of liquidating accounts judicially at common law, is obviously exposed to many disadvantages and delays; and, for this reason, the action of account has, in a great measure, fallen into disuse. In England, the parties in unsettled and litigated accounts have recourse to chancery; in Pennsylvania, to arbitrators, or to jurors acting in the character of arbitrators.

The numerous embarrassments, which arise from the want of a proper commercial forum, are well known and severely felt both by the gentlemen of the bar, and by the gentlemen of the exchange.

Impressed with these truths, the committee who were appointed to report a draught of a constitution for the consideration of the late convention of Pennsylvania, included, in their report, the plan of a chancery establishment. The convention thought it improper to fix that establishment as a part of the constitution, but have given ample powers to the legislature to adopt that or any similar one, and to model and alter it as the sage instructions of time may direct.

Impressed with these truths, which I have both witnessed and experienced, I have thought it my duty to bring this important subject fully into your view. Viewed in a commercial light, Pennsylvania, and particularly her metropolis, attracts solicitous attention both on this and on the other side of the Atlantick. Every friend to Pennsylvania, every friend to her metropolis, every enlightened friend to the interests of commerce, must wish ardently to see her commercial establishments complete. These observations apply to the United States on a scale still more extensive; and, as applied to them, therefore, acquire still an additional degree of importance.

With these observations I conclude, at last, my minute delineation — if drawn in a more masterly manner, it would be interesting as well as minute — of the juridical establishments of the United States and of Pennsylvania.

IV

OF THE NATURE OF COURTS

THE next subjects of my remarks are, the nature, and the constituent parts of courts.

That the judicial department should be independent, is a principle, which, in a former part of my lectures,[a] I had an opportunity of stating, explaining, and enforcing at large. In the review which we have now made of that department, as established in the United States and in this commonwealth, we see what a strict and uniform regard has been paid to the practical observance of this very important principle. To neither of the constitutions is a judicial magistrate known, who holds his office by a tenure less secure or less respectable than that of his own good behaviour.

All courts should be open. This is one of the rules, which, by the constitution of Pennsylvania,[b] is rendered inviolable by the legislature itself. It is a rule of the highest moment.

The place of administering justice was originally at the gates of the cities — in other words, in the presence of all the people. Such was the practice in the days of Job.[c] By Moses also, of legislators the first and wisest, the same ancient custom is mentioned.[d] Homer speaks of it as subsisting in the heroick ages.[e] In some countries, this simple and undisguised mode is still observed.[f]

Among the Saxons, as we are informed by Selden, their courts, like the heliastick court at Athens, were, for the most part, kept in the open air.[g]

By the ancient Romans, trials were held in publick, in the presence of the accused, and of all who wished to hear them. This procedure was open and noble; says the writer[h] who mentions it; it breathed Roman magnanimity.

In France, too, as appears, we are told, from some old manuscript law books, criminal processes were anciently carried on in publick, and in a form not very different from the publick judgments of the Romans. "The

[a] Ante. p. 297.   [b] Art. 9. s. 11.   [c] Job xxix. 7.   [d] Gen. xxiii. 18.
[e] Il. l. 18. v. 497.   [f] 1. Gog. Or. L. 28.   [g] Bac. on Gov. 10.
[h] Com. on Bec. c. 22.

witnesses," says Beaumanoir, one of the oldest writers on the laws of France, "ought to give their testimony in open court." [i]

All trials, says Beccaria,[j] should be publick; that opinion, which is the best, or, perhaps, the only cement of society, may curb the authority of the powerful, and the passions of the judge; and that the people, inspired with courage, may say, "We are not slaves; we are protected by the laws."

"Let not," says my Lord Bacon,[k] in the same spirit of sound sense, "decrees issue in silence: let judges give the reasons of their judgments: let them do this openly: that what is unrestrained in point of authority, may be circumscribed by a regard to character and fame."

But why, it may be asked, are examples produced in such numbers — why do we cite authorities of so much weight, in order to establish a principle, in itself so extremely plain? Is it not selfevident, that, in a court of justice, every one is entitled to a publick trial? Why, then, refer us to instances, in Asia, in Greece, in Rome, in France, of the enjoyment of a selfevident right?

Because, in Asia, in Greece, in Rome, in France, too, till very lately, the enjoyment of this selfevident right has been lost. Liberty, indeed, says it is selfevident: but tyranny holds a contrary language; and unfortunately for the human race, the voice of tyranny has been more loud and more powerful than the voice of freedom.

To states as well as to individuals, the lesson is salutary — let those, who stand, take heed lest they fall. Asia is fallen, Greece is fallen, Rome is fallen, France is fallen — I correct myself — she rises. Let the other monitory instances suggest caution: I offer them not to your imitation.

The slave who suffers, and the slave who dreads the inquisition — how would he exult to be able to say, in the irrevocable language of Pennsylvania, "all courts shall be open."

According to the rules of judicial architecture, a system of courts should resemble a pyramid. Its base should be broad and spacious: it should lessen as it rises: its summit should be a single point. To express myself without a metaphor — in every judicial department, well arranged and well organized, there should be a regular, progressive gradation of jurisdiction; and one supreme tribunal should superintend and govern all the others.

An arrangement in this manner is proper for two reasons. 1. The supreme tribunal produces and preserves a uniformity of decision through the whole judicial system. 2. It confines and it supports every inferiour court within the limits of its just jurisdiction.

If no superintending tribunal of this nature were established, different

---

[i] Mont. Sp. L. b. 28. c. 34.   [j] C. 14.   [k] 1. Ld. Bac. 252. Aph. 38.

courts might adopt different and even contradictory rules of decision; and the distractions, springing from these different and contradictory rules, would be without remedy and without end. Opposite determinations of the same question, in different courts, would be equally final and irreversible. But when, from those opposite determinations, an appeal to a jurisdiction superiour to both is provided, one of them will receive a sentence of confirmation, the other, of reversal. Upon future occasions, the determination confirmed will be considered as an authority; the determination reversed will be viewed as a beacon.

Ampliare jurisdictionem has been a principle avowed by some judges: it is natural, and will operate where it is not avowed. It will operate powerfully and irresistibly among a number of coordinate and independent jurisdictions; and, without a tribunal possessing a control over all, the pernicious and interfering claims could neither be checked nor adjusted. But a supreme court prohibits the abuse, and protects the exercise, of every inferiour judiciary power.

In France, before the present revolution, the establishment of a number of parliaments or independent tribunals produced, in the different provinces, a number of incongruous and jarring decisions. This has been assigned, and with much apparent reason, as the great source of that diversity of customs and laws, which prevailed, to an uncommon degree, in the different parts of the kingdom of France, in other respects so well compacted.

In England, the principles and the rules of law are, through the whole judiciary department, reduced to a standard, uniform in an exemplary degree. In no country, perhaps, does a stronger impression prevail of the advantages resulting from stability in the administration of justice. But by an unwise inattention, to say the least of it, to the inferiour establishments, the base of the exquisitely proportioned edifice, erected by Alfred, is narrowed and weakened; and its beauty and durability are consequently impaired.

In the United States and Pennsylvania — for here we must take the two constitutions in a collected view — a fine and regular gradation appears, from the justices of the peace in the commonwealth, to the supreme court of the national government. The justice of peace is, in criminal matters, assisting to the court of quarter sessions: in civil causes, his jurisdiction is subordinate to the court of common pleas. The courts of common pleas, and quarter sessions, and orphans' courts of each county are subordinate to the supreme court, whose jurisdiction extends over the commonwealth. The supreme court is, by a late law, rendered subordinate to the high court of errours and appeals. With regard to the register's court, an exception is introduced by the law just now mentioned. Though a county jurisdiction, it is not rendered subordinate to the supreme court by an appeal: that revisionary process is directed *per saltum* to the high court of errours and appeals. From the highest court of a state, a writ of errour lies, in federal causes, to the supreme court of the United States. In the national government, a writ of errour lies from a district to a circuit court, and from a circuit to the supreme court.

In controversies, to which the state or nation is a party, the state or nation itself ought to be amenable before the judicial powers. This principle, dignified because it is just, is expressly ratified by the constitution of Pennsylvania.[1] It declares, that suits may be brought against the commonwealth. The manner, the courts, and the cases, in which they may be brought, are left to the direction of the legislature. It was deemed sufficient to recognize the principle: its operation will be guided in such a way, as time and circumstances shall suggest. Upon the same principle, the judicial power of the national government "shall extend to controversies to which the United States are a party; and to controversies between two or more states." [m]

These provisions may be viewed by some as incompatible with the opinions, which they have formed concerning the sovereignty of the states.

In the introduction to my lectures,[n] I had an opportunity of showing the astonishing and intricate mazes, in which politicians and philosophers have, on this subject, bewildered themselves, and of evincing, that the dread and redoubtable sovereign, when traced to his ultimate and genuine source, is found, as he ought to be found, in the free and independent man. In one of my lectures,[o] I proved, I hope, that the only reason, why a free and independent man was bound by human laws, was this — that he bound himself. Upon the same principle on which he becomes bound by the laws, he becomes amenable before the courts of justice, which are formed and authorized by those laws. If one free and independent man, an original sovereign, may do all this; why may not an aggregate of free and independent men, a collection of original sovereigns, do this likewise? The dignity of the state is compounded of the dignity of its members. If the dignity of each singly is undiminished, the dignity of all jointly must be unimpaired. Is a man degraded by the manly declaration, that he renders himself amenable to justice? Can a similar declaration degrade a state?

To be privileged from the awards of equal justice, is a disgrace, instead of being an honour; but a state claims a privilege from the awards of equal justice, when she refuses to become a party, unless, in the same case, she becomes a judge.

"In any cause" — said the judge of the high court of admiralty of

[1] Art. 9. s. 11. [m] Cons. U.S. art. 3. s. 2. [n] Ante. pp. 80–81.
[o] Ante. p. 186. et seq.

England, in a very late decision[p] — "In any cause where the crown is a party, it can no more withhold evidence of documents in its possession, than a private person. If the court thinks proper to order the production of any publick instrument, that order must be obeyed."

In the Mirrour of Justices, we have an account of the first constitutions ordained by the ancient kings of England. When the writer of that book calls them ancient, they must be so indeed; for my Lord Coke[q] informs us, that most of it was written long before the conquest. Among these constitutions, we find the following very remarkable one. "It was ordained that the king's court should be open to all plaintiffs; from which they should have, without delay, remedial writs, as well against the king or the queen as against any *other* of the people." [r] You are pleased by tracing another instance, in which Saxon principles are renewed by our constitutions.

"Judges ought to know, that the poorest peasant is a man, as well as the king himself: all men ought to obtain justice; since in the eyes of justice, all men are equal; whether the prince complain of a peasant, or a peasant complain of the prince." [s] These are the words of a king — of the late Frederick of Prussia. In his courts of justice, that great man stood upon his native greatness, and disdained to mount upon the artificial stilts of sovereignty.

In England, there is a noted distinction, which runs through the whole system of courts. Some are courts of record: others are courts not of record.

A court of record is one, whose proceedings and acts are entered in rolls of parchment, and whose power is to hold pleas according to the course of the common law. These rolls, being the memorials of the judges, import in them such incontrollable credit, that they admit no averment, or plea, or proof, to the contrary of what they contain. Such a record can be tried only by itself.[t] No possible kind of evidence, not even that of the senses, can shake its authenticity; if we may rely on the authority of a well known story in Westminster Hall. A party, in perfect health, was hearing his cause; but his counsel, by an unfortunate stroke of his plea, had killed him on the record. The judges could, by no means, take notice of him, though he stood before their eyes. He averred that he was alive: his averment could not be received: it was against the record.[u]

A court, not of record, is one, whose acts are not enrolled in parchment, or whose proceedings are not according to the course of the common law.[v]

It deserves to be remarked, that the distinction between courts of

---

[p] 1. Col. Jur. 68.   [q] 10. Rep. Pref. 14.   [r] 4. Cou. Ang. Norm. 487.
[s] Warv. 343.   [t] 1. Inst. 260.   [u] Bar. on st. 248.   [v] Wood. Ins. 464.

record and courts not of record was unknown in England till after the Norman conquest.[w] The occasion and the cause of its introduction deserve also to be remarked. The Conqueror, averse to the Saxon law of liberty, but unwilling to run the risk of an attempt to overturn it at once, formed a plan, artful and too successful, for undermining it by degrees. He appointed all the judges of the *curia regis* from among the Normans, ignorant of the Saxon laws, and fond of their own. The language of the court was altered; and all pleadings and proceedings were entered in the Norman tongue. This introduced the technical terms and, imperceptibly, the rules and maxims of that foreign jurisprudence.

This introduction of a new language, the exaltation of the aula regis, and the consequent depression of the county courts, paved the way, in the opinion of a very sensible lawyer,[x] for the distinction between courts of record and not of record. Courts of record were those, whose proceedings were duly entered in the Norman tongue, and, unless reversed, could never be questioned or contradicted. To have allowed such a privilege to the county courts, in which the Saxon suitors were judges, and whose proceedings were in the English language, would have been inconsistent with the genius of the Conqueror's plan; for it would have had a tendency to confirm, rather than to depress, the Saxon system. The county courts, therefore, were considered as courts not of record.

From any thing I have said, no inference, I hope, will be drawn, that I deem fidelity and exactness in registering and preserving the acts of courts of justice as matters of small importance: they are of the greatest. I only mean to enter my protestation against a sacrifice of the principles of common sense, to a superstitious regard for the infallibility of records.

[w] 1. Reev. 68.   [x] Sulliv. 271.

V

OF THE CONSTITUENT PARTS
OF COURTS — OF THE JUDGES

I NOW proceed to consider the constituent parts of courts. The judges form one of those constituent parts. Let me introduce their character by the beautiful and correct description of the magna charta of King John. A judge should know the laws: he should be disposed to observe them.

It seems to be the opinion of some, that severity should be the striking feature in a judge's countenance. His countenance should reflect the sentiments of his heart. In his heart should be written the words of the law. If the law say, and the law does say, that, in all its judgments, justice shall be executed in mercy; on the heart of a judge will this heavenly maxim be deeply engraven; in his looks it will beam.

> —— Nec supplex turba timebunt.
> Judicis ora sui; sed erunt sub judice tuti.*
>
> OVID.

He ought, indeed, to be a terrour to evil doers; but he ought also to be a praise to those who do well. The more numerous as well as the more valuable part of the citizens are, we trust, of the latter description. Complacency, therefore, rather than vengeance, should habitually influence the sentiments, and habitually mark the features of a judge.

A judge is the blessing, or he is the curse of society. His powers are important: his character and conduct can never be objects of indifference.

When a judge is mentioned as the curse of society, Jefferies, of infamous memory, instantly starts into view. Some circumstances, which attended the fate of that odious man, place, in the strongest light, that deep detestation which is always entertained, and which is expressed whenever it can be expressed with safety, against the character and person of an oppressive and tyrannical judge.

When his master abdicated the throne, his own security lay only in flight. From the law, the law's worst assassin could expect no protection. That he might escape unknown, he shaved his eye brows, put on a

* [And that suppliant crowd will not fear the face of its judge, but they will be safe under the judge.]

seaman's habit, and, all alone, made the best of his way to Wapping, with a design to take shipping for a foreign country. But his countenance could not remain undiscovered under all this disguise: a man, whom, upon a trial, he had frightened almost into convulsions, no sooner got a glimpse of it, than, in a moment, he recollected all the terrours he had formerly felt. Notice was instantly given to the mob, who rushed in upon him like a herd of wolves. He was goaded on to the lord mayor: the lord mayor, seeing a man, on whom he had never looked without trembling, brought before him in this situation, fell into fits, was carried to his bed, and never rose from it. On his way to the tower, to which he was committed, he saw threatening faces on every side; he saw whips and halters held up around him; and cried out in agony, "for the Lord's sake, keep them off." I saw him, I heard him, says a cotemporary historian, and without pity too; though, without pity, I never saw any other malefactor.[a]

On the other hand — I now speak from Beccaria[b] — a man of enlightened understanding, appointed guardian of the laws, is the greatest blessing that a sovereign can bestow on a nation. Such a man is accustomed to behold truth, and not to fear it: unacquainted with the greatest part of those imaginary and insatiable necessities, which so often put virtue to the proof, and accustomed to contemplate mankind from the most elevated point of view, he considers the nation as his family, and his fellow citizens as brothers.

Patience of hearing, says the great Lord Bacon, is an essential part of justice; and an overspeaking judge is no well tuned cymbal. It is no grace to a judge, first to find that, which, in due time, he might have heard from the bar; or to show quickness of conceit in cutting witnesses or counsel off too short; or to prevent information by questions, even by pertinent ones. In hearing a cause, the parts of a judge are four — to direct the evidence — to moderate length, repetition, or impertinency of speech — to recapitulate, select, and collate the material parts of that which hath been said — to give the rule or sentence.[c]

A judge, particularly a judge of the common law, should bear a great regard to the sentiments and decisions of those, who have thought and decided before him.

It may be asked — why should a point be received as law, merely because one man or a succession of men have said it is law, any more than another point should be received as reason, merely because one philosopher or a set of philosophers have said it is reason? In law, as in philosophy, should not every one think and judge for himself? *Stare decisis* may prevent the trouble of investigation; but it will prevent also the pleasure and the advantages of improvement.

[a] 4. Guth. 1063.   [b] C. 42.   [c] 3. Ld. Bac. 377.

Implicit deference to authority, as I have declared on more occasions than one, I consider as the bane of science; and I honour the benefactors of mankind, who have broken the yoke of that intellectual tyranny, by which, in many ages and in many countries, men have been deprived of the inherent and inalienable right of judging for themselves. But how natural it is, from one extreme to vibrate with violence to its opposite one! Though authority be not permitted to tyrannise as a mistress; may she not be consulted as a skilful guide? May not respect be paid, though a blind assent be refused, to her dictates?

A man must have an uncommon confidence in his own talents, who, in forming his judgments and opinions, feels not a sensible and strong satisfaction in the concurrence of the judgments and opinions of others, equally or more conversant than himself with the subjects, on which those judgments and opinions are formed. Society of wise men in judgment is like the society of brave men in battle: each depends not merely on himself: each depends on others also: by this means, strength and courage are diffused over all. To human authority in matters of opinion, as well as to human testimony in matters of fact, a due regard ought to be paid. To rely on both these kinds of evidence, is a propensity planted, by nature, in the human mind.

In certain sciences, a peculiar degree of regard should be paid to authority. The common law is one of those sciences. Judicial decisions are the principal and most authentick evidence, which can be given, of the existence of such a custom as is entitled to form a part of the common law. Those who gave such decisions, were selected for that employment, on account of their learning and experience in the common law. As to the parties, and those who represent the parties to them, their judgments continue themselves to be effective laws, while they are unreversed. They should, in the cases of others, be considered as strong evidence of the law. As such, every prudent and cautious judge will appreciate them. He will remember, that his duty and his business is, not to make the law, but to interpret and apply it.

VI

THE SUBJECT CONTINUED—OF JURIES

JURIES form, with a few exceptions, another constituent part of courts: they form, especially, a constituent part of courts exercising criminal jurisdiction.

I mentioned, in a former lecture,[a] that I love and admire the trial by jury; and that my love and admiration of it spring from proper principles. Those principles I am now to unfold.

When I speak of juries, I feel no peculiar predilection for the number twelve: a grand jury consists of more, and its number is not precisely fixed.

When I speak of juries, I see no peculiar reason for confining my view to a unanimous verdict, unless that verdict be a conviction of a crime — particularly of a capital crime. In grand juries, unanimity is not required.

When I speak of juries, I mean a convenient number of citizens, selected and impartial, who, on particular occasions, or in particular causes, are vested with discretionary powers to try the truth of facts, on which depend the property, the liberty, the reputation, and the lives of their fellow citizens.

Having described what I mean when I speak of juries, it is proper that I should assign, in the fullest and clearest manner, my reasons for some parts of my description.

The first part in this description, which has drawn your most marked attention, is, probably, that which represents the powers, vested in juries, as discretionary. This part, therefore, merits the first illustration. It will be remembered all along, that the discretionary power vested in juries is a power to try the truth of facts. "Ad quæstionem facti respondent juratores."

The truth of facts is tried by evidence. The principal species of evidence, which comes before juries, is the testimony of witnesses.

In a former lecture,[b] I had occasion to observe, that human testimony is a source of evidence altogether original, suggested by our constitution; and not acquired, though it is sometimes corroborated, and more fre-

[a] Ante. p. 492.   [b] Ante. pp. 282–283.

quently corrected, by considerations arising from experience. I had occasion further to observe, that, in no case, the law orders a witness to be believed; for the testimony of a thousand witnesses may not produce belief; and that, in no case, the law orders a witness not to be believed; for belief may be the unavoidable result of his testimony. These general positions, then laid down, it is now our business to fortify and apply. If we shall be successful in fortifying and applying them; we shall see, in a new and in a very striking light, the sublime principle of the institution of juries.

It is tedious, and it is painful, to travel through all the numerous degrees, into which it has been attempted to arrange the force of evidence. Some writers on the subject have divided proofs into such as are near, and such as are remote. Others have been adventurous enough to define the precise number of each, which is necessary to superinduce the condemnation of a person, who is accused. One says, two will be sufficient: a second says, three are necessary: a third fixes upon a number different from either. They have never reflected, that evidence arises from the circumstances attending the fact: that those circumstances should be considered in a collected and not in a separate view; and that on the more or less intimate connexion which subsists between them, the strength or weakness of the evidence resulting from them depends.

The truth of this remark will sufficiently appear, if we consider separately any of the presumptions enumerated by those writers on the criminal law. There is not one of them, which may not appear favourable, or unfavourable, or indifferent to the person under trial. A man, with a bloody sword in his hand, is seen running from a house. On entering it, a person run through the body, and no other person, is found there. Would not the presumption be strong, that the man, who ran from the house was the assassin? But should a jury be compelled, on this evidence, to convict him? Should he not be allowed to prove, if he can, the connexion of this strong circumstance against him with another, in his favour, equally strong — that, passing the door of the house, he was drawn, by the cries of the person assassinated, to his assistance, and suddenly seized the poignard which the assassin had left in his side? The weight of any one circumstance cannot be ascertained independently of others: the number and connexion of those others cannot be specified, previously, in a didactick treatise upon the degrees of evidence.

Thus it is with regard to evidence arising from circumstances: will more success attend an attempt to ascertain systematically the degrees of evidence arising from positive testimony? This depends upon the character of him who delivers, and upon the character of him who receives it. That, which would be believed from the mouth of a witness famed for his integrity and good sense, would be disbelieved, if told by a witness remarkable for falsehood or credulity. A person, hackneyed in the ways and vices of the world, who has deceived and who has been deceived a thousand times, is slow to credit testimony. An undesigning countryman, who has never practised nor experienced the artifices of fraud, believes implicitly every thing he hears. Can the characters of witnesses — can the characters of jurors be graduated in a dissertation upon evidence? And yet, in each particular case, the force of evidence must depend upon the character both of witnesses and jurors.

For these reasons, we find, in the institutions of antiquity, no general rules prescribed concerning the force of testimony, or the weight of presumptions: the emperour Hadrian expressly declares the impracticability of prescribing them. When one of his judges applied to him for a rescript, containing particular directions upon this subject; the emperour wrote him an answer, in which the sentiment we have mentioned is beautifully exhibited. "No certain rule," says he, "can be given with regard to the degree of evidence, which will be sufficient in every cause that shall occur. This only I can recommend to you in general; that you by no means confine yourself to any one kind or degree; but that, according to the nature and the circumstances of every case, you estimate, in your own mind, what you believe, and what you do not think to be sufficiently proved." [e]

The evidence of the sciences is very different from the evidence of facts. In the sciences, evidence depends on causes which are fixed and immovable, liable to no fluctuation or uncertainty arising from the characters or conduct of men. In the sciences, truths, if selfevident, are instantly known. If their evidence depend on their connexions with other truths, it is evinced by tracing and discovering those connexions. In facts, it is otherwise. They consist not of principles which are selfevident; nor can their existence be traced or discovered by any necessary connexion with selfevident principles. As facts, therefore, are neither principles, nor necessarily connected with principles; the evidence of facts is unsusceptible of a general theory or rules.

Let us then forbear to attempt a graduated scale of this kind of evidence. It is the philosopher's stone of criminal jurisprudence. It is impossible to establish general rules, by which a complete proof may be distinguished from a proof that is incomplete, and presumptions slightly probable may be distinguished from conjectures altogether uncertain.

If, therefore, the evidence of facts can be ascertained, distinguished, and estimated by no system of general rules; the consequence unavoidably is, that, in every case, the evidence of facts must depend upon circumstances, which to that case are peculiar. The farther consequence unavoidably is, that the power of deciding on the evidence of facts must

[e] 2. M'D. Ins. 631.

be a discretionary power; for it is a power of deciding on a subject un-susceptible of general principles or rules.

And, after all, is it, at last, come to this? Do we live by discretionary power? Is this the final result of the boasted trial by jury? In Turkey, life and every thing precious in life depend on the nod of one man: here, it seems, on the nod of twelve. There is a difference, indeed, in number: but, in principle, where is the difference?

Such is, and such must be our doom. It is agreed, on all hands, that, in every state, there must be somewhere a power supreme, arbitrary, abso-lute, uncontrollable: these are strong expressions for discretionary power. There have been, it is true, different opinions concerning the question — where does this power reside?

What security, then, it may next be asked, is there, under any gov-ernment, for the enjoyment of property, character, freedom, and life; if, under every government, the last resolution of the tedious and expensive process is into arbitrary or discretionary power?

Let us not despair: perhaps, after a little investigation, we may be happy enough to discover some emerging isthmus, on which, amidst this unstable, watery scene that surrounds us, we may be able to find rest for the soles of our feet.

It has been shown, at large, that it is impracticable, by any determinate rules, to ascertain or graduate the force of evidence in facts; and that, consequently, juries, who decide on the evidence of facts, must possess discretionary powers. But though it be impracticable to ascertain this matter by determinate rules; is it, therefore, impracticable also to give and acquire some conception of it by a general reference? Perhaps not.

Let us try: let the reference be as comprehensive as possible: if we must live by discretion, let the exercise of that discretion be universally unani-mous. If there must be, in every political society, an absolute and dis-cretionary power over even the lives of the citizens; let the operations of that power be such, as would be sanctioned by unanimous and universal approbation. Suppose then, that, in pursuing this train of thought, we assume the following position — that the evidence, upon which a citizen is condemned, should be such as would govern the judgment of the whole society.

Let us, first, inquire, whether this position be reasonable: let us next inquire, whether, if this position is reasonable, the establishment of it would give, to the citizen, a just degree of security against the improper exercise of discretionary power: let us, in the last place, inquire, whether, if this theory is eligible, it be possible to reduce its principles to practice.

1. I am first to inquire, whether the position — that the evidence, upon which a citizen is condemned, should be such as would govern the judg-ment of the whole society — be a reasonable position.

We showed, at large, in a former part of these lectures,[d] that, in a society, the act or judgment of a majority is always considered as the act or judgment of the whole.

Before the formation of society, the right of punishment, or, to speak with more propriety, the right of preventing the repetition of crimes, belonged to him who had suffered the injury, arising from the crime which was committed. In a society formed and well constituted, the right of him who has suffered the injury is transferred to the community. To the community, therefore, instead of the injured individual, he who committed the injury is now to answer. To answer to the community for his conduct, was a part of the social contract, which, by becoming a member, he tacitly and voluntarily made.[e] In this manner, a complete right is vested in the society to punish; and a full obligation is laid on the individual offending, to be amenable to punishment.

The social contract is of a peculiar kind: when analyzed into its component parts, it is found to be a composition of agreements, equal in number to the number of all the members, of which the society is composed. To each of those agreements there are two parties. One member of the society is the party on one side: all the other members form the party on the other side.

The punishment of a crime in regulated society presupposes two things. 1. The crime must be authenticated. 2. The penalty must be ascertained. Upon the principles which we have laid down, each of those two prerequisites to punishment must be equally the act of the society — of the whole society.

With regard to each of these prerequisites, the society may act either collectively and personally, or by deputation and representation. If they act by deputation and representation, they may intrust one of the forementioned prerequisites to the management of one class of deputies and representatives; and, to another class, they may commit the management of the other prerequisite. With regard to both, however, the proceedings must be those of the whole society, or, at least, sanctioned by the authority of the whole society: for it must be remembered, that to the whole society the right of punishment was transferred, and with the whole society the engagement to be amenable to its justice was made.

On a nearer and more minute view of things, we shall discover a most material difference between the modes proper for the management of the different prerequisites; because, on a nearer and more minute view of things, we shall discover, in the management of those different pre-

[d] Ante. p. 242.

[e] Upon this principle of consent, all civil penalties are debts to the publick; from whence the Greeks and Romans used λυειν, and "pœnas solvere, luere," for undergoing a punishment, which was a conditional debt contracted by their own consent. Pet. on. Jur. 79.

requisites, a most material difference in the situation of the parties to the social contract.

Penalties may be adjusted, graduated, and ascertained by general rules, and against all the members of the society indiscriminately. In the consequences of the regulations made upon this subject, every member may be affected in a double capacity; he may be affected, either as the individual party to one agreement, or as forming one of the numerous party to each of the other agreements, of which we have seen the social contract to be composed. In other words, he may be affected either as the author or as the sufferer of the penalties. Impartiality, therefore, in the conduct of every member, may rationally be expected; and there will be little reason to use strong or numerous precautions against interestedness or its effects. If the society act by representatives, and a difference of sentiment takes place among them concerning any subject; the numbers on the different sides, in the representative body, will probably bear to one another a proportion nearly the same, as would be found if all the members of the society were personally assembled.

But when we attend to the management of the other prerequisite — that of authenticating the commission of a crime — a situation of men and things, extremely different, appears to our view. Here no general rules can be adopted — no measures can be taken, which will equally and indiscriminately affect all the different members of the community in their turn. Here, the parties to one of the agreements, which form the social contract, appear in their original stations — on one side, an individual — on the other, all the members of the society except himself — on one side, those who are to try — on the other, he who is to be tried.

In this isolated situation, in which he necessarily but unfortunately stands; and in which, if all the members of the society were present, his fate must, from the very nature of society, be decided by the voice of the majority — in this situation, if the society act by representatives, it is reasonable to demand, and it is just to grant the reasonable demand, that the unanimous voice of those who represent parties, and who themselves are parties as well as judges, should be necessary to warrant a sentence of condemnation. In such a situation, where the representatives are not indifferent, and, consequently, may not be impartial, their unanimous suffrage may be considered as nothing more, than what is necessary to found a fair presumption concerning the sentiments of a majority of the whole community, had the whole community been personally present. In such a situation, therefore, we may probably be justified in recurring to our position — that the evidence, upon which a citizen is condemned, should be such as would govern the judgment of the whole society: and we may require the unanimous suffrage of the deputed body who try, as the necessary and proper evidence of that judgment.

2. I am next to inquire, whether the establishment of this position would give, to the citizen, a just degree of security against the improper exercise of discretionary power.

In all states, as we have seen, discretionary powers must be placed somewhere. The great body of the people is their proper permanent depository. But on some occasions, and for some purposes, they must be delegated. When they are exercised by the people themselves, a majority, by the very constitution of society, is sufficient for the purpose. When they are exercised by a delegation from the people, in the case of an individual; it would be difficult to suggest, for his security, any provision more efficacious than one, that nothing shall be suffered to operate against him without the unanimous consent of the delegated body.

This provision, however, may still be fortified by a number of additional precautions. Care may be taken in the manner of forming the delegated body. As this body cannot, for reasons which will appear afterwards, be selected, on every occasion, by the great body of the people themselves; they may, on every occasion, be selected by an officer, confidential, impartial, and, by the people themselves, appointed for this very purpose. Notwithstanding this very guarded selection, yet if any improper character appear among the delegated body, every reasonable exception may be allowed against his competency to act. To a necessary exercise of discretionary powers on one hand, the indulgence of a discretionary power may be opposed, on the other. Leave may be given to reject any determinate number of the delegated body, even without disclosing any cause of rejection. Under all these guarded and generous precautions, the person who would undergo a trial might, with an almost literal propriety, be said to try himself.

If, even after all these precautions, conviction might, by possibility, take place improperly; a power might be vested in another body to set the improper conviction aside, and to remit the trial of the cause to a new abstract of the citizens.

Surrounded and fortified by establishments and provisions of this nature, innocence might certainly be secure.

3. I am now, in the last place, to inquire, whether these principles, so beautiful in theory, can possibly be reduced to practice.

Reduced to practice! It cannot have escaped you, that I have been describing the principles of our well known trial by jury.

Those principles, so illustrious in themselves, will receive a new degree of splendour from a more particular investigation concerning the history, the nature, and the properties of this admired institution.

To Athens, to Germany, and to Normandy, the institution of juries has been attempted to be severally traced. From Athens it has been supposed to be transplanted to Rome; from Rome, to England. Those who think it originated in Normandy or Germany, suppose it to have been brought into England from the place of its original establishment.

The great principle of Solon's system was, unquestionably, this noble one — that every citizen should enjoy the inestimable right of being tried by his peers, and bound only by laws to which he had given his consent. His laws were of the most extensive nature. They comprehended rules of right, maxims of morality, precepts of agriculture, and regulations of commerce. His institutions concerning marriage, succession, testaments, the rights of persons and of things, have been disseminated through the jurisprudence of every civilized nation in Europe.[f] The trial by jury, therefore, as well as other establishments, may, it is said, refer, with great propriety, its original to Athens.

In Athens, the citizens were all equally admitted to vote in the publick assembly, and in the courts of justice, whether civil or criminal.[g]

The trial by a jury in Athens was conducted, it is said, with the same forms as those of an English jury, with a few exceptions arising from the difference between the two political constitutions.[h] When the cause was ready for hearing, the jury, who were to try it, were chosen by ballot.[i] It was necessary that they should be competent in point of understanding, character, and disinterestedness.[j] The jury was very numerous: it consisted sometimes of five hundred, sometimes of a thousand, sometimes of fifteen hundred members.[k] If the defendant, in a criminal prosecution, had half the number of votes in his favour, he was acquitted.[l] The presiding archon settled the cause for trial, gave the ballot, received the verdict, and published it.[m]

In this mode of trial, we are told, equal law was open to all: it was favourable to liberty, because it could not be influenced by intrigues.[n]

In every particular cause, the jurors were chosen and sworn anew.[o] They were attended by proper officers of the court, that no one might mix with them, or corrupt them, or influence their decisions.[p] They were not obliged to follow testimony in cases immediately within their own knowledge: but when witnesses were the best evidence, they were admitted.[q] They were an important body of men, vested with great powers, patrons of liberty, enemies to tyranny.[r]

The antiquity of this institution among the most civilized people of the world, is urged as an argument, that it is founded in nature and original justice.[s] "The trial by a jury of our own equals seems to grow out of the idea of just government; and is founded in the nature of things." [t]

---

[f] 1. Gill. 461.   [g] Pet. on Jur. 57. 58. 1. Gill. 459.   [h] Pet. on Jur. 27.
[i] Id. 69.   [j] Id. 28. 29.   [k] Id. 29.   [l] Id. ibid.   [m] Id. 28. 50. 51.
[n] Id. 32.   [o] Pet. on Jur. 43.   [p] Id. 44.   [q] Id. 48. 69. 81.   [r] Id. 69.
[s] Id. 70.   [t] Id. 108.

From this institution, as it was established and observed by the Greeks, we pass to it as established and observed by the Romans.

About sixty years after the expulsion of the Tarquins, the Romans, agitated by the dissensions between the patricians and plebeians, on many subjects, and particularly on that of their judicial government, sent commissioners to Athens to obtain a transcript of the laws of Solon.

Among the Romans, there was a double selection of jurors. On the kalends of January, a number, different at different times, of citizens of best note were chosen by ballot. From these, all the juries were supplied, to the number of eighty one each, upon every new cause.[u] On each side, there was a liberty to challenge fifteen: fifty one remained to give the verdict. This *rejectio judicum* is often mentioned by Cicero.[v]

In Rome as in Athens, the jury were sworn; and the defendant was acquitted on an equality of votes.[w]

Both at Athens and Rome, the time allowed to the counsel for their pleadings, was measured by the dropping of a certain quantity of water.[x] When the counsel, on each side, had finished their arguments by saying, "dixi," the prætor sent out the jury to consult about their verdict. When they returned with their verdict, they delivered it to the prætor; and he published it.[y]

The Roman juries were judges of law as well as of fact.[z] They could give a verdict of condemnation, a verdict of acquittal, or a verdict of *non liquet*. This last has, by some, been considered as a special verdict; but improperly; for a special verdict furnishes the court with a statement of facts, on which they can found a decision of law; whereas a *non liquet* among the Romans immediately adjourned the cause for farther consideration. In some modern tribunals on the continent of Europe, a most scandalous use has, by judges, been made of their power to pronounce a *non liquet*.

In the celebrated cause of Milo, we can trace the vestiges of a special jury. Pompey, who was, at that time, sole consul, with the dictatorial power, "videre ne quid detrimenti respublica caperet," * appointed a jury, in all respects, of the most able and upright men. Of this jury, the celebrated Cato was one. "Te, M. Cato, testor," says Cicero, in his animated and particular address. The selection of a jury in this peculiar manner, instead of the usual way by ballot, was, probably, one instance, in which Pompey exercised his dictatorial authority.[a]

Julius Cæsar extended the Roman name and power into Gaul and Germany; and reduced those countries into the form of Roman provinces.

[u] Pet. on Jur. 113. 115.   [v] Id. 114. 115. 122.   [w] Id. 117.   [x] Id. 134.
[y] Id. 119. 120.   [z] Id. 121.
* [To see that the public interest suffered no damage.]   [a] Pet. on Jur. 133.

This is an expression of strong and peculiar import. When a country war reduced into the form of a Roman province, it lost its own laws, and was governed by those of Rome.[b]

Cæsar visited Britian: Claudius, one of his successours, achieved the conquest of a considerable part of the island. He planted in it four colonies. One of them — that at Malden — was intended, as we are told by Tacitus,[c] not so much as a check upon the rebel Britons, as to accustom the new conquests to a familiarity with the Roman laws — "imbuendis sociis ad officia legum." His designs were crowned with success. The Britons, who, at first, were disgusted even with the language of Rome, became soon the admirers of her language, her eloquence, and her laws.[d] Under the reign of Severus, the Roman laws were in their meridian splendour in Britian, and were illustrated by the talents and authority of the celebrated Papinian.[e]

When the Romans retired from England to guard the vitals of the empire, the Britons resumed, in part, their ancient customs; but blended them with the Roman institutions, with which they had long been familiar. As the trial by jury was a part of the Roman system of judicial polity, when her colonies were established in Britain, it is probable, that this, among other parts, was left and was continued among the Britons.[f]

Such is the train of observations, which has induced an opinion, that the trial by jury was introduced into England from Athens, through the intermediate channel of Rome. Others think they can trace this mode of trial through a different channel.

The very learned Selden is of opinion, that the Saxons derived the institution of juries immediately from the Grecians. The government of the Saxons, about the time of Tiberius, was, in general, as he informs us,[g] so suited to that of the Grecians, that it cannot be imagined but much of the Grecian wisdom was introduced among them, long before the glory of the Romans was exalted to its greatest height. It may be well supposed, he infers, that there is some consanguinity between the Saxons and the Grecians, though the degree of that consanguinity be not known. The people were a free people, because they were a law to themselves. This was a privilege belonging to all the Germans, in the same manner as to the Athenians and the Lacedemonians.

The most ordinary trial among the Saxons was, upon a traverse of the matter in fact, by witnesses before the jurors; their votes made the verdict, and determined the matter in fact. In former times, continues he, it was questionless a confused manner of trial by votes of the whole multitude, which made the verdict hard to be discerned. But time taught them

[b] Id. 140.   [c] Ann. l. 12.   [d] Pet. on Jur. 142.   [e] Id. 143.
[f] Pet. on Jur. 146. 179.   [g] Bac. on Gov. 9.

better advice, to bring the voters to a certain number, according to the Grecian way.[h]

The trial *per pares,* we are told by others, was common to all the northern nations, as well as to the Saxons.[i]

It is probable, says an ingenious and well informed writer, that, among the Saxons, every kind of law suit was, at first, determined in full assembly, and by a plurality of voices. But when the duty of these assemblies became burthensome by the increase of business, convenience introduced a practice of selecting a certain number of their members to assist their president in the detemination of each cause. Hence the origin of juries; the precise date of whose establishment is uncertain, because it probably arose from no general or publick regulation, but from the gradual and almost imperceptible changes, authorized by common usage in the several districts of the kingdom. The number of jurymen was, for some time, different upon different occasions; till the advantage of uniform practice introduced a general rule, which determined, that no less than twelve persons should be called in all ordinary causes.[j]

A third class of writers contend, that juries, properly so called, were first introduced into England from Normandy. They admit a near affinity between this institution and that known to the tribunals of the Saxons; but insist, that, among that people, the trial by jury, speaking correctly,[k] did not exist. The trial, say they, *per duodecim juratos,* called *nambda,* was established among the Scandinavians at a very early period; but having fallen into disuse, was revived by a law of Reignerus surnamed Lodbrog, about the year eight hundred and twenty. Seventy years after this time, Rollo made his settlement in Normandy; and, among other customs, carried with him this mode of trial. When the Normans transplanted themselves into England, they were anxious to legitimate this as well as other parts of their jurisprudence, and endeavoured to substitute it in the place of the Saxon *sectatores,* or suitors to the court. The earliest mention, they say, which we find of any thing like a jury, was in the reign of the Conqueror. He had referred a cause to the county, or *sectatores,* to determine in their county court, as the course then was according to the Saxon establishment. That court gave their opinion of the cause. But Odo, the bishop of Baieux, who presided at the hearing of the cause, was dissatisfied with their determination, and directed, that, if they were still sure they spoke truth, they should choose twelve from among themselves, who should confirm it upon their oaths. The old trial by an indefinite number of suitors of court continued, it is added, for many years after the conquest; but the precedent set by the Bishop of Baieux

---

[h] Bac. on Gov. 56.   [i] Millar. 440. Sulliv. 251.   [j] Millar. 123.
[k] 1. Reev. 18. 60.

had a great effect towards altering it. It was not, however, till the reign of Henry the second, that the trial by jurors became general.[1]

If this account possessed all the accuracy, with the want of which it contains an implied censure of others, still it would admit the principles and substantial rules of trial by jury, to have subsisted among the Saxons; and would establish, between their institution and that of the Normans, a difference only with regard to the number of jurors, and to their quali- fication by an oath. But, on farther examination, we shall find, that, in both these respects, the law was the same before as after the conquest — that the suitors of the court, in other words, the freemen, were the judges, or, as we now say, the jury.[m]

Before the conquest, we can discover the clearest vestiges of a jury qualified by an oath, and consisting of twelve men. The most ancient, says Selden,[n] are to be found in a law of King Ethelred. Its original is in the following words — "In singulis centuriis comitia sunto, atque liberæ con- ditionis viri duodeni, ætate superiores, una cum præposito sacra tenentes juranto se adeo verum aliquem innocentem haud damnaturos, sontemve absoluturos" — In every hundred let there be a court; and let twelve free- men of mature age, together with their foreman, swear, upon the holy relicks, that they will condemn no innocent, and will absolve no guilty person.[o]

Selden, as we find from his notes collected by Bacon, translates the word "præpositus" — the lord of the hundred. If his translation is just; then this is a strict instance of the duodecemviral judgment. I translate the word "præpositus" — the foreman of the jury: if my translation is just; then the jury, in this instance, consisted of thirteen members, in- cluding their foreman. I can only say, that, so far as I know, my transla- tion is the usual one of the word, præpositus; that it seems rather un- natural to designate the lord of the hundred by the name of the president of the jury; and that, I apprehend, it was never customary for the judge and jury to be sworn "together" — "una."

There were two Saxon kings of the name of Ethelred. The first was the immediate predecessor of the great Alfred: the second was one of his successours. Selden refers the law which we have mentioned, to the reign of the second Ethelred. Now, there must be some mistake here one way or the other. If this law describes the jury of twelve; it is not the most ancient vestige of it; for, as we shall soon see, it was unquestionably established in the reign of Alfred. The conjecture is far from being im- probable, that this law should be referred to the reign of the first Ethel- red; and that it describes a jury consisting of thirteen — a foreman and twelve others.

It has been already observed, that, among the Saxons, the number of

[1] Id. 60. 61.   [m] Sulliv. 247.   [n] Anal. b. 2. c. 6.   [o] Pet. on Jur. 159.

jurymen was probably different at different times. It may be observed here, that, before the era of which we now speak, we discover not the slightest traces of the principle of unanimity in juries. If a jury was equally divided in a criminal prosecution, we have seen that, in Athens and Rome, the defendant was acquitted: but what was to be done in a civil cause? To avoid frequent dilemmas of this kind, it is probable that juries consisted generally of an uneven number. This number might be fixed by the first Ethelred to thirteen. This, at least, was an improvement upon a larger and more inconvenient number.

But to the penetrating Alfred, this number, and the regulations connected with this number, would, probably, appear to require and to be susceptible of still greater improvement. A jury of thirteen sit on the life of a prisoner. Six vote for his condemnation: six vote for his acquittal: must his life depend on a single vote — perhaps not more to be relied on than the single throw of a die? Is it not probable, that such as this would be the soliloquy of the humane Alfred? If so; is it not probable, that, from this precarious situation, the family of Alfred — for his people were his children — would be relieved by the resources of a mind, no less distinguished by its vigorous exertion, than by its wise and benevolent reflections? We can only conjecture his motives, indeed: but we know his conduct. He fixed the number of jurors at twelve: to a conviction by that number, he rendered a unanimous vote indispensably necessary. To him the world is indebted for the unanimous duodecemviral judgment.

I establish these interesting facts.

I have already mentioned, on the authority of my Lord Coke, that the greatest part of the book called "The Mirrour of Justices," was written long before the conquest. In that book, we find an account of Alfred's acts and judgments, conjectured to have been originally composed by himself. Of that account, I give the following very literal translation from the old French — the language, in which Andrew Horne compiled and published the book. "He hanged Cadwine, because he judged Hackwy to death without the assent of all the jurors, in a case where he had put himself upon a jury of twelve men; and because three were for saving him against nine, Cadwine removed the three for others upon whom Hackwy did not put himself." "He hanged Frebern, because he judged Harpin to death, when the jurors were in doubt as to their verdict; for where there is a doubt, they should save rather than condemn." [p]

These texts are short: but they are pregnant with precious instruction.

1. Each juror may here find a salutary lesson for his conduct, in the most important of all the transactions of a man or a citizen — in voting whether a fellow man and a fellow citizen shall live or die. Does he

[p] Pet. on Jur. 166, 167.

doubt? he should acquit. It is only when the clearest conviction is in full and undivided possession of the mind, that the voice of conviction ought to be pronounced.

2. All the jurors may, in this transaction, of all human transactions the most important, find a salutary lesson for their conduct, in forming the collected verdict of the whole from the separate judgment of each.

I speak of criminal — I speak of capital cases; because the cases here mentioned were those, in which persons were "judged to death."

Is the judgment of a majority of the members — that the defendant should be convicted — a sufficient foundation for a verdict of conviction by the jury? It is not. That verdict must be composed of each separate judgment. In the case before us, a majority of three to one were for conviction. But the judge was hanged for pronouncing sentence of death upon the votes of this majority, though it was propped by an adventitious accession of three other votes.

3. Every citizen may here find most comfortable information of the jealous attention, with which the law watches over him, even when he is accused of violating the law. No jury can pass upon him, except that upon which he puts himself. "Hackwy," says the case before us, "did not put himself upon those others." For every trial there must be a new selection. The discretionary powers, which we have described, and which, in one view, appear so formidable, though, in every view, they are so necessary, can never be exercised against him by any body of men, to the exercise of whose powers he does not give his consent. He may suffer, indeed, in another way. He may suffer the pain of contumacy, direful and hard. His contumacy may, by a legislative process, be transformed into a confession of his guilt. But, by his country he can never suffer, unless, in the language of the law, he "put himself upon his country."

In the strictest and most correct meaning of the word, we have unquestionably, I think, traced the trial by jury to the Saxons. Selden thinks they derived it immediately from the Greeks: others think they derived it from the Greeks through the intermediate channel of the Romans. The latter seems the most probable opinion. From the Romans they might receive it, by their immediate intercourse with them in Germany, or they might receive it by still another intermediate channel — that of the Britons.

It has been already mentioned, that the Roman arms were followed constantly and rapidly by the Roman laws. If, therefore, we can trace the conquests of Rome to the Saxons; to them we may expect to trace the institutions of Rome likewise.

The loss of the legions under Varus was one of the most striking events in the reign of Augustus. On the mind of the emperour it made so deep an impression, that he was often heard to cry, in his interrupted slumbers — Varus! restore my legions! This remarkable disaster happened in or near the country of the Cherusci, which was itself a part of Saxony; and was, indeed, the consequence of the extraordinary pains employed by Varus, to diffuse among the inhabitants the laws and jurispudence of Rome.

By Velleius Paterculus we are informed, that when Varus commanded the army in Germany, he entertained an opinion, that men, who had nothing human about them but their form and their language, might be civilized by laws much more easily, and much more effectually, than they could be brought under subjection by the sword. Under the influence of this impression, he remained in his camp without military exertion; and, surrounded with enemies, sat in judgment on causes, which were brought before him, in the same manner as if he had been a prætor, presiding in the forum of Rome. Of this propensity, the Germans took an artful advantage. They instituted, before Varus, a continued series of litigation; they expressed, in the strongest terms, their gratitude at beholding their controversies terminated by Roman justice, and at seeing the mild energy of law substituted in the place of decisions by force. They expressed also their hopes, that, by the influence of this new discipline, their own ferocity would be gradually softened, and themselves would be gradually qualified to think and to act as the friends of Rome. The surprise of his legions was the first thing which roused him — but it roused him too late — from his delusive dream.

The Saxons, it is said, might see the benefit and retain the exercise of the Roman institutions, after they had expelled him who introduced them with so much zeal, and so much unguarded confidence.

The Saxons, who invaded and conquered England, might also learn the Roman forms of decision through the medium of the Britons. On a former occasion,[q] I mentioned, that there is, in truth, no reason to suppose that the destruction of the Britons by the Saxons, on their invasion of England, was so great or general as it has been frequently represented. After some time, there was, unquestionably, an intimate and a continued intercommunication of manners, customs, and laws between the two nations. Even an English historian admits, that a more minute and particular account of the Anglo-Saxon constitution might be extracted from the Welch laws of Howell Dha, which were collected in the year eight hundred and forty two, than even from the Saxon laws themselves. He indeed accounts for this similarity, by supposing that the Welch adopted the regulations of their ancient enemies. A Welch historian would, probably, admit the fact of the similarity, but, as to the inference drawn from it, he might, perhaps, be able to turn the tables upon the historian

[q] Ante. p. 346.

of England. It is, indeed, highly probable, that the Saxons borrowed more from the Britons, than the Britons borrowed from the Saxons.

I have now traced the trial by jury, in its principle, and in many parts of its practical rules, to the most splendid eras of Rome and Athens: and I have ascertained the reign, in which its present number was fixed, and the principle of unanimity in verdicts of conviction was introduced. On this principle of unanimity, farther attention ought to be bestowed.

We have seen an express and a very awful authority, that, in verdicts of conviction in criminal cases, it must be inviolably observed. Is the rule extended — ought it to be extended to verdicts of acquittal in criminal cases? Is it extended — ought it to be extended to any verdict in civil cases? I state the questions on the double grounds of fact and reason; because, in these lectures, we are entitled to consider the law as citizens as well as jurists. It may be our duty to obey, when it is not our duty, because, without any fault, it is not in our power, to approve.

I shall consider the questions historically and on principle. On this, as on other topicks of common law, we shall probably find that principle is illustrated by history.

I beg leave, before I proceed, to suggest one precaution — that the idea of a unanimous verdict should be carefully distinguished from the idea of a unanimous sentiment in those who give that unanimous verdict. This distinction, perhaps, will be found far from being unworthy of your attention. But let us proceed.

That verdicts in civil causes, as well as verdicts of conviction in criminal causes, must be unanimous in order to be valid, seems to be a rule unknown to the law of England for many ages after that of Alfred. During some reigns after the conquest, the law was, that if some of the jurors were for one party, and some for the other, new jurors were added, till twelve were found, who agreed in opinion for one of the parties.[r] In the reign of Henry the third, a unanimous verdict was still not deemed absolutely necessary; but the dissenting jurors were amerced, as guilty of a kind of offence, in obstinately maintaining a difference of opinion.[s]

In the next reign — that of Edward the first — it was laid down for law by a respectable writer,[t] that when the jurors differed in opinion, the judge, before whom the cause was tried, might, at his election, add others, till twelve were found unanimous; or might compel the jury to agree among themselves, by directing the sheriff to keep them without meat or drink, till they agreed on their verdict.[u] There was still another method, which, we are informed by a remarkable case in that reign, was the custom. The verdict of the minority as well as of the majority was ascer-

    [r] 1. Reev. 106.   [s] Id. 242.   [t] Fleta.   [u] 1. Reev. 480.

tained, and distinctly entered on the record; and then judgment was given according to the verdict of the majority.[v]

In the eighth year of Edward the third, when a juror delayed his companions a day and a night, without assenting or giving any good reason why he would not assent, the judge committed him to prison. In the forty first year of the same reign, the point was fully debated in the court of common pleas, and, as has been generally thought, finally settled. All the jurors, except one, were agreed. They were remanded, and remained all that day and the next without eating or drinking. Being then asked if they were agreed, the dissenting juror answered, no; and said that he would die first in prison. On this, the justices took the verdict of the eleven, and committed the single juror to prison. All this happened in an assize. But when judgment was prayed upon this verdict, in the court of common pleas, the justices were unanimously of opinion, "that a verdict from eleven jurors was no verdict at all." When it was urged, that former judges had taken verdicts of eleven both in assize and trespass, and one taken in the twentieth year of the king was particularly mentioned; Thorpe, one of the justices, said, that it was not an example for them to follow, for that judge had been greatly censured for it: and it was said by the bench, that the justices ought to have carried the jurors about with them in carts till they were agreed. Thus it was settled, we are told, that the jurors must be unanimous in the verdict; and that the justices may put them under restraint, if necessary, to produce such unanimity.[w]

Unanimity produced by restraint! Is this the principle of decision in a trial by jury? Is that trial, which has been so long considered as the palladium of freedom — Is that trial brought to its consummation by tyranny's most direful engine — force upon opinion — upon opinion given under all the sanctions and solemnities of an oath? Every other agreement produced by duress is invalid and unsatisfactory: what contrary principles can govern this?

Let us here make a pause — let us turn round and look back upon the point said to be settled, and the manner of settling it. Useful observations will probably be the result.

We see that, in civil cases, unanimity was not originally required from the jurors: the unanimous verdict of twelve was, indeed, deemed necessary; and, for this reason, new jurors were added, till twelve were found of the same mind. This mode must have been productive of very great inconveniences. It was necessary that the added jurors should be as fully informed concerning the cause, as those who had been impannelled origi-

[v] Id. ibid. 2. Hale. P. C. 297.   [w] 2. Reev. 191.

nally. Every new addition, therefore, must have been attended with all the trouble, and expense, and delay of a new trial. With a view, probably, to avoid those inconveniences, a custom was introduced to enter on the record the opinion of the minority as well as that of the majority; and to give judgment upon the latter opinion.[x]

From the record of the case, however, in which this is stated to have been the custom, it appears that another mode was adopted sometimes by the jurors among themselves, and without any communication of it to the court. A large extract of this record, of the twentieth year of Edward the first, is furnished us in one of the valuable notes annexed to my Lord Hale's history of the pleas of the crown.[y] The history of that case, and the conduct of the jury who tried it, deserve very particular attention.

Certain lands were recovered against a prior before two judges of assize, in the sixteenth year of Edward the first. The prior complained, that injustice had been done him at the assize; and the bishop of Winchester and others were appointed to hear the prior's complaint, and to do justice. The judges appealed, for their justification, to the record of the judgment, which they had given. In that record, the conduct of the jury was stated very minutely. John Pickering, one of the jurors, in narrating the verdict of the jury, was contrary to all the other jurors; for he narrated a different thing from what was agreed upon among them, as appeared by their examination. For this conduct he was amerced, and ordered into the custody of the sheriff, till he made satisfaction for his transgression. The judges, say the bishop and his associates, without specifying on the record, as was the custom in such cases, the opinions of the eleven, or the contradictory opinion of John Pickering, received the verdict, as if all had been of the same sentiment concerning it, and gave judgment accordingly. This judgment was, by the bishop and his associates, declared contrary to the law and custom of the kingdom. From this decision, a writ of errour was brought before the king, by the original plaintiff. But whether any final determination was given, or, if given, what it was, we are not informed.

From the record it appears, that, when the jurors could not agree in a verdict, it was the custom and deemed to be the law to enter the different sentiments upon the record, and give judgment according to those of the

---

[x] In the fifty sixth year of Henry the third, we have a precedent of the manner, in which the entry on the record was made — "And all the jury except —— say upon their oath, &c. and —— says upon his oath, &c. But because the aforesaid eleven say accordingly, &c. therefore it is considered," &c.

In a record of the fourteenth year of Edward the first, the reason is assigned in these words — "quia dicto majoris partis juratorum standum est." To the principle — that a majority is sufficient — and not — that unanimity is necessary — an appeal is made on the record. 2. Hale. P. C. 297.

[y] Vol. 2. p. 298.

majority. But from this record something more appears. It appears, that the jury might agree upon a verdict among themselves, and appoint one of their number to narrate it to the court — that if the person, thus appointed, narrated the verdict in a manner contrary to what was agreed on, he was guilty of a misdemeanor — that the verdict agreed on should not, however, be vitiated by the prevarication of the foreman, but should be received according to what was agreed upon among the jury. Such is the evident import of the record before the judges of assize, and of the judgment which they gave upon the proceedings.

The bishop and his associates are extremely inaccurate in stating the facts, upon which they ground their reprehension of the judges. From their statement one would be led to imagine, that Pickering narrated one verdict as the voice of the other eleven, and another as his own; and that the judges, without taking any notice of this contradiction, had received and entered the verdict as a unanimous one. But this was very far from being the fact, as it appears upon the record of the two judges of assize. Pickering specified in his narration no difference of sentiment. He, on the contrary, attempted to palm upon the court, as a unanimous verdict, one contradictory to that which had been agreed on among the jury. The other jurors disclosed the verdict agreed on. That verdict was received and entered as a unanimous one. Pickering himself appears not to have either denied or retracted his own agreement to it. The law and custom of the kingdom, therefore, concerning contradictory verdicts, were applied, with great inaccuracy, to the proceedings before the two judges.

Highly probable it is, however, that, before this verdict was formed, much diversity of sentiment was entertained concerning it, among the jurors. The expressions of the record are very remarkable — "inter illos fuit *provisum*" — the verdict was *provided* among them. Consideration, consultation, adjustment are all suggested by this emphatick phrase.

One important subject of their deliberation is mentioned; and it appears, that their sentiments were worthy of the subject, which employed their attention. The prior, it seems, claimed the plaintiff as his villain. The consequence of this claim, if established, would have been, that the plaintiff could not have recovered the lands in question. For a villain could acquire no property in lands or goods; but if he purchased either, the lord might enter upon them, or seize them for his own use.[z]

The jury found, that the father of the plaintiff was a free man, and of free condition; and that although the father and his issue held, of the prior and his predecessors, their tenements in villainage and by villain services, this should not prejudice them as to the freedom of their persons. They assign the reason — because no prescription of time can reduce free blood

[z] 2. Bl. Com. 93.

to a condition of slavery; therefore the plaintiff should recover. This position, indeed, the bishop and his associates declare to be altogether false; and some of the jury themselves, perhaps, entertained a degree of hesitation concerning it, and did not adopt it till after much deliberation and advisement. They provided, however, a verdict, founded on this position, and instructed one of their number to narrate that verdict to the court.

The conduct of this jury in forming their verdict deserves the attention — perhaps, as we shall afterwards find, the imitation of their successours. Sentiments, somewhat discordant when taken separately, may, by a proper process, be melted down into a unanimous verdict.

Hitherto we have discovered no law or authority, which, in civil causes, requires unanimity in the verdicts, far less in the sentiments, of jurors. In this reign, however, an approach seems, at first sight, to be made towards the rule. The author of Fleta, who wrote in the time of Edward the first, gives, as we have seen, the election to the judges, either to increase the number of jurors till twelve are found unanimous, or to compel the first twelve, by hunger and thirst, to agree.

The author of Fleta was a writer very respectable: great deference is due to his sentiments: but the sentiments of no writer have, on the balance of authority, the weight of judicial determinations. Besides, the practice of withholding from jurors the causes of torpor and the incentives of passion, while they ponder and deliberate concerning their verdict, will, perhaps, be traced to a source and to principles, very different from those assigned by the author of Fleta.

The case decided in the forty first year of the reign of Edward the third may, perhaps, be urged as a leading and governing authority for the principle of unanimity in the verdicts and opinions of jurors. In that case, the court said, that the justices ought to have carried the jurors about with them in carts, till they were agreed. But, as to this saying of the court, I crave the liberty of proposing two questions.

Is it supported by any previous custom or adjudication? Our investigations hitherto lead us to conclude, that it has no such support.

Is it the point of adjudication in this very case? It is not. The question in judgment before the court was this — Is the verdict from eleven jurors only a good verdict? This question the court determined judicially; and their determination was in the negative. But was the other question — what shall be done with a disagreeing jury? — was this question in judgment before them? It was not. Was the answer given to this question a necessary consequence of their adjudication on the point judicially before them? It was not. The verdict of eleven jurors only might be an erroneous verdict. Does it follow, that the errour can be prevented or rectified only by carting the jury till they agree? According to the practice previous to this saying of the court, it would have been rectified by entering on the record the opinion of the dissenting juror. According to the practice subsequent to this saying, the errour would have been prevented by directing a juror to be withdrawn. According to the principles of jury trial, it might be prevented or rectified by a variety of modes other and more eligible than that of carting the jury. Some of those modes will soon be suggested.

"I would know," says my Lord Chief Justice Vaughan, in the celebrated cause of Bushell,[a] "whether any thing be more common, than for two men, students, barristers, or judges, to deduce contrary and opposite conclusions from the same case in law? And is there any difference, that two men should infer distinct conclusions from the same testimony? Is any thing more known, than that the same author, and the same place in that author, is forcibly urged to maintain contrary conclusions; and the decision is hard which is in the right? Is any thing more frequent in the controversies of religion, than to press the same text for opposite tenets? How then comes it to pass, that two persons may not, with reason and honesty, apprehend what a witness says, to prove one thing in the understanding of one, and a contrary thing clearly in the understanding of the other? Must, therefore, one of these," asks his Lordship, "merit fine and imprisonment?"

Must, therefore, both of these, I beg leave to ask, merit what is worse than imprisonment and fine? Must they be exposed, in carts, to publick derision, because they act a part which is common, innocent, unavoidable? Must they suffer all the extremities of hunger and thirst, till, at last, agonizing nature makes the necessary but disgraceful barter of unsufferable punishment for degrading prevarication? Are instruments subscribed by pain, by infamy, and by shame — are these the letters recommendatory, which our law despatches, or wishes to despatch, to the remotest regions of the globe, in order to concentre in the trial by jury the admiration and imitation of all?

It must, however, be confessed, that though no judicial determinations, so far as I know, are precisely in the point; yet the forms of our law, rendered venerable by the immemorial practice of ages, seem at least to countenance, if not to presuppose, the principle of unanimity in the trial by jury. When the jury retire, a bailiff is sworn to keep them together till they be agreed of their verdict. When they return to the bar, the first question asked of them is — are you agreed of your verdict? This question must be answered in the affirmative, before the verdict can be received. Such are the established forms of the law. They seem to require a unanimous verdict.

Every juror swears that he will give a true verdict according to his

[a] Vaughan, 141.

evidence. The sacred obligation of this oath demands, that to unanimity truth shall not be made a sacrifice.

In this situation are the jury placed. Truth and unanimity — qualities very distinct — qualities, on some occasions, seemingly irreconcilable — must unite in the composition of their verdict. To extricate them from such a labyrinth, where the law seems to point to one direction, and their oaths seem to point to another, is there no affectionate hand to furnish them a clue?

What is a verdict? It is the joint declaration of twelve jurymen upon their oaths. Littleton calls it "the verdict of twelve men." [b]

"Veredictum," says my Lord Coke, in his valuable Commentary, "quasi dictum veritatis, as judicium is quasi juris dictum. Et sicut ad quæstionem juris non respondent juratores, sed judices; sic ad quæstionem facti, non respondent judices, sed juratores." A verdict is a declaration of the fact: a judgment is a declaration of the law. To a question of law the judges, not the jury, shall answer: so, to a question of fact, the jury, not the judges, shall answer. So far the parallel holds exactly between the duties of judges and of jurors, in their respective provinces of law and of fact. So far the parallel holds between a verdict and a judgment.

We have seen what a verdict is: it is a joint declaration of the jury. What is a judgment? It is, I apprehend, the joint declaration of the court. It is not merely a declaration of a majority of the judges: it is the declaration of the *court*. When it is solemnly pronounced, even by a dissenting president, it must be announced as "the judgment of this court" — not as the "judgment of a majority of the judges." Why should not the parallel hold, in this instance too, with regard to a jury, except in a case of conviction, which has been already shown to stand upon its own peculiar foundation?

We have seen, that, in this instance too, the parallel did hold formerly with regard to the jury. We have seen, that the declaration of the majority operated as the verdict of the jury. For some time, indeed, the dissent of the minority was noticed on the record; but was it necessary to notice that dissent? Was it necessary to continue that practice? Every one knows, that judgments are entered as the acts of the court generally, even when there is a dissenting minority. Why should not the same practice prevail — why should we not presume that the same practice has prevailed, with regard to juries? On the record, the transactions of the court bear the same stamps of unanimity with the transactions of the jury: whence, then, can it be inferred, that a degree of unanimity is, in reality, required from the jurors, which, on all hands, is acknowledged to be unnecessary in the judges?

Whether, therefore, we consult the suggestions of the records, or the

[b] 1. Ins. 226.

information of etymology, the inferences of analogy, or the language of adjudications, we shall find no authority to conclude, that, in civil causes, the verdict of a jury must be founded on unanimous opinion.

But recurrence will still be had to those venerable forms, immemorially established, which countenance or presuppose the doctrine of unanimity in the trial by jury. Before a verdict can be received, it will be urged, the jury must declare, that of that verdict they are agreed.

Permit me, on this occasion, to have recourse to a conjecture. I propose it with diffidence: I pursue it with caution: if my expressions concerning it become sanguine, it shall not be till I think I have established it. My conjecture is, that by the phrase, "agreed of a verdict," nothing more is meant, than that the jury are willing and prepared to give a verdict; and by that means, bring to a decision the controversy submitted to them.

In early times, a verdict, as we have seen, could not be prevented by the contrary vote or sentiment of one or of a minority of the jurors. The jury was increased till twelve were unanimous; or the vote of a majority was received as a decision. But the effect of an obstinate refusal to give any vote was very different. We have seen, that all the votes were required to be disposed of on the record; and that though eleven votes on one side, and one on the other, formed materials for a verdict; yet eleven votes, unopposed by the dissenting one, were deemed insufficient for that purpose. Those, therefore, who wished to obstruct the administration of justice in the trial by jury, accomplished their wishes by refusing to give any vote on either side. In turbulent times — and the times I allude to were turbulent — this expedient would be often used, by the friends of a powerful usurper in possession, against a legal recovery by him who had right. To restrain and to prevent the pernicious effects of such a conduct, every juror was sworn to give a verdict; the bailiff was sworn to confine him till he should agree to give it; and no declaration was received by the court, till it was unanimously declared, that, as to the point of *giving* a verdict, they were all agreed.

These observations will throw a new light upon some points, which have been already mentioned. The case of an obstinate juror, of the species now described, happened, as we before noticed, in the eighth year of the reign of Edward the third. Upon that case, my Lord Chief Justice Vaughan makes the following remarks: "This book," says he, "rightly understood, is law: that he staid his fellows a day and a night, without any reason or assenting, may be understood, that he would not, at that time, intend the verdict at all, more than if he had been absent from his fellows; but wilfully not find for either side. In this sense, it was a misdemeanor against his oath; for his oath was truly to try the issue, which he could never do, who resolved not to confer with his fellows." "And in this sense," adds he, "it is the same with the case 34. Ed. III. where

twelve being sworn, and put together to treat of their verdict, one secretly withdrew himself, and went away, for which he was justly fined
and imprisoned; and it differs not to withdraw from a man's duty, by
departing from his fellows; and to withdraw from it though he stay in
the same room: and so is that book to be understood." [c] These remarks
corroborate what I have mentioned — that the great object seems to have
been to secure a decision, not a unanimous decision, by verdict. For both
the cases, just now noticed, happened before that which is alleged to have
settled the principle of unanimity. I hope, I have now established my conjecture.

I have asked, "since judgments are entered as the acts of the court
generally, when there is a dissenting minority; why should not the same
practice prevail — why should we not presume that the same practice
has prevailed, with regard to juries?" I now go farther, and undertake to
evince, that the reason for that practice is much greater, and that, consequently, the presumption in its favour is much stronger, in the case of
jurors, than it is in the case of judges. This will appear from a variety of
considerations.

In the turbulent times, to which I allude, the jurors, as we are told by
Montesquieu, were obliged to fight either of the parties who might give
them the lie. When there was no dissent, or which, as to this point, was
the same thing — when no dissent appeared, a party who gave the lie to
one, must engage in single combat with each. Their number would render
him circumspect. A regard, therefore, to the security of jurors would
superinduce every prudent appearance of unanimity in their opinions
and verdicts. But this reason applied not to the judges.

In times the most civilized and tranquil, it is improper to expose jurors
unnecessarily to the concealed resentment of those, who may be affected
by the parts they severally take in the juries, of which they are members.
This reason is applicable, but not so strongly applicable, to the judges.

In this argument, whatever shows a greater reason for preserving the
vestiges of diversity in the sentiments of the judges, than in those of the
jurors, will have the same effect, as that which shows a greater reason for
preserving the appearance of unanimity in the sentiments of the jurors,
than in those of the judges. We have seen,[d] that "a judge, particularly a
judge of the common law, should bear a great regard to the sentiments
and decisions of those, who have thought and decided before him." We
have seen,[e] "that the evidence of facts — and facts are the province of
juries — cannot be ascertained, distinguished, or estimated by any system
of general rules; and that, for this reason, the evidence of facts must, in
every case, depend on circumstances, which to that case are peculiar."
The natural consequences from these two positions are, that it might be

      [c] Vaugh. 151.   [d] Ante. p. 501.   [e] Ante. p. 505.

useful, perhaps material, to preserve, on the record, evidences of the unanimity or diversity of sentiments, with which judgments are given, so that they may make the slighter or deeper impression on the minds of succeeding judges; and that such a measure, with regard to verdicts, would be altogether useless and immaterial; since every verdict rests on its own peculiar circumstances, without precedent and without example.

The result is, that the reasons for apparent unanimity on the record are not so great, nor the presumption arising from them so strong, in the case of judges as in the case of jurors: an apparent unanimity, however, is preserved, while a real diversity of sentiment subsists, in the case of judges: there is, therefore, much greater reason to presume, that a real diversity of sentiment may subsist, though an apparent unanimity be preserved, in the case of juries.

It may be naturally asked — if this principle of unanimity in the trial by jury be unfounded; how has it happened, that the opinion of its existence has been so general and so permanent, not only among the people at large, but even among professional characters? This has already been accounted for in part. It was prudent to preserve the appearance of unanimity: this uniform appearance would naturally produce and disseminate an opinion that the unanimity was real. Besides, in one species — in the most important species of verdicts — those of conviction in criminal, still more in capital cases — this unanimity, upon the principles which have been explained, was not only apparent, but real and indispensable. Farther; the awful precedents set by Alfred, to establish the principle of unanimity in this species of verdicts, would naturally make a deep and lasting impression upon all — upon professional characters, as well as upon others. Impressions, deep and lasting, are always diffusive: their influence, therefore, extended beyond those causes, which had originally produced them. Unanimity, confined, in its principle, to verdicts of conviction in criminal cases, was applied indiscriminately to cases and verdicts of every kind — to verdicts of acquittal, as well as to those of conviction — to cases civil, as well as to cases criminal.

This subject, so very interesting to juries and to all who, and whose causes, are tried by juries, I have investigated minutely and carefully, historically and upon principle. Of many late *dicta* I have taken no notice, because they are suspended on those of a more early period. To trace matters to their remotest sources, is the most satisfactory and the most successful mode of detecting errours, as well as of discovering truths. In doing both, I hope that, on this subject, I have had some success: if so, I shall have much satisfaction; for I shall have contributed to dispel a cloud, dark and heavy, which has hitherto shaded and hung over the trial by jury, so luminous when beheld in its unintercepted lustre.

If I have been successful, many practical advantages will result to parties, to jurors, and to judges. My theory is shortly this. To the conviction of a crime, the undoubting and the unanimous sentiment of the twelve jurors is of indispensable necessity. In civil causes, the sentiment of a majority of the jurors forms the verdict of the jury, in the same manner as the sentiment of a majority of the judges forms the judgment of the court. In many cases, a verdict may, with great propriety, be composed of the separate sentiments of the several jurors, reduced to what may be called their average result. This will be explained. Hitherto, I have said nothing concerning verdicts of acquittal in criminal cases. After what has been observed, it is unnecessary to say much concerning them. If to a verdict of conviction, the undoubted and the unanimous sentiment of the twelve jurors be of indispensable necessity; the consequence unquestionably is, that a single doubt or a single dissent must produce a verdict of acquittal.

Let us now see whether this theory, short and plain, may not be reduced to practice, with great security and advantage to parties, to juries, and to judges.

In criminal prosecutions, the state or society is always a party. From the necessity of the case, it is also always a judge. For we have seen, that, in the social contract, the party injured transfers to the publick his right of punishment, and that, by the publick, the party injuring agrees to be judged. The state acts by the medium of the selected jury. Can the voice of the state be indicated more strongly, than by the unanimous voice of this selected jury? Again; the state, though a party on one side, has a deep interest in the party on the other side; for to a well organized state, every citizen is precious. According to the theory which we are now trying by its application to practice, the state can lose no precious part of herself, unless on the strongest indication that she herself, if consulted on the occasion, would say,

—— immedicabile vulnus
Ense recidendum est; ne pars sincera trahatur.*

By the practice of this theory, the state will lose no member by the malice or resentment of a single individual, who, with a constitution as strong as his heart is hard, can starve his fellow jurors into a reluctant and prevaricating verdict of conviction.

How stands the other party to a criminal prosecution? He stands single and unconnected. He is accused of a crime. For his trial on this accusation, he is brought before those who, if he is guilty, represent his offended judge. If it were possible, the characters of party and judge

* [An incurable wound must be cut away with the sword to keep the healthy part from being drawn with it.]

should be separated altogether. When that is impossible, the greatest security imaginable should be provided against the dangers, which may result from their union. The greatest security is provided by declaring, and by reducing to practice the declaration, that he shall not suffer, unless the selected body who act for his country say unanimously and without hesitation — he deserves to suffer. By this practice, the party accused will be effectually protected from the concealed and poisoned darts of private malice and malignity, and can never suffer but by the voice of his country.

By this practice, we are led to see the beautiful and exquisite propriety and emphasis of a form, which is used every day in criminal trials; but which is the object of little attention, because it is used every day. When the jury are sworn to try a person for a crime, the clerk of the court informs them succinctly of the nature of the charge; that the prisoner has pleaded to it, that he is not guilty; that for trial he has put himself upon his country — "which country," adds he, "you are." Upon the principles which I have stated and explained, a jury, in criminal cases, may, indeed, be called the country of the person accused, and the trial by jury may, indeed, be denominated the trial *per patriam.*

"In a well tempered government," says the Empress of Russia, in the excellent instructions which she gave concerning a code of laws for her extensive empire, "In a well tempered government, no person is deprived of his life, unless his country rise up against him." [f] Let others know, and teach, and publish, and recommend fine political principles: it is ours to reduce them to practice.

We may now conclude, that the practice of the theory, which we have explained, is advantageous and secure for the parties in criminal causes. Let us next examine it in relation to causes of a civil nature. Here, we say, the sentiment of a majority of the jurors forms the verdict of the jury, in the same manner as the sentiment of a majority of the judges forms the judgment of the court.

That the sentiments of the majority shall govern, is, as we before showed at large,[g] the general rule of society. To this rule we have seen the strongest reason to introduce an exception, with regard to verdicts of conviction in criminal prosecutions. Does the same reason extend to civil causes? We presume not. In civil causes, the jury stand equally indifferent to the parties on either side. As the juridical balance thus hangs in perfect equipoise between them; it is for their security, and for their advantage too, that the scales should clearly indicate the proportional weight of law and truth which is thrown into them, and that a preponderancy on the whole should direct the decision. To insist that a jury

[f] 3. War. Bib. 67.   [g] Ante. p. 242.

should be unanimous, is eventually, in many cases, to ordain, that their verdict shall not be the legitimate offspring of free deliberation and candid discussion; but shall be the spurious brood of strength of constitution and obstinacy of temper. For the advantage and security of the parties this cannot be; the other must.

Let us now consider this subject as it respects juries. From the principle of unanimity, as it has been often understood, he who will be obliged to discharge the important trusts and duties of a juryman has but a comfortless prospect before him. He must perform the most interesting business of society — he must decide upon fortune, upon character, upon liberty, upon life: all this he must perform in conjunction with others, whom he does not choose, whom, perhaps, he does not know, with whom, perhaps, he would not wish to associate; for though jurors are selected, they are not selected by one another: all this, too, he must perform in real or in counterfeited unanimity with eleven others, each of whom is summoned and appears on this business under the same untoward circumstances with himself. What must he do? In the affairs of life, real unanimity among such a number is little to be expected; least of all is it to be expected in matters which are litigated, and concerning which, if there had been no doubt, it is to be presumed there would have been no controversy. If real unanimity cannot be expected, he must either counterfeit it himself, or he must be an accessory before the fact to the counterfeiting of it by others. The first is the principal, the second is inferiour only to the principal degree of disingenuity. Such a situation can never be desirable: on some occasions, it may be dreadful.

Let us suppose, that matters are brought to the sad alternative — that a juror must ruin his constitution, or, perhaps, literally starve himself; or, to avoid immediate death or a languishing life, he must, contrary to his conscience, doom a fellow man and a fellow citizen to die — what must he do? In this crisis of distress, he prays direction from the laws of his country: the laws of his country, as often understood, tell him — you must starve: for it cannot be insinuated, that the laws will advise him to belie his conscience. He obeys the hard mandate: by the virtue of obedience he loses his life: by his death the jury are discharged: for now there is a natural, as well as a moral impossibility of obtaining the unanimous verdict of twelve men. The former produces what, on every principle of morality and jurisprudence, the latter ought most unquestionably to have produced. But what must be the consequence of the jury's discharge? Does it discharge the person accused? No. A second jury must sit upon him; and before that second jury must be brought all those inextricable difficulties, which produced such calamity in the first.

Where is this to end? By the practice of the principles which I have explained, this can never begin. It is no hardship for each juror to speak his genuine and undisguised sentiment. Is it for conviction? Let him declare it. Let every other, in the same manner, declare his genuine and undisguised sentiment. If the sentiment of every other is for conviction; the verdict of conviction is unanimous. If a single sentiment is not for conviction; then a verdict of acquittal is the immediate consequence. To this verdict of acquittal, every one whose private sentiment was for conviction ought immediately to agree. For by the law, as it has been stated, twelve votes of conviction are necessary to compose a verdict of conviction: but eleven votes of conviction and one against it compose a verdict of acquittal.

Thus it is as to criminal matters. Under this disposition of things, can an honest and conscientious juror dread or suffer any inconvenience, in discharging his important trust, and performing his important duty, honestly and conscientiously? Under this disposition of things, will the citizens discover that strong reluctance, which they often and naturally discover, against serving on juries in criminal, especially in capital cases? Under this disposition of things, will those who have influence with the returning officer, exert that influence to prevent their being returned; and will those who cannot prevent their being returned, but can pay a fine, pay the fine rather than perform the service? Under this disposition, will juries, in criminal, especially in capital cases, be composed — as we have seen them too often composed — chiefly of such as have neither influence enough to avoid being returned, nor money enough to pay a fine for their non-attendance?

In civil causes, the business of the jury will be managed and directed in the same manner as the business of the court, and of every other publick body. Unanimity will always be acceptable: free and candid discussion will always be used: if they produce unanimity, it is well: if they reach not this high aim, acquiescence will be shown in the sentiment of the majority. This is the conduct of legislators: this is the conduct of judges: why should not this be the conduct of jurors?

I mentioned, that, in many cases, a verdict may, with great propriety, be composed of the separate sentiments of the several jurors, reduced to what may be called their average result. This I now explain.

It has been observed — and the observation has been illustrated at great length — that the power of juries is a discretionary power. This discretionary power arises from the nature of their office. Their office is to try the truth of facts: the truth of facts is tried by their evidence: the force of evidence cannot be digested by rules, nor formed into a regular system.

In many causes, there can be but two different sentiments. If, for instance, a suit be brought for the recovery of a horse; there can be, among the jury, only two opinions — that the plaintiff ought, and that he ought not, to recover. If there is a majority on either side, the voice of the majority should govern the verdict. If, on each side, there be an equal number of opinions, the verdict should be in favour of the possessor. "Melior est conditio possidentis." *

But there are many other causes, in which twenty different opinions may be entertained, as well as two; and there is no fixed rule, by which the accuracy or inaccuracy of any one of them can be ascertained. An action of slander, for instance, is brought by a young woman to recover damages for an injury, which she has sustained by the defamation of her character. A variety of opinions may be formed, without end, concerning the particular sum which she ought to recover. Each of those various opinions may be composed from a variety of combining circumstances, the precise force of any of which can never be liquidated by any known methods of calculation. Those combining circumstances will arise from the situation and character of the plaintiff, from the situation and character of the defendant, from the nature and kind of the injury, and from the nature and extent of the loss. In the mind of each of the jurors, according to his situation and character, each of those combining circumstances may produce an effect, different from that which is produced by them in the mind of every other juror. The opinions, which are composed of those circumstances operating thus differently, must, of necessity, be different. Each juror forms his own. The opinion of each has an equal title to regard. How shall a verdict be collected from twelve opinions, no two of which are the same? Let each pronounce the particular sum, which, he thinks, the plaintiff ought to recover: let the sums be added together: let the amount of the whole be divided by twelve: let the sum produced by this division form the verdict of the jury. In this manner I explain what I mean by a verdict, "composed of the separate sentiments of the several jurors, reduced to what may be called their average result." This mode of forming a verdict will, on many occasions, be found useful and satisfactory.

Let us, in the last place, consider this subject as it regards judges. Judges do not, indeed, undergo, but, with melancholy, sympathetick feelings, they are obliged to witness — nay, they are obliged to be instrumental in — the feelings which jurors undergo, from the principle and the practice of unanimity, as it is frequently understood.

How natural is it for a jury, worn down by thirst, and hunger, and want of sleep, distracted by altercations and debates, bewildered by the difficulties and embarrassments by which those debates and altercations were produced — how natural is it for them to fly, for relief and instruction, to the court! Before the court they appear, pale, anxious, dejected; and beg the court to instruct and relieve them. On the principle of unanimity, as often received, what can the court do or advise? If they are

---

* [The condition of the possessor is the better one.]

well disposed — and we will presume them well disposed — they will, with every mark of compassionate attention and regard, advise them to do — what, if they could have done, there would have been no application for advice — "gentlemen, we advise you to agree: return to your chamber; confer together; reason together; come to an agreement; for you must agree; otherwise we cannot receive your verdict."

I have presumed the court to be well disposed: for this presumption, there is not always a sufficient ground. In the celebrated trial of William Penn and William Meade, four of the jurors dissented from the others. The recorder of London, before whom the cause was tried, addressing himself to Mr. Bushel, one of the four dissenters, said, Sir, you are the cause of this disturbance, and manifestly show yourself an abettor of faction; I shall set a mark on you, Sir. Gentlemen, said he to the whole jury, you shall not be dismissed, till we have a verdict that the court will accept; and you shall be locked up without meat, drink, fire, and tobacco: we will have a verdict, by the help of God, or you shall starve for it.[h]

But I have presumed the court to be well disposed. If they really are so, their situation is, indeed, a distressful one. They see before them a body of men, intrusted by their country with the greatest and most interesting powers: in the execution of this high trust, they see them suffering, though not offending: from those unmerited sufferings, they feel themselves altogether incapable of affording relief. What, in this situation, is left to the court? The alternate emotions of compassion and regret — compassion for those, whom they cannot aid — regret, because they cannot aid them.

By reducing to practice the theory, which I have stated and explained, the judges will be disburthened of all that uneasiness, under which they otherwise must labour; and will, on every occasion, have it in their power to relieve and advise satisfactorily every jury, who may apply to them for advice and relief.

Is the jury sitting in a criminal cause? Are they at a loss what to do? Do they pray the direction of the court? The court may give them a series of directions, which, one would imagine, must contain a remedy for every complaint. — Gentlemen, each of you must know the state of his own mind. Each of you must be clearly of opinion that the prisoner ought to be convicted, or that he ought to be acquitted; or you must be doubtful what opinion you must form. If the first be the case, you ought to vote for a conviction: if either of the two last be the case, you ought to vote for an acquittal. What we say in the case of one, we say in the case of every one. Let every one, therefore, govern his own vote by these directions. When the vote of each is formed; the next step is to compose the verdict of all from the vote of each. Let the votes, then, be

[h] 2. St. Tr. 613. 614.

taken: they must be either unanimous or not unanimous: if they are not unanimous, let all agree to a verdict of acquittal: if they are unanimous, they must be unanimous for acquittal, or for conviction: if the former, the verdict is a verdict of acquittal: if the latter, the verdict is a verdict of conviction.

Is the jury sitting in a civil cause? Are they, in this cause too, at a loss what to do? Do they pray the direction of the court? The court may, in this cause too, give them a series of satisfactory directions. — Gentlemen, can only two opinions be entertained concerning the cause before you? If so; after freely and candidly discussing the matter by friendly conference among yourselves, let each make up his own opinion: let all the opinions be collected: if there be a majority on either side, let all agree to a verdict in favour of that side: if there is an equality of votes on each side, let the verdict be given in favour of possession. May any indefinite number of opinions be entertained concerning the cause before you? Let each juror form his own: let the verdict consist of the average result of all.

I trust, I have now shown, that, by reducing to practice the theory, which I have advanced on the subject of unanimity in jury trials, many solid advantages would result from it to judges, to juries, and to parties. I trust, I have established this theory on every pillar on which a legal theory can be built — on precedent — on authority — on principle.

To all the nations, which swarmed from the northern hive, the trial by jury was common: to none of them, the principle of unanimity was known.

I here finish what, at present, I propose to say, concerning the doctrine of unanimity in the trial by jury.

Of juries there are two kinds; a grand jury, and a traverse jury. The institution of the grand jury is, at least in the present times, the peculiar boast of the common law. In the annals of the world, there cannot be found an institution so well fitted for avoiding abuses, which might otherwise arise from malice, from rigour, from negligence, or from partiality, in the prosecution of crimes.

In Athens, we can discover the vestiges of an institution, which bears a resemblance, though a very slight one, to that of grand juries. There was among them a previous inquiry before that trial, in which the final sentence was pronounced.

In cases of murder, the relations of the deceased alone had a right to prosecute.[1] There is an evident resemblance between this regulation, and that part of the law of England, which relates to prosecutions by appeal. When crimes were committed immediately against the government of Athens, every citizen might step forward as the prosecutor; for an in-

[1] 2. Gog. Or. L. 71.

jury offered to the commonwealth was considered as personal to each of its members.

Among the Romans, too, any one of the citizens was permitted to prosecute a publick offence. With all our predilection, however, for those celebrated republicks, we must admit, that these regulations were extremely injudicious, and produced mischiefs of very dangerous, though of very opposite kinds. Prosecutions were, on some occasions, undertaken from motives of rancour and revenge. On other occasions, a friend, a dependent, perhaps a confederate, of the criminal officiously engaged to prosecute him, with a view to ensure his impunity. Of this we have a remarkable instance, in the case of the infamous Verres. Cœcilius, his creature and associate, disputed with Cicero the right of accusing him. The preference was adjudged to Cicero, in a process known by the name of *divination*.

There was a time, says Beccaria, when the crimes of the subjects were the inheritance of the prince.[j] At such a time probably it was, that the judge himself became the prosecutor. In several of the feudal nations, this was, indeed, the case. The gross impropriety of this regulation appears at the first view. The prosecutor is a party: without the last necessity, the prosecutor ought not to be both a party and a judge.

Among the Saxons, as we are informed by Mr. Selden, besides the satisfaction recovered by the party injured, there was a way found out to punish the offender by indictment. The difference, adds he, between former indictments and those in these days, consists in this, that the ancient indictments were in the name of one man; those of the latter sort are in the name of the jury. Time and experience, continues he, refined this way of trial into a more excellent condition.[k]

In the reign of Henry the third, the presentment of offences was made by a jury of twelve, returned for every hundred in the county. But towards the latter end of the reign of Edward the third, another improvement was introduced into the institution of grand juries. Besides the jury for every hundred, the sheriff returned a jury for the county, which was termed "the grand inquest." When this grand inquest inquired for the whole body of the county, the business of the hundred inquest, and the whole trust and duty of making presentments and finding indictments, naturally devolved upon the grand jury.[l]

A presentment is an accusation brought forward by the grand jury of their own mere motion. An indictment is a particular charge laid, by the publick prosecutor, before the grand jury, and found by them to be true.

The trust reposed in grand juries is of great and general concernment. To them is committed the custody of the portals of the law, that into the hallowed dome no injustice may be permitted to enter. They make, in

[j] Bec. c. 17.   [k] Bac. on Gov. 53, 54, 57.   [l] 2. Reev. 210, 211.

the first instance, the important discrimination between the innocent and the guilty. To the former, they give a passport of security: the latter they consign to a final trial by a traverse jury.

The manner, in which grand juries ought to make their inquiries, well deserves to be attentively considered. It has been declared by some, that grand juries are only to inquire, "whether what they hear be any reason to put the party to answer" — "that a probable cause to call him to answer, is as much as is required by law." But, indeed, such a declaration is very little consonant to the oath — the best evidence of the law — which every grand juryman is obliged to take. He swears, that he will inquire diligently. As little is such a declaration consonant to ancient authority and practice. "In those days," says my Lord Coke,[m] speaking of the reign of Edward the first — "in those days (as yet it ought to be) indictments, taken in the absence of the party, were formed upon plain and direct proof, and not upon probabilities or inferences." Still as little is such a declaration consonant to the voice of reason and sound sense. An indictment has been styled, and with no small degree of propriety, the verdict of the grand jury. "It ought to import all the truth which is requisite by law; and every part material ought to be found by the oath of the indictors." Now, is it consistent with reason or sound sense, that a verdict found upon oath — upon an oath to make diligent inquiry — should be the vague, perhaps the visionary, result merely of probability? Ought not moral certainty to be deemed the necessary basis of what is delivered, under the sanction of an obligation so solemn and so strict?

The doctrine, that a grand jury may rest satisfied merely with probabilities, is a doctrine dangerous as well as unfounded: it is a doctrine, which may be applied to countenance and promote the vilest and most oppressive purposes: it may be used, in pernicious rotation, as a snare, in which the innocent may be entrapped, and as a screen, under the cover of which the guilty may escape.

It has been alleged, that grand juries are confined, in their inquiries, to the bills offered to them, to the crimes given them in charge, and to the evidence brought before them by the prosecutor. But these conceptions are much too contracted: they present but a very imperfect and unsatisfactory view of the duty required from grand jurors, and of the trust reposed in them. They are not appointed for the procecutor or for the court: they are appointed for the government and for the people: and of both the government and people it is surely the concernment, that, on one hand, all crimes, whether given or not given in charge, whether described or not described with professional skill, should receive the punishment, which the law denounces; and that, on the other hand, in-

---

[m] 2. Ins. 384.

nocence, however strongly assailed by accusations drawn up in regular form, and by accusers marshalled in legal array, should, on full investigation, be secure in that protection, which the law engages that she shall enjoy inviolate.

The oath of a grand juryman — and his oath is the commission, under which he acts — assigns no limits, except those marked by diligence itself, to the course of his inquiries: why, then, should it be circumscribed by more contracted boundaries? Shall diligent inquiry be enjoined? And shall the means and opportunities of inquiry be prohibited or restrained?

The grand jury are a great channel of communication, between those who make and administer the laws, and those for whom the laws are made and administered. All the operations of government, and of its ministers and officers, are within the compass of their view and research. They may suggest publick improvements, and the modes of removing publick inconveniences: they may expose to publick inspection, or to publick punishment, publick bad men, and publick bad measures.

The relative powers of courts and juries form an interesting subject of inquiry. Concerning it, different opinions have been entertained; and it is of much consequence, in the study and in the practice too of the law, that it be clearly and fully understood. I shall treat it in the same manner, in which I have treated other questions of great importance: I shall examine it historically and on principle.

From a statute made in the thirteenth year of Edward the first, usually called the statute of Westminster the second,[n] it appears that the contest between judges and juries concerning their relative powers ran, at that time, in a direction very different from that which it has taken since. The judges, then, were disposed to compel the jury to find the law as well as the fact: the jury were disposed to show the truth of the fact only, and to refer to the court the determination of the law. The statute interposed, and declared the discretionary power of the jury to do which of the two they thought most proper. "It is ordained, that the justices assigned to take assizes shall not compel the jurors to say precisely, whether it is or is not a disseisin." A general verdict of this kind included the question of law as well as the question of fact. "It is sufficient that they show the truth of the fact, and pray the assistance of the justices. But if they will voluntarily say, whether it is or is not a disseisin, their verdict shall be received at their own peril."

This statute recognised the law as it then stood, but introduced no new law. We are informed by my Lord Coke, in his commentary on it,[o] that in all actions, real, personal, and mixed, and upon all issues joined, general or special, the jury might find the special matter of fact pertinent

[n] C. 30.   [o] 2. Ins. 425.

and tending only to the issue joined, and might pray the discretion of the court for the law. This the jurors might do at the common law, not only in cases between party and party, of which the statute puts an example of the assize; but also in pleas of the crown at the suit of the king. This statute, therefore, like many others of the ancient statutes, is only in affirmance of the common law.[p]

Bracton, who wrote in the reign of Henry the third, tells us,[q] that a distinction was commonly taken between the provinces of the judges and jurors in this manner — truth is to be displayed by the jury; justice and judgment by the court. Yet, says he, it seems that judgment sometimes belongs to the jurors, when they declare upon their oath, whether such a one disseised or did not disseise such a one; according to which declaration, the judgment of the court is rendered. But, adds he, as it belongs to the judges to pronounce a just judgment, it is incumbent on them diligently to weigh and examine what is said by the jury, that they themselves may not be misled by the jury's mistakes.

We have the high authority of Littleton, that, in cases where the jury may give their verdict at large — in other words, a special verdict, stating the facts, and praying the decision of the court as to the law — they may, if they will take upon them the knowledge of the law, give their verdict generally, as is put in their charge.[r]

In a case determined in the reign of Queen Elizabeth, it was objected, that a jury could not give a special verdict upon a special and collateral issue; but that, in such case, the jury ought to give a precise and categorical answer to the question arising from such special issue. It was resolved, however, unanimously by the court, that the law will not compel the jurors to take upon them the knowledge of points in law, either in cases of property, or in those which concern life; and that it will not compel even the judges to give their opinions of questions and doubts in law upon the sudden; but, in such cases, the truth of the facts should be found; and, after consideration and conference, the question should be determined according to the law.[s]

In the famous trial of John Lilburne, for publishing a book, entitled, an impeachment of high treason against Oliver Cromwell, we hear a language, very different from that, to which we have hitherto been accustomed. "Let all the hearers know" — said Mr. Justice Jermin, a judge of the upper bench, as it was called during the commonwealth, and who was one of the commissioners appointed in the extraordinary commission of oyer and terminer for the trial of Mr. Lilburne — "Let all the hearers know, the jury ought to take notice of it, that the judges, that are sworn, that are twelve in number, they have ever been the judges of the law,

[p] 9. Rep. 13.   [q] Bract. 186 b.   [r] Lit. s. 368. 1. Ins. 228.
[s] 9. Rep. 11. b. 13.

from the first time that ever we can read or hear that the law was truly expressed in England: and the jury are only judges, whether such a thing were done or no; they are only judges of matter of fact." [t] Lord Commissioner Keble delivers it as the opinion of the court, that "the jury are judges of matter of fact altogether; but that they are not judges of matter of law." [u] The prisoner urged the authority of my Lord Coke, that the jury were judges of the law as well as of the fact; but, by a mistake, mentioned the book as a commentary upon Plowden instead of Littleton. The court told him there was no such book; that they knew it a little better than he did. He pressed to read it; and said that it was an easy matter for an abler man than him, in so many interruptions as he met with, to mistake Plowden for Littleton. "You cannot" — these are the words of Judge Jermin, as mentioned in the report of the trial — "you cannot be suffered to read the law: you have broached an erroneous opinion, that the jury are the judges of the law, which is enough to destroy all the law in the land; there was never such a damnable heresy broached in this nation before." [v] Mr. Lilburne persisted, however, and read his authorities.

"Extremes in nature equal ends produce." As were some of the judges under Cromwell, so were some of the judges under Charles the second. We have had occasion to take some notice of the trial of William Penn and William Meade. The jury, at last, agreed on a verdict of acquittal. This verdict the court could not refuse; but they fined each of the jurors forty marks for giving it, "because it was against the direction of the court in matter of law." [w] The jurors were imprisoned till they should pay the fines. Mr. Bushell, one of them, sued a writ of habeas corpus out of the court of common pleas. His case was heard and determined there; and the cause of commitment was adjudged to be insufficient, and Mr. Bushell was discharged.

To what end — said Lord Chief Justice Vaughan, in delivering the opinion of the court — to what end are jurors challenged so scrupulously to the array and the poll? To what end must they be true and lawful men, and not of affinity with the parties concerned? To what end must they have, in many cases, the view, for their exacter information chiefly? To what end must they undergo the heavy punishment of the villainous judgment; if, after all this, they must implicitly give a verdict by the dictates and authority of another man, under pain of fines and imprisonment, when sworn to do it according to the best of their own knowledge? A man cannot see by another's eye, nor hear by another's ear; no more can a man conclude or infer the thing to be resolved, by another's understanding or reasoning.

Upon all general issues, the jury find not the fact of every case by

[t] 2. St. Tri. 19.　　[u] Id. 69.　　[v] Id. ibid.　　[w] Vaugh. 136.

itself, leaving the law to the court; but find for the plaintiff or defendant upon the issue tried, wherein they resolve both law and fact complicately, and not the fact by itself.[x]

In every case, says the late Sir Michael Foster, where the point turneth upon the question, whether the homicide was committed wilfully and maliciously, or under circumstances justifying, excusing, or alleviating; the matter of fact, to wit, whether the facts alleged by way of justification, excuse, or alleviation be true, is the proper and only province of the jury. But whether, upon a supposition of the truth of the facts, such homicide be justified, excused, or alleviated, must be submitted to the judgment of the court.[y]

It is of the greatest consequence, says my Lord Hardwicke, to the law of England, that the powers of the judges and jury be kept distinct: that the judges determine the law, and that the jury determine the fact.[z]

This well known division between their provinces has been long recognised and established. When the question of law and the question of fact can be decided separately; there is no doubt or difficulty in saying, by whom the separate decision shall be made. If, between the parties litigant, there is no contention concerning the facts, but an issue is joined upon a question of law, as is the case in a demurrer; the determination of this question, and the trial of this issue, belongs exclusively to the judges. On the other hand, when there is no question concerning the law, and the controversy between the parties depends entirely upon a matter of fact; the determination of this matter, brought to an issue, belongs exclusively to the jury. But, in many cases, the question of law is intimately and inseparably blended with the question of fact: and when this is the case, the decision of one necessarily involves the decision of the other. When this is the case, it is incumbent on the judges to inform the jury concerning the law; and it is incumbent on the jury to pay much regard to the information, which they receive from the judges. But now the difficulty, in this interesting subject, begins to press upon us. Suppose that, after all the precautions taken to avoid it, a difference of sentiment takes place between the judges and the jury, with regard to a point of law: suppose the law and the fact to be so closely interwoven, that a determination of one must, at the same time, embrace the determination of the other: suppose a matter of this description to come in trial before a jury — what must the jury do? — The jury must do their duty, and their whole duty; they must decide the law as well as the fact.

This doctrine is peculiarly applicable to criminal cases; and from them, indeed, derives its peculiar importance. When a person is to be tried for a crime, the accusation charges against him, not only the particular fact

[x] Vaugh. 148. 150.   [y] Fost. 255.   [z] Hardw. 28.

which he has committed, but also the motive, to which it owed its origin, and from which it receives its complexion. The first is neither the only, nor the principal object of examination and discussion. On the second, depends the innocence or criminality of the action. The verdict must decide not only upon the first, but also, and principally, upon the second: for the verdict must be coextensive and commensurate with the charge.

It may seem, at first view, to be somewhat extraordinary, that twelve men, untutored in the study of jurisprudence, should be the ultimate interpreters of the law, with a power to overrule the directions of the judges, who have made it the subject of their long and elaborate researchers, and have been raised to the seat of judgment for their professional abilities and skill.

But a deeper examination of the subject will reconcile us to what, at first, may appear incongruous. In criminal cases, the design, as has been already intimated, is closely interwoven with the transaction; and the elucidation of both depends on a collected view of particulars, arising not only from the testimony, but also from the character and conduct of the witnesses, and sometimes also from the character and conduct of the prisoner. Of all these, the jury are fittest to make the proper comparison and estimate; and, therefore, it is most eligible to leave it to them, after receiving the direction of the court in matters of law, to take into their consideration all the circumstances of the case, the intention as well as the facts, and to determine, upon the whole, whether the prisoner has or has not been guilty of the crime, with which he is charged.

Juries undoubtedly may make mistakes: they may commit errours: they may commit gross ones. But changed as they constantly are, their errours and mistakes can never grow into a dangerous system. The native uprightness of their sentiments will not be bent under the weight of precedent and authority. The esprit du corps will not be introduced among them; nor will society experience from them those mischiefs, of which the esprit du corps, unchecked, is sometimes productive. Besides, their mistakes and their errours, except the venial ones on the side of mercy made by traverse juries, are not without redress. Of an indictment found by a grand jury, the person indicted may be acquitted on his trial. If a bill be returned "ignoramus" improperly, the accusation may be renewed before another grand jury. With regard to the traverse jury, the court, if dissatisfied with their verdict, have the power, and will exercise the power, of granting a new trial. This power, while it prevents or corrects the effects of their errours, preserves the jurisdiction of juries unimpaired. The cause is not evoked before a tribunal of another kind. A jury of the country — an abstract, as it has been called, of the citizens at large, — summoned, selected, impannelled, and sworn as the former, must still decide.

One thing, however, must not escape our attention. In the cases and on the principles, which we have mentioned, jurors possess the power of determining legal questions. But they must determine those questions, as judges must determine them, according to law. The discretionary powers of jurors find no place for exertion here. Those powers they possess as triers of facts; because, as we have already observed, the trial of facts depends on evidence; and because the force of evidence cannot be ascertained by any general system of rules. But law, particularly the common law, is governed by precedents, and customs, and authorities, and maxims: those precedents, and customs, and authorities, and maxims are alike obligatory upon jurors as upon judges, in deciding questions of law.

True it is, according to the sentiment of my Lord Hardwicke, that it is of the greatest consequence to preserve the separate and distinct powers of the judges and the juries. But equally true it is, that those separate and distinct powers may be rendered reciprocally beneficial, by the most pleasing and harmonious cooperation.

In favour of a conclusion of this kind, the conduct of juries bears ample testimony. The examples of their resisting the advice of a judge, in points of law, are rare, except where they have been provoked into such an opposition by the grossness of his own misconduct, or betrayed into an unjust suspicion of his integrity by the misrepresentation of others. In civil cases, juries almost universally find a special verdict, as often as the judges recommend it to them. In criminal cases, indeed, special verdicts are less frequent: but this happens, not because juries have an aversion to them, but because such cases depend more on the evidence of facts, than on any difficulties arising in points of law.

Nor is it a small merit in this arrangement, that, by means of it, every one who is accused of a crime may, on his plea of "not guilty," enjoy the advantages of a trial, in which the judges and the jury are to one another a mutual check, and a mutual assistance. This point deserves from us a full illustration.

Some things appear, at the first view, to be alike, which, upon a close inspection, are found to be materially different. To a superficial observer, no very important distinction would seem to arise, between the credibility and the competency of evidence. Between them, however, a most important distinction subsists. They spring from different sources; they run in different directions; and, in the division of power between the court and the jury, they are, with great propriety, allotted to different provinces. In some instances, indeed, the line of division is scarcely perceptible; but, even in those instances, the law points out a proper mode of management.

Evidence is of two kinds, written and oral. In each kind, the important distinction between its competency and its credibility takes place. In oral evidence, however, or the testimony of witnesses, the distinction is the most important; and, for this reason, it should be clearly known and strictly preserved.

The excellency of the trial by jury, says the great and good Lord Chief Justice Hale, is, that they are the triers of the credit of the witnesses, as well as the truth of the fact: it is one thing whether a witness is admissible to be heard: whether, when he is heard, he is to be believed, is another thing.[a]

It is a known distinction, says Lord Chief Justice Willes, in a very celebrated cause, that the evidence, though admitted, must still be left to the persons who try the causes, to give what credit to it they please.[b]

That I may observe it once for all, says Lord Chief Justice Hale, in another place, the exceptions to a witness are of two kinds. 1. Exceptions to the credit of the witness, which do not at all disable him from being sworn, but yet may blemish the credibility of his testimony; in such case, the witness is to be allowed, but the credit of his testimony is left to the jury, who are judges of the fact, and likewise of the probability or improbability, credibility or incredibility of the witness and his testimony; these exceptions are of such great variety and multiplicity, that they cannot easily be reduced under rules or instances. 2. Exceptions to the competency of the witness, which exclude him from giving his testimony: and of these exceptions the court is the judge.[c]

The writers on the civil law, to which the trial by jury has, for many ages, been unknown, have attempted to reduce the credibility and incredibility of testimony under rules and instances: but their attempts have shown, what, indeed, has been likewise shown from the nature of the thing, that such a reduction is not only not easy, as my Lord Hale says, but is altogether and absolutely impracticable.

Evidence is, by those civilians, distinguished into different degrees — into full probation; into probation less than full; into half probation. The deficiency in half probation is made up, sometimes by torture, sometimes by the suppletory oath of the party. Concerning circumstantial proofs, rules, unsatisfactory because unfounded, have been heaped upon rules, volumes have been heaped upon volumes, and evidence has been added, and divided, and subtracted, and multiplied, like pounds, and

[a] 1. Hale. P. C. 635.   [b] 1. Atk. 45. Omychund v. Barker.
[c] 2. Hale. P. C. 276.

shillings, and pence, and farthings. In the parliament of Toulouse, we are told by Voltaire,[d] they admitted of quarters and eighths of a proof. For instance, one hearsay was considered as a quarter; another hearsay, more vague, as an eighth; so that eight vague hearsays, which, in fact, are no more than the reverberated echos of a report, perhaps originally groundless, constitute a full proof. Upon this principle it was, that poor Calas was condemned to the wheel.

Evidence is that which produces belief. Belief is a simple act of the mind, more easily experienced than described. Its degrees of strength or weakness cannot, like those of heat and cold, be ascertained by the precise scale of an artificial thermometer. Their effects, however, are naturally felt and distinguished by a sound and healthful mind. With great propriety, therefore, the common law forbears to attempt a scale or system of rules, concerning the force or credibility of evidence: it wisely leaves them to the unbiassed and unadulterated sentiments and impressions of the jury. But with regard to the propriety or competency of evidence, the case is very different. This subject is susceptible of system and of rule. This subject, therefore, is wisely committed to the information and experience of the judges.

The most general and the most conspicuous rule with regard to the competency of evidence, is, that the best, of which the nature of the fact in question is capable, must be produced, if it can be produced: if it cannot be produced, then the best evidence, which can be obtained, shall be admitted. Both the parts of this rule are founded on the most solid reason. To reject, as incompetent, the strongest evidence which can be procured, would be rigid, and unaccommodating to the various vicissitudes of life and business. To admit an inferiour kind of evidence, when evidence of a superiour nature is withheld, would prevent that degree of satisfaction in the minds of the jurors, which evidence should be fitted to produce. Evidence produces belief: the strongest evidence produces the strongest belief: why is the strongest evidence withheld? The party, in whose power it is, can have no motive for withholding it, unless he is conscious that it would disclose something, which his interest requires to be concealed. The satisfactory administration of justice, therefore, demands, that it should be laid before the jury.

The application of this rule is most extensive. What ought or ought not to be presumed in the power of the party, must be collected by a full and intimate knowledge or information concerning the business and transactions of life. The most authentick materials of information and knowledge are furnished by juridical history — a subject deservedly the professional study of judges of the common law.

[d] Com. on Bec. c. 22.

Another rule, of high import in the administration of justice, is, that evidence, in order to be admitted, must have a proper degree of connexion with the question to be tried: in legal language, it must be pertinent to the issue. A variety of evidence, unconnected with the point specified by the record for the examination of the jury, would have a tendency to bewilder their minds, and to prevent that strict and undivided attention, which is so indispensable to the satisfactory investigation of that, which they are empowered and intrusted to decide.

The evidence proper to be given in each of the numerous kinds of issues, which come before a jury, forms a very interesting portion of legal knowledge. At present, we can only show the principle and the importance of that accuracy, which the law requires in the admission of evidence. The preservation of this accuracy is fitly committed to the experience of the judges.

With regard to oral evidence, or the testimony of witnesses, the rule of the law is, that proper testimony may be received from the mouth of every intelligent person, who is not infamous or interested. Concerning the points of intelligence, of infamy, and of interestedness, a great variety of rules are established by the law. To apply those rules to cases which occur in the course of practice, is, with obvious propriety, allotted to the judges.

In one of those subjects, however — I mean the interest of witnesses — the line of division, between the province of the judges and that of the jury, is faintly marked, and difficult to be ascertained. The degrees of interest are so numerous, and the effects of the same degree of interest upon different characters and in different situations are so diversified, that it is impracticable, in many instances, to define exactly the precise boundary, at which the question of competency ends, and the question of credibility begins. In doubtful cases of this description, the judges, especially of late years, presume in favour of the province of the jury. This is done with great reason. For an objection, urged, without success, against the competency of a witness, may be urged successfully against the credibility of his testimony; and to the objecting party it is altogether immaterial, whether the testimony of the witness is rejected or disbelieved. When an objection, says my Lord Hardwick, is made against a witness, it is best to restrain it to his credit, unless it is like to introduce great perjury; because it tends to let in light to the cause.[e]

In arranging and in summing up the evidence, the court, from their knowledge and experience of business, can give great assistance to the jury. In questions of law emerging from the evidence, the assistance of the court is still more necessary and essential. Lord Chief Justice Hale

[e] Hardw. 360.

observes, that a judge may be of much advantage to the jury, by showing them his opinion even in matter of fact.[f] Of the sentiment of a
judge so exemplary in his delicacy as well as in his candour, I risk not
the disapprobation; but I add, that this power can never be exercised
with a reserve too cautious.

We have seen, by a number of instances, how, in the administration
of justice, the jury receive assistance from the judges. Let us now see
how the judges receive assistance from the jury.

"Ex facto oritur jus." * The jury lay the foundation of truth, on which
the judges erect the superstructure of law. A correct statement of the
facts, every professional gentleman knows, is necessary to an accurate
report. A true verdict given by the jury, is an essential prerequisite to a
just judgment pronounced by the court. Judgments in supposed cases
may abundantly evince professional skill; but they will never have a
decisive influence over society — they will never come home to the
business and bosoms of the citizens — unless they are practically founded
on the manners, and characters, and rights of men. The manners, the
characters, and the rights of men are truly and practically reported by
the verdicts of juries.

To judges of a proper disposition, the assistance of juries is soothing
as well as salutary. In criminal cases, it is unquestionably so. "To say the
truth" — I use the language of the humane Lord Chief Justice Hale —
"it were the most unhappy case that could be to the judge, if he, at his
peril, must take upon him the guilt or innocence of the prisoner, and
if the judge's opinion must rule the matter of fact." [g]

Take upon him the guilt or innocence of the prisoner! It may be
soothing, indeed, to judges, to be relieved from this mental burthen, of
all the most anxious: but upon whom — methinks I hear a citizen ask
— upon whom must this most anxious of all mental burthens be laid?
How must it be born by those on whom it is laid?

This very serious and momentous question brings before us the trial
by jury in a view, the sublimity of which I have often admired in
silence; but which now — though I feel myself far inferiour to the task
— I must endeavour to describe and explain. I solicit your candid indulgence, while I attempt to delineate the particulars, of which this
prospect, magnificent and interesting, is composed; and then try, with
unequal efforts, to convey the impression which naturally will result from
the combination of the whole.

It will be necessary to review some principles, of which notice has
been already taken in the course of my lectures. In a former part of
them[h] I observed, that, when society was formed, it possessed jointly all

[f] Hale. Hist. 256.   * [A law arises from what has been done.]
[g] 2. Hale. P. C. 313.   [h] Ante. pp. 173–174.

the previously separate and independent powers and rights of the individuals who formed it, and all those other powers and rights which result from the social union. I observed, that all those powers and rights were collected, in order to be enjoyed and exercised; that, in a numerous and extended society, all those powers could not, indeed, be exercised personally; but that they might be exercised by representation. I asked, whether one power might not be delegated to one set of men? and whether another power might not be delegated to another set of men? alluding to the legislative and executive departments. I mentioned a third power of society — that of administering justice under the laws. I asked, whether this power might not be partly delegated, and partly retained in personal exercise; because, in the most extended communities, an important part of the administration of justice may be discharged by the people themselves. I mentioned, that all this has been done, as I should have the pleasure of showing, when I should come to examine our governments, and to point out, by an enumeration and comparison of particulars, how beautifully, how regularly, and how usefully, we have established, by our practice in this country, principles concerning the distribution, the arrangement, the reservation, the direction, and the uses of that publick power, of which the just theory is still unknown in other nations.

I have had the pleasure of explaining the powers, legislative, executive, and judicial, which the people have delegated: I come now to that part of the judicial authority, which they retain in personal exercise — I mean, the authority to decide in criminal cases; in cases, especially, of life and death.

This may be considered in two different points of light; as a power, and as a burthen. As a burthen, it is considered as too heavy to be imposed, as a power, it is considered as too great to be conferred, permanently upon any man, or any organized body of men. We have seen it a discretionary — so far it partakes of a legislative power. We have seen that, in large and extended communities, necessity directs the delegation of other legislative power. This is a species of legislative power, which may, and therefore should, be exercised in person. In cases of life and death, the standing jurisdiction remains with the people at large. As emergencies occur, an abstract of the people is selected for the occasional exercise of it. The moment that the occasion is over, the abstracted selection disappears among the general body of the citizens. No one citizen, therefore, any more than any other, can complain of this as an uneasy burthen. Except on particular occasions, and during those occasions, it is imposed on no one.

If jurisdiction in cases of life and death, considered as a burthen, is uneasy to those who bear it; considered as a power, it is tremendous to those who behold it. A man, or a body of men, habitually clothed with a power over the lives of their fellow citizens! These are objects formidable indeed. By an operation, beautiful and sublime, of our juridical system, objects so formidable are withdrawn from before the eyes of our citizens — objects so formidable do not exist. To promote an habitual courage, and dignity, and independence of sentiment and of actions in the citizens, should be the aim of every wise and good government. How much are these principles promoted, by this beautiful and sublime effect of our judicial system. No particular citizen can threaten the exercise of this tremendous power: with the exercise of this tremendous power, no particular citizen can be threatened. Even the unfortunate prisoner, the day of whose trial is come, the jury for whose trial are selected, impannelled, and returned — even this unfortunate prisoner cannot be threatened with the exercise of this tremendous power by any particular citizen. When he comes to the bar and looks upon the prisoner, a single supercilious look will produce a peremptory rejection.

Uncommonly jealous is the constitution of the United States and that of Pennsylvania upon this subject, so interesting to the personal independence of the citizens. The formidable power we have mentioned is interdicted even to the legislatures themselves. Neither congress nor the general assembly of this commonwealth, can pass any act of attainer for treason or felony.[1] Now, an act of attainder is a legislative verdict.

I have said, that this authority remains with the people at large. Potentially, indeed, it does; actually, it cannot be said to remain even with them. The contrivance is so admirably exquisite concerning this tremendous jurisdiction, that, in the general course of things, it exists actually no where. But no sooner does any particular emergency call for its operations, than it starts into immediate existence.

But it remains, that I give satisfaction with regard to the inquiry — how shall this burthen, attended with so much uneasiness, be born by those, upon whom, though only occasionally, it is laid?

It is, we acknowledge, a most weighty burthen. That man must, indeed, be callous to sensibility, who, without emotion and anxiety, can deliberate on the question — whether, by his voice, his fellow man and fellow citizen shall live or die. But while capital punishments continue to be inflicted, the burthen must be borne, and while it must be borne, every citizen, who, in the service of his country, may be called to bear it, is bound to qualify himself for bearing it in such a manner, as will ensure peace of mind to himself, justice to him whose fate he may determine, and honour to the judicial administration of his country. By so qualifying himself, though, in the discharge of his duty, he will feel

[1] Cons. U.S. Art. 1. s. 9. Cons. Penn. Art. 9. s. 18.

strong emotions, he will, from the performance of it, feel no remorse.

I must again enter upon a review of some principles, of which notice has already been taken.

With regard to the law in criminal cases, every citizen, in a government such as ours, should endeavour to acquire a reasonable knowledge of its principles and rules, for the direction of his conduct, when he is called to obey, when he is called to answer, and when he is called to judge. On questions of law, his deficiencies will be supplied by the professional directions of the judges, whose duty and whose business it is professionally to direct him. For, as we have seen, verdicts, in criminal cases, generally determine the question of law, as well as the question of fact. Questions of fact, it is his exclusive province to determine. With the consideration of evidence unconnected with the question which he is to try, his attention will not be distracted; for every thing of that nature, we presume, will be excluded by the court. The collected powers of his mind, therefore, will be fixed, steadily and without interruption, upon the issue which he is sworn to try. This issue is an issue of fact. Its trial will depend upon the evidence. Evidence, in every cause, is that which produces: evidence, in a capital cause, is that which *forces* belief.

Belief, as we have seen, is an act of the mind, not easily described, indeed, but easily felt. Does the juror feel its force? Let him obey the constitution of his nature, and yield to the strong conviction. If the evidence produce, upon the mind of each of his fellow jurors, the same strong conviction, which it produces on his, their sentiments will be unanimous; and the unanimous sentiments of all will still corroborate the strong conviction of each. If a single doubt remain in the mind of any juror, that doubt should produce his dissent; and the dissent of a single juror, according to the principles which we have explained, and, we trust, established, will produce a verdict of acquittal by all.

Considered in this manner, is the duty of a juror, in a capital case, intolerably burthensome? It cannot, indeed, as we have said, be discharged without emotion: but the unbiassed dictates of his own constitution will teach — will force him to discharge it properly.

In criminal — in capital cases, with what sublime majesty does the trial by jury now appear to its ravished beholders! In the first and purest principles of society its foundations are laid: by the most exquisite skill, united with consummate benignity, the grand and finely proportioned edifice has been raised: within its walls, strong and lofty as well as finely proportioned, freedom enjoys protection, and innocence rests secure.

VII

THE SUBJECT CONTINUED—OF SHERIFFS AND CORONERS

THE sheriff is an officer of high respectability in our juridical system, and was known to the most early ages of the common law.

Among the Saxons, his power was very great and extensive — judicial as well as ministerial. In his ministerial character, he executed the writs of the king and the judgments of his courts: in his judicial character, the sheriff presided in the several courts of justice comprehended within the sphere of his jurisdiction. He was chosen in the county court by the votes of the freeholders; and, like the king himself, says Selden,[a] was entitled to his honour by the people's favour.

All the other nations of Gothick and German origin, who, on the ruins of the Roman empire, founded kingdoms in the different parts of Europe, had officers of the same kind with the sheriffs of the Anglo-Saxons. This is a strong evidence of their high antiquity, as well as general respectability.[b] In some of the Gothick constitutions, the sheriffs were elected by the people, but confirmed by the king. The election and appointment were made in this manner: the people chose twelve electors; those electors nominated three persons to the king; from those three the king selected one, who was the confirmed sheriff.[c]

The popular elections of the sheriffs, in England, were lost by the people in the reigns of Edward the second and Edward the third; and a new mode of appointment was substituted in their place.[d] In the time of Lord Chancellor Fortescue, the manner of the election of sheriffs was as follows. Every year there met, in the court of exchequer, all the king's counsellors, as well lords spiritual and temporal, as all other the king's justices, all the barons of the exchequer, the master of the rolls, and certain other officers. All these, by common consent, nominated of every county three persons of distinction, such as they deemed best qualified for the office of sheriff, and presented them to the king. Of the persons so nominated and returned, the king made choice of one, who, by virtue of the king's letters patent, was constituted high sheriff of that county,

[a] Bac. on Gov. 41.   [b] 2. Hen. 245.   [c] 1. Bl. Com. 340.
[d] 4. Bl. Com. 420.

for which he was so chosen.[e] This mode of nomination and appointment still continues in England.[f]

It has been usual to appoint them annually. But in the reign of Henry the fifth, we find from this custom a parliamentary exception, rendered very remarkable by the reason assigned for it. The king is permitted to appoint sheriffs for four years; "because by wars and pestilence there are not a sufficient number remaining, in the different counties, to discharge this office from year to year." [g]

By a parliamentary regulation made in the reign of Edward the second, and repeated in that of Edward the third, it was directed that sheriffs should be chosen from such persons as had lands in their shires; and that those lands should be sufficient to answer to the king and his people, if grieved.[h]

By a law of the United States, a marshal is appointed for each district for the term of four years; but is removable from his office at pleasure.[i] As no particular mode is specified by the law for appointing the marshal, his appointment falls, of course, under the general provision made by the national constitution.[j] The president nominates, and, with the advice and consent of the senate, appoints him. His powers and his duties are, in general, coincident with those of a sheriff.[k]

By the constitution of Pennsylvania,[l] sheriffs are chosen by the citizens of each county: two persons are chosen for the office; one of the two is appointed by the governour. We observe, here, another instance of the old Saxon and German customs revived in the constitution of this commonwealth.

Our sheriffs are elected and hold their offices for three years, if they behave themselves well; but no person shall be twice chosen or appointed sheriff in any term of six years. The converse of this regulation we find in an act of parliament — No man, who has served the office of sheriff for one year, can be *compelled* to serve it again within three years afterwards.[m] The reason of this converse regulation may be collected from another act of parliament. The expense which custom had introduced in serving the office of high sheriff became so burthensome, that it was enacted, that no sheriff should keep any table at the assizes, except for his own family, or give any presents to the judges or their servants, or have more than forty men in livery: yet, for the sake of safety and decency, he

---

[e] Fort. de laud. c. 24. [f] Wood. 70. [g] Bar. on St. 386. [h] 2. Reev. 78.
[i] Laws. U.S. 1. cong. 1. sess. c. 20. s. 27. [j] Art. 2. s. 2.
[k] "The marshals of the several districts, and their deputies, shall have the same powers in executing the laws of the United States, as sheriffs and their deputies, in the several states, have by law, in executing the laws of the respective states." Laws U.S. 3. cong. 2. sess. c. 101. s. 9. The same provision was contained in a prior law, repealed by that above cited. Laws U.S. 2. cong. 1. sess. c. 28. s. 9. *Ed.*
[l] Art. 6. s. 1. [m] St. 1. R. 2. c. 11. 1. Bl. Com. 343.

may not have less than twenty men in England and twelve in Wales.[n]

An attention to the powers and duties of the sheriff will disclose, I think, a peculiar propriety in the compound mode of election and appointment, directed by our constitution. He executes the process of courts, and, in his county, is the principal conservator of the peace: so far he is an executive officer, and should be appointed by the governour. He returns jurors: for this reason, he should be chosen by the people. Invested with the double character, he should receive his authority partly from both. As he is elected and appointed for three years, and can serve only once in the period of six years; he is, in a considerable degree, independent, and may, therefore, be presumed impartial in the exercise of his very important duties and powers. Those duties and powers we are now concisely to describe.

The judicial power of the sheriff, which, in former times, was very great and extensive, is, by our juridicial system, transferred, with great propriety, to other establishments: for it is obviously incongruous, that executive and judicial authority should be united in the same person.

Permit me here to observe, that the accumulation of unnecessary and even inconsistent powers seems to be the principal objection against the old Saxon institutions. In most other respects, they are not more venerable on account of their antiquity, than on account of their matured excellence. Permit me also here to observe, that, in the correct distribution of the powers of government, the constitution of Pennsylvania approaches, if it does not reach, theoretick perfection.

The ministerial power of the sheriff is of great importance to the impartial administration of justice, and to the internal peace and tranquillity of the commonwealth. He is the chief officer, says my Lord Coke, within the shire. To his custody the county is committed. This custody is threefold. 1. Of the life of justice; for no suit begins, and no process is served, but by the sheriff. It belongs to him also to return indifferent juries, for the trials of men's properties, liberties, and lives. 2. Of the life of the law; for, after suits long and chargeable, he makes execution, which is the life and fruit of the law. 3. Of the life of the republick; for, within the county, he is the principal conservator of the peace, which is the life of the commonwealth.[o]

With regard to process issuing from the courts of justice, the sheriff's power and duty is, to execute it, not to dispute its validity: though the writ be illegal, the sheriff is protected and indemnified in serving it.[p] From this general rule, however, one exception must be taken and allowed. He must judge, at his peril, whether the court, from which the process issued, has or has not jurisdiction of the cause.[q]

[n] St. 13 and 14. C. 2. c. 21. 1. Bl. Com. 346.   [o] 1. Ins. 168. a.
[p] 6. Rep. 54. 9. Rep. 68.   [q] 10. Rep. 76. 2. Wil. 384.

The selection and the return of jurors is a most momentous part of the power and duty of a sheriff. It is that part, in which abuses are most fatal: it is that part, in which there is the greatest opportunity and temptation to commit them. Let us speak of former times. In the reign of Edward the first, the parliament was obliged to interpose its authority to give relief to the people against sheriffs, who harassed jurors unnecessarily, by summoning them from a great distance, and who returned such as would not give an impartial verdict. This last abuse, says a modern writer[r] on the English law, was never perfectly removed till the late act was made for balloting juries. In an account of Cornwall, written by Mr. Carew, we are informed, that, in the reign of Henry the seventh, an article of charge for the "friendship of the sheriff," was common in an attorney's bill.[s]

As the principal conservator of the peace in his county, and as the calm irresistible minister of the law, the authority of a sheriff is important; his duty is proportionably great. To preserve or restore the publick tranquil-. lity, to ensure or enforce the effectual execution of the law, he is invested with the high power of ordering to his assistance the whole strength of the county over which he presides.

The law is mild in its mandates; but it will be obeyed. It knows, it presumes, it will suffer none of its ministers to know or to presume, any power superiour to its own. If any man, says my Lord Coke, however great, might resist the sheriff in executing the king's writs; it would be regular and justifiable in the sheriff to return such resistance: but such a return would redound greatly to the dishonour of the king and his crown: what redounds to the dishonour of the king and his crown, is against the common law: and, therefore, if necessity require it for the due execution of the king's writs, the sheriff may, by the common law, take the *posse comitatus* to suppress such unlawful force and resistance.[t]

When necessity requires it, the sheriff not only may, but must at his peril, employ the strength of his county. In the reign of Edward the second, a sheriff had the king's writ to deliver possession of land: the sheriff returned that he could not execute the writ by reason of resistance. This was considered as an insult upon the authority, with which he was invested; and because he took not the power of the county in aid of the execution, he was amerced at twenty marks.[u]

Besides the warrant of the common law, continues my Lord Coke, the sheriff has his letters patent of assistance, by which the king commands, that all archbishops, bishops, dukes, earls, barons, knights, freemen, and all others of the county shall attend, assist, and answer to the sheriff, in every thing which belongs to his office. No man above fifteen and under

[r] Bar. on St. 185. [s] Bar. on St. 458. [t] 2. Ins. 193. [u] 2. Ins. 194.

seventy years of age, ecclesiastical or temporal, is exempted from this service: for so it is by construction of law.

How easily are these cases applied to the United States and to Pennsylvania, under the operation of the fine rule, that the empire of the law is stronger as well as safer than the empire of man!

I proceed to consider the office of coroner. This office, though much neglected, though, perhaps, despised, is an office, both ancient and dignified. It forms no inconsiderable part of a complete juridical system.

In the time of the Saxons, as we are informed by Mr. Selden, he was one of the two chief governours of the county. He was made by election of the freeholders in their county court, as the sheriff was, and from among the men of the chiefest rank in the county.[v]

By the constitution[w] of this commonwealth, sheriffs and coroners are chosen and appointed in the same manner. We see here another revival of the Saxon and German institutions.

To the office of sheriff, that of coroner is, in many instances, a necessary substitute: for if the sheriff is interested in a suit, or if he is of affinity with one of the parties to a suit, the coroner must execute and return the process of the courts of justice.[x]

But the most important duty and business of a coroner is of another nature. When any person is killed, or dies suddenly, or dies in prison, the coroner must hold an inquest concerning the manner of his death. This inquest must be held upon the view of the body; for if the body cannot be found, the coroner cannot sit. He must certify his inquisition to the court of king's bench or to the next assizes.[y]

The lord chief justice of the king's bench is the supreme coroner of all England, and may exercise that jurisdiction in any part of the kingdom.[z]

From the statute of Wales, made in the twelfth year of Edward the first, and which, by the remedies provided for Wales, informs us, at the same time, what was the law and practice of England — from this statute we learn, that the coroner was directed to attend and summon a jury, when a man was wounded so dangerously, that his life was despaired. This branch of a coroner's duty is now totally neglected. "It is a regulation, however," says the learned observer upon the ancient statutes, "which deserves much to be revived: and I should conceive that this attendance of the coroner with a jury, when a dangerous wound had been received, was to prevent the dying words of the person murdered from being evidence; as this kind of proof, though allowed at present, cannot be too cautiously admitted. It is presumed, indeed, that the words of a person expiring cannot but be true, considering the situation, under which he gives the information. But may not a dying man, though a good chris-

[v] Bac. on Gov. 41.   [w] Art. 6. s. 1.   [x] 4. Ins. 271.   [y] 1. Bl. Com. 349.
[z] 4. Rep. 57 b.

tian, deprived of expected happiness in life by a wound, received, perhaps, from an enemy, rather wish his punishment more eagerly than he should do? And may not those about the dying person, who are generally relations, repeat what he said more strongly on the trial, than possibly the words were delivered?" [a]

[a] Bar. on St. 124.

VIII

THE SUBJECT CONTINUED—OF COUNSELLORS AND ATTORNIES

IN our courts of justice there are counsellors and attornies. In England, there are two degrees of counsellors — serjeants and barristers. How ancient and honourable the state and degree of a serjeant is, has been the ample theme of many learned and elaborate treatises.

My Lord Coke, in a speech which he made upon a call of serjeants, compares the serjeants' coif — a cap of a particular form — to Minerva's helmet; for Minerva was the goddess of counsel. He also discovers, that the four corners of that cap indicate four excellent qualities — science, experience, observation, recordation.[a]

Pace tanti viri, shall the truth be disclosed? If the origin of coifs is investigated, we shall, perhaps, find that Mercury, and not Minerva, is entitled to the merit of the invention. At one period, the clergy were almost the only lawyers known in England; but, in a fit of resentment, they were banished from the bar. Its sweets — for its profits were sweet — could not be easily relinquished. The clerk still pleaded, but disguised in the serjeant's robe, and, by contriving the coif, concealed his clerical tonsure.

But, like many other things, its first origin was lost in its subsequent splendour. The institution became honourable and venerable; and, as such, is still considered and preserved in England. "A serjeant at law," says my Lord Chancellor Fortescue,[b] "shall not take off his coif, though he be in the royal presence, and talking with his majesty. No one can be made a judge of the courts of king's bench or common pleas, until he is called to the state and dignity of a serjeant." To America, however, it has not been transplanted. We leave it to continue and flourish in its native soil.

In the first ages of Athens, the parties pleaded for themselves; but, in later times, they were allowed to have the benefit of counsel.[c] That the length of their speeches might not exhaust the patience of the judges, or prevent other business equally necessary, it was usual — perhaps the spirit of the custom might be revived with no disadvantage — to measure their allotted portion of time by an hour glass, in which they used water in-

---

[a] Bar. on St. 453.   [b] De Laud. c. 50.   [c] 1. Pot. Ant. 106.

stead of sand. So scrupulously exact were they in this particular, that an officer, whose name denoted his office — Εφυδωρ — was appointed to distribute the water equally to each side. While strict justice was required from the advocates, strict justice was done them: the glass was stopped while the proper officer recited the laws which they quoted. Nay, the water remaining at the conclusion of an argument might be transferred to the use of another speaker. Hence this expression — Let such a one speak till my water be run out.[d]

This custom was practised by the Romans. The time allowed, by the law, for the speeches of the advocates is termed, by Cicero, "legitimæ horæ." The patient and indulgent Antoninus, who was a philosopher as well as an emperour, ordered, as we are told by his historian, plenty of water for the speakers at the bar; in other words, he allowed them full time for their speeches. "Quoties judico," says the younger Pliny, "quantum quis plurimum postulat aquæ do" — when I sit in judgment, I give to every advocate as much water as he desires.[e]

This instance of resemblance between the Athenian and Roman bars is not mentioned on account of its intrinsick importance, but because it proves, more strongly than an important instance could prove, the principle of imitation. The coincident practice could be dictated by no common principle of nature or of society.

Counsellors, or barristers at law, have been long known in England. Formerly they were styled "apprenticii ad legem," apprentices to the law; because they were considered only as learners, and were not permitted to exercise the full office of an advocate, till they were qualified by the knowledge and experience acquired during the long probationship of sixteen years.[f] Edward the first, it is said, introduced the practice of permitting them to plead in the court of king's bench, before they attained the rank and dignity of serjeants.[g]

Attorney, says my Lord Coke, is an ancient English word, and signifies one who is set in the turn, stead, or place of another. Of these, some are private; and some are publick, as attornies at law.[h] The business of an attorney at law is to manage the practical part of a suit, and to follow the advice of the serjeants or barristers, who are of counsel in it.[i]

At the common law, no person could appear by an attorney, without the king's writ or letters patent.[j] In one part of his works, my Lord Coke admires the policy of this regulation. Its genius was to prevent the increase and multiplication of suits. But when statutes permitted the parties to appear by attorney, it is not credible, says he, how suits at law increased and multiplied. Such ill success has ever had the breach of the

---

[d] Pet. on Jur. 59. 63. 1. Pot. Ant. 118.   [e] Pli. Ep. l. 6. ep. 2. Pet. on Jur. 134.
[f] Forte. de Laud. c. 50.   [g] 1. Reev. 491.   [h] 1. Ins. 51. b.
[i] 2. Ins. 564. Wood. Ins. 466.   [j] Wood. Ins. 466.

maxims and the ancient rules of the common law.[k] In another part of
his works, he expresses sentiments more favourable to the appointment of
attornies. The act commanding the judges to admit them, he styles "an
act of grace," because the king gave his royal assent to a law for the
quiet and safety of his subjects, giving them power to make attornies,
whereby he lost such profit of the great seal, as he formerly received in
such cases.[l]

To correct the abuses, which arose from the admission of attornies,
whose heads and whose hearts were equally unqualified for the trust, it
was enacted, so early as the reign of Henry the fourth,[m] that all the attornies shall be examined by the judges; and such as are good and virtuous
and of good fame shall, by the discretion of the court, be received and
sworn well and faithfully to serve in their offices; and their names shall
be entered on the roll.

A barrister is not sworn.[n]

According to the law of the United States, parties may plead and manage their own causes personally, or by the assistance of such counsel or
attornies at law, as, by the rules of the several courts, shall be permitted
to manage and conduct causes.[o]

By a rule of the supreme court, it is ordered, that it shall be requisite to
the admission of attornies and counsellors to practise in that court, that
they shall have been such for three years in the supreme court of the state
to which they respectively belong, and that their private and professional
character shall appear to be fair. In the circuit court for the Pennsylvania district, the same rule is made with the only difference of "two"
instead of "three" years.[p]

By a law of Pennsylvania[q] it is provided, that a competent number of
persons, learned in the law, and of an honest disposition, may be admitted
by the justices of the several courts to practise as attornies in them. No
attorney shall be admitted, without taking an oath or affirmation — that
he will behave himself in the office of attorney within the court, according to the best of his learning and ability, and with all good fidelity, as
well to the court as to the client; that he will use no falsehood, nor delay
any person's cause for lucre or malice.[r]

---

[k] 2. Ins. 249.   [l] 2. Ins. 378.   [m] St. 4. H. 4. c. 18.   [n] 2. Ins. 214.
[o] Laws U.S. 1. cong. 1. sess. c. 20. s. 35.
[p] At April sessions, 1804, the abovementioned rule of the circuit court was re-
scinded, and the following established. "ORDERED, that no person shall be admitted
to practise as counsel or attorney of this court, unless he shall have previously studied three years, been admitted two years in a court of common pleas, and in the supreme court of a state: or unless he shall have studied four years, been admitted one
year in a court of common pleas, and in the supreme court of a state: or unless he
shall have studied five years, and been admitted in the supreme court of a state.
Satisfaction also of moral character will be required." *Ed.*
[q] 1. Laws. Penn. 185. s. 28.   [r] Id. 360. s. 38.

Attornies at law, on one hand, enjoy privileges on account of their attendance in courts: on the other, they are peculiarly subject to the censure and animadversion of the judges.[s]

In all the courts of Pennsylvania, and in all those of the United States, except the supreme court, the same person may act as counsel and as attorney. In the supreme court, the different offices must be exercised by different persons.

The law has not, in every age, nor in every country, been formed into a separate profession. Doubts have been entertained, whether, in any country, or in any age, it should be so formed. Every man, it has been often said, ought to be his own lawyer.

In a system of lectures, addressed peculiarly, though by no means exclusively, to those who are designed for the profession of the law, this question deserves our particular notice. It deserves our notice more especially as we are told, in a very late and a very sensible performance concerning the revolution in France, that those, who have been most active in this mighty event, mean to destroy the separate profession of the law. An event, so auspicious to man, will diffuse a winning appearance over every thing, with which it seems to be, in the slightest manner, connected. But it is our business to examine the foundations, and not merely the external appearances of things.

It may be asked — when you have taken so much pains, in the introduction to these lectures, and in many parts of them, to persuade us, that the knowledge of the law should, especially among a free people, be disseminated universally; will you now turn suddenly in an opposite direction, and endeavour to persuade us, that a distinct and separate profession should be formed of the law? The result, perhaps, of investigating this subject will be, that unless the law is made the peculiar study and profession of some, it will never become the object of knowledge to all.

We have heard the complaint of my Lord Coke, that the admission of attornies at law into the courts of justice is an innovation upon the practice and the policy of the common law. It must be confessed that this is the case. At the common law, both the plaintiff and the defendant appeared in their proper persons. "The plaintiff offers himself," and "the defendant comes" are the immemorial and authentick forms of entry — "Querens obtulit se" — "Defendens venit." These, on both sides, denote a personal appearance.

In the early and simple periods of society, the personal appearance of the parties was all that was necessary. Such were the periods of which we speak. Among the ancient Saxons, few and plain were the forms and circumstances, under which property was litigated and decided in their courts of justice; uniform and short were the proceedings in those courts.

[s] 3. Bl. Com. 26.

Among the ancient Saxons, therefore, professional characters were not
necessary for the management or the determination of suits. The king,
or the earl, as the case might be, was qualified to judge; and the parties to
plead.

An adherence to principle often dictates a variation in practice. In the
progress of society, the business of society became more complex and
intricate; and the controversies arising from it became more frequent and
embarrassed. This new order of things introduced a new order of professions. To the king were substituted the judges: to the earls, the sheriffs;
and to the parties, attornies or counsel learned in the law: "After the
Anglo-Saxon laws were committed to writing," says Dr. Henry in his
history of Britain, "it became necessary that some persons should read
and study them with particular attention, in order to understand their
true intent and meaning. This gave rise to lawyers by profession, who,
in the language of England in those times, were called *rœdboran*, or
lahmen, and, in latin, *rhetores*, or *causidici*. Some of these law men, after
having undergone an examination as to their knowledge of the law, were
appointed assessors to the aldermen and hundredaries: others of them
acted as advocates and pleaders at the bar." [t]

But it will be replied — and still on the authority of my Lord Coke —
that the introduction of lawyers multiplies suits at law. The unnecessary
"multiplication of lawyers", rather say: for that is the amount of my
Lord Coke's complaint: and, even in the ground of his complaint, he appears not altogether steady or consistent. But elsewhere, my Lord Coke
traces the multiplication of law suits to causes very different from the
establishment of the law as a profession. Their two general causes, says
he, are peace and plenty. Peace is the mother of plenty; and plenty the
nurse of suits.[u] Instead of wishing the removal of those general causes,
he prays for their continuance.

In a country governed by the common law, the separate profession of
lawyers ought to be established for a peculiar reason. The common law is
the law of experience. Far is it, indeed, from being without its general
principles; but these general principles are formed strictly upon the plan
of the *regulae philosophandi*, which, in another science, Sir Isaac Newton
prescribed and observed with such glorious success — they are formed
from the coincidence, or the analogy, or the opposition of numberless
experiments, the accurate history of which is contained in records and
reports of judicial determinations. To peruse those reports — to consult
those records, requires much time and industry. To methodise them under the proper heads, requires much attention and patient sagacity. From
a variety of particular cases to draw conclusions, neither too wide nor too

[t] 2. Hen. 245.   [u] 4. Ins. 76.

narrow, requires a judgment habitually exercised, as well as naturally strong. These are the requisites, by which the common lawyer must be formed. From these requisites we may easily infer the propriety of establishing the law as a separate profession. To acquire these requisites is a sufficient employment.

In the common law, principles are collected slowly and with difficulty; but, when once collected, they may be communicated soon and easily. The principles may be known, and may be reduced to practice too, by men who never heard or witnessed one of the legal experiments, from the lengthened series of which those principles are drawn.

In this manner I reconcile my positions — that the knowledge of the law should be disseminated universally — and — that the law should be formed into a separate profession. In this manner, too, I prove — that unless the law is made the peculiar study and profession of some, it will never become the object of knowledge to all.

Should the profession of the law be merely honorary? Or should it be a source of profit as well as of fame? These questions have undergone ample discussion; and have, at different times, received contrary authoritative resolutions. In a government truly republican, the subject will not admit of dispute.

By the Cincian law, every gratification whatever was interdicted to the Roman advocates. What was the consequence? Between citizen and citizen an inequality inconsistent with the government of a free country. Those who had and those who might have causes depending, and were unqualified for pleading them — this is the description of the many — were kept in a state of vassalage to those, by whom they might be pleaded without a fee — this is the description of the few. Hence the well known relation of client and patron: hence the tyranny and servility, to which that well known relation gave rise. Besides, this regulation was as liable to be eluded as it was certain to be abused. Presents, said to be voluntary, might easily supply the place of stipulated fees. We are told of a lawyer, who practised this art with great address and advantage. A piece of plate, which a client had thrown at his feet, was placed conspicuous in his office,[v] with this inscription — "lucri neglecti lucrum."

What can be more honourable that that gain, which is acquired by virtue and talents? In a state of republican equality, what can be more reasonable, than that one citizen should receive a compensation for the services, which he performs to another? still more so, for those which he performs to the state?

It may be expected, that I should here say something concerning the studies which a lawyer should pursue, the accomplishments which he

[v] Bar. on St. 415.

should acquire, and the character which he should support. Something concerning each of these topicks I mean to say, but with a diffidence proportioned to the delicacy of the subject.

I think I may venture the position — that in no science can richer materials be found, and that, in no science, have rich materials been more neglected or abused, than in the science of law — particularly of the common law. Listen to the sentiments of my Lord Bacon, in his book on the advancement of learning. It is well known, that the vast object of this exalted and most comprehensive genius was, to erect a new and lasting fabrick of philosophy, founded, not on hypothesis or conjecture, but on experience and truth. To the accomplishment of this design, it was necessary that he should previously review, in all its provinces and divisions, the state of learning as it then stood. To do this effectually required knowledge and discernment, exquisite and universal: such were happily employed in the arduous task. Whatever, in science, is erroneous or defective, he has pointed out. He has done more; he has suggested the proper means of correcting errours and supplying defects. Of the science of law, he thus speaks — Those, who have written concerning laws, have treated the subject like speculative philosophers, or like mere practising lawyers. The philosophers propose many things, which, in appearance, are beautiful, but, in fact, are without utility. They make imaginary laws for imaginary commonwealths; and their discourses are as the stars, which give little light, because they are so high. The lawyers, on the other hand, attached implicitly to the institutions of their country, or to the tenets of their sect, exert not their judgment unbiassed, but harangue as if they were in chains.

But certainly, continues he, the knowledge of this subject properly belongs *ad viros civiles*. Those *viri civiles* — "practical statesmen" is, perhaps, the nearest translation, of which our language will admit — he describes in the following manner. They know what appertains to human society, what, to the publick welfare, what, to natural equity, what, to the manners of nations, what, to the different forms of commonwealths. These are qualified to judge concerning laws, by the principles and rules of genuine policy and natural justice. For there are certain fountains of justice, from which all civil laws should flow like streams. To those fountains of justice and publick utility let us have recourse.ᵂ He then goes on, according to his plan, to give a specimen of a treatise concerning universal justice, or the fountains of law.

I have said that the law, particularly the common law abounds in rich materials. For the truth of this observation, can I appeal to stronger evidence than to a series — continued, almost without interruption, for five hundred years — of cases which actually happened, and were judicially

---

ᵂ 1. Ld. Bac. 248. 2. Ld. Bac. 537.

determined? Many of these cases are related in the most accurate and masterly manner; witness the reports of my Lord Coke, of Mr. Peere Williams, and of Sir James Burrow: others, too, deserve to be mentioned. These are the precious materials of the common law. These are authentick experiments, on which a sound system of legal philosophy must be formed. On these experiments, the most indefatigable industry has been frequently employed. But has it been employed in a proper manner? Upon cases, cases have been accumulated: to collections, collections have been superadded: but they have been directed, generally, by no order more eligible that that of the alphabet. To one who is already a lawyer, abridgments may, on particular occasions, be of use: but surely they are not calculated to inspire or to guide the liberal and enlightened study of the law.

The Institutes of my Lord Coke are a cabinet richly stored with the jewels of the law: but are not those jewels strewed about in endless and bewildering confusion?

In expression, as well as in arrangement, the compositions of the law have been glaringly imperfect; and have had an injurious tendency to deter those, whose attachment they should have been fitted to attract. Hear the natural and pathetick description which the celebrated Sir Henry Spelman gives of his situation and feelings, when he commenced his study of the common law: "My mother sent me to London to learn the law: when I entered on its threshold, and encountered a foreign language, a barbarous dialect, an inelegant arrangement, and a collection of matter, not only immense, but disposed in such a manner as to be a perpetual load upon the memory; my spirits, I own it, failed within me." [x]

Since his time, indeed, very considerable assistance has been furnished to young gentlemen, engaged in the acquirement of legal knowledge. Of this assistance, the short but very excellent analysis digested by my Lord Chief Justice Hale forms a most valuable part; whether we consider it in itself, or as the foundation of what has been erected upon it. The distribution of this scientifical performance has, as we are informed by Sir William Blackstone, been principally followed in his celebrated Commentaries on the laws of England. It is but justice to add, that, in those Commentaries, the method of Hale's analysis is improved as well as regarded. I have formerly observed, that, in point of expression, the Commentaries are elegant and pure.

But something more is wanting still. Excellent materials, a correct arrangement of those materials, and a proper expression of the arranged form are all necessary; but they are not all that is necessary to a sound system of the law. For a system founded on principles truly political and philosophical, we still look around us in vain. On such principles

[x] 1. Bl. Com. 31. n.

alone, can a system solid and permanent be erected. To confirm my sentiments, let me again resort to the high authority, before whose splendour
the whole host of sciolists hide their diminished heads. "The reasons of
municipal laws," says my Lord Bacon, "severed from the grounds of nature, manners, and policy, are like wall flowers, which, though they grow
high upon the crest of states, yet they have no deep root." [y]

Let me again repeat it — that we have no such system of the common
law as I have described, is by no means owing to the want of the materials proper for the erection of so noble a fabrick. "I do not a little admire
the wisdom of the laws of England," says my Lord Bacon in another
place,[z] "and the consent, which they have with the wisdom of philosophy
and nature itself."

By this time, you are at no loss to discover my sentiments concerning
the studies which a lawyer ought to pursue, and the accomplishments
which he ought to acquire. He ought to know men and societies of men,
in every state and in every relation in which they can be placed: in every
state and in every relation in which men or societies of men can be
placed, he ought to know what appertains to justice — to comprehensive
morality. From the fountains of justice, we have seen, the civil laws
should spring. To that fountain, ever full and ever flowing, let the stu-
dent of the law intrepidly ascend: he will then, with ease, with pleasure, and with certainty, follow the meandering courses of its numerous
streams.

It is an opinion, far from being uncommon, that the only institution
necessary for a practising lawyer is, to observe the practice in a lawyer's
office. No opinion was ever more unfounded: no opinion, perhaps, ever
entailed more mischief upon those, who have been its unfortunate victims. I certainly shall not be misunderstood as if I meant to speak with
contempt of the practice, which is to be observed in a lawyer's office.
Nothing can be more remote from my intention and from my sentiments.
To the most accomplished lawyer, even the *minutiae* of practice are
objects of regard; and, in his hands, they can be employed to useful, nay,
to splendid purposes. In nature, the greatest bodies, the greatest systems
of bodies, are composed of the smallest particles; and the microscope, as
well as the telescope, discloses a world of wonders to our view. So in the
sciences — so, particularly, in the science of law. But to be confined to
microsopick observations is the doom of an insect, not the birthright of a
man.

I have said that the opinion just mentioned entails much mischief upon
its unfortunate victims. I have said the truth. Law, studied and practised
as a science founded in principle, is among the most delightful of occupations: followed as a trade depending merely upon precedent, it be-

[y] 4. Ld. Bac. 101.   [z] Id. 103.

comes and continues a drudgery, severe and insupportable. One, who follows it in this manner, lives in a state of continual distrust and alarm. To such a one, every thing new is something odious: for he has been taught to approve of things, not because they are proper or right, but because he has seen them before. To such a one, the least deviation from even the most unessential form, appears equally fatal with the greatest departure from the most important principles: for they agree in the only circumstance, by which he can distinguish either: they are not within the sphere of his practice. Tied to the centre of precedent, he treads, for life, the same dull, and small, and uniform circle around it, without daring to view or to enjoy a single object on either side.

How very different is the situation of him, who ranges, not without rule, but without restraint, in the rich, the variegated, and the spacious fields of science! To his observation and research every thing is open: he is accustomed to examine and to compare the appearances and the realities of things; to contemplate their beauty, to investigate their utility, and to admire the wonderful harmony, with which beauty and utility coincide. To him an object is not dangerous because it is new: he measures it by the correct standard of his principles: he discovers what purposes it is fitted to answer, and what other purposes it is fitted to destroy: he learns when to use it, and when to lay the use of it aside. The discovery of one improvement leads him to the discovery of another: the discovery of that other leads him, in delightful progression, to another still.

I am now to make some remarks concerning the character which a lawyer ought to support.

Laws and law suits seem, in the apprehension of some, to be synonimous or nearly synonimous terms. In the opinion of such, the business and the character of a lawyer will be, to produce and to manage controversies at law. Part of the opinion may be admitted to be just. To manage controversies at law, when they have been produced by another cause, is part of the business of a lawyer: to produce them is no part of it. Even to manage law suits, though a part, is not the principal part, of a lawyer's business: the principal part of his business is to prevent them. The professional pride of a lawyer is, that no controversy arises from any opinion which he gives, nor from the construction of any instrument which he draws. Like a skilful pilot, he has studied correctly the chart of the law: he has marked the places which are dangerous, as well as those which are safe. Like a pilot, honest and benevolent as well as skilful, he cautiously avoids every danger, and through the channels of security steers the fortunes of those, who intrust them to his care.

One reason, why the association between lawyers and law suits is so strong in the minds of some people, may be this, that they never think of the former, till they are plunged in the latter, or in the necessary causes of the latter. But even in this situation, the association is not a correct one; for when they are in this situation, the tardy recourse to a lawyer is to help them out of it.

To give honest and sound advice in questions of law, to those who ask it in matters relating to their business or conduct, forms the character, which a lawyer ought to support. I speak now of his private character: his publick character and conduct come under a different consideration.

A general prejudice against the professional character of the bar has arisen, I believe, from observing, that the gentlemen of the profession appear equally ready to undertake either side of the same cause. Both sides, it is said, and said with truth, cannot be right: and to undertake either with equal alacrity evinces, it is thought, an insensibility — presumed professional — to the natural and important distinction between right and wrong.

This subject deserves to be placed in its true light. That this insensibility is sometimes found at the bar cannot be denied. That it is often imputed when it is not found, ought also to be admitted. A few observations will easily disclose the origin of this prejudice: and its origin ought to be disclosed; for I deem it of publick importance, especially in a free country, that the professional character of the bar should stand in a respectable point of view.

Let it be observed, that by far the greatest number of law suits originate from disputed facts. Of these a lawyer cannot judge, but from the representation of them, which he receives from his client. A dishonest client will impose upon his counsel: an honest client, from the blindness and partiality of self interest, is often imposed upon himself: the imposition, in this case, operates upon the counsel equally as in the other. In both cases, the lawyer, instead of deserving censure, deserves sympathy; for it is always disagreeable to be engaged in a bad and unsuccessful cause.

Again; even when law suits originate from disputed points of law, they frequently spring from positive institutions, particularly from intricate and artificial regulations concerning property. To such questions, the natural distinction between right and wrong is susceptible of no other application, than that they be decided according to the law of the land.

But further; in such cases, the rule of positive law may be really doubtful; and this doubt may be the true cause of the controversy. How often do we see juries and judges divided, nay equally divided, in opinion? If this is so, a difference of sentiment in two gentlemen of the bar should not be viewed as either pretended or reprehensible. The court frequently direct arguments of counsel on each side: can it be improper for the counsel to obey those directions?

These remarks explain and justify the conduct of counsel in the cases which I have described, and are fitted to remove the prejudice, which, in such cases, is entertained against them. If a lawyer is so lost to a sense of his duty and character, as to advocate a cause which he knows to be morally and certainly unjust, his conduct requires not to be explained; and I mean not to justify it.

To the court, as well as to his client, a duty is owing by a gentleman of the bar: these obligations are, by no means, incompatible: both will be discharged by uniform candour, and by a decent firmness properly blended with a dignified respect.

Thus much concerning counsel and attornies at law. I have been full and particular upon this head, because it personally and immediately concerns the future conduct and prospects of many of my hearers.

IX

THE SUBJECT CONTINUED—OF CONSTABLES

I AM now to consider the office of a constable. This officer, and the office which he holds, are often treated with a degree of disrespect; but very improperly and very unwisely. In a government founded on the authority of the people, every publick officer is respectable; for every publick officer is a free citizen: he is more; by other free citizens he is invested with a portion of their power.

Besides; the powers and duties of constables, if properly and effectually exercised and discharged, are of real importance to the community; and their publick utility should rescue them from contempt. The antiquity as well as the usefulness of the office is very great. Of its original it may be said, as we are informed by my Lord Bacon,[a] *caput inter nubila condit;* for its authority was granted upon the ancient laws and customs of the kingdom, practised long before the conquest. It was intended and instituted for the conservation of the peace, and for repressing every kind of annoyance and disturbance of the people. This was done by way of prevention and not of punishment; for a constable has no judicial power to hear or determine any cause.

Upon a probability of a breach of the peace, as when warm words have passed, the constable may command the parties to keep the peace, and depart and forbear. When an affray is made, he may part those engaged in it, and keep them asunder. He may arrest and commit the breakers of the peace; and, if they will not obey, he may call power to his assistance.[b] If an affray is in a house, he may break the doors open to restore and preserve the peace. If an offender fly into another district or county, the constable may make fresh pursuit and take him. To prevent as well as to quell a breach of the peace, he may command all persons to assist him; and those, who refuse, may be bound over to the sessions and fined.[c]

It is the duty of a constable to execute, with speed and secrecy, all warrants directed to him; and not to dispute the authority of him who issues them; provided the matter in question is within his jurisdiction.[d]

The power and duty of constables are extended to a great variety of in-

---

[a] 4. Ld. Bac. 94. [The head disappears among the clouds; *i.e.* the source is lost in obscurity.]
[b] Ld. Bac. 96.   [c] Wood. Ins. 87.   [d] Id. ibid.

stances by a number of acts of assembly, which have been passed in Pennsylvania.

In cases of necessity, a constable has power to appoint a deputy.[e]

There are two kinds of constables; a high constable and a petty constable. Their authority is the same in substance, and differs only in point of extent.[f]

To appoint men of low condition to the office of constable, is, according to my Lord Bacon,[g] a mere abuse and degeneracy from the first institution. They ought, says he, to be chosen from among the better sort of residents.

I have now finished my account of the judicial departments of the United States and Pennsylvania; and, with it, the description of their governments and constitutions. To the government and constitution of every other state in the Union, my remarks and illustrations will, generally, be found applicable. In those instances, in which a strict application cannot be made, still, I flatter myself, my remarks and illustrations will throw some light upon the respective advantages or disadvantages of institutions, which cannot be measured by the same common standard.

[e] Ld. Bac. 98.   [f] 4. Ld. Bac. 98.   [g] Id. 96.

X

OF CORPORATIONS

IN a former part of my lectures,[a] after having described a state, I observed, that, in a state, smaller societies may be formed by a part of its members: that these smaller societies, like states, are deemed to be moral persons, but not in a state of natural liberty; because their actions are cognizable by the superiour power of the state, and are regulated by its laws. I mentioned, that, to these societies, the name of corporations is generally appropriated, though somewhat improperly; for that the term is strictly applicable to supreme as well as to inferiour bodies politick. In obedience, however, to the arbitress of language, I shall designate those smaller societies by the name of corporations; and to the consideration of them I now proceed.

A corporation is described to be a person in a political capacity created by the law, to endure in perpetual succession.[b] Of these artificial persons a great variety is known to the law. They have been formed to promote and to perpetuate the interests of commerce, of learning, and of religion. It must be admitted, however, that, in too many instances, those bodies politick have, in their progress, counteracted the design of their original formation. Monopoly, superstition, and ignorance have been the unnatural offspring of literary, religious, and commercial corporations. This is not mentioned with a view to insinuate, that such establishments ought to be prevented or destroyed: I mean only to intimate, that they should be erected with caution, and inspected with care.

In England, corporations may exist by the common law, by act of parliament, by prescription, and by charter from the king.[c] The king and the parliament are corporations by the force of the common law.[d]

In the United States, and in Pennsylvania, corporations can only exist by the common law, or by virtue of legislative authority. This authority, however, may be exercised by a power delegated by the legislature; as has been done, in this connmonwealth,[e] with regard to churches. Upon the same principle, the king, in England, may communicate to a subject the power of erecting corporations, and may permit him to name the persons of whom they shall be composed, and the authority which they

[a] Ante. pp. 239–240. [b] Wood. Ins. 111. [c] 10. Rep. 29 b. [d] Wood. Ins. 112.
[e] 3. Laws. Penn. 40.

shall enjoy. Still, however, it is the king, who really erects them; the subject is only his instrument; and the act of the instrument becomes the act of its mover, under the well known maxim, "qui facit per alium, facit per se." [f]

To every corporation a name must be assigned; and by that name alone it can perform legal acts.[g]

When a corporation is duly established, there are many powers, rights, and capacities, which are annexed to it tacitly and of course.

It has perpetual succession, unless a period of limitation be expressed in the instrument of its establishment. This succession is, indeed, the great end of an incorporation; and, for this reason, there is, in all aggregate bodies politick, a power necessarily implied of filling vacancies by the election of new members.[h]

The power of removing any of its members for just cause, is a power incident to a corporation. To the order and good government of corporate bodies, it is adjudged necessary that there should be such a power.[i]

Another and a most important power, tacitly annexed to corporations by the very act of their establishment, is the power of making by-laws.[j] This, indeed, is the principal reason for erecting many of the bodies corporate. Their nature or their circumstances are peculiar; and provisions peculiarly adapted to them cannot be expected from the general law of the land. For this reason, they are invested with authority to make regulations for the management of their own interests and affairs. These regulations, however, must not be contrary to the overruling laws of the state; for it will be remembered, that these smaller societies, though moral persons, are not in a state of natural liberty. Their private statutes are *leges sub graviore lege.* "Sodales, legem quam volent, dum nequid ex publica lege corrumpant, sibi ferunto," is a rule as old as the twelve tables of Rome.[k]

The general duties of every corporation may be collected from the nature and design of its institution: it should act agreeably to its nature, and fulfil the purposes for which it was formed.

But corporations are composed of individuals; those individuals are not exempted from the failings and frailties of humanity; those failings and frailties may lead to a deviation from the end of their establishment. For this reason, as has already been observed, they ought to be inspected with care. The law has provided proper persons with proper powers to visit those institutions, and to correct every irregularity, which may

[f] 10. Rep. 33 b. 1. Bl. Com. 474. [Who acts through another, acts for himself.]
[g] 10. Rep. 122.   [h] 1. Bl. Com. 475.   [i] 1. Burr. 539.
[j] Ld. Ray. 498. Hob. 211. 1. Bl. Com. 475.
[k] 1. Bl. Com. 476. [Let societies make for themselves the law they want so long as they destroy nothing from the public law.]

arise within them. In England, it has, by immemorial usage, appointed them to be visited and inspected, in the court of king's bench, according to the rules of the common law.[1] We have formerly seen,[m] that the powers of the court of king's bench are vested in the supreme court of Pennsylvania.

A corporation may surrender its legal existence into the hands of that power, from which it was received. From such a surrender, the dissolution of the body corporate ensues. An aggregate corporation is dissolved by the natural death of all its members.[n] By a judgment of forfeiture against a corporation itself, it may be dissolved; but not by a judgment of ouster against individuals. God forbid — such is the sentiment of Mr. Justice Wilmot[o] — that the rights of the body should be lost or destroyed by the offences of the members.

Suffice it to have said thus much concerning corporations, or subordinate societies established within the society at large.

[1] Id. 481.   [m] Ante. p. 460.   [n] 3. Burr. 1867.   [o] Id. 1871.

XI

OF CITIZENS AND ALIENS

LET us proceed to investigate still farther the component parts of which civil government and all its subordinate establishments consist. They consist of citizens.

I have already observed [a] that the social contract is a contract of a peculiar kind; that when correctly analyzed, it is found to be an assemblage of agreements equal, in number, to the number of individuals who form the society; and that, to each of those agreements, a single individual is one party, and all the other individuals of the society are the other party.

The latter party I have considered heretofore; and have called it the people. The former party I am now to consider; and, in order to avoid confusion, I call it, in this discussion, the citizen; and when I shall have occasion to refer to more subordinate agreements than one, I shall call the individuals, parties to them, by the name of citizens.

I know that the term *citizen* is often applied to one of the more numerous party — to one of the people: and I shall be obliged to take the description of a citizen from the character which he supports as one of the people. But you will easily perceive, that the same person may, at different times, act or be viewed in different characters; and though his description be taken from one of them, the account of his duties and of his rights too may, on a particular occasion, be referred to the other. This I have chosen to do, rather than to introduce an unknown phrase, or to use a known phrase in a new signification. Besides, the expression is frequently employed also in the sense in which I now use it. "Generally speaking," says the great political authority,[b] Aristotle, "a citizen is one partaking equally of power and of subordination."

A citizen then — to draw his description as *one* of the *people* — I deem him, who acts a personal or a represented part in the legislation of his country. He has other rights; but his legislative I consider as his characteristick right. In this view, a citizen of the United States is he, who is a citizen of at least some one state in the Union: for the members of the house of representatives in the national legislature are chosen, in each state, by electors, who, in that state, have the qualifications requisite for

[a] Ante. p. 507.　　[b] 1. Rus. Anc. Eur. 362.

electors of the most numerous branch of the state legislature.[e] In this view, a citizen of Pennsylvania is he, who has resided in the state two years; and, within that time, has paid a state or county tax: or he is between the ages of twenty one and twenty two years, and the son of a citizen.[d]

I have, on another occasion,[e] traced the description of a citizen in every other state of the Union: to your recollection of that investigation, and to the constitutions of the several states, I now refer you.

When a man acts as one of the numerous party to the agreements, of which I have taken notice; it is his right, according to the tenour of his agreements, to govern; he is one of the *people*. When he acts as the single party to that agreement, which he has made with all the other members of the society; it is his duty, according to the tenour of his agreement, to obey; he is a *single citizen*. Of this agreement, indeed, it is impossible to ascertain all the articles. From the most obvious deduction of reason, however, one article may be specified, beyond all possibility of doubt. This article, of prime importance, is — that to the publick will of the society, the private will of every associated member must, in matters respecting the social union, be subordinate and submissive. The publick will of the society is declared by the laws. Obedience, therefore — civil obedience — obedience to the laws and to the administration of the laws — this is a distinguishing feature in the countenance of a citizen, when he is seen from this point of view.

That men ought to be governed, seems to have been agreed on all hands: the reason is, that, without government, they could never attain any high or permanent share of perfection or happiness. But the question has been — by whom should they be governed? And this has been made a question, by reason of two others — by whom *can* they be governed? — are they capable of governing themselves?

To this last question, Mr. Burke, in the spirit of his late creed,[f] has answered in the negative. "Society," says he, "requires not only that the passions of individuals should be subjected, but that even in the mass and body as well as in the individuals, the inclinations of men should frequently be thwarted, their will controlled, and their passions brought into subjection. This can only be done *by a power out of themselves*." This negative answer has been, from time immemorial, the strong hold of tyranny: and if this negative answer be the true one, the strong hold of tyranny is, in fact, impregnable to all the artillery of freedom. If men should be governed; and if they cannot govern themselves; what is the consequence? They must be governed by other masters.

[e] Cons. U.S. art. 1. s. 2.   [d] Cons. Penn. art. 3. s. 1.   [e] Ante. pp. 408–410.
[f] Refl. on Fr. Rev. 47.

An opinion, however, has, by some, been entertained, that the question, which I last mentioned, may receive an answer in the affirmative. Men, it has been thought, are capable of governing themselves. In the United States, this opinion, which heretofore rested chiefly on theory, has lately been put in a train of fair practical experiment. That this experiment, to human happiness so interesting, may be crowned with abundant and glorious success, is, of all things in this world, the "consummation most devoutly to be wished."

But to its glorious and abundant success, the obedience of the citizens is of a necessity, absolute and supreme. The question, which has been proposed — the question, in the negative answer to which, tyranny has triumphed so long and so generally — the question, concerning which philosophers and patriots have indulged, and been pleased with indulging, a contrary sentiment — the question, which, in the United States, is now put upon an experiment — this all-important question is — not merely nor chiefly — are men capable of governing? Of this, even tyrants will admit the affirmative; and will point to themselves as living proofs of its truth. But the question is — are men capable of governing *themselves?* In other words; are they qualified — and are they disposed to be their *own* masters? For a moral as well as an intellectual capability is involved in the question. In still other words; are they qualified — and are they disposed to *obey themselves?* For to government, the correlative inseparable is obedience. To think, to speak, or to act, as if the former may be exercised, and, at the same time, the latter may not be performed, is to think, to speak, or to act, in a manner the most contradictory and absurd.

By a long and minute deduction, proved, in a former lecture,[g] that, on the true principles of freedom, a man is the only human power, by whom he himself can be *bound*. It requires but a very small variation of phrase, and none of sentiment, to say, that on the true principles of freedom, man is the only human power, by whom he himself can be *governed*.

Are we made so waywardly, that what, in principle, is true and right, must, in practice, be false and wrong? Surely not.

Is the *safety* of man endangered by obedience? What can be a source of greater security, than to be governed only by a law, which has been made by himself, and by others, with whom he participates a general identity of interest, and a perfect equality of duties and of rights?

Is the *freedom* of man infringed by performing the service of obedience to such a law, made as has been mentioned? This service bears, we think, a resemblance as near as, being human, it can bear, to that service,

[g] Ante. p. 186. et seq.

which, with a propriety truly striking and strong, is denominated "perfect freedom."

Is the *dignity* of man degraded by observing a law? The Supreme of Being! — he himself worketh not without a rule!

In a *moral* view, self government increases, instead of impairing, the security, the liberty, and the dignity of the *man;* in a *political* view, self government increases, instead of impairing, the security, the liberty, and the dignity of the *citizen.*

Attend now to the result of the whole. — In a free and well constituted government, the first duty of its every member is — obedience to the laws. That they be true and faithful to themselves, is the allegiance, which a legitimate republick requires from her citizens: to themselves they cannot be true and faithful, unless they obey as well as make the laws — unless, in the terms in which a citizen has been defined, they partake of subordination as well as of power.

As a citizen of a republican government owes obedience to the laws; so he owes a decent, though a dignified respect to those who administer the laws. In monarchies, there is a political respect of person: in commonwealths, there should be a political respect to office. In monarchies, there are ranks, preeminences, and dignities, all personal and hereditary. In commonwealths, too, there are ranks, preeminences, and dignities; but all official and successive. In monarchies, respect is paid without a prospect of return. In commonwealths, one may, next year, succeed, as an officer, to the respect, which, this year, he pays as a citizen. The dignities of office are open to all.

You will be pleased to hear, that, with regard to this as well as to many other subjects, we have renewed, in our governments, the principles and the practice of the ancient Saxons. Between dignity and duty, no separation was made by them. In the early period of the Anglo-Saxon state, the allodial proprietors were numerous; their estates were generally small; and all were understood to be of the same rank and condition. Some, indeed, were distinguished above others by their character and their talents; but the superiority derived from this source was accompanied with no legal preeminence or power.[h]

So likewise it was in the heroick ages of Greece: no distinction was then known among men, except the distinction, truly honourable, which arose from a difference of abilities and merit.[i]

Titles of nobility in England, though now merely personal, were, in their origin, altogether official. The heretoch or duke was intrusted with a military department: the marquis was appointed to guard the frontiers or marches of the country: the alderman or earl was, as we formerly saw, the first civil officer of the shire. In the juridical history of England, the

[h] Millar. 236. [i] 1. Gill. 49.

first arbitrary title of honour, without the shadow of office or duty annexed to it, makes its appearance so late as the reign of Henry the sixth.

Under a republican government, it is prudent as well as proper — it is the interest as well as the duty of the citizens, to show a political respect for office. In the government they have an interest: in every office and department of the government they have an interest: this interest requires, that every department and every office should be well filled: in a commonwealth, respect attached to office is frequently the principal inducement to its acceptance by those, who are qualified to fill it well.

On the citizen under a republican government, a third duty, more severe, it may be thought, than either of the former, is strictly incumbent. Whenever a competition unavoidably takes place between his interest and that of the publick, to the latter the former must be the devoted sacrifice. By the will and by the interest of the community, every private will and every private interest must be bound and overruled. Unless this maxim be established and observed; it is impossible that civil government could be formed or supported. Fortunate, however, it is, that in a government formed wisely and administered impartially, this unavoidable competition can seldom take place, at least in any very great degree.

If the sacrifice, which I have mentioned, is demanded and enforced by the publick, when the competition does not unavoidably take place; or if it is demanded and enforced farther or longer than the existing competition indispensably requires; it is tyranny; it is not government.

The citizen has rights as well as duties: the latter he is obliged to perform: the former he is entitled to enjoy or recover. To that original contract of association, to which, in our reasonings concerning government, an appeal must so often be made, he is a party; nay, in point of right, a party, voluntary, independent, equal. On one side, indeed, there stands a single individual: on the other side, perhaps, there stand millions: but right is weighed by principle; it is not estimated by numbers. From the necessity of the case, as was shown on a former occasion,[j] if a controversy arises between the parties to the social agreement, the numbers, or a selection from the numbers, must be the judges as well as one of the parties. But, because those of one party must, from the necessity of the peculiar case, be the judges likewise; does it follow, that they are absolved from that strict obligation, by which every judge is sacredly bound to administer impartial justice? Does it follow, that they may, with avidity, listen to all the interested suggestions, the advice of which a party would pursue? When the same person is and must be both judge and party; the character of the judge ought not to be sunk in that of

[j] Ante. p. 507.

the party; but the character of the party should be exalted to that of the judge.

When questions — especially pecuniary questions — arise between a state and a citizen — more especially still, when those questions are, as they generally must be, submitted to the decision of those, who are not only parties and judges, but legislators also; the sacred impartiality of the second character, it must be owned, is too frequently lost in the sordid interestedness of the first, and in the arrogant power of the third. This, I repeat it, is tyranny: and tyranny, though it may be more formidable and more oppressive, is neither less odious nor less unjust — is neither less dishonourable to the character of one party, nor less hostile to the rights of the other, because it is proudly prefaced by the epithet — legislative. He, who refuses the payment of an honest demand upon the publick, because it is in his power to refuse it, would refuse the payment of his private debt, if he was equally protected in the refusal. He, who robs as a legislator, *because* he dares, would rob as a highwayman — *if* he dared.

And are the publick gainers by this? Even if they were, it would be no consideration. The paltry gain would be but as dust in the balance, when weighed against the loss of character — for as the world becomes more enlightened, and as the principles of justice become better understood, states as well as individuals have a character to lose — the paltry gain, I say, would be but as dust in the balance, when weighed against the loss of character, and against the many other pernicious effects which must flow from the example of publick injustice. But the truth is, that the publick must be losers, instead of being gainers, by a conduct of this kind. The mouth, which will not utter the sentiments of truth in favour of an honest demand, may be easily taught to repeat the lessons of falsehood in favour of an unjust one. To refuse fair claims, is to encourage fraudulent ones, upon the commonwealth. Little logick is required to show, that the same vicious principles and dispositions, which oppose the former, will exert their selfish, or their worse than selfish, influence to support the latter.

I think I have proved, that if the sacrifice, which has been mentioned, is demanded and enforced by the publick, when the competition between publick and private interest does not take place, it is tyranny, and not government; folly, and not wisdom. I have added, that if this sacrifice is demanded and enforced farther or longer than the competition indispensably requires, this, too, is tyranny, and not government. This likewise it is easy to prove.

There may be times, when, to the interest, perhaps to the liberty of the state, every private interest and regard ought to be devoted. At those times, such may be the situation and the peril of the commonwealth —

for it is in perilous and distracted times, that, by the citizens, extraordinary exertions of duty ought to be made — at those times, a citizen obeys his duty's and his country's sacred call; he makes the necessary sacrifices, without expressly stipulating for a recompense: of demanding such a stipulation, the impropriety and the indelicacy may be equally evident. Great sacrifices and great exertions are made with faithfulness and zeal; perhaps, with considerable success. The perils disappear: to distraction and danger, peace and serenity succeed: the commonwealth becomes flourishing and opulent. Ought the sacrifice, which, in the hour of her distress and danger, was made at her call, to be continually enforced and demanded by her, after the danger and distress are over? But this sacrifice is demanded and enforced continually, if this citizen has neither received, nor had it in his power to recover, that recompense, which is just. This case — if such a case has ever happened — may go without any actual redress; but it can never go without well grounded complaint.

There is a sacrifice of another kind, not indeed so great, but, on some occasions, very vexatious, which is required of a citizen under a republican government, unnecessarily, and against his rights. He is frequently pestered with a number of frivolous, ambiguous, perplexed, and contradictory laws. The very best constitutions are liable to some complaints. What may be called the rage of legislation is a distemper prevalent and epidemical among republican governments.

Every article of the social contract cannot be ascertained: some of its leading principles cannot easily be mistaken. One certainly is, that, in a free state, the law should impose no restraint upon the will of the citizen, but such as will be productive of advantage, publick or private, sufficient to overbalance the disadvantages of the restraint: for, after all, we shall find that the *citizen* was made for the sake of the *man*. The proof of this advantage lies upon the legislature. If a law is even harmless, the very circumstance of its being a law, is itself a harm. This remark might be remembered, with profit, in the revision of many codes of law. In a word; government and human laws are necessary; if good, they are inestimable, in the present state. It must be admitted, however, that they are a burthen and a yoke: they should resemble that yoke which is easy, and that burthen which is light.

The citizen under a free government has a right to think, to speak, to write, to print, and to publish freely, but with decency and truth, concerning publick men, publick bodies, and publick measures.

Thus much concerning the duties and the rights of a private citizen.

I am next to treat of aliens.

——— homo sum;
Nihil humani alienum a me puto.*

* [I am a human being; therefore I consider nothing human alien to me.]

If this humane maxim had prevailed, as it ought to have prevailed, in the establishment of government, and the formation of laws; the title, which relates to aliens, would have been of an import very different from what we generally find it to be.

The contracted and debasing spirit of monopoly has not been peculiar to commerce; it has raged, with equal violence, and with equal mischief, in law and politicks.

In ancient times, every alien was considered as an enemy. The rule, I think, should be reversed. None but an enemy should be considered as an alien — I mean — as to the acquisition and the enjoyment of property. The rights of citizenship are the rights of parties to the social compact. Even to these, aliens should be permitted to accede upon easy terms.

This subject is of high importance to the United States; to Pennsylvania, in particular.

When I speak of the contracted rule, which prevailed in ancient times, I mean to speak, and I wish to be understood, with some illustrious exceptions. These deserve to be distinctly pointed out. From them, valuable instruction may be drawn.

The general policy of the Egyptians was unfriendly to strangers. It is even said of them, that they were accustomed to kill, or reduce to slavery, all those whom they found upon their coasts; except at one city only, at which they were allowed to land and trade. But Psammeticus, one of their princes, observed maxims of a more humane and enlightened nature. He favoured navigation in his seas; he opened his ports to the commerce of all nations; and he granted every kind of encouragement to every one, who would settle in Egypt. Amasis, one of his successours, governed, by the same principles, his behaviour towards foreigners. He conferred many benefits upon the Grecians; and even allowed them to erect altars and temples. Under the government of Amasis, it is observed, Egypt was perfectly happy.[k]

Under the famous Theseus, the rival and the friend of Hercules, strangers were invited to participate in the privileges of Athens: from all parts the invitation was accepted; and the new citizens were incorporated with the ancient Athenians. Every thing now, it is added, seemed favourable to his views: he governed a free people with moderation and benevolence; he was esteemed and beloved by the neighbouring nations; and he enjoyed a foretaste of that profound veneration, with which succeeding ages gradually honour the memory of great men.[l]

This policy, enlarged and generous, was continued in Attica, during many ages after Theseus; and rendered that celebrated country the most frequent resource of the miserable. On a particular occasion, the descendants of the great Hercules, devested of their possessions and driven into

[k] 3. Gog Or. Laws. 15. 16.   [l] 1. Anac. 31. 32.

banishment by one of the vicissitudes of the times, enjoyed the advantages of the policy introduced by the friend of their ancestor: they were received by the Athenians.[m]

When it was, in the time of Lysias, attempted to contract the foundation of the Athenian government; this part of their ancient policy is, in his oration against that attempt, mentioned with particular respect. "As to myself, I hold it to be the best security for the state, that all have an equal share in the government. When formerly we built walls, and acquired a fleet, and money, and allies; we regarded not these advantages as obtained only for ourselves; we shared them with the Eubæans, by establishing the right of intermarriage. Such were once our principles: by bestowing on strangers the honours of our country, we rendered them our friends: shall we now, by degrading our fellow citizens, render them our enemies? Never let this take place." [n]

"By those states," says my Lord Bacon, in his book concerning the augmentation of the sciences, "who have easily and liberally communicated the right of citizenship, greatness has been most successfully acquired. No commonwealth opened its bosom so wide for the reception of new citizens, as the commonwealth of Rome. The fortune of the empire was correspondent to the wisdom of the institution; for it became the largest on the face of the earth. It was their custom to confer the right of citizenship in the most speedy manner; and in the highest degree too — I mean not only the right of commerce, the right of marriage, the right of inheritance; but even the right of suffrage, and the right to the offices and the honours of the republick. So that it may be said, not that the Romans extended themselves over the whole globe, but that the inhabitants of the globe poured themselves upon the Romans. This is the most secure method of enlarging an empire." [o]

My Lord Hale, another lawyer of eminent name, speaks in the same spirit. "The shutting out of aliens," says he, "tends to the loss of people, which, laboriously employed, are the true riches of any country." [p]

In the law of England, there is a distinction between two kinds of aliens — those who are friends, and those who are enemies. Among alien enemies a subdivision is made, or at least was made till lately, which must occasion some degree of astonishment. Alien enemies are distinguished into such as are temporary, and such as are perpetual. Nay; what is more; this line of distinction, certainly never drawn by the peaceful spirit of christianity, is attempted to be marked by the progress of the christian system. "All infidels"— these are the expressions of my Lord Coke in the report of Calvin's case — "all infidels are perpetual enemies; the law presumes not that they will be converted; between them, as with the

[m] 1. Gill. 69.   [n] Gil. Lys. and Isoc. 319.   [o] 1. Ld. Bac. 245.
[p] 1. Bac. 76. Vent. 427.

devils, whose subjects they are, and the christian, there is perpetual hostility; and can be no peace;" — for he fortifies the favourite sentiment by a pleonasm: he goes farther — he attempts to fortify it by the language, tortured surely, of christianity itself. "Quæ autem conventio Christi ad Belial; aut quæ pars fideli cum infideli." [q]

"Upon this ground," continues he, "there is a diversity between a conquest of the kingdom of a christian king, and the conquest of that of an infidel. In the former case, the ancient laws of the kingdom remain, till they are altered by the conqueror: in the latter case, they are immediately abrogated; and, till new laws be established, the conqueror shall judge them according to natural equity." [r]

The character of an opinion, like the character of a man, may be illustrated by tracing its history and pedigree. The opinion, that "the common law of England, as such, has no allowance or authority in the American plantations," is the bastard child of this bastard mother, begotten on her body by the Commentaries[s] on the laws of England. This very case of Calvin, and this very part of Calvin's case, is cited — none better could be cited — as the authority for an opinion, which was calculated to cut off the noblest inheritance of the colonies: to use, for once, a language *technically* legal, the colonies were *mulier*, though they were *puisne* — they were legitimate, though they were young.

But to return to the subject of alienage — an alien, according to the notion commonly received as law, is one born in a strange country and in a foreign society, to which he is presumed to have a natural and a necessary allegiance.[t]

Errour, as well as truth, is sometimes connected by a regular chain. A man is deemed a dangerous enemy or a suspicious friend to that country in which he wishes to reside, because he is previously deemed an appurtenant or a slave to that country in which he chanced to be born. Such is *one* of the consequences of "natural and necessary allegiance."

Between alien friends, who are temporary subjects, and subjects naturalized or natural born, a species of subjects intermediate is known to the law of England. They are distinguished by the appellation of denizens. The power of denization is a high and incommunicable portion[u] of the prerogative royal. A denizen is received into the nation, like a person who is dropt from the clouds. He may acquire rights, but he cannot inherit them, not even from his own parent: he may transmit rights to his children, who are born after his letters patent of denization; but not to those who were born before. A denizen may be moulded into a thousand

[q] 2. Cor. VI. 15. [And what agreement pray is there of Christ toward Belial; or what part has the faithful person in common with the infidel?]
[r] 6. Rep. 17.   [s] 1. Bl. Com. 107.   [t] 1. Bac. 76.   [u] 1. Bl. Com. 374.

fantastical shapes: he may be a denizen in tail, a denizen for life, a denizen for years, a denizen upon condition, a denizen in one court of justice, and an alien in another.[v] Of those modifications, however, a subject naturalized is unsusceptible; because, we are told, they would be inconsistent with the purity, the absoluteness, and the indelibility of natural allegiance.[w] For a sound rule, we receive an unsound reason.

Between a subject naturalized and a subject natural born, the distinction is merely nominal as to private rights: it applies only to the manner, in which those rights are devolved. On one they are devolved by his birth: on the other, by the consent of the nation, expressed in the parliament. With regard, however, to publick rights, the case is widely different. By statutes made even since the revolution, no subject naturalized can be a member of parliament; and no bill for naturalization can be received in either house of parliament, without such a disabling clause.[x]

Britain seems determined to merit and to perpetuate, in political as well as geographical accuracy, the description, by which it was marked many centuries ago — *divisos* toto orbe Britannos.*

What a very different spirit animates and pervades her American sons! Indeed it is proper that it should do so. The insulated policy of the British nation would as ill befit the expansive genius of our institutions, as the hills, the ponds, and the rivulets which are scattered over their island, would adequately represent the mountains, and rivers, and lakes of the United States. "In the new world" — I speak now from one of the finest writers of Britain [y] — "in the new world nature seems to have carried on her operations with a bolder hand, and to have distinguished the features of the country by a peculiar magnificence. The mountains of America are much superiour in height to those in the other divisions of the globe. From those lofty mountains descend rivers proportionably large. Its lakes are no less conspicuous for grandeur, than its mountains and rivers." We imitate, for we ought to imitate, the operations of nature; and the features of our policy, like those of our country, are distinguished by a peculiar magnificence.

In a former lecture,[z] we have seen how easily the essential rights of citizenship can be acquired in the United States, and in every state of the Union. Let us now see, how liberally the doors are thrown open for admission to the publick trusts and honours, as well as to the private rights and privileges, of our country.

At the end of two years from the time, at which a foreigner "of good character" — for numbers without virtue are not our object — a former

<hr/>

[v] 1. Ins. 129. a.　　[w] 1. Ins. 129. a.　　[x] 1. Bl. Com. 374.
* [The Britons separated from the whole world.]
[y] 2. Rob. Amer. 3. 4.　　[z] Ante. p. 408. et seq.

mode of "*better* peopling his majesty's plantations" is now fallen into dis-
repute — at the end of two years from the time,[a] at which a foreigner of
good character sets his foot in this land of generosity as well as freedom,
he is entitled to become, if he chooses,[b] a citizen of our national government. At the end of seven years, a term not longer than that which is frequently required for an apprenticeship to the plainest trade, the citizen
may become legislator; for he is eligible as a representative in the congress of the United States.[c] After having, in that capacity, undergone the
honourable but short probationship of two years, the doors even of our
national senate are opened as far as to receive him.[d]

In Pennsylvania, the citizen may become a representative[e] at the end of
three, a senator,[f] at the end of four, and governour[g] of the commonwealth, at the end of seven years.

It would be tedious, and it is unnecessary, to multiply particulars, by
going through all the sister states. In this, as in other respects, in which
we have viewed them, we are still pleased with the

—— facies, qualis decet esse sororum.[*]

The rights and the disabilities of aliens with regard to property, especially with regard to landed property, forms a subject of investigation
both interesting and nice. But, according to my uniform method, I post-
pone it until I arrive at the second great division of my system. The examination of general principles should precede that of particular rules.

One opinion, however, I will now mention: it seems to be founded on
the authority of Sir Henry Spelman and the Grand Custumier of Normandy. The opinion is, that the law, by which an alien is prohibited from
holding lands, is an original branch of the feudal system; because, by that
system, no one could purchase lands, unless he did fealty to the lords, of
whom they were holden; and because an alien, who owed a previous
faith to another prince, could not take an oath of fidelity in a second
sovereign's dominions.[h]

---

[a] By the law now in force, a residence of five years is required. Laws U.S. 7. cong.
1. sess. c. 28. *Ed.*
[b] Laws U.S. 1. cong. 2. sess. 3. 3.   [c] Cons. U.S. art. 1. s. 2.
[d] Cons. U.S. art. 1. s. 3.   [e] Cons. Penn. art. 1. s. 3.
[f] Cons. Penn. art. 1. s. 8.   [g] Art. 2. s. 4.
[*] [Appearance, such as it befits sisters to have (cf. p. 265).]
[h] 1. Bac. 76. Tit. Alien.

XII

OF THE NATURAL RIGHTS OF INDIVIDUALS

W E have now viewed the whole structure of government; we have now ranged over its numerous apartments and divisions; and we have examined the materials of which it is formed. For what purpose has this magnificent palace been erected? For the residence and accommodation of the sovereign, Man.

Does man exist for the sake of government? Or is government instituted for the sake of man?

Is it possible, that these questions were ever seriously proposed? Is it possible, that they have been long seriously debated? Is it possible, that a resolution, diametrically opposite to principle, has been frequently and generally given of them in theory? Is it possible, that a decision, diametrically opposite to justice, has been still more frequently and still more generally given concerning them in practice? All this is possible: and I must add, all this is true. It is true in the dark; it is true even in the enlightened portions of the globe.

At, and nearly at the commencement of these lectures, a sense of duty obliged me to enter into a controversial discussion concerning the rights of society: the same sense of duty now obliges me to enter into a similar discussion concerning the rights of the constituent parts of society — concerning the rights of men. To enter upon a discussion of this nature, is neither the most pleasant nor the most easy part of my business. But when the voice of obligation is heard, ease and pleasure must preserve the respectful silence, and show the cheerful acquiescence, which become them.

What was the primary and the principal object in the institution of government? Was it — I speak of the primary and principal object — was it to acquire new rights by a human establishment? Or was it, by a human establishment, to acquire a new security for the possession or the recovery of those rights, to the enjoyment or acquisition of which we were previously entitled by the immediate gift, or by the unerring law, of our all-wise and all-beneficent Creator?

The latter, I presume, was the case: and yet we are told, that, in order to acquire the latter, we must surrender the former; in other words, in order to acquire the security, we must surrender the great objects to be secured. That man "may secure *some* liberty, he makes a surrender in trust of the *whole* of it." — These expressions are copied literally from the late publication of Mr. Burke.[a]

Tyranny, at some times, is uniform in her principles. The feudal system was introduced by a specious and successful maxim, the exact counterpart of that, which has been advanced by Mr. Burke — exact in every particular but one; and, in that one, it was more generous. The free and allodial proprietors of land were told that they must surrender it to the king, and take back — not merely "some," but — the whole of it, under some certain provisions, which, it was said, would procure a valuable object — the very object was security — security for their property. What was the result? They received their land back again, indeed; but they received it, loaded with all the oppressive burthens of the feudal servitude — cruel, indeed; so far as the epithet cruel can be applied to matters merely of property.

But all the other rights of men are in question here. For liberty is frequently used to denote all the absolute rights of men. "The absolute rights of every Englishman," says Sir William Blackstone, "are, in a political and extensive sense, usually called their liberties." [b]

And must we surrender to government the *whole* of those absolute rights? But we are to surrender them only — in *trust:* — another brat of dishonest parentage is now attempted to be imposed upon us: but for what purpose? Has government provided for us a superintending court of equity to compel a faithful performance of the trust? If it had; why should we part with the legal title to our rights?

After all; what is the mighty boon, which is to allure us into this surrender? We are to surrender all that we may secure "some:" and this "some," both as to its quantity and its certainty, is to depend on the pleasure of that power, to which the surrender is made. Is this a bargain to be proposed to those, who are both intelligent and free? No. Freemen, who know and love their rights, will not exchange their armour of pure and massy gold, for one of a baser and lighter metal, however finely it may be blazoned with tinsel: but they will not refuse to make an exchange upon terms, which are honest and honourable — terms, which may be advantageous to all, and injurious to none.

The opinion has been very general, that, in order to obtain the blessings of a good government, a sacrifice must be made of a part of our natural liberty. I am much inclined to believe, that, upon examination, this opinion will prove to be fallacious. It will, I think, be found, that wise and good government — I speak, at present, of no other — instead

[a] Refl. on Fr. Rev. 47.   [b] 1. Bl. Com. 127.

of contracting, enlarges as well as secures the exercise of the natural liberty of man: and what I say of his natural liberty, I mean to extend, and wish to be understood, through all this argument, as extended, to all his other natural rights.

This investigation will open to our prospect, from a new and striking point of view, the very close and interesting connexion, which subsists between the law of nature and municipal law. This investigation, therefore, will richly repay us for all the pains we may employ, and all the attention we may bestow, in making it.

"The law," says Sir William Blackstone, "which restrains a man from doing mischief to his fellow citizens, though it diminishes the natural, increases the civil liberty of mankind." [e] Is it a part of natural liberty to do mischief to any one?

In a former part of these lectures, I had occasion to describe what natural liberty is: let us recur to the description, which was then given.[d] "Nature has implanted in man the desire of his own happiness; she has inspired him with many tender affections towards others, especially in the near relations of life; she has endowed him with intellectual and with active powers; she has furnished him with a natural impulse to exercise his powers for his own happiness, and the happiness of those for whom he entertains such tender affections. If all this be true, the undeniable consequence is, that he has a right to exert those powers for the accomplishment of those purposes, in such a manner, and upon such objects, as his inclination and judgment shall direct; provided he does no injury to others; and provided some publick interests do not demand his labours. This right is natural liberty."

If this description of natural liberty is a just one, it will teach us, that selfishness and injury are as little countenanced by the law of nature as by the law of man. Positive penalties, indeed, may, by human laws, be annexed to both. But these penalties are a restraint only upon injustice and overweening self-love, not upon the exercise of natural liberty.

In a state of natural liberty, every one is allowed to act according to his own inclination, provided he transgress not those limits, which are assigned to him by the law of nature: in a state of civil liberty, he is allowed to act according to his inclination, provided he transgress not those limits, which are assigned to him by the municipal law. True it is, that, by the municipal law, some things may be prohibited, which are not prohibited by the law of nature: but equally true it is, that, under a government which is wise and good, every citizen will gain more liberty than he can lose by these prohibitions. He will gain more by the limitation of other men's freedom, than he can lose by the diminution

[e] 1. Bl. Com. 125. 126.   [d] Ante. pp. 241–242.

of his own. He will gain more by the enlarged and undisturbed exercise of his natural liberty in innumerable instances, than he can lose by the restriction of it in a few.

Upon the whole, therefore, man's natural liberty, instead of being abridged, may be increased and secured in a government, which is good and wise. As it is with regard to his natural liberty, so it is with regard to his other natural rights.

But even if a part was to be given up, does it follow that *all* must be surrendered? "Man," says Mr. Burke,[e] "cannot enjoy the rights of an uncivil and of a civil state together." By an "uncivil" contradistinguished from a "civil" state, he must here mean a state of nature: by the rights of this uncivil state, he must mean the rights of nature: and is it possible that natural and civil rights cannot be enjoyed together? Are they really incompatible? Must our rights be removed from the stable foundation of nature, and placed on the precarious and fluctuating basis of human institution? Such seems to be the sentiment of Mr. Burke: and such too seems to have been the sentiment of a much higher authority than Mr. Burke — Sir William Blackstone.

In the Analysis of his Commentaries,[f] he mentions "the right of personal security, of personal liberty, and of private property" — not as the natural rights, which, I confess, I should have expected, but — as the "civil liberties" of Englishmen. In his Commentaries, speaking of the same three rights, he admits that they are founded on nature and reason; but adds[g] "their establishment, excellent as it is, is still human." Each of those rights he traces severally and particularly to magna charta, which he justly considers as for the most part declaratory of the principal grounds of the fundamental laws of England.[h] He says indeed,[i] that they are "either that *residuum* of natural liberty, which is not required by the laws of society to be sacrified to publick convenience; or else those civil privileges, which society has engaged to provide, in lieu of the natural liberties so given up by individuals." He makes no explicit declaration which of the two, in his opinion, they are; but since he traces them to magna charta and the fundamental laws of England; since he calls them "civil liberties;" and since he says expressly, that their establishment is human; we have reason to think, that he viewed them as coming under the latter part of his description — as civil privileges, provided by society, in lieu of the natural liberties given up by individuals. Considered in this view, there is no material difference between the doctrine of Sir William Blackstone, and that delivered by Mr. Burke.

If this view be a just view of things, the consequence, undeniable and

---

[e] Refl. on Fr. Rev. 47.   [f] B. 1. c. 1. s. 8.   [g] 1. Com. 127.   [h] Id. 128.
[i] Id. 129.

unavoidable, is, that, under civil government, individuals have "given up" or "surrendered" their rights, to which they were entitled by nature and by nature's law; and have received, in lieu of them, those "civil privileges, which society has engaged to provide."

If this view be a just view of things, then the consequence, undeniable and unavoidable, is, that, under civil government, the right of individuals to their private property, to their personal liberty, to their health, to their reputation, and to their life, flow from a human establishment, and can be traced to no higher source. The connexion between man and his natural rights is intercepted by the institution of civil society.

If this view be a just view of things, then, under civil society, man is not only made *for*, but made *by* the government: he is nothing but what the society frames: he can claim nothing but what the society provides. His natural state and his natural rights are withdrawn altogether from notice: "It is the *civil social* man," says Mr. Burke,[j] "and *no other*, whom I have in my contemplation."

If this view be a just view of things, why should we not subscribe the following articles of a political creed, proposed by Mr. Burke.

"We wished, at the period of the revolution, and we now wish to derive all we possess, *as an inheritance from our forefathers*. Upon that body and stock of inheritance, we have taken care not to innoculate any cyon alien to the nature of the original plant. All the reformations we have hitherto made, have proceeded upon the principle of reference to antiquity; and I hope, nay I am persuaded, that all those, which possibly may be made hereafter, will be carefully formed upon analogical precedent, authority, and example."

"Our oldest reformation is that of magna charta. You will see that Sir Edward Coke, that great oracle of our law, and indeed all the great men who follow him, to Blackstone, are industrious to prove the pedigree of our liberties."

Let us observe, by the way, that the only position, relating to this subject, for which I find the authority of my Lord Coke quoted,[k] is a position, to which every one, who knows the history of the common law, will give his immediate and most unreserved assent: the position is — "that magna charta was, for the most part, declaratory of the principal grounds of the fundamental laws of England." But Mr. Burke proceeds.

"They endeavour to prove, that the ancient charter, the magna charta of King John, was connected with another positive charter from Henry the first; and that both the one and the other were nothing more than a reaffirmance of the still more ancient standing law of the kingdom. In the matter of fact, for the greater part, these authors appear to be in the

[j] Refl. on Fr. Rev. 47.   [k] 1. Bl. Com. 127. 128.

right; perhaps not always: but if the lawyers mistake in some particulars, it proves my position still the more strongly; because it demonstrates the powerful prepossession towards antiquity, with which the minds of all our lawyers and legislators, and of all the people whom they wish to influence, have been always filled; and the stationary policy of this kingdom in considering their most sacred rights and franchises as an *inheritance*." [1]

It is proper to pause here a little. — If, in tracing the pedigree of our "most sacred rights," one was permitted to indulge the same train of argument and reflection, which would be just and natural in the investigation of inferiour titles, we should be prompted to inquire, how it happens, that "mistakes in some particulars" would prove more strongly the general point to be established. Would mistakes in some particulars respecting a title to land, or the genealogy of a family, prove more strongly the validity of one, or the antiquity of the other?

But I must do Mr. Burke justice. The reason, which he assigns, why the making of those mistakes proves his position the more strongly, is, because it proves the "powerful *prepossession* towards antiquity." Of this prepossession I will controvert neither the existence nor the strength: but I will ask — does it prove the point in question? — Does it prove the truth and correctness of even the *civil* pedigree of the liberties of England? Is predilection an evidence of right? Is property or any thing else, which is in litigation, decided to belong to him, who shows the strongest affection for it? If, in a controversy concerning an inferiour object, the person, who claims it, and who undertakes to substantiate his claim, should own, that, in deducing his chain of title, some mistakes were made; but should urge even those mistakes as an argument in his behalf, because his perseverance in his suit, notwithstanding those mistakes, demonstrates his powerful attachment for the thing in dispute; what would a discerning court — what would an unbiassed jury think of his conduct? I believe they would not think that it paid any extraordinary compliment, either to their impartiality or to their understanding.

I begin now to hesitate, whether we should subscribe the political creed of Mr. Burke. Let us, however, proceed and examine some of its other articles.

Some one, it seems, had been so hardy as to allege, that the king of Great Britain owes his crown to "the choice of his people." This doctrine, says Mr. Burke, "affirms a most unfounded, dangerous, illegal, and unconstitutional position." "Nothing can be more untrue, than that the crown of this kingdom is so held by his majesty." [m] To disprove the assertion, "that the king of Great Britain owes his crown to the choice of his

---

[1] Refl. on Fr. Rev. 24.   [m] Refl. on Fr. Rev. 9.

people," Mr. Burke has recourse to the declaration of rights, which was made at the accession of King William and Queen Mary. "This declaration of right," says he, "is the corner stone of our constitution, as *re-enforced*, explained, improved, and in its fundamental principles *for ever* settled. It is called an 'act for declaring the rights and liberties of the subject, and for *settling* the succession of the crown.' These rights and this succession are declared in one body, and bound indissolubly together." [n] "It is curious," adds he, "with what address the *temporary* solution of continuity in the line of succession" — for it was impossible for Mr. Burke not to admit that from this line a temporary deviation was made — "it is curious with what address this *temporary* solution is kept from the eye; whilst all that could be found in this act of necessity, to countenance the idea of an *hereditary succession* is brought forward, and fostered, and made the most of by the legislature." "The legislature," he proceeds, "had plainly in view the act of recognition of the first of Queen Elizabeth, and that of James the first, both acts strongly declaratory of the inheritable nature of the crown; and, in many parts, they follow, with a nearly literal precision, the words and even the form, which is found in these old declaratory statutes." [o] "They give the most solemn pledge, taken from the act of Queen Elizabeth, as solemn a pledge as ever was or can be given in favour of an hereditary succession. 'The lords spiritual and temporal, and commons, do, in the name of all the people aforesaid, most humbly and faithfully submit *themselves, their heirs and posterities for ever;* and do faithfully promise, that they will stand to, maintain, and defend their said majesties, and also the *limitation of the crown, herein* specified and contained, to the utmost of their power." [p]

I have mentioned above, that tyranny, at some times, is uniform in her principles: I have done her full justice: she is not so at all times. Of truth, liberty, and virtue, it is the exclusive prerogative to be always consistent.

Let us, for a moment, adopt the statement, which Mr. Burke has given us. Upon that statement I ask — if the humble and faithful submission of the parliament, in the name of all the people, was sufficient, in the time of Elizabeth, to bind themselves, their heirs and posterity for ever, to the line of hereditary succession; how came it to pass, that, in the time of William and Mary, the parliament, in the name of all the people, was justified in deviating, even for an instant, from the succession in that hereditary line? I ask again — if the humble and faithful submission of the parliament, in the name of all the people, was, in the sixteenth century, insufficient to bind their heirs and posterity in the seventeenth

century; how comes it to pass that, in the seventeenth century, the
humble and faithful submission of the parliament, in the name of all the
people, could bind their heirs and posterity in the eighteenth century?
Such a submission was either sufficient or it was not sufficient for that
binding purpose: let the disciples of the doctrine, which rests on this
dilemma, choose between the alternatives.

I have now no hesitation whether we should or should not subscribe
the creed of Mr. Burke: that creed, which is contradictory to itself, cannot, in every part, be sound and orthodox.

But, to say the truth, I should not have given myself the trouble of
delivering, nor you, of hearing these annotations upon it; unless it had
derived the support, which it claims, from the Commentaries on the laws
of England. The principles delivered in those Commentaries are never
matters of indifference: I have already mentioned,[q] "that when they are
not proper objects of imitation, they furnish excellent materials of
contrast."

Government, in my humble opinion, should be formed to secure and
to enlarge the exercise of the natural rights of its members; and every
government, which has not this in view, as its principal object, is not a
government of the legitimate kind.

Those rights result from the natural state of man; from that situation,
in which he would find himself, if no civil government was instituted.
In such a situation, a man finds himself, in some respects, unrelated to
others; in other respects, peculiarly related to some; in still other
respects, bearing a general relation to all. From his unrelated state, one
class of rights arises: from his peculiar relations, another class of rights
arises: from his general relations, a third class of rights arises. To each
class of rights, a class of duties is correspondent; as we had occasion to
observe and illustrate, when we treated concerning the general principles
of natural law.

In his unrelated state, man has a natural right to his property, to his
character, to liberty, and to safety. From his peculiar relations, as a husband, as a father, as a son, he is entitled to the enjoyment of peculiar
rights, and obliged to the performance of peculiar duties. These will be
specified in their due course. From his general relations, he is entitled to
other rights, simple in their principle, but, in their operation, fruitful
and extensive. His duties, in their principle and in their operation, may
be characterized in the same manner as his rights. In these general relations, his rights are, to be free from injury, and to receive the fulfilment
of the engagements, which are made to him: his duties are, to do no
injury, and to fulfil the engagements, which he has made. On these two

---

[q] Ante. p. 80.

pillars principally and respectively rest the criminal and the civil codes of the municipal law. These are the pillars of justice.

Of municipal law, the rights and the duties of benevolence are sometimes, though rarely, the objects. When they are so, they will receive the pleasing and the merited attention.

You now see the distribution, short, and simple, and plain, which will govern the subsequent part of my system of lectures. From this distribution, short, and simple, and plain as it is, you see the close and very interesting connexion between natural and municipal law. You see, to use again my Lord Bacon's language, how the streams of civil institutions flow from the fountain of justice.

I am first to show, that a man has a natural right to his property, to his character, to liberty, and to safety.

His natural right to his property, you will permit me, at present, to assume as a principle granted. I assume it for this reason; because I wish not to anticipate now what will be introduced, with much greater propriety and advantage, when I come to the second great division of my lectures, in which I am to treat concerning things.

To his character, every one has a natural right. A man's character may, I think, be described as the just result of those opinions, which ought to be formed concerning his talents, his sentiments, and his conduct. Opinions, upon this as upon every other subject, ought to be founded in truth. Justice, as well as truth, requires, concerning characters, accuracy and impartiality of opinion.

Under some aspects, character may be considered as a species of property; but, of all, the nearest, the dearest, and the most interesting. In this light it is viewed by the Poet of nature —

> The purest treasure mortal times afford
> Is spotless reputation.
> Who steals my purse, steals trash.
> 'Twas mine; 'tis his; and has been slave to thousands;
> But he who filches from me my good name,
> Takes from me that, which not enriches him,
> But makes me poor indeed.

By the exertion of the same talents and virtues, property and character both are often acquired: by vice and indolence, both are often lost or destroyed.

The love of reputation and the fear of dishonour are, by the all-gracious Author of our existence, implanted in our breasts, for purposes the most beneficent and wise. Let not these principles be deemed the growth of dispositions only which are weak or vain; they flourish most luxuriantly in minds, the strongest and, let me add, the most humble. Of the happiness of heaven, a part of the unerring description is — that it is "full of glory."

Well may character, then, be considered as one of the natural rights of man: well may it be classed among those rights, the enjoyment of which it is the design of good government and laws to secure and enlarge: well does it deserve their encouragement and protection; for, in its turn, it assists their operations, and supplies their deficiencies.

I remarked, a little while ago, that the rights and the duties of benevolence are but rarely, though they are at some times, the objects of municipal law. The remark may be extended to rights and duties of many other kinds. To many virtues, legal rewards are not, nor can they be, assigned: with legal impunity, many vices are, and must be, suffered to escape. But before a court of honour those qualities and sentiments and actions are amenable, which despise the subtlest process of the tribunals of law, and elude the keenest vigilance of the ministers of justice. This court, powerful in its sentences as well as extensive in its jurisdiction, decrees to virtue, and to the virtuous exertion of talents, a crown of fame, pure and splendid: vice, and idleness, less odious only than vice, it dooms to wear the badges of infamy, dirty and discoloured. This court, therefore, in a government of which virtue is the principle and vice is the bane, ought to receive, from all its institutions, the just degree of favour and regard.

> Honour 's a sacred tie —
> The noble mind's distinguishing perfection,
> That aids and strengthens virtue, where it meets her.

The Poet adds —

> And imitates her actions, where she is not.

The moral descriptions of Mr. Addison are seldom inaccurate. On this occasion, however, I must declare that I think him liable to the charge of inaccuracy. The counterfeit of virtue should not be dignified with the appellation of honour.

It is the sentiment of some writers, highly distinguished too by their liberal and manly principles, that honour is peculiar to governments which are monarchical. "In extreme political liberty," says the Marquis of Beccaria, "and in absolute despotism, all ideas of honour disappear, or are confounded with others. In the first case, reputation becomes useless from the despotism of the laws; and, in the second, the despotism of one man, annulling all civil existence, reduces the rest to a precarious temporary personality. Honour, then, is one of the fundamental principles of those monarchies, which are a limited despotism; and in these, like revolutions in despotick states, it is a momentary return to a state of nature and original equality." [r]

How prevalent even among enlightened writers, is the mistaken opinion, that government is subversive of equality and nature! Is it necessarily so? By no means. When I speak thus, I speak confidently, because I speak from principle fortified by fact. Let the constitution of the United States — let that of Pennsylvania be examined from the beginning to the end. No right is conferred, no obligation is laid on any, which is not laid or conferred on every, citizen of the commonwealth or Union — I think I may defy the world to produce a single exception to the truth of this remark. Now, as I showed at large in a former part of my lectures,[s] the original equality of mankind consists in an equality of their duties and rights.

That honour is the principle of monarchical governments, is the well known doctrine of the celebrated Montesquieu. But let us examine the nature and qualities of that honour which he describes. It is that honour which can subsist without honesty; for he says expressly,[t] that, in well policied monarchies, there are very few honest men. It is that honour which forbids not adulation, nor cunning, nor craft. It is that honour which judges of actions not as they are good, but as they are showy; not as they are just, but as they are grand; not as they are reasonable, but as they are extraordinary. It is, in one word, that honour, which fashions the virtues just as it pleases, and extends or limits our duties by its own whimsical taste. To this honour, indeed, truth in conversation is a necessary point: but is this for the sake of truth? By no means.

For the possession of this honour — vicious in its practice, and, even when right in its practice, vicious in its principle — a republican government will not, I presume, contend. But to that honour, whose connexion with virtue is indissoluble, a republican government produces the most unquestionable title. The principle of virtue is allowed to be hers: if she possesses virtue, she also possesses honour. I admire the fine moral and political instruction, as well as the elegant architectural taste, exhibited by the justly framed structure, in which the temple of honour was accessible only through the temple of virtue.

Viewed in this light, the honour of character is a property, which is, indeed, precious. But let it be remembered, that, in this view, it is a property, which must be purchased. To claim that reputation which we do not deserve, is as absurd, though it is not as bare-faced, as to claim that property which is not ours. The only difference is, that, in the former case, we claim generally that which belongs to another, while, in

[r] Bec. c. 9.   [s] Ante. pp. 240–241.   [t] Sp. L. b. 3. c. 6.

the latter case, we claim that which only does not belong to ourselves. In both cases, the claim is equally unfounded.

To bestow on another that reputation which he does not deserve, is equally profuse, and, in many instances, is more unjust than to bestow on him that property, to which he is not, on the principles either of justice, or charity, or benevolence, entitled. As it is equally profuse, it is more to be guarded against. In the latter case, we bestow what is our own, and, therefore, are inclined to be cautious: in the former case, we are apt to be inconsiderate, because what we bestow is not ours. Indiscriminate pride is not so odious, but it is as useless and it is as heedless as indiscriminate censure. In one important particular they precisely coincide. They have an equal tendency to destroy and to render inefficacious the great distinction between right and wrong, approbation and disapprobation, virtue and vice.

If it is unwarrantable to bestow reputation where it is not due, what epithet shall we assign to that conduct, which plucks the wreath of honour from those temples, around which it has been meritoriously placed? Robbery itself flows not from a fountain so rankly poisoned as that, which throws out the waters of malicious defamation.

The subject of reputation will again come under your view, when I treat concerning prosecutions for libels and actions of slander: both of which suppose an unjustifiable aggression of character. What I have now said will suffice to point to the general principles, on which those actions and prosecutions should be defended, supported, and determined.

Property must often — reputation must always be purchased: liberty and life are the gratuitous gifts of heaven.

That man is naturally free, was evinced in a former lecture:[u] I will not reiterate what has been advanced.

I shall certainly be excused from adducing any formal arguments to evince, that life, and whatever is necessary for the safety of life, are the natural rights of man. Some things are so difficult; others are so plain, that they cannot be proved. It will be more to our purpose to show the anxiety, with which some legal systems spare and preserve human life; the levity and the cruelty which others discover in destroying or sporting with it; and the inconsistency, with which, in others, it is, at some times, wantonly sacrificed, and, at other times, religiously guarded.

In Sparta, nothing was deemed so precious as the life of a citizen. And yet in Sparta, if an infant, newly born, appeared, to those who were appointed to examine him, ill formed or unhealthy, he was, without any further ceremony, thrown into a gulph near mount Taygetus.[v] Fortunate it was for Mr. Pope — fortunate it was for England, which boasts

_____

[u] Ante. p. 241.   [v] 4. Anac. 161. 162.

Mr. Pope — that he was not born in the neighbourhood of mount Taygetus.

At Athens,[w] the parent was empowered, when a child was born, to pronounce on its life or its death. At his feet it was laid: if he took it in his arms, this was received as the gracious signal for its preservation: if he deigned not a look of compassion on the fruit of his loins, it was removed and exposed. Over almost all the rest of Greece,[x] this barbarity was permitted or authorized.

In China, the practice of exposing new born children is said to have prevailed immemorially, and to prevail still. As the institutions of that empire are never changed, its situation is never improved.

Tacitus records it to the honour of the Germans, that, among them, to kill infants newly born was deemed a most flagitious crime. Over them, adds he, good manners have more power, than good laws have over other nations. This shows, that, in his time, the restraints of law began to be imposed on this unnatural practice; but that its inveteracy had rendered them still inefficacious.

Under the Roman commonwealth, no citizen of Rome was liable to suffer a capital punishment by the sentence of the law. But at Rome, the son held his life by the tenure of his father's pleasure. In the forum, the senate, or the camp, the adult son of a Roman citizen enjoyed the publick and private rights of a *person*: in his father's house, he was a mere *thing;*[y] confounded, by the laws, with the cattle, whom the capricious master might alienate or destroy, without being responsible to any tribunal on earth.

The gentle Hindoo is laudably averse to the shedding of blood; but he carries his worn out friend or benefactor to perish on the banks of the Ganges.

With consistency, beautiful and undeviating, human life, from its commencement to its close, is protected by the common law. In the contemplation of law, life begins when the infant is first able to stir in the womb.[z] By the law, life is protected not only from immediate destruction, but from every degree of actual violence, and, in some cases, from every degree of danger.

The grades of solicitude, discovered, by the law, on the subject of life, are marked, in the clearest manner, by the long and regular series of the different degrees of aggression, which it enumerates and describes — threatening, assault, battery, wounding, mayhem, homicide. How those different degrees may be justified, excused, alleviated, aggravated, redressed, or punished, will appear both in the criminal and in the civil code of our municipal law.

[w] 3. Anac. 4.   [x] Id. ibid.   [y] 8. Gibbon. 52.   [z] 1. Bl. Com. 129.

Thus much concerning the natural rights of man in what has been termed his unrelated state. I come now to specify and to consider those peculiar relations, by virtue of which a man is entitled to the enjoyment of peculiar rights, and obliged to the performance of peculiar duties.

I begin with marriage, which forms the near relation between husband and wife.

Whether we consult the soundest deductions of reason, or resort to the best information conveyed to us by history, or listen to the undoubted intelligence communicated in holy writ, we shall find, that to the institution of marriage the true origin of society must be traced. By that institution the felicity of Paradise was consummated; and since the unhappy expulsion from thence, to that institution, more than to any other, have mankind been indebted for the share of peace and harmony which has been distributed among them. "Prima societas in ipso conjugio est," says Cicero in his book of offices;[a] a work which does honour to the human understanding and the human heart.

The most ancient traditions of every country ascribe to its first legislators and founders, the regulations concerning the union between the sexes. The honour of instituting marriage among the Chinese, is assigned to their first sovereign,[b] Fo-hi. In order to render this great foundation of society respectable, he adjusted, as we are told,[c] the ceremonies, with which the contracts of marriage were accompanied.

Among the Egyptians, the law of marriage is said to have been established by Menes,[d] whose name is transmitted to us as that of their first king. The history of Abraham[e] affords a striking instance of the profound respect, which in his day was paid, in Egypt, to the conjugal union.

Cecrops has been already mentioned as the first great legislator of the Athenians, and as borrowing his institutions from those of the Egyptians. Accordingly we are informed, that he established, at Athens, the laws and ceremonies of marriage, in the same manner as they were observed and practised in Egypt. Polygamy was not permitted.[f] These regulations are described as the sources of virtues and enjoyments. They evinced the advantages of decency, the attractions of modesty, the happiness of loving, and the necessity of constancy in love.[g]

The founder of Rome made, concerning marriages, a law, which, on many accounts, will deserve our particular attention. It was expressed in these words: "let every wife, who by the holy laws of marriage falls into the power of a husband, enter with him into a community of goods and sacrifices." [h]

As marriage has been instituted by the first, it has always been en-

[a] L. 1. c. 17. [The first bond of union is in marriage itself.]
[b] 1. Gog. Or. L. 22.   [c] 3. Gog. Or. L. 313.   [d] 1. Gog. Or. L. 22.
[e] Gen. xii. 19.   [f] 2. Gog. Or. L. 19.   [g] 1. Anac. 7.   [h] 1. Rol. R. H. 32.

couraged by the wisest legislators. By the law of Moses,[i] a man, during one year after his marriage, was exempted from publick burthens, and from going to war. A regulation nearly similar, as we are told, was established by the Incas of Peru.[j] The *jus trium liberorum*, introduced by the prudent policy of Augustus, was a permanent inducement to matrimony at Rome.[k]

Legislators have, with great propriety, carried their views still farther; they have provided, as far as municipal law can provide, against the violation of rights, indispensably essential to the purity and harmony of the matrimonial union. Treachery, upon any occasion, is sufficient to stain a page in the annals of life; but perfidy against the solemn engagements of marriage obliterates the impression of happiness from every subsequent part of the conjugal history. Upon this subject, however, so interesting to the finest sentiments and emotions of the heart, every thing, that might be wished, cannot, we fear, be expected from the operation of human laws. Much must be left to the influence of that legitimate honour, which we have described as the inseparable friend and companion of virtue. From the bastard honour, which we likewise described, it would be ridiculous, in this case, to hope for any assistance. In this case, as in many others, that honour glories in its shame.

Concerning the ancient Germans, Tacitus, in his short but masterly account of their manners,[l] informs us, that among them the laws of marriage were rigidly observed; and that no part of their conduct was more exemplary.

We have seen the first institution of marriage among the Athenians and the Romans: a concise view of its history will be instructive and interesting.

In the heroick ages of Greece, we are told,[m] the rights of beauty and feminine weakness were highly respected and tenderly observed. The simplicity of those ages was equally remote from the cruel tyranny of savages, which condemns the fair sex to servitude, and the sordid selfishness of luxury, which considers them solely as instruments of pleasure. Hence those affecting scenes so exquisitely described by Homer, which, in the interviews of Hector and Andromache, exhibit the most striking image of nuptial felicity and love. But this beautiful picture of ancient manners was soon miserably defaced; and, in the degenerate periods of Greece, the fair sex were as much neglected and despised, as they had been loved and admired in the heroick ages.

In those degraded times, of which I am now obliged to speak, no pains were employed to render the Grecian females agreeable members of society, in any one part of their lives. Education was either entirely

---

[i] Deuter. xxiv. 5.   [j] 1. Gog. Or. L. 23.   [k] Mont. Sp. L. b. 23. c. 21.
[l] C. 18.   [m] 1. Gill. 52. 56.

withheld from them; or it was directed to such objects as were fitted to contract and debase, instead of elevating and enlarging the mind. When they were grown up, they were thrown away in marriage, without being consulted in the choice; and by entering into this new state, they found the severe guardianship of a father succeeded by the absolute dominion of a husband. At this period, even the laws of Athens countenanced this unworthy tenour of conduct: to secure the fortune of the husband was deemed an object of greater importance, than to protect the person and honour of the wife, from the outrage so peculiarly dreaded by female virtue.[n]

Let us now turn our attention to Rome. You recollect, that, by a law of Romulus, "the wife fell into the power of the husband." The law, which, on the whole, was very susceptible of a construction mild and generous, received from this part of it an interpretation most unwarrantable and severe. By this interpretation, coloured with the unnatural fiction, that, on a solemn marriage, the wife was adopted by the husband, he acquired over her all the tremendous plentitude of Roman paternal power. This extreme, as is usual, soon produced its opposite; and female servitude was exchanged for female licentiousness. The solemnities of the ancient nuptials were declined, in order to avoid the odious consequences superinduced upon them by the construction and fiction of law; and the parties, without losing, on either side, their independence or their name, subscribed definite and stipulated articles of a marriage contract. Their cohabitation, and the appearances of a common interest which they exhibited, were received, without investigation, as sufficient evidence of a regular and solemn marriage. Hence the detestable train of conjugal vice, infidelity, rage, rancour, and revenge, with which so many volumes of the Roman story are crowded and disgraced.

By the precepts of christianity, and the practice of the christians, the dignity of marriage was, however, restored.

In the eye of the common law, marriage appears in no other light than that of a civil contract: and to this contract the agreement of the parties, the essence of every rational contract, is indispensably required. If, therefore, either of the parties is incapable of agreeing, is unwilling to agree, or has not, in fact, as well as in ability and will, concluded the agreement; the marriage cannot be established by the principles of the common law.

Disability to contract marriage may arise from immature age. A man, as we have seen before,[o] may consent to marriage at fourteen; a woman, at twelve years of age. If, before those respective ages, a marriage take place, either party may, at the age of consent, but not before or after that age, disagree, declare the marriage void, and marry again: but if, at the age of consent, they agree to continue together, there is no occa-

---

[n] Gill. Lys. and Isoc. Inc. c.   [o] Ante. p. 412.

sion for another marriage between them; that which has taken place being deemed a marriage, though only an inchoate and imperfect one. If, at the time of the inchoate marriage, one of the parties is, and the other is not of the age of consent, when the last arrives at that age, the first as well as the last may disagree; for in a contract of marriage, both or neither must be bound.[p]

Disability to contract marriage may arise from the want of reason. Consent, as has been already observed, is essential to this, as to every other contract; but those who enjoy not a competent share of reason, are incapable of giving consent.[q]

By a law of Pennsylvania, certain degrees of consanguinity and affinity, specified in a table subjoined to the law, are disabilities to contract matrimony: and all marriages within those degrees are declared to be void. I refer you to the table specifying the degrees.[r]

One marriage undissolved, forms a disability to contract another. In such a case the second marriage is void as well as criminal.[s]

"Consensus non concubitus facit matrimonium," * is a maxim of our law; marriage, therefore, must be the effect of willingness as well as of capacity to contract it.[t]

When to the ability and will to contract, an actual contract is added; then the marriage is complete.

Before the time of Pope Innocent the third, there was no solemnization of marriage in the church; but the man came to the house where the woman inhabited, and led her home to his own house; which was all the ceremony then used.[u]

By an act of the legislature of Pennsylvania, all marriages, not forbidden by the law of God, shall be encouraged.[v] In the construction of legacies, it is a general rule, that all conditions are unlawful, which would operate against the liberty of marriage.[w]

It will be proper, in the next place, to consider the consequences of marriage.

The most important consequence of marriage is, that the husband and the wife become, in law, only one person: the legal existence of the wife is consolidated into that of the husband. Upon this principle of union, almost all the other legal consequences of marriage depend. This principle, sublime and refined, deserves to be viewed and examined on every side. Among human institutions, it seems to be peculiar to the common law. Peculiar as it is, however, among human institutions, it seems not uncongenial to the spirit of a declaration from a source higher than human — "They twain shall be one flesh."

[p] 1. Ins. 79. a. b.   [q] 1 Bl. Com. 438.   [r] 1. Laws Penn. 46.
[s] 1. Bl. Com. 436.   * [Mutual consent, not cohabitation, makes a marriage.]
[t] 1. Ins. 33.   [u] 3. Bac. 575.   [v] 1. Laws Penn. 36.   [w] Swin. 266.

Even of the common law, this was not always a principle. We are told by the learned Selden, that the Saxon wives were never one with their husbands; nor were they, as wives, under the view of the frank-pledge: a Saxon wife was obliged to give pledge by her friends, that she would do no wrong. She passed as an appurtenant to her husband, rather than one in unity with him: and her estate was rather appurtenant to her than to him: for if she failed in her good carriage to her husband, she was to make him amends out of her own estate; and if that was insufficient, then her pledges were to make satisfaction for her.[x] This interposition of friends between husband and wife, in matters respecting either their conduct or their claims, seems alien to the delicacy and nearness of the matrimonial connexion. On very pressing emergencies, indeed, it is necessary that the law should interfere, and on such emergencies we shall see that it does interfere; but the general presumption and the universal wish ought to be, that, between husband and wife, there subsist or may subsist no difference of will or of interest. Such accordingly, during many centuries past, has been the language of the law. Bracton, in the reign of Henry the third, informs us, that "husband and wife are as one person, because they are one flesh and blood."[y] Littleton, whose sayings are of such high authority, tells us repeatedly, "that the husband and the wife are but one person in the law."[z]

In pursuance of this principle, a crime, except treason and murder,[a] committed by the husband and wife, shall be charged against him solely; because the law will suppose that she acted under his influence or coercion. In pursuance of the same principle, a husband and wife cannot be witnesses for or against one another: if they were permitted to give testimony for one another, one maxim of the law would be violated — No one can be a witness in his own cause: if they were permitted to give testimony against one another, another maxim of the law would be violated — No one is obliged to accuse himself.

But, as has before been intimated, whenever urgent emergencies arise; whenever any outrage is threatened or committed against the peace or safety of society, as well as against the refined rules of the conjugal union; the law will interpose its authority, and, though it will not order, because it cannot enforce its orders for observing the latter, it will order, because it can enforce its orders for preserving the former.

The refined delicacy of the maxim — that husband and wife are considered as one person by our law — appears now in a beautiful and striking point of view. The rights, the enjoyments, the obligations, and the infelicities of the matrimonial state are so far removed from her protection or redress, that she will not appear as an arbitress; but, like a candid

---

[x] Bac. on Gov. 65.   [y] 1. Ins. 187 b.   [z] S. 168. 291.   [a] 1. Bl. Com. 444.

and benevolent neighbour, will presume, for she wishes, all to be well.

To the other rights and to the other duties of a marriage life, we must extend the observations which we have already applied to one of them. Reliance must be placed on that honour, which is the inseparable friend and companion of virtue.

I have spoken concerning those consequences of marriage, which relate to the persons of the husband and wife: the consequences which relate to their property, will be fully considered under the second great division of my system: you observe, that I carefully avoid the blending of the two divisions.

By that event which closes the scene of all sublunary enjoyments, marriage is dissolved: it may be dissolved sooner — by divorce.

To the law of England, two kinds of divorce are known — a divorce from the bed and the table — and a divorce from the chains — the metaphor is proper on this occasion — a divorce from the chains of matrimony. The propriety of the first kind, I am, I confess, at a loss to explain: that of the second kind is frequently obvious. When, as we have seen, the impression of happiness must be obliterated from every succeeding part of the conjugal history, why should any more blackened pages be added to the inauspicious volume? But of causes which are slight or trivial, a divorce should, by no means, be permitted to be the effect. When divorces can be summoned to the aid of levity, of vanity, or of avarice, a state of marriage becomes frequently a state of war or stratagem; still more frequently, a state of premeditated and active preparation for successful stratagems and war. Such was the case in ancient Rome. "Passion, interest, or caprice," says the Historian of her falling state, "suggested daily motives for the dissolution of marriage; a word, a sign, a message, the mandate of a freeman declared the separation; the most tender of human connexions was degraded to a transient society of profit or pleasure." [b]

—— Sic fiunt octo mariti
Quinque per autumnos.*

Juv. sat. VI. 20.

Non consulum numero, sed maritorum annos suos computant.†

Sen. de. Benef. III. 16.

Both these remarks are levelled particularly at the female sex: but who drew the picture, in which the lion was injuriously represented?

Cicero, after having said, as we have seen, "prima societas in ipso con-

[b] 8. Gibbon. 62.
* [Thus eight husbands are made in the space of five autumns.]
† [They compute their years not by the number of consuls, but by the number of their husbands.]

jugio est," adds, "proxima in liberis." I consider, in the next place, the relation of parent and child.

The transition is, indeed, a natural one. The sentiments of parental affection are generally warm and tender, in proportion to those of conjugal love. The sentiments of filial duty are generally sincere and respectful, in proportion to those of parental affection.

It is the duty of parents to maintain their children decently, and according to their circumstances; to protect them according to the dictates of prudence; and to educate them according to the suggestions of a judicious and zealous regard for their usefulness, their respectability, and their happiness.

The formidable power of a Roman father is unknown to the common law. But it vests in the parent such authority as is conducive to the advantage of the child. When it is necessary — and a real necessity exists much more rarely than is often imagined — a moderate chastening may be administered; but every milder means should be previously used. Part of his authority he may delegate to the person intrusted with his child's education:[e] that person acts then in the place, and he ought to act with the disposition, of a parent. The legal power of a father ceases, when the child attains the age of twenty one years.

But, — for we now turn to the duties of children — as obedience and subjection to their parents are due from them during their minority; honour and reverence are naturally and justly expected from them ever afterwards. If it become necessary, the child should, according to his circumstances, maintain the parent: 'tis but a natural and grateful return for the maintenance, which the parent has given to the child.

The decent reserve which the common law has shown, with regard to the relation between parent and child, should be admired, and may be accounted for on the same principles, which were observed under the relation of husband and wife. The civil law interposed in the nice feelings and tender transactions of both relations, with a rude and indelicate management. In that law, we find an enumeration of fourteen different reasons, for which a father may disinherit his child. Would it not have been much more natural, to have left, as the common law has left, this subject to the decision of that judge, which holds its tribunal in every parent's breast?

But, here as on former occasions, I refer the questions of property — and there are very important ones — arising from this relation, to the full discussion, which will be given under the second division of my system.

A bastard is one who is born out of lawful marriage. By law, he is

---

[e] 1. Bl. Com. 453.

considered *quasi nullius filius.* But surely it is the natural duty of his parents to maintain, to protect, and to educate him.

The rules which govern the relation between a father and his child, govern, but in an inferiour degree, and for a shorter time, that relation, which is substituted in the place of the other, between a guardian and his ward. On this subject, therefore, it will not be necessary to descend into particulars.

I come now to examine the relation between a master and his servants.

Slavery, or an absolute and unlimited power, in the master, over the life and fortune of the slave, is unauthorized by the common law. Indeed, it is repugnant to the principles of natural law, that such a state should subsist in any social system. The reasons, which we sometimes see assigned for the origin and the continuance of slavery, appear, when examined to the bottom, to be built upon a false foundation. In the enjoyment of their persons and of their property, the common law protects all. With regard, however, to any right, which one man may have acquired to the personal service of another, the case is very different. This right the common law will support.[d] He, to whose service this right is acquired, is only in the same state of subjection, to which every servant and apprentice is obliged, and finds it his interest, to submit.

The contract between a master and a servant arises upon the hiring. If a servant is retained generally, without expressing any limited time, the law will construe it to be for a year:[e] the reasonable foundation of this rule is, that, through the revolutions of the seasons, equality shall be preserved in the contract; that the master shall not have it in his power to dismiss the servant when there is little work to be done; nor the servant have it in his power to depart when there is much. The contract, however, may be made for any term longer or shorter than a year.[f] If, during the term of the contract, the servant become sick, this is a condition incident to humanity. In his sickness, the master is bound to take care of him, and provide for him; nor can a deduction of wages be made for the time, during which he is detained from service.[g]

If a servant marry, the marriage dissolves not the contract to serve:[h] if, without any reasonable cause, he depart from his service, within the term, for which he is retained; he can recover no wages.[i] A contract for service is, on both sides, personal, and is discharged by the death of either of the parties.[j] This is the rule at the common law.

A master, we are told, may justify an assault in defence of his servant; and a servant, in defence of his master; the former, because he has an interest in the service of the latter; the latter, because the defence of the

[d] 1. Bl. Com. 423. 425.   [e] Ins. 42. b.   [f] 1. Bl. Com. 425.   [g] 2. Burr. 948.
[h] F. N. B. 168.   [i] Wood. Ins. 51.   [j] Str. 1267. Wood. Ins. 51.

former is considered as part of the consideration, for which wages are stipulated and received.[k] The law is unquestionably so as is here stated: the reasons assigned for it, I am inclined to believe, are founded on principles much too narrow. The defence of one's own person is a part of the law of all self preservation. The defence of the person of another is, I think, a part of the law of humanity. This point, however, which is of a very general importance to the peace and security of society, will merit an investigation in another place.

The common law, retaining the refined delicacy which we have observed oftener than once, will not, without strong necessity, inspect or interpose in the interiour government of a family. That sufficient authority, however, may exist to preserve order in the domestick department — a department of mighty moment to human happiness — the law invests the master with a power to correct, but moderately, his servant or apprentice, for negligence or for other misbehaviour. We have seen that "sine imperio, nulla domus stare potest." [1] Besides; in the regulation which the law has drawn concerning an atrocious outrage, in which she found it necessary to interpose, she has with a pencil exquisitely fine, but whose strokes can be traced by a discerning eye, marked a line of general direction for the relative rights and duties of a master and servant. From the latter to the former, she expressly requires a species, though an inferiour species, of allegiance: from the former to the latter, she, by a necessary consequence, strongly inculcates a species, though an interiour species, of protection. These remarks will receive illustration, when the crime of petty treason shall come under our view.

Apprentices are a species of servants. They are usually bound for a term of years, to serve and to be instructed by their masters in their profession or trade.

Persons under the age of twenty one years cannot, by the common law, bind themselves apprentices, in such a manner as to become liable to an action for departing from their service, or for other breaches of their indentures. For this reason, it is necessary that the parent, guardian, or some friend of the apprentice be bound for the faithful discharge of his duty.[m] But it is not every minor, who has such connexions, willing to be bound for him.

By the custom of London, an infant, unmarried and above the age of fourteen years, may bind himself apprentice to a freeman of London; and the covenants in the indenture of apprenticeship shall be as valid, as if the apprentice had been of full age.[n] The spirit of this custom has been adopted and enlarged by the legislature of Pennsylvania. A minor, bound an apprentice with the assent of the parent, the guardian, or the next

[k] 1. Bl. Com. 429.   [1] Cic. de leg. 1. 3.   [m] 3. Bac. 547.   [n] Id. 347.

friend, or with the assent of the overseers of the poor, and approbation of any two justices, is bound as fully as if of age at the time of making the indentures. But an apprenticeship under this very excellent law must expire, in the case of a male, at twenty one, in the case of a female, at eighteen years of age.[o]

To qualify one for the skilful and successful exercise of a trade or profession, an apprenticeship is certainly useful; but, by the common law, it is not necessary. It was resolved, as we are informed in one of the reports of my Lord Coke, that, at the common law, no man can be prohibited from exercising his industry in any lawful occupation; for the law hates idleness, the mother of all evil, and especially in young men, who, in their youth, which is their seed time, ought to learn lawful trades and sciences, which are profitable to the commonwealth, and of which they themselves may reap the harvest in their future years. Besides; the common law abhors all monopolies, which forbid any from working in any lawful trade. If he who undertakes to work is unskillful, his ignorance is his sufficient punishment; for "quilibet quærit in qualibet arte peritos;" * and if, in performing his work, he injures his employer, the law has provided an action to recover damages for the injury done.[p] To every monopoly, we are told by the same book in another place,[q] there are three inseparable incidents against the commonwealth. 1. The price of the commodity is raised. 2. The quality of the commodity is debased. 3. Those who formerly maintained themselves and their families by the same profession or trade, are impoverished, and reduced to a state of beggary and idleness.

Besides apprentices, and those to whom the name of servant is appropriated in the language of common life, the relation of servant is extended, by the language and by many rules of the law, to others in a superiour ministerial capacity — to bailiffs, to stewards, to agents, to factors, to attornies, and to the masters of vessels considered in their relation to the owners of them.[r]

Of many acts of the servant, the master is entitled to receive the advantage: of many others, he is obliged to suffer or to compensate for the injury. In each series of cases — it would be, here, improper to attempt an enumeration of particulars — In each series of cases, the principle is the same. Whatever is done by the servant, in the usual course of his business, is presumed, and fairly presumed, to be done by the command, or the authority, tacit or express, of the master; whatever is done by the master's command, is considered, and justly considered, as done by the master in person: "Qui facit per alium, facit per se." †

[o] 1. Laws Penn. 540. s. 1.　　* [Experts are sought in any occupation.]
[p] 11. Rep. 53. b. 54.　　[q] Id. 86. b.　　[r] 3. Bac. 544.
† [Who acts through another, acts himself.]

Thus much concerning the relation between master and servant: and thus much concerning the component parts of that important and respectable, though small and sometimes neglected establishment, which is denominated a family. "Id autem est" — says Cicero,[s] in the fine and just passage already cited oftener than once — "id autem est principium urbis, et quasi seminarium reipublicæ." It is the principle of the community; it is that seminary, on which the commonwealth, for its manners as well as for its numbers, must ultimately depend. As its establishment is the source, so its happiness is the end, of every institution of government, which is wise and good.

In the introduction to my lectures[t] I told my hearers, that "publick law and publick government were not made for themselves;" but that "they were made for something better;" that "I meant society;" that "I meant particularly domestick society." Perhaps, it was then thought, by some, that all this was introduced merely for the sake of an encomium — but, by the way, an encomium severely just — with which it was accompanied. In the regular course of my system, the sentiment has now undergone a scrutinizing analysis in the most minute detail. I can appeal to such, if any such, who thought otherwise then — I can appeal to all, who have formed their opinion now, whether the sentiment, in all its parts, and in all its objects too, is not founded in sound politicks and genuine philosophy.

In digesting a system of English law a little more than a century ago, it would have been necessary to notice and explain another domestick relation — not, indeed, founded in nature — that of lord and villain. Of the feudal city, however, we can still recollect the exteriour battlements and towers, cumbrous, but disproportioned and insecure, and the interiour buildings and halls, spacious, but comfortless and inconvenient. In ruins it now lies. With sentiments very different from those of regret, we can exclaim over it — *fuit servitus.*[u]

I have now done with considering the peculiar relations of man in a state of society, independent of civil government. But in that state, as he bears peculiar relations to some, so he bears a general relation to all. From that general relation, rights and duties result. His rights are, to receive the fulfilment of the engagements which are made to him, and to be free from injury to his peculiar relations, to his property, to his character, to his liberty, to his person. His duties are, to fulfil the engagements, which he has made; and to do no injury, in the same extensive meaning, in which he would wish and has a right to suffer none.

[s] De Off. 1. 1. c. 17. [Moreover it is the beginning of the city, and the nursery, as it were, of the commonwealth.]

[t] Ante. p. 86.

[u] Fuit Ilium. [*Fuit servitus:* slavery is a thing of the past; *fuit Ilium:* Troy is a thing of the past.]

In a former lecture,[v] when I delineated at large the principles and the character of the social man, these rights and duties received their illustration, and were shown to be laid deeply in the human frame. To your recollection of what was then said, I beg leave to refer you. These rights and duties are indeed, as has been observed, great pillars on which chiefly rest the criminal and the civil codes of the municipal law. It would surely be preposterous to undermine their foundation, with a view to give strength or stability to what they support — to unfix what rests on the immovable basis of nature, and to place it on the tottering institutions of man.

I here close my examination into those natural rights, which, in my humble opinion, it is the business of civil government to protect, and not to subvert, and the exercise of which it is the duty of civil government to enlarge, and not to restrain. I go farther; and now proceed to show, that in peculiar instances, in which those rights can receive neither protection nor reparation from civil government, they are, notwithstanding its institution, entitled still to that defence, and to those methods of recovery, which are justified and demanded in a state of nature.

The defence of one's self, justly called the primary law of nature,[w] is not, nor can it be abrogated by any regulation of municipal law.[x] This principle of defence is not confined merely to the person; it extends to the liberty and the property of a man: it is not confined merely to his own person; it extends to the persons of all those, to whom he bears a peculiar relation — of his wife, of his parent, of his child, of his master, of his servant:[y] nay, it extends to the person of every one, who is in danger;[z] perhaps, to the liberty of every one, whose liberty is unjustly and forcibly attacked. It becomes humanity as well as justice.

The particular occasions on which the defensive principle may be exercised, and the degrees to which the exercise of it may be carried, will appear in subsequent parts of my lectures: for instead of being disavowed, it is expressly recognised by our municipal institutions.

[v] Ante. pp. 232–233.
[w] Est igitur, judices, hæc non scripta, sed nata lex; quam non dedicimus, accepimus, legimus; verum ex natura ipsa arripuimus, hausimus, expressimus; ad quam non docti, sed facti, non instituti, sed imbuti sumus; ut si vita nostra in aliquas insidias, si in vim, si in tela aut latronum aut inimicorum incidisset, omnis honesta ratio esset expediendæ salutis: silent enim leges inter arma; nec se expectari jubent, cum ei qui expectare velit, ante injusta pœna luenda sit, quam justa repetenda. Cic. pro Mil. [There exists, Judges, this law which is not written, but inborn; we have not learned it, received it, or read it, but from nature herself we have snatched, imbibed, and extorted it; a law to which we are not trained, but in which we are made; in which we are not instructed, but with which we are imbued; the law, namely, that whenever our life falls into some ambush, is attacked, or is set upon by brigands or enemies, there is every honest reason for saving one's self: for amid arms the laws are silent, and they do not order a man to wait around, since he who will wait must suffer an unjust penalty before he obtains a just retribution.]
[x] 3. Bl. Com. 4.   [y] Id. 3.   [z] 1. Haw. 131.

As a man is justified in defending, so he is justified in retaking, his property, or his peculiar relations, when from him they are unjustly taken and detained. When and how this recaption may be made, will also appear in the proper places. For this redress, dictated by nature, is also recognised by municipal law.

Under the same description, the right of abating or removing nuisances may, in many instances, be classed.

This long investigation concerning natural rights and natural remedies, I conclude by answering the question, with which I introduced it: man does not exist for the sake of government, but government is instituted for the sake of man. The course of it has naturally led me to consider a number of interesting subjects, in a view somewhat different, perhaps, from that, in which we see them considered in some of our law books; but in a view perfectly consonant to the soundest rules and principles of our law.

PART THREE

I

OF THE NATURE OF CRIMES; AND THE NECESSITY AND PROPORTION OF PUNISHMENTS

HITHERTO, we have considered the rights of men, of citizens, of publick officers, and of publick bodies: we must now turn our eyes to objects less pleasing — the violations of those rights must be brought under our view. Man is sometimes unjust: sometimes he is even criminal: injuries and crimes must, therefore, find their place in every legal system, calculated for man. One consolatory reflection, however, will greatly support us in our progress through this uninviting part of our journey: we shall be richly compensated when we reach its conclusion. The end of criminal jurisprudence is the *prevention* of crimes.

What is an injury? — What is a crime? — What is reparation? — What is punishment? — These are questions, which ought to be considered in a separate, and also in a connected, point of view. At some times, they have been too much blended. In some instances, the injury and the reparation have been lost in the crime and the punishment. In other instances, the crime and the punishment have, with equal impropriety, been sunk in the reparation and injury. At other times, they have been kept too much apart. The crime has been considered as altogether unconnected with the injury, and the punishment as altogether unconnected with reparation. In other instances, the reparation only has been regarded, and no attention has been given to the punishment: the injury only has been calculated; but no computation has been made concerning the crime.

An injury is a loss arising to an individual, from the violation or infringement of his right.

A reparation is that, which compensates for the loss sustained by an injury.

A crime is an injury, so atrocious in nature, or so dangerous in its example, that, besides the loss which it occasions to the individual who suffers by it, it affects, in its immediate operation or in its consequences, the interest, the peace, the dignity, or the security of the publick. Offences and misdemeanors denote inferiour crimes.

A punishment is the infliction of that evil, superadded to the reparation, which the crime, superadded to the injury, renders necessary, for the purposes of a wise and good administration of government.

Concerning an injury and a reparation, and the measures by which each of them ought to be estimated, it will not be necessary to say much; because, with regard to them, much confusion or mistake has not been introduced into the theory or practice of the law.

Concerning crimes and punishments, and concerning the relation between a crime and an injury, and between punishment and reparation, the case is widely different indeed. On those subjects, an endless confusion has prevailed, and mistakes innumerable have been committed. On those subjects, therefore, it will be proper to be full; and it will certainly be attempted — I promise not success in the attempt — to be both accurate and perspicuous.

From an inattention or a disregard to the great principle — that government was made for the sake of man, some writers have been led to consider crimes, in their origin and nature as well as in their degrees and effects, as different from injuries; and have, consequently, taught, that without any injury to an individual, a crime might be committed against the government. Suppose, says one of the learned commentators on Grotius, that one has done neither wrong nor injury to any individual, yet if he has committed something which the law has prohibited, it is a crime, which demands reparation; because the right of the superiour is violated, and because an injury is offered to the dignity of his character.[a] How naturally one mistake leads to another! A mistake in legislation produces one in criminal jurisprudence. A law which prohibits what is neither a wrong nor an injury to any one! What name does it deserve? We have seen[b] that a law which is merely harmless without being tyrannical, is itself a harm; and should be removed.

But this doctrine is unsupported by sound legal principle. Every crime includes an injury: every offence is also a private wrong: it affects the publick, but it affects the individual likewise. It is true indeed, that, in very gross injuries, we seldom hear of any satisfaction being awarded to the individual, for reasons, the propriety of which will, by and by, be examined. But in offences of an inferiour nature, the distinction, and, at the same time, the connexion between the crime and the injury is most

[a] 2. War. Bib. 15.   [b] Ante. p. 579.

accurately marked and preserved. For a battery, he who commits it may be indicted. Violence against the person of an individual is a disturbance of the publick peace. On this disturbance punishment may be inflicted. But in the crime and the punishment, the injury is not sunk, nor is the reparation lost. The party who has suffered the violence may bring his action against the party who has committed it: and recover in damages a satisfaction for the loss, which has been sustained.

The doctrine, that a crime may be committed against the publick, without any injury being done to an individual, is as little consonant to the history, as it is to the principles of criminal jurisprudence. Among the Saxons, as we are informed by Mr. Selden, the most ancient way of proceeding, in criminal causes, was by an appeal of the party complaining. But afterwards, in cases which concerned damage, injury, or violence done to the body of a man or to his estate, the king — who represented the publick — was found to be therein prejudiced, beside the prejudice done immediately to the subject: and upon this ground, a way was found out to punish the offender by indictment, beside the satisfaction done to the party wronged.[c]

In the very early periods of society, those actions, even the most atrocious, which now are viewed and prosecuted as solely crimes against the state, were considered and resented merely as private injuries. In those ages, the conceptions of men were too crude to consider an injury done to an individual, as a crime committed against the publick; they viewed it only as a prejudice to the party, or the relations of the party, who were immediately affected. The privilege of resenting private injuries, in the opinion of a very ingenious writer on the history of the criminal law,[d] was that private right which was the latest of being surrendered to society. An improvement in government, so opposite to a strong propensity of human nature, could not have been instantaneous. The progressive steps leading to its completion were slow and almost imperceptible.

Coincident, in a very considerable degree, with these sentiments and observations, is a part of the law and practice of England, which at this moment subsists in its full force — I mean the law and practice concerning appeals, particularly appeals of death. An appeal is the party's private action, seeking satisfaction for the injury done him; and at the same time, prosecuting for the crown in respect of the offence against the publick. On an appeal, the benign prerogative of mercy cannot be exercised; because, saith the law,[e] the plaintiff has an interest in the judgment. This interest, however, may be released; and the release will be a bar to the proceedings on an appeal.

[c] Bac. on Gov. 53.   [d] Kaims. Hist. L. Tr. 19, 20.   [e] 5. Rep. 506.

These observations, drawn from so many separate sources, combine in the result, that a crime against the publick has its foundation in an injury against an individual. We shall see, in the progress of our investigation, that as, in the rude ages of society, the crime was too much overlooked; so, in times more refined, there has been a disposition, too strong, to overlook the injury.

Concerning the standard, by which crimes should be measured in municipal law, there has been much diversity of sentiment among writers, even the wisest and most enlightened. The law of nature, it is admitted on all hands, measures crimes by the intention, and not by the event. Should a standard, different from that which has been established by unerring wisdom, be adopted by uninformed man? Should not that rule, which is observed by the law divine, be observed, in humble imitation, by laws which are human? It is said, not; and it is said, that this difference must be accounted for by those peculiar attributes of the divine nature, which distinguish the dispensations of supreme wisdom from the proceedings of human tribunals. A being whose all-seeing eye observes the inmost recesses of the heart, and whose outstretched arm no flight or stratagem can elude or escape — such a being may consider and may punish every crime in exact proportion to the quantity of intrinsick guilt, which is contained in it. But with those to whom the trust and authority of human government is committed, the case is greatly different. Their power and their knowledge are limited by many imperfections: speed may remove, artifice may cover the object of punishment from their view or their grasp: by them, therefore, crimes must be considered in proportion to the ease and security with which they are committed or concealed, and not in strict proportion to their degrees of inherent criminality. Such, or nearly such, seem to be the sentiments of Mr. Paley.[f]

The Marquis of Beccaria goes farther: he thinks himself authorized to assert, that crimes are to be measured only by the injury done to society. They err, therefore, says he, who imagine that a crime is greater or less according to the intention of the person by whom it is committed; for this will depend on the actual impression of objects on the senses, and on the previous disposition of the mind; and both of these will vary in different persons, and even in the same person at different times, according to the succession of ideas, passions, and circumstances. Upon that system, it would be necessary to form, not only a particular code for every individual, but a new penal law for every crime. Men with the best intentions, do the greatest injury, and with the worst, the most essential services to society. That crimes are to be estimated by the injury done to society, adds he, is one of those palpable truths, which, though

[f] 2. Paley, 291. 292.

evident to the meanest capacity, yet, by a combination of circumstances, are known only to a few thinking men, in every nation and in every age.[g]

Sir William Blackstone, in one part of his Commentaries, seems to adopt these sentiments. All crimes, says he, are to be estimated according to the mischiefs which they produce in civil society.[h]

Mr. Eden, in one part of his book on the principles of penal law, tells us, agreeably to the same sentiments, that crimes are of temporal creation, and to be estimated in proportion to their pernicious effects on society:[i] in another part, he says, that, in some cases, it is necessary to punish the offence without any research into its motive; and that, in every case, it is impracticable for lawgivers to assume the divine attribute of animadverting upon the fact, only according to the internal malice of the intention:[j] in a third place, however, he expresses himself in the following manner: "It is true, that crimes are to be estimated, in some degree, by the actual mischief done to society; because the internal malignity of mankind is not within the cognizance of human tribunals. But if this position were received in its fullest latitude, it would prove too much; it would prove that every act of homicide is equally criminal; and that the intention is, in no case, to be considered:"[k] in a fourth place, he considers its flagitiousness as the standard, by which a crime should be measured; and informs us, that, by its flagitiousness, he means its abstract nature and turpitude, in proportion to which, the criminal should be considered as more or less dangerous to society:[l] in a fifth place, he intimates the same sentiment, that "the malignity of the fact is the true measure of the crime."[m]

Is it not shocking to reason, says Mr. Dagge, and destructive of virtue, to contend, that the ill consequence of an act is more to be considered than its immorality? To disregard a crime, however heinous, because it may be supposed not to have a bad effect on society; and to punish slight offences severely, because they tend more immediately to disturb the publick peace, is to sacrifice moral equity to political expediency. But, in fact, there is no real necessity for making such a sacrifice. If we would effectually provide for the lasting peace of society, we should first regard private offences, which are the sources of publick crimes. The subtle distinctions, which casuists make between moral and political delinquencies, are offensive to common sense.[n]

Concerning the standard by which punishments should be measured in municipal law, there has been, as might be expected, as much diversity of sentiment, as concerning the standard for the measure of crimes.

Publick utility, says Mr. Eden, is the measure of human punishments; and that utility is proportioned to the efficacy of the example.[o]

[g] Bec. c. 7. 8.　　[h] 4. Bl. Com. 41.　　[i] Eden. 89.　　[j] Id. 12.
[k] Eden. 12.　　[l] Id. 8.　　[m] Id. 10.　　[n] 1. Dag. 335. 343.　　[o] Eden. 151.

Liberty, says Montesquieu,[p] is in its highest perfection, when criminal laws derive each punishment from the particular nature of the crime. Then the punishment does not flow from the capriciousness of the legislator, but from the very nature of the thing; and man uses no violence to man.

Among crimes of different natures, says Sir William Blackstone, those should be most severely punished, which are most destructive to the publick safety and happiness: and, among crimes of an equal malignity, those, which a man has the most frequent and easy opportunities of committing, which cannot be so easily guarded against as others; and which, therefore, the offender has the greatest inducement to commit.[q]

Much to the same purpose are the expressions of Mr. Paley — the punishment should be in a proportion compounded of the mischief of the crime, and the ease with which it is executed.[r]

The end of human punishment, says Mr. Paley, in another place, should regulate the measure of its severity.[s] To the propriety of this rule every one will subscribe; but it throws us back upon another, concerning which there is an equal variety and opposition of sentiment.

Criminals, says Plato in his book concerning laws, are punished, not because they have offended, for what is done can never be undone, but that they may not offend.[t]

The very learned Mr. Selden objects to this doctrine, and says, that the antecedent crime is the essence of punishment.[u]

The amendment of the criminal is assigned by some as the end of punishment. To put it out of his power to do future mischief, is the end proposed by others. To deter from the imitation of his example, is that proposed by a third class of writers. Reparation to the injured, is an end recommended by a fourth class.

Almost all agree, that between crimes and punishments there ought to be a proportion: but how can this proportion be fixed among those, who are so much at variance with regard to the measure of the objects, between which it confessedly ought to subsist?

If there is so much diversity and contrariety of opinion respecting the principles, how much greater diversity and contrariety of conduct may we expect to find with regard to the execution, of the criminal law. Nay, how often shall we find those rules violated in its practice, the propriety of which is agreed in its theory.

The theory of criminal law has not, till lately, been a subject of much attention or investigation. The Marquis of Beccaria led the way. His performance derives much importance from the sentiments and principles, which it contains: it derives, perhaps, more from those, which its appear-

[p] Sp. L. b. 12. c. 4.   [q] 4. Bl. Com. 16.   [r] 2. Paley. 290.   [s] Id. 287.
[t] 1. Dag. 203. Eden. 6.   [u] 1. Dag. 203.

ance has excited in others. It induced several of the most celebrated
literati in Europe to think upon the subject. The science, however, is, as
yet, but in a weak and infantine state. To convince you that it is so, I
need only refer you to the unsatisfactory, nay, the contradictory sentiments, of which I have given you an account, with regard to the two
great heads of crimes and punishments. That account has been extracted
from the most celebrated writers on the subject — from writers, indeed,
who, on any subject, would deserve celebrity.

To give you a history of the practice of criminal law would be a task,
not difficult, because the materials are very copious; but it would be very
disgusting both to you and to me. I draw the character of this practice
from one, who appears to have a head and a heart well qualified to feel
and to judge upon the subject — I mean the Author of the principles of
penal law. "The perusal of the first volume of the English State Trials," ᵛ
says he, "is a most disgustful drudgery." "The proceedings of our criminal courts at this era" — meaning that which preceded the revolution —
"are so disgraceful, not only to the nation, but to human nature, that, as
they cannot be disbelieved, I wish them to be buried in oblivion. From
oblivion, it is neither my duty nor inclination to rescue them." — No; nor
to rescue from oblivion the proceedings of other ages and of other countries, equally disgraceful and disgustful. I recite only a single instance.

Mr. Pope, in his picturesque and interesting retrospect of the barbarous
reigns of the Conqueror and his son, asks, alluding to the laws of the
forests —

> What wonder then, if beast or subject slain
> Were equal crimes in a despotick reign?
> Both, doom'd alike, for sportive tyrants bled,
> But while the subject starv'd, the beast was fed.ʷ

Many, I dare say, have considered this as a fine fanciful description of
the Poet. It has, however, been exceeded by the strict severity of fact.
We are, in the Life of Mr. Turgot, told in plain and sober prose, that so
rigorous were the forest laws of France even so lately, that a peasant,
charged with having killed a wild boar, alleged as an alleviation of the
charge, that he thought it was a man.ˣ

In these lectures, I have had frequent occasion to observe and to regret
the imperfection and the impropriety, which are seen too plainly in the
civil codes and institutions of Europe: it is the remark — it is the just
remark of Sir William Blackstone, that, "in every country of Europe,
the criminal law is more rude and imperfect than the civil." ʸ Instead of
being, as it ought to be, an emanation from the law of nature and morality; it has too often been avowedly and systematically the reverse. It

---

ᵛ Eden. 199. ʷ Windsor Forest. ˣ Pri. Lect. 297. ʸ 4. Bl. Com. 3.

has been a combination of the strong against the weak, of the rich against the poor, of pride and interest against justice and humanity. Unfortunately, indeed, it is, that this has been the case; for we may truly say, that on the excellence of the criminal law, the liberty and the happiness of the people chiefly depend.

By this time, you see very clearly, that I was well warranted to announce, even in the summary of my system, that the criminal law greatly needs reformation. I added — In the United States, the seeds of reformation are sown. Those seeds, and the tender plants which from some of them are now beginning to spring, let it be our care to discover and to cultivate. From those weeds, luxuriant and strong, with which they are still intermingled, and by which, if they continue so, they will indubitably be choked, let it be our business industriously to separate them. From those beasts of the forest, by whom, if left unguarded, they will unquestionably be devoured, let it be our effort vigorously to defend them.

In the fields of the common law, which, for ages past, have lain waste and neglected, some of those seeds and plants will, on an accurate inquiry, be found. In the gardens of the American constitutions, others, and the most choice of them, have been sown and planted by liberal hands.

The generical term used immemorially by the common law, to denote a crime, is *felony*. True indeed it is, that the idea of felony is now very generally and very strongly connected with capital punishment; so generally and so strongly, that if an act of parliament denominates any new offence a felony, the legal inference drawn from it is, that the offender shall be punished for it capitally. But this inference, whatever legal authority it may now have acquired, is by no means entitled to the merit of critical accuracy. At this moment, every felony does not, in England, receive a punishment which is capital: petit larceny is a felony. At this moment, one felony escapes in England, as it must in all other countries, every degree of punishment that is human: suicide is a felony. At the common law, few felonies, indeed, were punished with death.

Treason is now considered, both in legal and in vernacular language, as a species of crime distinct from that of felony; but originally it was not so considered. "In ancient time," says my Lord Coke,[z] "every treason was comprehended under the name of felony." Indeed it was so, down even to the time of Edward the third; for the famous statute of treasons, made in his reign, uses these expressions — "treason or *other* felony."

It will be very important to ascertain the true meaning of a term, employed so extensively and so long by the common law, to convey the idea of a crime.

In order to ascertain the true meaning, it is frequently of importance

[z] 3. Ins. 15.

to ascertain the true etymology, of a term; and in order to ascertain that of the term *felony*, much learned labour has been bestowed by juridical lexicographers and criticks.

Sir William Blackstone asserts that its original is undoubtedly feudal; and being so, we ought to look for its derivation in the Teutonick or German language; and he prefers that given by Sir Henry Spelman; according to whom, *felon* is taken from two northern words, *fee*, which signifies, as all know, the fief, feud, or beneficiary estate; and *lon*, which signifies price or value. Felony is, therefore, the same as *pretium feudi*, the consideration, for which a man gives up his fief; as we say, in common speech, such an act is as much as your life or estate is worth. "In this sense," says Sir William, "it will clearly signify the feudal forfeiture, or act, by which an estate is forfeited or escheats to the lord." [a] He mentions two other derivations, and adds — "Sir Edward Coke, as his manner is, has given us a still stranger etymology; that it is, "crimen animo *felleo* perpetratum," with a bitter or gallish inclination.[b]

The authority of Sir Henry Spelman, in matters of legal antiquity, is unquestionably respectable: it is unfortunate, on this as on many other occasions, that his Glossary, the work here cited, is not in my power; and, therefore, I cannot examine particularly what he says upon the subject.

Serjeant Hawkins, so noted for his painful accuracy and his guarded caution, cites, in his treatise of the pleas of the crown, both the places which are cited by the Author of the Commentaries. The Serjeant had probably examined both: he follows the description of my Lord Coke. From this, I infer one of the two things — that Mr. Hawkins either found something in the Glossary, which prevented his assent to the conclusion drawn from it, or preferred the authority of my Lord Coke to that of Sir Henry Spelman. Thus, on one side we find Sir Henry Spelman and Sir William Blackstone; on the other, my Lord Coke and Serjeant Hawkins. In each scale of authority the weight is great; but, in both, it is equal: the beam of decision inclines at neither end.

If an estate could be purchased, instead of being forfeited, by a felony, I can easily conceive how the crime might be viewed as the consideration of the purchase: if a fee signified a crime, instead of signifying a fief, I can easily conceive how the estate might be viewed as the value forfeited by its commission. But the "pretium feudi," applied in the manner and arrangement in which the application is made here, appears, in my humble conception, to be etymology inverted. Thus stand the propriety and the authority of the derivation adopted by the Author of the Commentaries.

[a] 4. Bl. Com. 95. 96.
[b] 4. Bl. Com. 95. 1. Ins. 291 a.

My Lord Coke, when he refers the meaning and the description of felony to the motive, and not to the event, to the disposition which produced it, and not to the forfeiture which it incurs, cites, in the margin, the authority of Glanville, the oldest book now extant in law, and two very ancient statutes; one made in the reign of Henry the third; the other in that of his son, Edward the first. With regard to Glanville, there must be some numerical mistake in the margin; for it refers us to the fifteenth chapter of the fourteenth book: in that book, there are only eight chapters. The statutes I have examined: you shall judge whether they support that meaning of felony, for the truth of which they are cited.

The first is the twenty fifth chapter of the statute of Marlbridge, which was made in the fifty second year of Henry the third. It is very short. "In future, it shall not, by our justices, be adjudged murder, where it is found misfortune only; but it shall take place as to such as are slain by felony — interfectis per feloniam — and not otherwise." Felony is here put most obviously in a contrasted opposition to misfortune; intention to accident. But what is peculiarly unfortunate for the etymology of Sir William Blackstone, a forfeiture was incurred at that time, and, according to the reprehensible theory retained in England for the sake of fees and not for the sake of justice, a forfeiture is still incurred, where a homicide happens by misfortune,[e] as well as where it is committed feloniously. If felony, therefore, "signifies clearly," as he says, "such a crime as works a forfeiture of the offender's lands or goods," the distinction mentioned in the statute would be absurd and ridiculous; referring felony to the principle, and not to the consequences of the fact, the provision in the statute is just and humane.

The other statute cited by my Lord Coke is the sixteenth chapter of Westminster the first, made in the third year of the first Edward. It distinguishes between those criminals who may be bailed, and those who ought not to be bailed. In the latter class are ranked those, who are taken for house burning *feloniously* done — "felonieusement fait." — Does this direct our view to the punishment, or to the intention?

But I am able to produce instances still more ancient and still more strong. The Mirrour of Justices, as has been mentioned oftener than once, contains a collection of the law, chiefly as it stood before the conquest; and consequently before the feudal system was introduced into England. In that collection there is a chapter concerning incendiaries: they are thus described — Incendiaries are those who burn a city, a town, a house, a man, a beast or other chattels *of their felony* — "de leur felony," — in time of peace for hatred or vengeance. Do the words *of their felony* describe that principle, which gives the crime its "body

---

[e] 4. Bl. Com. 188.

and its form?" or do they relate to a feudal forfeiture, then unknown?

But to put the matter in a light still more striking and clear: in the next sentence, a case is supposed, in which the intention existed, the fact was committed; but the effect did not take place; and, consequently, the punishment was not to be inflicted: yet the action is said to be done feloniously. "If one puts fire to a man *feloniously* — felonieusement — so that he is scorched or hurt, but not killed by the fire; it is not a capital crime." [d]

I suggest another argument, the legal force of which will, by every professional gentleman, be seen immediately to be irresistible. In every indictment for felony, the fact charged must be laid to have been done feloniously. To express this meaning, no other term in our language is legally adequate.[e] The antiquity of indictments, and the high authority of their essential forms, I pretend not to ascertain or to circumscribe.

But Sir William Blackstone, in this passage, is opposed not only by principle, by precedent, and by other authority; he is, I think, clearly opposed by his own. He says here, as we have seen, that felony clearly signifies the feudal forfeiture, or act, by which an estate is *forfeited, or escheats to the lord*. And yet, in another place,[f] he recommends great care in distinguishing between escheat to the lord, and forfeiture to the king; and traces them very properly to different sources. "Forfeiture of lands," says he, "and of whatever else the offender possessed, was the doctrine of the old Saxon law, as a part of the punishment for the offence; and does not at all relate to the feudal system, nor is the consequence of any signiory or lordship paramount; but being a prerogative vested in the crown, was neither superseded nor diminished by the introduction of the Norman tenures; a fruit and consequence of which escheat must undoubtedly be reckoned. Escheat, therefore, operates in subordination to the more ancient and superiour law of forfeiture.

"The doctrine of escheat upon attainder, taken singly, is this, that the blood of the tenant, by the commission of any felony (under which denomination all treasons were formerly comprised) is corrupted and stained, and the original donation of the feud is thereby determined, it being always granted to the vassal on the implied condition of *dum bene se gesserit*. Upon the thorough demonstration of which guilt by legal attainder, the feudal covenant and mutual bond of fealty are held to be broken, the estate instantly falls back from the offender to the lord of the fee, and the inheritable quality of his blood is extinguished and blotted out for ever. In this situation the law of feudal escheat was brought into England at the conquest, and in general superadded to the ancient law of fortfeiture. In consequence of which corruption and extinction of hereditary blood, the land of all felons would immediately revest in the lord, but

<hr>

[d] 4. Cou. Ang. Nor. 504.   [e] 1. Haw. 65.   [f] 2. Bl. Com. 251. 252.

that the superiour law of forfeiture intervenes, and intercepts it in its passage; in case of treason for ever; in case of the other felony, for only a year and a day; after which time, it goes to the lord in a regular course of escheat, as it would have done to the heir of the felon, in case the feudal tenures had never been introduced. And that this is the true opera-tion and genuine history of escheats, will most evidently appear from this incident to gavelkind lands (which seem to be the old Saxon tenure) that they are in no case subject to escheat for felony, though they are liable to forfeiture for treason."

Instead, therefore, of considering felony as a feudal forfeiture or escheat, we are here taught, and properly taught, to view them as flowing from different sources, and, in their operations, not only distinct, but incompatible.

Having thus traced the true meaning of felony, not to the event or part of the punishment, but to the principle and disposition from which it proceeds; our next step will be to ascertain, as plainly and as correctly as possible, the nature and character of that principle and disposition. It is characterized by the epithet *felleo*. Some derive it from the Latin verb *fallo*, which signifies, to deceive, others from the Greek word φηλος, which signifies an impostor or deceiver. In language, these derivations are different: in sentiment, they are the same. Perhaps they may lead us to as just a conception as can well be formed of felony — the generical term employed by the common law to denote a crime.

Without mutual confidence between its members, society, it is evident, could not exist. This mutual and pervading confidence may well be con-sidered as the attractive principle of the associating contract. To place that confidence in all the others is the social right, to deserve that con-fidence from all the others is the social duty, of every member. To en-tertain a disposition, in which that confidence cannot with propriety be placed, is a breach of the social duty, and a violation of the social right: it is a crime inchoate. When an injury, atrocious in its nature, or evil in its example, is committed voluntarily against any one member, the author of that voluntary injury has, by his conduct, shown to all, that their right is violated; that his duty is broken; that they cannot enjoy any longer their right of placing confidence in him; that he entertains a disposition unworthy of this confidence; that he is false, deceitful, and treacherous: the crime is now completed.

A disposition, regardless of social duty to all, and discovered by an injury, voluntary, and atrocious or dangerous, committed against one — this is a crime against society. Neither the disposition separated from the injury, nor the injury separated from the disposition, constitutes a crime. But though both the ingredients are necessary, they have not an equal operation in forming that character, from which a crime receives its denomination. In the consideration of crimes, the intention is chiefly to be regarded.

As the injuries, and the breaches of social trust and confidence, which we have mentioned, may relate to a great variety of objects, and, in their own nature, may be more or less aggravated, it follows, that crimes may be distinguished into many different species, and are susceptible of many different degrees.

Some think, that, at common law, the disposition, separated from the injury, constituted a crime. The saying, that "voluntas reputabitur pro facto," * seems to have given rise to this opinion. On a close examination, however, it will, I imagine, appear, that, in all the cases, on which the opinion is founded, and from which the saying is drawn, an injury was done, though not the injury intended to be done.

A very ancient case is reported in the following manner. A man's wife went away with her adulterer; and they compassed the death of the husband; and as he was riding towards the sessions of oyer and terminer and gaol delivery, they assaulted and beat him with weapons, so that he fell down as dead: upon this they fled. The husband recovered, and made hue and cry, and came to the sessions, and showed all this matter to the justices; and, upon the warrant of the justices, the woman and her adulterer were taken, indicted, and arraigned. All this special matter was found by a verdict; and it was adjudged, that the man should be hanged, and the woman burnt.^g Here, indeed, the injury intended and compassed — for to compass is, in legal understanding, to intend — was not carried into complete execution: an atrocious injury, however, was perpetrated.

Another case is mentioned to the following purpose. A young man was arraigned, because he intended to have stolen his master's goods, and came to his master's bed, where he lay asleep, and, with a knife, attempted, with all his force, to have cut his throat; and, thinking that he had indeed cut it, fled; upon this, the master cried out; and his neighbours apprehended the young man. All this matter was found by a special verdict; and, in the end, the young man was adjudged to be hanged. Quia voluntas reputabitur pro facto. But upon this case it is to be observed, that there was much more than mere intention: a barbarous outrage was committed on the person of a man; and was even thought by the aggressor to have been fully completed in its most extreme extent. For the young man, it is said, thought that he had indeed cut his master's throat. Accordingly, my Lord Coke says upon this subject, that it was not a bare compassing or plotting of the death of a man, either by word, or even by writing; but that some overt deed to manifest that compassing or plotting was necessary.

* [The intention is to be taken for the deed.]   ^g 3. Ins. 5.

In a species of high treason, and in a species of felony, the rule is still observed — that the intention manifested by a degree of injury, though not the degree intended, constitutes the crime. This is the case in compassing the death of the king. Though this intention be not completed by his death; the crime is completed by what is called an *overt act*, manifesting that intention by injurious and disloyal conduct. Indeed this rule is so strictly observed in this species of treason, that even when the intention is carried into full effect by putting the king to death, this completion itself, connected with the intention, is not considered as constituting the crime: it is viewed only as the injurious and overt act which manifests that intention. Agreeably to these principles, the regicides of Charles the first were indicted as compassing his death, and the fact of beheading him was specified and made use of as one of the overt acts to prove this compassing.[h]

The species of felony, in which the rule above mentioned still governs, is burglary. A burglar, says my Lord Coke, is, by the common law, a felon, who, in the night, breaketh and entereth into a mansion house of another, with intent to commit some felony within it.[i] The intention in this crime is to commit a felony; but, in order to constitute the crime, it is not necessary that the intention should be executed; the injurious acts done at the time and the place and in the manner described are sufficient: nay more; if the intention be completed by committing the felony, yet, if it be not committed at the time and the place, and in the manner described, it is not a burglary, though it is a felony of another species.

The foregoing cases, the view under which I have stated them, and the observations which I have drawn from them, show strongly the spirit of the common law in its estimation of crimes. In those cases, the felony or treason is traced to the malignity of the principle, not to the mischief of the consequences: the crime is constituted, though the event fail.

In other cases, indeed, the completion of the event is necessary to the constitution of the crime; but even in these, the intention is much more considered than the act. "Actus non facit reum, nisi mens sit rea," [j] is, I believe, a rule of immemorial antiquity in the common law. If, indeed, it is an errour, as the Marquis of Beccaria alleges it to be, to think a crime greater or less according to the intention of him by whom it is committed, it is, in the common law, an errour of the most inveterate kind; it is an errour which the experience of ages has not been able to correct. "Justitia," said Bracton many hundred years ago, "est voluntarium bonum; nec enim potest dici bonum proprie, nisi intercedente voluntate:

---

[h] Kel. 8.   [i] 3. Ins. 63.
[j] 3. Ins. 6. [The act does not make a man guilty, unless the mind is guilty.]

tolle enim voluntatem, et erit omnis actus indifferens. Affectio quidem tua nomen imponit operi tuo. Crimen non contrahitur nisi voluntas nocendi[k] intercedat. Voluntas et propositum distinguunt maleficia. Furtum omnino non committitur sine affectu furandi. In maleficiis spectatur *voluntas* et non *exitus*." [1]

But, on one hand as well as on the other, there is an extreme. The intention governs; the intention communicates its colours to the act: but the act — the *injurious* act must be done. Abstract turpitude is not, I apprehend, a subject of cognizance in a human forum. The breach of our duty to man and to society alone is the object of municipal reprehension. For those sentiments, for those principles, nay for those actions, by which no other member of society can be affected, no one member is accountable to the others. For such sentiments, for such principles, and for such actions, he is amenable only to the tribunal within, and the tribunal above him. In the human code we have seen it to be a rule, that without an injury there is no crime.

Let us not, however, confine our conceptions of injury to the loss or to the risk merely of property. Of injury, all our rights, natural and civil, absolute and relative, are susceptible. Every injurious violation, therefore, of any of those rights may lay the foundation of a crime. The strings of society are sometimes stretched in the nicest unison: strike one, and all emit a complaining tone. Is a single member of society menaced? He who threatens is bound in a recognisance to keep the peace towards every other citizen, as well as towards him, to whom the immediate cause of alarm was given.[m]

I have now traced and described the principles of the common law with regard to the measure of crimes. We have seen with what wise and experienced caution its rules are guarded from every extreme. The result seems to be, that the common law estimates crimes by the design chiefly, but pays a proportionate attention to the fact — by the malignity, without overlooking the injury, of the transaction. After ideal perfection in her calculations concerning those amounts and proportions she aspires not; she is satisfied with that practical degree of accuracy, which a long and careful experience can attain.

From the consideration of crimes I pass to the consideration of punishments. On this subject some rules, and some valuable ones too, may be gleaned from the principles and the practice of the common law; but we

---

[k] Brac. 26. [Justice is a voluntary good, for it cannot be strictly called good, unless with the will interceding; for take away the will, and every act will become neither good nor evil. Your desire gives the name to your act. No crime is committed unless the desire of doing wrong enter in. Desire and purpose distinguish crimes. No theft is ever committed without the desire to steal. In wrongdoings the desire is to be scrutinized and not the result.]

[1] Id. 136 b.   [m] Bl. Com. 250.

must have recourse chiefly to those which are founded on our new but improved political establishments, and to those which result from the general principles of criminal jurisprudence.

Every crime, we have seen, includes an injury: this I consider as a leading maxim in the doctrine of crimes. In the punishment of every crime, reparation for the included injury ought to be involved: this I consider as a leading maxim in the doctrine of punishments.

In this particular, the law of England is defective to a degree both gross and cruel. The father of a family, whose subsistance depends on his personal industry, is, in the arms of his wife, and amidst his surrounding children, stabbed by the order of an insolent and barbarous neighbour. The miserable sufferers by the event are the miserable witnesses of the crime. The assassin, who has ordered it, is opulent and powerful. To the honour of the English law and of its administration be it said, that no degree of opulence or power will purchase or command impunity to the guilty: this assassin will feel its avenging arm. But to the honour of the English law and of its administration can it be added, that every degree of injury shall find its proportioned degree of reparation; and that as the assassin is not above its power, so those who suffer by the assassination are not beneath its care? No. This addition cannot be made. The widow and the orphans, who were the witnesses of the crime and the sufferers by the loss, are recognized in the former, but not in the latter character. They attend to give their testimony on the trial. The rich culprit is condemned as he ought to be. They apply to obtain reparation for the loss — of the life? That is irreparable — of the industry of their husband and father, from the ample patrimony of the criminal, who occasioned the loss? To this application, reasonable and just, what is the answer which must be given in the spirit of the law? His property is forfeited by the crime; no funds remain to make you reparation for your loss. They are dismissed, without being reimbursed the expense of their attendance in consequence of their duty and the order of the law; for the king pays no costs. Can this be right?

It was, in ancient times, ordered otherwise and better. In the early part of our juridical history, we find that a part of the composition or forfeiture for homicide was given to the relations of the person deceased.[n] We find likewise, that, in those times, penalties in cases of personal injury had so far the nature of a civil redress, that they were given as a compensation to the person injured.[p] Thus it was among the ancient Saxons. Reparation, indeed, was one great object in the Anglo-Saxon system of criminal law. The principle may be traced to the Germans as described by Tacitus.[q] "Recipitque satisfactionem universa domus." In one of the

[n] 2. Henry 289. 2. Dag. 90. Eden. 217.   [p] 1. Reev. 12.

[q] De. Mor. Germ. c. 21. 2. Dag. 77. [And the entire household receives satisfaction.]

very early laws of Pennsylvania, it is directed that "those next of kin shall be considered in the loss occasioned by the death of the party killed." [r]

Another quality of the Saxon jurisprudence in criminal matters deserves our attention — I add, our imitation: they inflicted very few capital punishments.[s] Such was the case, we are told, formerly in Scotland; such was it originally in Ireland; and such was it anciently in Wales.[t]

In every case before judgment, the Romans allowed an accused citizen to withdraw himself from the consequences of conviction into a voluntary exile. To this institution, the former practice of abjuration in England bore a strong resemblance. This was permitted, as my Lord Coke says, when the criminal chose rather "perdere patriam, quam vitam." [u] On the same principles, a liberty was given, in Greece, to a person accused to disappear after his first defense, and retire into voluntary banishment — in the language of the English law, to abjure the realm after the indictment was found.[v]

Sabacos, one of the legislators of Egypt, went still further. He abolished capital punishments, and ordained, that such criminals as were judged worthy of death should be employed in the publick works. Egypt, he thought, would derive more advantage from this kind of punishment; which, being imposed for life, appeared equally adapted to punish and to repress crimes.[w]

Punishments ought unquestionably to be moderate and mild. I know the opinion advanced by some writers, that the number of crimes is diminished by the severity of punishments: I know, that if we inspect the greatest part of the criminal codes, their unwieldy size and their ensanguined hue will force us to acknowledge, that the opinion has been general and prevalent. On accurate and unbiassed examination, however, it will appear to be an opinion unfounded and pernicious, inconsistent with the principles of our nature, and, by a necessary consequence, with those of wise and good government.

So far as any sentiment of generous sympathy is suffered, by a merciless code, to remain among the citizens, their abhorrence of crimes is, by the barbarous exhibitions of human agony, sunk in the commiseration of criminals. These barbarous exhibitions are productive of another bad effect — a latent and gradual, but a powerful, because a natural, aversion to the laws. Can laws, which are a natural and a just object of aversion, receive a cheerful obedience, or secure a regular and uniform execution? The expectation is forbidden by some of the strongest principles in the

---

[r] R. O. Book A. p. 49.   [s] 4. Bl. Com. 406.   [t] Whitak. 278.
[u] Eden. 31. [To lose his fatherland, than his life.]   [v] 2. Gog. Or. L. 72.
[w] 3. Gog. Or. L. 15.

human frame. Such laws, while they excite the compassion of society for those who suffer, rouse its indignation against those who are active in the steps preparatory to their sufferings.

The result of those combined emotions, operating vigorously in concert, may be easily conjectured. The criminal will probably be dismissed without prosecution, by those whom he has injured. If prosecuted and tried, the jury will probably find, or think they find, some decent ground, on which they may be justified or, at least, excused in giving a verdict of acquittal. If convicted, the judges will, with avidity, receive and support every, the nicest, exception to the proceedings against him; and, if all other things should fail, will have recourse to the last expedient within their reach for exempting him from rigorous punishment — that of recommending him to the mercy of the pardoning power. In this manner the acerbity of punishment deadens the execution of the law.

The criminal, pardoned, repeats the crime, under the expectation that the impunity also will be repeated. The habits of vice and depravity are gradually formed within him. Those habits acquire, by exercise, continued accessions of strength and inveteracy. In the progress of his course, he is led to engage in some desperate attempt. From one desperate attempt he boldly proceeds to another; till, at last, he necessarily becomes the victim of that preposterous rigour, which repeated impunity had taught him to despise, because it had persuaded him that he might always escape.

When, on the other hand, punishments are moderate and mild, every one will, from a sense of interest and of duty, take his proper part in detecting, in exposing, in trying, and in passing sentence on crimes. The consequence will be, that criminals will seldom elude the vigilance, or baffle the energy of publick justice.

True it is, that, on some emergencies, excesses of a temporary nature may receive a sudden check from rigorous penalties: but their continuance and their frequency introduce and diffuse a hardened insensibility among the citizens; and this insensibility, in its turn, gives occasion or pretence to the further extension and multiplication of those penalties. Thus one degree of severity opens and smooths the way for another, till, at length, under the specious appearance of necessary justice, a system of cruelty is established by law. Such a system is calculated to eradicate all the manly sentiments of the soul, and to substitute in their place dispositions of the most depraved and degrading kind.

The principles both of utility and of justice require, that the commission of a crime should be followed by a speedy infliction of the punishment.

The association of ideas has vast power over the sentiments, the passions, and the conduct of men. When a penalty marches close in the rear of the offence, against which it is denounced, an association, strong and striking, is produced between them, and they are viewed in the inseparable relation of cause and effect. When, on the contrary, the punishment is procrastinated to a remote period, this connexion is considered as weak and precarious, and the execution of the law is beheld and suffered as a detached instance of severity, warranted by no cogent reason, and springing from no laudable motive.

It is just, as well as useful, that the punishment should be inflicted soon after the commission of the crime. It should never be forgotten, that imprisonment, though often necessary for the safe custody of the person accused, is, nevertheless, in itself a punishment — a punishment galling to some of the finest feelings of the heart — a punishment, too, which, as it precedes conviction, may be as undeserved as it is distressing.

But imprisonment is not the only penalty, which an accused person undergoes before his trial. He undergoes also the corroding torment of suspense — the keenest agony, perhaps, which falls to the lot of suffering humanity. This agony is by no means to be estimated by the real probability or danger of conviction: it bears a compound proportion to the delicacy of sentiment and the strength of imagination possessed by him, who is doomed to become its prey.

These observations show, that those accused of crimes should be speedily tried; and that those convicted of them should be speedily punished. But with regard to this, as with regard to almost every other subject, there is an extreme on one hand as well as on the other; and the extremes on each hand should be avoided with equal care. In some cases, at some times, and under some circumstances, a delay of the trial and of the punishment, instead of being hurtful or pernicious, may, in the highest degree, be salutary and beneficial, both to the publick and to him who is accused or convicted.

Prejudices may naturally arise, or may be artfully fomented, against the crime, or against the man who is charged with having committed it. A delay should be allowed, that those prejudices may subside, and that neither the judges nor jurors may, at the trial, act under the fascinating impressions of sentiments conceived before the evidence is heard, instead of the calm influence of those which should be its impartial and deliberate result. A sufficient time should be given to prepare the prosecution on the part of the state, and the defence of it on the part of the prisoner. This time must vary according to different persons, different crimes, and different situations.

After conviction, the punishment assigned to an inferiour offence should be inflicted with much expedition. This will strengthen the useful association between them; one appearing as the immediate and unavoidable consequence of the other. When a sentence of death is pronounced, such an interval should be permitted to elapse before its execution, as will render the language of political expediency consonant to the language of religion.

Under these qualifications, the speedy punishment of crimes should form a part in every system of criminal jurisprudence. The constitution of Pennsylvania[x] declares, that in all criminal prosecutions, the accused has a "right to a speedy trial."

The certainty of punishments is a quality of the greatest importance. This quality is, in its operation, most merciful as well as most powerful. When a criminal determines on the commission of a crime, he is not so much influenced by the lenity of the punishment, as by the expectation, that, in some way or other, he may be fortunate enough to avoid it. This is particularly the case with him, when this expectation is cherished by the example or by the experience of impunity. It was the saying of Solon, that he had completed his system of laws by the combined energy of justice and strength. By this expression he meant to denote, that laws, of themselves, would be of very little service, unless they were enforced by a faithful and an effectual execution of them. The strict execution of every criminal law is the dictate of humanity as well as of wisdom.

By this rule, important as well as general, I mean not to exclude the pardoning power from my system of criminal jurisprudence. That power ought to continue till the system and the proceedings under it become absolutely perfect — in other words — it ought to continue while laws are made and administered by men. But I mean that the exercise of the pardoning power should be confined to exceptions, well ascertained, from the general rule. Confined in this manner, instead of shaking the truth or diminishing the force of the rule, the exercise of the power to pardon will confirm the former and increase the latter.

Need I mention it as a rule, that punishments ought to be inflicted upon those persons only, who have committed crimes — that the innocent ought not to be blended in cruel and ruinous confusion with the guilty?

Yes; it is necessary to mention this as a rule: for, however plain and straight it is, when viewed through the pure and clear ether of reason and humanity, it has not been seen by those whom pride and avarice have blinded; nay, it has been represented as a rule, crooked and distorted, by those who have beheld it through the gross and refracting atmosphere of false policy and false philosophy. The doctrines of forfeiture and corruption of blood have found their ingenious advocates, as well as their powerful patrons.

There have been countries and times — there still are countries and times, when and where the rule, founded in justice and nature, that the property of the parent is the inheritance of his children, has been inter-

[x] Art. 9. s. 9.

cepted in its benign operation by the cruel interference of another rule, founded in tyranny and avarice — the crimes of the subject are the inheritance of the prince. At those times, and in those countries, an insult to society becomes a pecuniary favour to the crown; the appointed guardian of the publick security becomes interested in the violation of the law; and the hallowed ministers of justice become the rapacious agents of the treasury.

A poisoned fountain throws out its bitter waters in every direction. This rule, hostile to the nearest domestick connexions, was unfriendly also to the safety of the publick. If the inheritance was reaped by the prince; it was, by him, deemed a matter of small moment, that impunity was stipulated for the crime. Accordingly, we are told, that, in the thirteenth century, one of the methods, by which the kings of England and of other parts of Europe supplied their exchequers, was the sale of pardons for crimes.[y] When crimes were the sources of princely wealth, it is no wonder if they were objects of princely indulgence. In this manner we may naturally account for the disorder and violence, which, in those ages, prevailed so universally over Europe.

The law of forfeiture it has been attempted to defend by considerations drawn from utility, and also from natural justice. The high authority of Cicero is also[z] produced upon this occasion — "Nec vero me fugit, quam sit acerbum, parentum scelera filiorum pœnis lui; sed hoc præclare legibus comparatum est, ut caritas liberorum amiciores parentes reipublicæ redderet." [a] Amicus Cicero — sed magis amica veritas.[*] For the high authority of Cicero, I certainly entertain a proportionate degree of respect; but implicit deference should be paid to none. Besides; in the passage quoted, Cicero does not speak in a character of authority. He decides not as a judge: he pleads his own cause as a culprit; he defends, before Brutus, a rigorous vote, which he had given in the senate, against the sons of Lepidus.

But farther; upon a closer investigation, it will, perhaps, be found, that the principle of policy, on which Cicero rests his defence, as it certainly is not of the most generous, neither is it of the most enlarged kind; since forfeitures, far from preventing publick crimes and publick dangers, may have the strongest tendency to multiply and to perpetuate both. When the law says, that the children of him, who has been guilty of crimes, shall be bereaved of all their hopes and all their rights of inheritance; that they shall languish in perpetual indigence and distress; that

---

[y] Bar. on St. 27.   [z] 4. Bl. Com. 375.
[a] Ep. ad Brut. 12. [Nor indeed has it escaped my notice, what a harsh thing it is to pay for the crimes of parents through the punishment of their sons. But this has most plainly been provided for by the laws, that the love for their children might render parents more loving toward the commonwealth.]
[*] [Dear is Cicero, but dearer Truth.]

their whole life shall be one dark scene of punishment, unintermitted and unabating; and that death alone shall provide for them an asylum from their misery — when such is the language, or such is the effect of the law; with what sentiments must it inspire those, who are doomed to become its unfortunate though unoffending victims? — with what sentiments must it inspire those, who from humanity feel, or by nature are bound to take, an interest in the fortunes and in the fate of those victims, unfortunate though unoffending? With sentiments of pain and disgust — with sentiments of irritation and disappointment — with sentiments of a deadly feud against the state which has adopted, and, perhaps, against the citizens also who have enforced it.

Vain is the attempt to range the cold and timid suggestions of policy against the vivid and the indelible feelings of nature, and against the warm though impartial dictates of humanity. Who will undertake to satisfy an innocent son, that he is the victim — who will undertake to persuade his relations — his virtuous — his patriotick — his meritoriously patriotick relations, that one so nearly connected with them is the victim, whom the publick good indispensably demands to be offered up as a sacrifice to atone for the guilt of his father? The sons of Lepidus were the children of the sister of Brutus. "Contra patrem Lepidum Brutus avunculus," says he very naturally in his answer to Cicero.*

An attempt has been likewise made to support the law of forfeiture on the foundation of natural justice.[b] "All property," says Sir William Blackstone,[c] "is derived from society, being one of those civil[d] rights which are conferred upon individuals, in exchange for that degree of natural freedom, which every man must sacrifice when he enters into social communities. If therefore a member of any national community violates the fundamental contract of his association, by transgressing the municipal law, he forfeits his right to such privileges as he claims by that contract; and the state may very justly resume that portion of property, or any part of it, which the laws have before assigned him. Hence in every offence of an atrocious kind, the laws of England have exacted a total confiscation of the movables or personal estate; and in many cases a perpetual, in others only a temporary, loss of the offender's immovables or landed property; and have vested them both in the king, who is the person supposed to be offended, being the only visible magistrate in whom the majesty of the publick resides."

It has often been said, that, at elections, the people of England sell their liberty for their own money; but this, I presume, is the first time that this kind of exchange has been brought forward as a fundamental article of their *original* contract.

* [In contrast to their father Lepidus, Brutus is their uncle.]   [b] 4. Bl. Com. 375.
[c] 1. Bl. Com. 299.   [d] 4. Bl. Com. 9.

A philosophizing is, on some occasions, an unfortunate turn. It was, we are told, an opinion long received in China, that the globe of the earth was supported on the back of an elephant. The people were satisfied and inquired no farther. An ingenious philosopher, however, was not satisfied so easily. If the earth, reasoned he, must be supported on the back of an elephant, *pari ratione*, the elephant must stand on the back of something else. Exactly fitted for his design, he found a broad backed tortoise. He placed the elephant upon it, and published his new theory of the manner in which the globe was supported. Unfortunately, the spirit of his *ars philosophandi* caught; and he was asked — on whose back will you place the tortoise? To this a satisfactory answer is not yet found in the history of this Chinese philosophy.

The sceptres of princes required a support: the political creed of Europe rested them on forfeitures. The people paid and inquired not. But the attempt is now made to find a rational foundation for forfeitures: they are rested on property as a civil, and not as a natural right.

In both instances, the mistake was made, and the wrong direction was pursued, in the first step which was taken. Forfeitures for crimes, according to the true principles of political philosophy, were a foundation as improper for the revenue of princes, as an elephant, according to the true principles of natural philosophy, was inadequate to sustain the weight of the globe.

But the investigation of the doctrine — that property is a civil right — will, as I have already mentioned, find its appropriated place in the second division of my system.

The observations which we have made are equally applicable to the forfeiture of dower, as to the forfeiture of inheritance.

Corruption of blood is another principle, ruinous and unjust, by which the innocent are involved in the punishment of the guilty. It extends both upwards and downwards. A person attainted cannot inherit lands from his ancestors: he cannot transmit them to any heir: he even obstructs all descents to his posterity, whenever they must, through him, deduce their right from a more remote ancestor.[e]

This unnatural principle — I call it unnatural, because it dissolves, as far as human laws can dissolve, the closest and the dearest ties of nature — this unnatural principle was introduced by the feudal system, pregnant with so many other principles of the most mischievous kind: and it still continues to disgrace the criminal jurisprudence of England. It begins now, however, to be very generally deserted as to its principle. The ingenious and elegant Mr. Eden, who seems to cling to forfeiture, at least in a qualified degree, as "to a branch of the penal system, which will not be suffered to fall from the body of our law, without serious con-

[e] 4. Bl. Com. 381.

sideration," [f] admits very freely, that it is not so easy to reconcile, either to reason or benevolence, that corruption of blood, by which the inheritable quality is for ever extinguished.[g] Sir William Blackstone intimates a very laudable wish, that the whole doctrine may, in England, be antiquated by one undistinguishing law.[h]

This subject of extending punishments beyond the guilty, I conclude with a passage from one of the laws of Arcadius and Honorius, the Roman emperours. "Sancimus ibi esse pœnam, ubi et noxa est; propinquos, natos, familiares, procul a calumnia submovemus, quos reos sceleris societas non facit. Nec enim affinitas, vel amicitia, nefarium crimen admittunt; peccata igitur suos teneant auctores; nec ulterius progrediatur metus quam reperiatur delictum." [i]

As the punishment ought to be confined to the criminal; so it ought to bear a proportion, it ought, if possible, to bear even an analogy, to the crime.[j] This is a principle, the truth of which requires little proof; but the application of which requires much illustration.

"It is not only," says the Marquis of Beccaria, "the common interest of mankind that crimes should not be committed; but it is their interest also that crimes of every kind should be less frequent, in proportion to the mischief which they produce in society. The means, therefore, which the legislature use to prevent crimes, should be more powerful in proportion as they are destructive of the publick safety and happiness. Therefore there ought to be a fixed proportion between punishments and crimes." "A scale of crimes," adds he, "may be formed, of which the first degree should consist of such as tend immediately to the dissolution of society; and the last, of the smallest possible injustice done to a private member of that society." [k]

To a scale of crimes, a corresponding scale of punishments should be added, each of which ought to be modified, as far as possible, according to the nature, the kind, and the degree of the crime, to which it is annexed. To select, where it can be done, a punishment analogous to the crime, is an excellent method to strengthen that association of ideas, which it is very important to establish between them.

In the graduation of each of these scales, and in the relative adjustment between them, a perfect accuracy is unquestionably unattainable. The different shades both of crimes and of punishments are so numerous, and run so much into one another, that it is impossible for human skill to

[f] Eden 48. [g] Id. 39. [h] 4. Bl. Com. 382.
[i] Eden. 49. [We deem it sanctioned that the punishment should lie where the guilt is; relations, children, friends we keep far removed from any calumny, whom mere social intercourse does not make guilty of the crime; for neither blood relationship nor friendship incurs a nefarious charge. Therefore let sins bind only their own doers, and let fear proceed no further than wrongdoing is proved.]
[j] Id. 83. [k] Bec. c. 6. p. 17. 19.

mark them, in every instance, distinctly and correctly. How many intervening degrees of criminality are there between a larceny of the petty kind and a robbery committed with every degree of personal insult and outrage — between a private slander and a publick inflammatory libel — between a simple menace and a premeditated murder — between an unfounded murmur and a daring rebellion against the government?

But though every thing cannot, much may be done. If a complete detail cannot be accomplished; certain leading rules may be established: if every minute grade cannot be precisely ascertained; yet the principal divisions may be marked by wise and sagacious legislation. Crimes and punishments too may be distributed into their proper classes; and the general principles of proportion and analogy may be maintained without any gross or flagrant violation.

To maintain them is a matter of the first moment in criminal jurisprudence. Every citizen ought to know when he is guilty: every citizen ought to know, as far as possible, the degree of his guilt. This knowledge is as necessary to regulate the verdicts of jurors and the decisions of judges, as it is to regulate the conduct of citizens. This knowledge ought certainly to be in the possession of those who make laws to regulate all.

"Optima est lex," says my Lord Bacon, "quæ minimum relinquit arbitrio judicis." [1] If this is true with regard to law in general; it must be very true, and very important too, with regard to the law of crimes and punishments. What kind of legislation must that have been, by which "not only ignorant and rude unlearned people, but also learned and expert people, minding honesty, were often and many times trapped and snared!" Yet such is the character of the criminal legislation under Henry the eighth, given by the first parliament assembled in the reign of his daughter Mary;[m] which could well describe, for it still smarted under the legislative rod. The *candour*, at least, of legislation should be inviolable.

"Misera est servitus, ubi jus est incognitum." * When a citizen first knows the law from the jury who convict, or from the judges who condemn him; it appears as if his life and his liberty were laid prostrate before a new and arbitrary power; and the sense of general safety, so necessary to the enjoyment of general happiness, is weakened or destroyed. But a law uncertain is, so far, a law unknown. To punish by a law indefinite and unintelligible! — Is it better than to punish without any law?

A laudable, though, perhaps, an improvable degree of accuracy has

---

[1] 1. Ld. Bac. 249. [That law is best which leaves the least to the discretion of the judge.]

[m] St. 1. Mary. c. 1.

* [It is a miserable state of slavery where the law is unknown.]

been attained by the common law, in its descriptions of crimes and punishments. On this subject, I now enter into a particular detail. To the description of each crime, I shall subjoin that of its punishment; and shall mention, as I proceed, the alterations introduced by the constitution and laws of the United States and of Pennsylvania. The laws of other nations will frequently be considered in a comparative view.

II

OF CRIMES AGAINST THE RIGHT OF INDIVIDUALS TO THEIR PROPERTY

EVERY crime includes an injury: every injury includes a violation of a right. The investigations, which we have hitherto made concerning rights, will direct our course in that which we are now to make concerning wrongs.

I assumed, though, for the reasons assigned, I have not yet proved, that a man has a right to his property. I begin my enumeration of crimes with those which infringe this right.

I have observed that every injurious violation of our rights, natural and civil, absolute and relative, *may* lay the foundation of a crime.[a] I did not mean, however, to insinuate, by this observation, that every injury *ought* to be considered by the law in a criminal point of view. For every injury let reparation be made by the civil code, in proportion to the loss sustained; but let those injuries alone, which become formidable to society by their intrinsick atrocity, or by their dangerous example, be resented by society and prosecuted as crimes. Agreeably to this principle, a private injury done without actual violence, cannot be prosecuted by an indictment.[b] It is not considered as affecting the community.

This principle, however, seems to have gained its full establishment only by the liberality of modern times. It is remarkable, that a law made on this liberal principle, in an early period of Pennsylvania, was repealed by the king in council.[c] But this is not the only instance, in which the improving spirit of our legislation has been at first checked, but has received subsequent countenance by late decisions in England.

With the enjoyment and security of property, the security and the authenticity of its evidences is intimately connected. For this reason, dangerous and deliberate attacks upon that security or authenticity are crimes by the common law.

Forgery, at the common law, may be described "the fraudulent making or alteration of a writing, to the prejudice of another man's right."

[a] Ante. p. 625.   [b] 3. Burr. 1703. 1733.   [c] R. O. book A. vol. 1. p. 14.

For this crime, the punishment of fine, imprisonment, and pillory may, by the common law, be inflicted on the criminal.[d]

Among the Egyptians, publick notaries, who forged false deeds, or who suppressed or added any thing to the writings, which they had received to copy, were condemned to lose both their hands. They were punished in that part, which had been particularly instrumental in the crime.[e] In Lorrain, so long ago as the fourteenth century, forgery was punished with banishment.[f]

The first act of parliament, which appears against it, was made in the reign of Henry the fifth. This act punishes it by satisfaction to the party injured, and by a fine to the king.[g] But this first statute has been the fruitful mother of a thousand more. True it is, that the increase of commerce, the invention of negotiable and even current paper, the institution of national funds, and the many complex securities and evidences of real property have justly rendered the crime of forgery, beside its intrinsick baseness — for it is a species of the *crimen falsi* — a consideration of great importance and extent. But is it equally true, that all this is a sufficient reason, why, in almost all cases possible to be conceived, every forgery, which *tends* to defraud, either in the name of a real or of a fictitious person, should be made, as in England it is now made, a capital crime? [h] "Pluet super populum laqueos." There is a learned civilian, says my Lord Bacon, who expounds this curse of the prophet, of a multitude of penal laws; which are worse than showers of hail or tempest upon cattle; for they fall upon men.[i]

By a law of Pennsylvania, whoever shall forge, deface, corrupt, or embezzle deeds and other instruments of writing, shall forfeit double the value of the damage sustained, one half of which shall go to the party injured; and shall in the pillory, or otherwise, be disgraced as a false person.[j]

By a law of the United States it is enacted, that if any person shall falsely make, alter, forge, or counterfeit, or cause or procure to be falsely made, altered, forged, or counterfeited, or willingly act or assist in the false making, altering, forging, or counterfeiting any certificate, indent, or other publick security of the United States; or shall utter, put off, or offer, or cause to be uttered, put off, or offered in payment or for sale, any such false, forged, altered, or counterfeited certificate, indent, or other publick security, with intent to defraud any person, knowing the same to be false, altered, forged, or counterfeited, and shall be thereof convicted; every such person shall suffer death.[k]

To forge, says my Lord Coke, is metaphorically taken from the smith,

[d] 4. Bl. Com. 245.   [e] 1. Gog. Or. L. 59.   [f] Bar. on St. 380.   [g] Id. ib.
[h] 4. Bl. Com. 247.   [i] 4. Ld. Bac. 3.   [j] 1. Laws Penn. 5.
[k] Laws U.S. 1. cong. 2. sess. c. 9. s. 14.

who beateth upon his anvil, and forgeth what fashion or shape he will. The offence is called *crimen falsi*, and the offender *falsarius;* and the Latin word to forge is *falsare* or *fabricare*. And this is properly taken when the act is done in the name of another person.[1] "Falsely to make," says he, are larger words than "to forge;" for one may make a false writing within this act (he speaks of the 5th. Eliz. c. 14. in which, as to the present point, the words used are substantially the same with the words of the law now under consideration) though it be not forged in the name of another, nor his seal nor hand counterfeited. As if a man make a true deed of feoffment under his hand and seal of the manor of Dale unto B.; and B. or some other rase out D and put in S, and then when the true deed was of the manor of Dale, now it is falsely altered and made the manor of Sale; this is a false writing within the purview of the statute.[m]

Another crime against the right of property is larceny. Larceny is described — the felonious and fraudulent taking and carrying away of the personal goods of another.[n] The Mirrour describes the crime as committed, "treacherousement." [o] More indictments are to be found for larceny, among the records of England, than for all the other crimes known to the law. It is computed that nineteen criminals out of twenty are prosecuted for this crime.[p]

According as the opinions and sentiments of men concerning property have been more or less correct, their notions concerning larceny have been more or less pure. Indeed, in the nature of things, this must be the case. Theft, or the secret acquisition of property, was, at Sparta, thought neither a crime nor a shame. Why? Because at Sparta, Lycurgus had established a community of goods; and when one got hold of a larger share than his neighbours, especially among the young people, it was considered merely as an instance of juvenile address, and as indicating a superiour degree of future dexterity. The senatorial order at Rome, we are told, enjoyed the distinguished privilege of being exempted from every prosecution for larceny.[q] What is still more remarkable, a similar claim of privilege was, in the time of Charles the second, insisted on by the house of lords in England, when a bill was sent to them from the commons' to punish — wood stealers! [r] This anecdote we have on the authority of my Lord Clarendon, a peer, the chancellor, and the speaker of the house of lords.

Much has been said, in the English law books, concerning the distinction between grand and petit larceny. The distinction, however ancient, was never founded upon any rational principle; and the farther it flowed from its original source, the more unreasonable and cruel it became. Well

[1] 3. Ins. 169.   [m] 3. Ins. 169.   [n] Id. 107. 4. Bl. Com. 230.
[o] C. 1. s. 10. 2. Reev. 42.   [p] Bar. on St. 443.   [q] Bar. on St. 491.
[r] Id. ibid.

might Sir Henry Spelman complain, that, while every thing else became daily dearer, the life of a man became more and more cheap.[s] But, what is more, this distinction, irrational and really oppressive, appears never to have been established with any degree of accuracy. The Author of Fleta says, if a person steals the value of twelve pence *and* more, he shall be punished capitally. Britton, in one place, says, if it is twelve pence *or* more. At this time, therefore — that is, in the reign of Edward the first — it was unsettled whether twelve pence was sufficient, or more than twelve pence was necessary, to superinduce the capital punishment.[t] A similar diversity and uncertainty of opinion appears in the reign of Edward the third.[u]

In the description of larceny, the taking is an essential part. For every felony includes a trespass; and if the person is guilty of no trespass in taking the goods, he can be guilty of no felony in carrying them away.[v] This is precisely the law language, conveying the doctrine, which I have illustrated generally and fully — that, without an injury, there can be no crime. A real trespass must be committed; but a real trespass will not be covered or excused by any artful stratagem to prevent the appearance of it. If one, who intends to steal the goods of another, obtains, with that intention, the process of the law to get them into his possession, in a manner apparently legal; this contrivance — an abuse of the law — will not excuse him from a charge of a felonious taking.[w]

To a larceny it is as necessary that the goods be carried away, as that they be taken. But the least removal of the goods is sufficient to satisfy this part of the description. To remove them from one place to another, even in the same room, is, in legal understanding, to carry them away. One, who intended to steal plate, took it out of a trunk, and laid it upon the floor, but was surprised before he could do more; he was adjudged guilty of larceny.[x]

The taking and carrying away, says Sir William Blackstone, and very truly, must also be *felonious*, that is, done *animo furandi*. This, by the way, is a clear and decided instance, that, in the meaning of the common law, felony is referred to the intention, and not to the event. As we saw in the former part of the description, that the crime could not exist without the injury; we see now, that the injury will not constitute the crime without the criminal intention. For, as the Author of the Commentaries next observes, this requisite indemnifies mere trespassers, and other petty offenders.[y]

The last part of the description of larceny at the common law is, that the goods must be personal. Land, or any thing that is adhering to

[s] 4. Bl. Com. 238.   [t] 1. Reev. 485.   [u] 2. Reev. 204.
[v] 1. Haw. 89. Kel. 24.   [w] 1. Haw. 90.   [x] Kel. 31. 1. Haw. 93.
[y] 4. Bl. Com. 232.

the soil or to the freehold, cannot in one transaction be made the subject of larceny. But if any thing of this kind is, at one time, separated from the freehold, so as to become a chattel; and is, at another time, taken and carried away; larceny is now committed.[z]

In different nations, and in the same nation at different times, larceny or theft has received very different punishments. It would be tedious minutely to recite them. On no subject has there been more fluctuation in the criminal laws both of Greece and Rome. Seldom, however, was larceny punished capitally at Athens; never among the Romans. In the early part of the Anglo-Saxon period in England, theft of the worst kind did not expose the thief to any corporal punishment. But the compensation which he was obliged by law to make, rendered larceny a very unprofitable business when it was detected. Ina, the king of Wessex, declared stealing to be a capital crime; but allowed the offender or his friends to redeem his life, by paying the price at which it was valued by the law.[a]

The distinction between punishing theft as a crime, and exacting compensation for it as an injury, is strongly marked in a law of Howel Dha, the celebrated legislator of Wales: "If a thief is condemned to death, he shall not suffer in his goods; for it is unreasonable both to exact compensation, and to inflict punishment."

In the ninth year of Henry the first, larceny above the value of twelve pence was, in England, made a capital crime, and continues so to this day; and, in a vast number of instances, it is, by modern statutes, deprived of the benefit of clergy. These statutes, says Mr. Eden, are so complicated in their limitations, and so intricate in their distinctions, that it would be painful, on many accounts, to attempt the detail of them. It is a melancholy truth, but it may, without exaggeration, be asserted, that, exclusive of those who are obliged by their profession to be conversant in the niceties of the law, there are not ten subjects in England, who have any clear conception of the several sanguinary restrictions, to which, on this point, they are made liable.[b]

By a law of the United States, larceny is punished with a fine not exceeding the fourfold value of the property stolen, and with publick whipping not exceeding thirty nine stripes.[c] In Pennsylvania, a person convicted of larceny to the value of twenty shillings and upwards, shall restore the goods or pay their value to the owner, shall also forfeit to the commonwealth the value of the goods, shall undergo a servitude for any term not exceeding three years, and shall be confined and kept to hard labour: a person convicted of larceny under twenty shillings, shall restore the goods or pay their value to the owner, shall forfeit the same

---

[z] 1. Haw. 93. [a] 2. Henry 290. [b] Eden. 289.
[c] Laws U.S. 1. cong. 2. sess. c. 9. s. 16.

value to the commonwealth, shall undergo a servitude not exceeding one year, and shall be confined and kept to hard labour.[d]

Forgery and larceny seem to be the only crimes against the right of private property known to the common law.

Robbery is generally classed among the crimes against the right of private property; but somewhat improperly, in my opinion. Robbery receives its deep dye from outrage committed on the person; but as property also enters into the description of this crime, I shall consider it here.

Robbery, at the common law, is a violent and felonious taking from the person of another, of money or goods to any value, putting him in fear.[e] From this description it appears, that, to constitute a robbery, the three following ingredients are indispensable: 1. a felonious intention, or *animus furandi*. 2. Some degree of violence and putting in fear. 3. A taking from the person of another.

1. There must be a felonious intention to steal: larceny is a necessary, though by no means the most important ingredient, which enters into the composition of a robbery. The circumstances which are calculated and proper to evince this felonious intention, it is impossible to describe or recount: they must, in this as in other crimes, be left to the attentive consideration of those, by whom the person accused is tried. The value, however, of the property on which the larceny is committed, is, as to the robbery, totally immaterial. In this respect, a penny is equivalent to a pound.[f]

2. There must be some degree of violence and putting in fear. This indeed is the characteristick circumstance, which distinguishes robbery from other larcenies. If one assault another with such circumstances of terrour as put him in fear, and he, in consequence of this fear, deliver his money; this is a sufficient degree of violence; for he was put in fear by the assault; and gave his money to escape the danger.[g] To constitute a robbery, it is sufficient that the force used be such as might create an apprehension of danger, or oblige one to part with his property against his consent. Thus, if a man be knocked down without any previous warning, and stripped of his money while he lies senseless; this, though he cannot strictly be said to be *put in fear*, is undoubtedly a robbery.[h]

3. There must be a taking from the person of another. The thief must be in the possession of the thing stolen. If he go even so far as to cut the girdle, by which a purse hangs, so that it fall to the ground; yet if he do not take it up, he has not completed the robbery, because the purse was not in his possession.[i] The taking must be from the person; but this part

---

[d] 2. Laws. Penn. 803. s. 3. 4. [e] 3. Ins. 68. 1. Haw. 95. [f] 3. Ins. 69.
[g] 1. Haw. 96, 97. [h] Fost. 128. 4. Bl. Com. 242. [i] 3. Ins. 69.

of the description is answered, not only by taking the money out of one's pocket, or forcing from him the horse on which he actually rides, but by taking from him, openly and before his face, any thing which is under his immediate and personal care and protection. If one, wishing to save his money, throw it into a bush, and the thief take it up; this is a taking from the person.[j]

We are told by Mr. Selden, that, before the conquest, robbery was punished differently, by the different nations who came from the continent of Europe. By the Saxons, it was punished with death: by the Angles, and by the Danes, it was punished only with fine.[k] After the conquest, these different laws were settled by the Normans in the more merciful way; and if the delinquent fled, his pledge satisfied the law for him. But in the times of Henry the first, the law was again reduced to the punishment of this crime by death: and so it has continued ever since.[l]

In the ancient laws of Wales, it is expressly declared, that robbery shall never be punished with death; "because (say these laws) it is a sufficient satisfaction for this crime, if the goods taken be restored, and a fine paid to the person from whom they were taken, according to his station, for the violence offered him, and another to the king for the breach of the peace." [m]

Robbery, by a law of the United States, is punished capitally.[n] By a law of Pennsylvania, a person convicted of robbery forfeits to the commonwealth his lands and goods, and undergoes a servitude not exceeding ten years, in the gaol or house of correction.[o]

I proceed now to the consideration of two other crimes at the common law, which, though property, as in the case of robbery, enters into their description, yet receive their deep dye from outrages against personal security. This cannot be enjoyed without a legal guard around the *residence* of the person.

"A man's house is his castle" was the expression, in times rude and boisterous, when the idea of security was found only on its association with the idea of strength; and in such times, no expression more emphatical could have been used. In happier times, when the blessings of peace and law are expected and due — in such times, a man's house is entitled to an appellation more emphatick still — in such times, a man's house is his *sanctuary*. "Quid enim sanctius, quid omni religione munitius, quam domus uniuscujusque civium?" [p] Into this sanctuary, the law herself,

---

[j] 3. Ins. 69. 1. Haw. 96.   [k] Bac. on Gov. 63.   [l] Id. 88.   [m] 2. Henry 292.
[n] Laws U.S. 1. cong. 2. sess. c. 9. s. 8.   [o] 2. Laws Penn. 802. s. 2.
[p] Cic. pro dom. 41. [For what is more protected in any religion than the home of each and every one of the citizens?]

unless upon the most urgent emergencies, presumes not to look or enter. We have seen, on many occasions, with what a delicate — I may add, with what a respectful — reserve, she treats the near and dear domestick connexions. We may well suppose, that she will guard, with peculiar vigilance, the favoured spot in which a family reside. Even those who endeavour clandestinely to pry into its recesses — such are[q] eaves-droppers — receive her reprehension: and unless the peace or security of the publick require it, she will not suffer its doors to be broken, to execute even her own imperial mandates. When she thus solicitously protects the residence of a family from inferiour insults, we may rely, that she will zealously defend it from atrocious crimes. Such are arson and burglary.

Arson is a felony at common law, in maliciously and voluntarily burning the house of another.[r] This is not intended merely of the dwelling house itself, but extends to the outhouses; as the barn, the stable, the cow house, the dairy house, the mill house, the sheep house; which are parcel of the mansion house.[s]

This crime may be committed by wilfully burning one's own house, if the house of another is also burnt; but if no mischief is done to that of another, it is not felony, though the fire was kindled with an intention to burn the house of that other.[t] But if the intention is to burn the house of another person, and by the burning of this the house of a third person is also burned; the burning of the house of this third person is felony; because the pernicious event shall be coupled with the felonious intention.[u]

Neither the mere intention to burn a house, nor even an actual attempt to burn it, by putting fire to it, will, if no part of it be burnt, amount to felony; but if any part of the house be burnt, it is arson, though the fire afterwards go out of itself, or be extinguished.[v] No misfortune, nor even culpable negligence or imprudence, will amount to arson: it must be voluntary and malicious. A person, by shooting with a gun, set fire to the roof of a house; this was determined not to be felony.[w]

Arson is a crime of deep malignity. The object of other felonies against the right to property, is merely to give it a new master; the object of arson is to destroy it — to lose it to society, as well as to its owner. The confusion and terrour which attend arson, and the continued apprehension which follows it, are mischiefs frequently more distressing than even the loss of the property.

The crime of arson was one of the very few punished capitally by the Saxon law. In the reign of Edward the first, those who perpetrated this crime were burnt, that they might suffer in the same manner, in

[q] 4. Bl. Com. 169.　　[r] 3. Ins. 66. 1. Haw. 105.　　[s] 3. Ins. 67.
[t] Cro. Car. 376.　　[u] 3. Ins. 67.　　[v] 1. Haw. 106.　　[w] 1. Hale. P. C. 569.

which they had been criminal.[x] This crime is also one of the very few still punished capitally in Pennsylvania.[y] [z]

Burglary is a felony at the common law, in breaking and entering, by night, the mansion house of another, with intent to commit a felony.[a]

There have been some opinions, that this crime, on a construction of the phrase "by night," may be committed at any time after the setting and before the rising of the sun; because the day was deemed to begin at the end, and to end at the beginning of those times; but the later and better opinion is, that if there be day light enough to discern the countenance of a man when the crime is committed, it cannot amount to a burglary.[b]

To a burglary it is necessary, that the house be both broken and entered. The breaking must be actual, and not merely such as the law implies in every unlawful entry on the possession of another. To open a window; to unlock the door; to break a hole in the wall; to enter an open door and unlatch a chamber door; to come down the chimney; to knock at the door and rush in when it is opened; to gain admittance by an abuse of legal process, or by the means of a conspiring servant; all these are actual breaches. The least degree of entry with any part of the body, or with an instrument held in the hand, or even a load discharged from a gun, is sufficient to satisfy that entry, which the law deems necessary to constitute the crime of burglary.[c]

In a dwelling house only burglary can be committed. But a house in which one sometimes resides, and has left with an intention to return; a house which one has hired, and into which he has brought part of his goods, though he has not lodged in it; a chamber in a college; a room occupied in a private house by a lodger; the outhouses *adjoining* to the principal house; all these are mansion houses within the meaning of the law.[d] A shop may be parcel of a mansion house; but if it is severed by a lease to one who works in it by day only, and does not lodge in it, it is not burglary to break and enter it in the night time.

To a burglary, an intention to commit some felony, and not merely a trespass, is indispensable;[e] but, as was shown on another occasion,[f] it is not necessary that the felony intended be committed; and it is immaterial whether that felony be by common or by statute law.[g]

[x] 1. Reev. 485.   [y] 1. Laws. Penn. 137. 476.
[z] By an act of assembly passed 22d April, 1794, arson is punished by imprisonment at hard labour, for a period not less than five, nor more than twelve years. 3. Laws. Penn. 600. *Ed.*
[a] 3. Ins. 63. 1. Haw. 101.   [b] 1. Haw. 101.   [c] 1. Haw. 103.
[d] 3. Ins. 64. 1. Haw. 103. 104. 4. Bl. Com. 226.   [e] Wood. Ins. 388.
[f] Ante. p. 624.   [g] 4. Bl. Com. 227.

By the law of Athens, burglary was a capital crime.[h] Among the Saxons also, *burgessours* were to be punished with death.[i] In Pennsylvania, burglary and robbery receive precisely the same punishment.[j] The punishment for robbery has been already mentioned.

[h] 1. Pot. Ant. c. 26.   [i] 1. Reev. 485.   [j] 2. Laws. Penn. 802. s. 2.

III

OF CRIMES AGAINST THE RIGHT OF INDIVIDUALS TO LIBERTY, AND TO REPUTATION

LIBERTY, as we have seen on former occasions, is one of the natural rights of man; and one of the most important of those natural rights. This right, as well as others, may be violated; and its violations, like those of other rights, ought to be punished, in order to be prevented. Yet these violations are scarcely discernible in our code of criminal law.

This we must ascribe to one of two causes. Either this right has been enjoyed inviolably: or the law has suffered the violations of it to escape with shameful impunity. The latter is the truth: I am compelled to add, that the latter, bad as it is, is not the *whole* truth. Violations of liberty have not only been overlooked: they have also been protected; they have also been encouraged; they have also been made; they have also been enjoined by the law. I speak this not only concerning the statute law; I am compelled to speak it also concerning the common law of England: I speak this not only concerning the law as it was received in the American States before their revolution; I am compelled to speak it also concerning the law as it is received in them still: I speak this not only concerning the law as it is received generally in the other sister states; I am compelled to speak it also concerning the law as it is received in Pennsylvania: nay, I am farther compelled to speak it also of the law as it is recently received in our national government.

Our *publick* liberty we have indeed secured; — *esto perpetua* — But, notwithstanding all our boasted improvements — and they are improvements of which we may well boast — the most formidable enemy to *private* liberty is, at this moment, the law of the land.

In some former parts of my lectures,[a] I have had occasion to remark, and I have remarked with pleasure, that solicitous degree of attention which the law gives to personal security. Its most distant avenues are watchfully guarded. To decide questions, by which it may be affected in the highest, or even in inferiour degrees, I have shown, in a sublime part

[a] Ante. p. 547. et seq.

of our system, to be the incommunicable prerogative of sovereignty or selected sovereignty itself. I have shown, that, by an operation inexpressibly fine, personal safety never sees the arm which holds the sword of justice, but at the moment when it is found necessary that its stroke should be made. Inferiour to personal safety only, if indeed inferiour even to that, is the consideration of personal liberty. And yet, while personal safety can be authoritatively affected only by the community, or a body selected from the community impartially and for the occasion, the law implicitly, causelessly, unconditionally, and continually prostrates personal liberty at the feet of every wretch who is unprincipled enough to trample upon it. I say, unprincipled; because a citizen, who has principle, will not wound it by using the authority of the law. In every state of the union — in every county of every state, there are shops opened, nay licensed, nay established by the law, at which its authority may be purchased, for a trifle, by the worst citizen, in order to infringe the personal liberty of the best.

From the disgrace of these enormities against the rights of liberty, I gladly rescue the character and principles of the common law. The history of the several processes of capias, and orders and rules of commitment will show, when we come to it, that this part of our municipal law is of statute original; and that it was produced in the darkest and rudest, though its existence has continued in the most enlightened and the most refined times.

With another part of these enormities against the rights of liberty, however, impartiality obliges me to charge the common law. Man is composed of a soul and of a body. To mental as well as to bodily freedom, he has a natural and an unquestionable right. The former was grossly violated by the common law. Witness the many overgrown titles, by which the volumes of the law are still distended: witness, in particular, the customs *de modo decimandi*, and the writs *de excommunicato capiendo* and *de heretico comburendo*.[b] These parts I only mention; because from these parts we are happily relieved: they are parts of the common law, which did not suit those who emigrated to America: they were, therefore, left behind them.

But, in some respects, private liberty is still the orphan neglected; in others, she is still the victim devoted by our municipal law. So inveterate, indeed, is the vice of the law in this particular, that it has infected its very language. The terms, which denote the diminution or the destruction of personal safety — homicide, wounding, battery, assault — are all *prima facie* understood in an unfavourable meaning; though they are sometimes excused, or justified, or even enjoined, as well as sometimes prohibited and punished by the law: but to imprisonment, the idea of

[b] 4. Bl. Com. 46.

legal authority seems, in legal understanding, to be *prima facie* annexed: and when it speaks of the unauthorized kind, it is obliged to distinguish it by adding the epithets *false* or *unlawful*.

But legislators should bear in their minds, and should practically observe — and well persuaded I am, that our American legislators bear in their minds, and, whenever the necessary resettlement of things after a revolution can possibly admit of it, will practically observe, with regard to this interesting subject — the following great and important political maxim: — Every wanton, or causeless, or unnecessary act of authority, exerted, or authorized, or encouraged by the legislature over the citizens, is wrong, and unjustifiable, and tyrannical: for every citizen is, of right, entitled to liberty, personal as well as mental, in the highest possible degree, which can consist with the safety and welfare of the state. "Legum" — I repeat it — "servi sumus, ut *liberi* esse possimus." * In the course of my future investigations into this point, I shall be able to evince, in the clearest manner, that our municipal regulations concerning it are not less hostile to the true principles of utility, than they are to those of the superiour law of liberty.

Having made these preliminary observations on a subject, which so greatly needs, and so richly deserves them, I proceed to search the little that is said in some of our systems of criminal law — in others nothing is said — concerning it.

False imprisonment is punishable by indictment, like assaults and batteries; and the delinquent may be fined and imprisoned.[c]

Thus much concerning the crime of violating the personal liberty of man.

Reputation, except that of official characters, seems not, of late times, any more than personal liberty, to have attracted the distinguished regard of our publick law: and even when it deigns a little degree of regard to it, that regard flows from a wrong principle, and is referred to a wrong end. Libels are considered as objects of publick cognizance, not because the character, but because the tranquillity of the citizens is precious to the publick; and therefore, crimes of this nature are classed and prosecuted and punished as breaches of the peace, and as much resembling challenges to fight.[d] But it was not always so.

I said, on a former occasion,[e] that robbery itself does not flow from a fountain more rankly poisoned, than that which throws out the waters of calumny and defamation. In saying so, I was warranted by authority respectable and ancient. By the laws of the Saxons, the felon, who robbed, was punished less severely than the wretch who calumniated. By a law, made, towards the end of the seventh century, by

* [We are servants of the law so that we can be free.]
[c] 4. Bl. Com. 218. 2. Haw. 90.   [d] 4. Bl. Com. 150.   [e] Ante. p. 596.

Lothere, one of the kings of Kent, a calumniator was obliged to pay one shilling to him in whose house or lands he uttered the calumny. It was conceived, it seems, to diffuse a degree of contamination over things inanimate. He was obliged to pay six shillings to the person whom he calumniated, and twelve shillings to the king. When we recollect, that, long *after* this time, a shilling could purchase a fatted ox; we may judge concerning the light, in which defamation was viewed *at* this time. But Edgar the peaceable, who flourished about two centuries afterwards, made, against this crime, a law much more severe: it decreed, that a person convicted of gross and dangerous defamation should have his tongue cut out, unless he redeemed it by paying his full *were*, as it was called, or the price of his life. This law was confirmed by Canute the great.[f]

By the laws of Egypt, a defamer was condemned to the same punishment, which would have been inflicted on the defamed, if the defamation had been true.[g] Solon, in one of his laws, ordained, that a delinquent in slander should make reparation in money to the party injured, and should also pay a fine into the publick treasury.[h]

A libel may be described — a malicious defamation of any person, published by writing, or printing, or signs, or pictures, and tending to expose him to publick hatred, contempt, or ridicule.[i] It is clearly a crime at the common law.[j]

It has been often observed in the course of these lectures, that one extreme naturally produces its opposite. An unwarrantable attempt made in the star chamber, during the reign of James the first, to wrest the law of libels to the purposes of ministers, and an effort continued ever since to carry that attempt into execution, and even to go beyond some of its worst principles, have, in England, lost to the community the benefits of that law, wise and salutary when administered properly; and by the proper persons. The decision in that case has ever since been considered, in England, as the foundation of the law on this subject. It will be proper, therefore, to examine the parts of that decision with some degree of minuteness.

The libel, prosecuted and condemned, was a satyrical ballad on a deceased archbishop of Canterbury and his living successour.[k]

The first resolution is, that a libel against a magistrate, or other public person, is a greater offence than one against a private man. This, in the unqualified manner here expressed, cannot be rationally admitted. Other circumstances being equal, that of office ought to incline the beam, if the libel refer to his official character or conduct; because an officer is a citizen and more. But a libel of one kind against a private citizen, may

---

[f] 2. Henry. 293.   [g] 2. Gog. Or. L. 58.   [h] 1. Pot. Ant. 179.
[i] 1. Haw. 193.   [j] 3. Ins. 174.   [k] 5. Rep. 125.

certainly be more atrocious, and of example more atrociously evil, than a libel of another kind against a publick officer.

Another and a more important resolution in that case is — that it is immaterial whether the libel be false or true. This resolution is clearly extrajudicial, because it appears, from the state of the case, that the author of the libel was proceeded against on his own confession. The rule, however, has been followed by more modern determinations; and reasons have been offered to support it on the principles of law. The provocation and not the falsity, says Sir William Blackstone, is the thing to be punished criminally. In a civil action, he admits, a libel must appear to be false as well as scandalous; for, if the charge be true, the plaintiff has received no private injury, and has no ground to demand a compensation for himself, whatever offence it may be against the publick peace; and, therefore, upon a civil action, the truth of the accusation may be pleaded in bar of the suit. But in a criminal prosecution, the tendency which all libels have to create animosities, and to disturb the publick peace, is the sole consideration of the law.[1]

Upon this passage, I observe, in the first place, that a libel is a violation of the right of character, and not of the right of personal safety. It is no wonder if the reasonings on this crime are inaccurate, when its very principle is mistaken.

I observe, in the second place, that these inaccurate reasonings are attempted to be established by a gross inconsistency. When they refer to the *effects* of the libel, they suppose the tendency to produce disturbances of the peace: when they refer to the *causes* of the libel, they say to him who is actuated by them — you ought, in a settled government, to complain for every injury in the ordinary course of law, and by no means to revenge yourself.[m] Why is not this advice given consistently, to the person provoked by the libel? If he has received an injury — if on that injury a crime is superinduced; the law will repair the former, and punish the latter: if no injury has been sustained, no foundation has been laid for a crime.

I observe, in the third place, that Sir William Blackstone here seems not to have been sufficiently attentive to a principle, which he properly subscribes in another part of his Commentaries:[n] the crime includes an injury: every publick offence is also a private wrong, and somewhat more: it affects the individual, and it likewise affects the community.

The only points, it is said, to be considered in the prosecution for a libel, are, first, the making or publishing of the book or writing: secondly, whether the matter be criminal.[o]

On the last of these two points, a celebrated controversy has subsisted between judges and juries; the former claiming its decision as a question

[1] 4. Bl. Com. 150.   [m] 5. Rep. 125 b.   [n] 4. Bl. Com. 5.   [o] Id. 151.

of law; the latter claiming it as a question of fact, or, at least, necessarily involved in the decision of a question of fact. After what I have said, in a former lecture,[p] concerning the general duties and powers of juries, you will be at no loss to know my sentiments on this controverted subject. I only remark, at present, that if a libel be, as I think it is, a crime against the right of reputation; the trial on a libel must be the trial of a character, or some part of a character. Of all questions, almost, which can be proposed, I think this the most remote from a question of law.

The constitution of Pennsylvania has put this matter upon an explicit footing, consonant, or nearly consonant in my opinion, to the true principles of the common law: "in all indictments for libels, the jury shall have a right to determine the law and the facts, under the direction of the court, as in other cases." [q]

The punishment of a libel is a fine, or a fine and corporal punishment.[r]

[p] Ante. p. 520.   [q] Art. 9. s. 7.   [r] 1. Haw. 196.

IV

OF CRIMES AGAINST THE RIGHT OF INDIVIDUALS TO PERSONAL SAFETY

THE crimes which are next to be enumerated and considered are those against the right of personal safety. On this subject, the common law has been peculiarly accurate and attentive.

An assault is an attempt or offer, with force and violence, to do a corporal hurt to another; as by striking at him; by holding up the fist at him; by pointing a pitchfork at him, if he be within its reach; by presenting a gun at him, if he be within the distance to which it will carry; or by any other act of a similar kind, done in an angry and threatening manner.[a] An assault is violence inchoate.[b]

A battery is violence completed by beating another. Any injury done to the person of a man, in an angry, or revengeful, or rude, or insolent manner, as by touching him in any manner, or by spitting in his face, is a battery in the eye of the law.[c] In that eye, the person of every man is sacred: between the different degrees of violence it is impossible to draw a line: with great propriety, therefore, its very first degree is prohibited.[d]

Wounding is a dangerous hurt given to another; and is an aggravated species of battery.[e]

These offences may unquestionably be considered as private injuries, for which compensation ought to be decreed to those who suffer them. But viewed in a publick light, they are breaches of the publick peace: as such they may be prosecuted; and as such they may be punished. The punishment is fine, or fine and imprisonment.[f]

A battery or an assault, violence or an offer of violence, is susceptible of deep criminality from the atrocious intention, with which it is sometimes offered or done. An assault with a design to murder, to perpetrate the last outrage upon the honour of the fair sex, or to commit the crime which ought not to be even named — these are instances of what I mention: in these instances, to a heavy fine and imprisonment, it is usual to add the judgment of the pillory.[g]

Assaults, batteries, and woundings may be sometimes excused, and

[a] 1. Haw. 133.   [b] 3. Bl. Com. 120.   [c] 1. Haw. 134.   [d] 3. Bl. Com. 120.
[e] Id. 121,   [f] 1. Haw. 134. 4. Bl. Com. 217.   [g] 4. Bl. Com. 217.

sometimes justified. The particular cases in which this may be done, will be explained with more propriety, when we come to consider them as private injuries, and not as publick offences.

Affrays are crimes against the personal safety of the citizens; for in their personal safety, their personal security and peace are undoubtedly comprehended. An affray is a fighting of persons in a publick place, to the terrour of the citizens. They are considered as common nuisances. They may, and ought to be suppressed by every person present; and the law, as it gives authority, so it gives protection, to those who obey its authority in suppressing them, and in apprehending such as are engaged in them; if by every person present; then still more strongly by the officers of peace and justice.[h] In some cases, there may be an affray, where there is no actual violence; as where a man arms himself with dangerous and unusual weapons, in such a manner, as will naturally diffuse a terrour among the people.[i]

To challenge another, by word or letter, to fight a duel, or to be the messenger of such a challenge, or to provoke, or even to endeavour to provoke, another to send such a challenge, is a crime of a very high nature, and is severely reprehended by the law:[j] duels are direct and insolent contempts of the justice of the state.[k]

Affrays are punished by fine and imprisonment, the measure of which must be regulated by the circumstances of the case.[l] For sending a challenge, the offenders have been adjudged to pay a fine, to be imprisoned, to make a publick acknowledgment of their offence, and to be bound to their good behaviour.

It cannot have escaped your observation, with what a judicious mixture of poignant contempt the common law seasons its indignation against those, who are so lost to true sentiment as to deem it honourable to insult the justice of their country. They are not treated as criminals of dignity: they are considered in the very degraded view of common nuisances: the putrid offals of the shambles are viewed, as we shall see, in the same light.

Neither can it have escaped your observation, with what a deep knowledge of human nature, the common law traces and pursues duels to what is frequently their cowardly as well as their cruel source. Many are vain and base enough to wish and aspire at that importance, which, in their perverted notions, arises from being even the second in a quarrel of this nature, who have not spirit enough to face that danger, which arises from being the first. Hence often the officious and the insidious offers of friendship, as it is called, on these occasions, by those who, with hearts pusillanimous and malignant, inflame, instead of endeavouring, as those

[h] 3. Ins. 158. 4. Bl. Com. 145.　　　[i] 1. Haw. 135.　　　[j] 3. Ins. 158. 1. Haw. 135.
[k] 1. Haw. 138.　　　[l] Id. ibid.

possessed of bravery and humanity would endeavour, to extinguish an unhappy dispute — a dispute, perhaps, unpremeditated as well as unhappy — regretted as well as unintended by the immediate parties — and to rescue them from the consequences of which, without any violation of the rules of true honour, and even without any departure from the rules of false honour, which every one has not the calm courage to violate, nothing is wanting but a conduct diametrically opposite to that of these pretended friends — a conduct which will prevent extremities, without wounding a sentiment which, without necessity, ought not to be wounded, because it is delicate though it be mistaken.

Animated with a just degree of blended resentment and disdain against the conduct first described, the common law wisely and humanely extends disgrace and censure and punishment to those who provoke, even to those who *endeavour* to provoke, another to send a challenge.

On the same principles on which affrays are prohibited and punished, riots, routs, and unlawful assemblies are also prohibited and punished by the common law. Two persons may commit an affray; but to a riot, a rout, or an unlawful assembly, three are necessary. A riot is a tumultuous disturbance of the peace by persons unlawfully assembled with a view to execute, and actually executing, some unlawful act, in a violent and turbulent manner, to the terrour of the people.[m] A rout is a riot unfinished; and is committed by persons unlawfully assembled with a view to execute, and actually making a *motion* to execute, an unlawful act, the execution of which would render the riot complete. An unlawful assembly is an unfinished rout; and is committed by persons unlawfully assembled with a view, but without actually making a motion, to execute an unlawful act, to the execution of which, if they had made an actual motion, they would have been guilty of a rout.[n] The punishment of these offences, at the common law, has generally been by fine and imprisonment only: cases, however, very enormous have been punished by the pillory also.[o]

Mayhem is a crime committed by violently depriving one of the use of any part of his body, by losing the use of which he becomes less able, in fighting, to annoy his adversary or to defend himself.[p] This is an atrocious breach of the publick peace and security. By it, one of the citizens is disabled from defending himself; by it, his fellow citizens are debarred from receiving that social aid which they are obliged to give; by it, the state loses those services, which it had a right to exact and expect. In ancient times, this crime was punished according to the law of retaliation: it is now punished with fine and imprisonment.[q]

The forcible abduction or stealing of a person from his country, is a

---

[m] 1. Haw. 155. Salk. 594. 3. Ins. 176.   [n] 1. Haw. 158.   [o] Id. 159.
[p] 1. Haw. 111.   [q] 4. Bl. Com. 206.

gross violation of the right of personal safety. To this crime the term *kidnapping* is appropriated by the law. It robs the state of a citizen; it banishes the citizen from his country; and it may be productive of mischiefs of the most lasting and humiliating kind. By the common law, it is punished with fine, with imprisonment, and with the pillory.[r]

A rape is an irreparable and a most atrocious aggression on the right of personal safety. Besides the thousand excruciating, but nameless circumstances by which it is aggravated, some may be mentioned with propriety. It is a crime committed not only against the citizen, but against the woman; not only against the common rights of society, but against the peculiar rights of the sex: it is committed by one from whom, on every virtuous and manly principle, her sex is entitled to inviolable protection, and her honour to the most sacred regard. This crime is one of the selected few, which, by the laws of the Saxons, were punished with death. The same punishment[s] it still undergoes in the commonwealth of Pennsylvania.[t] On this subject, for an obvious reason, particular observations will not be expected from a lecture in the hall: they are fit for the book and the closet only: for even the book and the closet they are fit, only because they are necessary.

The crime not to be named, I pass in a total silence.

I now proceed to consider homicide, and all its different species. Homicide is the generical term used by the law to denote every human act, by which a man is deprived of his life. It may be arranged under the following divisions — enjoined homicide — justifiable homicide — homicide by misfortune — excusable homicide — alleviated homicide — malicious homicide — treasonable homicide.

I. 1. Homicide is enjoined, when it is necessary for the defence of the United States, or of Pennsylvania. At present, it is not necessary for me, and, therefore, I decline to examine the general and very important subject concerning the rights of war. I confine myself merely to that kind of war, which is defensive: and even that kind I now consider solely as a municipal regulation, established by the constitution of the nation, and that of this commonwealth.

The constitution of the nation is ordained to "provide for the common defence." In order to make "provision" for that defence, congress have the power to "provide for arming the militia," and "for calling them forth," "to repel invasions:" they have power "to provide a navy," "to raise and support armies," "to declare war." [u] Whenever the primary

---

[r] Id. 219.   [s] 1. Laws Penn. 135.

[t] By the act of assembly of 22d. April 1794, the punishment of this crime is changed into imprisonment at hard labour, for a period not less than ten, nor more than twenty one years. 3. Laws Penn. 600. *Ed.*

[u] Cons. U.S. art. 1. s. 8.

object, "the common defence," renders it necessary, the power becomes the duty of congress: and it requires no formal deduction of logick to point to the duty, when necessity shall require, of military bodies, "raised, supported, and armed." In Pennsylvania, it is explicitly declared upon the very point, that "the freemen of this commonwealth shall be armed for its defence."[v]

2. Homicide is enjoined, when it is necessary for the defence of one's person or house.

With regard to the first, it is the great natural law of self preservation, which, as we have seen,[w] cannot be repealed, or superseded, or suspended by any human institution. This law, however, is expressly recognised in the constitution of Pennsylvania.[x] "The right of the citizens to bear arms in the defence of themselves shall not be questioned." This is one of our many renewals of the Saxon regulations. "They were bound," says Mr. Selden, "to keep arms for the preservation of the kingdom, and of their own persons."[y]

With regard to the second; every man's house is deemed, by the law, to be his castle; and the law, while it invests him with the power, enjoins on him the duty, of the commanding officer. "Every man's house is his castle," says my Lord Coke, in one of his reports, "and he ought to keep and defend it at his peril; and if any one be robbed in it, it shall be esteemed his own default and negligence."[z] For this reason, one may assemble people together in order to protect and defend his house.[a]

3. Homicide is frequently enjoined by the judgment of courts agreeably to the directions of the law. This is the case in all capital punishments. This species of homicide is usually classed with those kinds which are justifiable. The epithet is true so far as it goes. But it goes not far enough to characterize the conduct of the officer to whom it relates. One may be justifiable in doing a thing, in omitting to do which he may be equally justified. But this is not the case with a sheriff, or other ministerial officer of justice. He is *commanded* to do execution.

II. As homicide is enjoined, when a sentence of death is to be executed; so it is sometimes justified in the execution of other process from the courts of justice. When persons, who have authority to arrest, and who use the proper means for that purpose, are resisted in doing so, and the party making resistance is killed in the struggle; this homicide is justifiable.[b] If a person, who interposes to part the combatants in an affray, and gives notice to them of his friendly intention, is assaulted by any of them, and, in the struggle, happens to kill; this is justifiable homicide. For, in such cases, it is the duty of every man to interpose, that mischief

[v] Cons. Penn. art. 6. s. 2.　[w] Ante. p. 609.　[x] Art. 9. s. 21.
[y] Bac. on Gov. 40.　[z] 7. Rep. 6.　[a] 1. Hale. P. C. 547. 4. Bl. Com. 223.
[b] Eden. 209. Fost. 270. 1. Hale. P. C. 494.

may be prevented, and the peace may be preserved. This rule is founded in the principles of social duty.[e] If a woman, in defence of her honour, kill him who attempts the last outrage against it; this homicide is justifiable.[d] In the same manner, the husband or father may justify the killing of one, who makes a similar attempt upon his daughter or wife.[e] In these instances of justifiable homicide, the person who has done it is to be acquitted and discharged, with commendation rather than censure.[f]

III. Homicide by misfortune happens, when a man, in the execution of a lawful act, and without intending any harm, unfortunately kills another.[g] The act must not only be lawful, but must also be done in a lawful manner. If a master, correcting his servant moderately, happens to occasion his death, it is only misadventure; for the act of correction was lawful: but it is much otherwise, if he exceed in the manner, the instrument, or the quantity of the correction.[h]

This species of homicide, if found by a jury, still, in strict law, as it is received in England, subjects the unfortunate — I cannot call him the guilty — party, to a forfeiture of his personal estate; or, as some say, only a part of it. He has, it is true, his pardon, and a writ for restoring his goods, as a matter of course, when he pays the fees for them.[i] Sir William Blackstone seems to make an apology for this forfeiture, by observing, that, in the case of homicide by misadventure, the law presumes negligence, or, at least, a want of sufficient caution, in him who was so unfortunate as to commit it; who, therefore, is not altogether faultless.[j] The law itself is severe in this instance — confessedly so: but the apology for it seems to be founded on a principle, rigorous and totally inadmissible.

Shall the unfortunate be necessarily viewed as also incautious? Shall negligence be presumed by the law, when misadventure has been found by the jury? No. The doctrine is inadmissible. It is rigorous. Accidents of this lamentable kind may be the lot of the wisest and most cautious, and of the best and most humane among men: they most frequently happen among those who are relations or friends; because those associate most frequently together. In such cases, to ascribe the calamity to a conduct "not altogether faultless;" to "presume negligence," when nothing existed but bitter misfortune, would, indeed, be to "heap affliction upon the head of the afflicted," and to stab afresh a heart still bleeding with its former wound. It would be to aggravate the loss of even a brother, a parent, a child, a wife; if of aggravation such a loss, in such circumstances, is susceptible.[k]

The law itself, in this instance, is, as has been mentioned, severe —

---

[e] Fost. 272. Eden. 209.   [d] Fost. 274. Eden. 210.   [e] 4. Bl. Com. 181.
[f] Id. 182. Fost. 279.   [g] Fost. 258.   [h] 4. Bl. Com. 182. Fost. 262.
[i] 4. Bl. Com. 188.   [j] Id. 186.   [k] Fost. 264.

confessedly so. The fees of office have probably, in this as in too many other instances, prevented improvement. "I therefore think," to use the expressions of a great master of criminal law, "those judges, who have taken general verdicts of acquittal in plain cases of homicide by misfortune, have not been to blame. They have, to say the worst, deviated from ancient practice in favour of innocence, and have prevented an expense of time and money, with which an application to the great seal, though in a matter of course, as this undoubtedly is, must be constantly attended." [1] It is proper to observe that this late practice of the judges is mentioned by Sir William Blackstone, in terms which intimate his approbation.[m]

IV. Excusable homicide is that which, on a sudden affray[n] between parties, is given in the necessary defence of him who wishes and endeavours to quit the combat. This is carefully to be distinguished, because it is materially different, from that kind of self defence which is justified or enjoined to prevent the perpetration of the most atrocious outrage upon one's person or habitation.[o]

The species of homicide, which we are now to consider, though excusable by the benignity of the law, is still culpable. It is done, when a person, engaged in a sudden affray, quits the combat before a mortal wound is given, and retreats or flies as far as he can with safety; and then, urged by mere necessity, kills his adversary for the preservation of his own life.[p] This species approaches near to manslaughter; and, in experience, the boundary between them is, in some places, difficult to be discerned: it is marked, however, in the consideration of law. In both species, it is supposed that passion has kindled on each side; and that blows have passed between the parties. But in the case of manslaughter, either the combat on both sides continues till the mortal stroke is given, or the party giving it is not in imminent danger: whereas, in the case of excusable homicide, he who is excused declines, before a mortal stroke given, any further combat, and retreats as far as he can with safety; and then, through mere necessity, and to avoid immediate death, kills his adversary.[q]

Though this species of homicide is very different from that which happens by misfortune; yet the judges, in one as well as the other, permit, if not direct, a general verdict of acquittal.[r]

V. To alleviated homicide, the term *manslaughter* is appropriated. When the epithet *alleviated* is applied to this species of homicide, it must be understood only as compared with that which is malicious: for manslaughter, though in this view an alleviated, is a felonious homicide. It is the unlawful killing of another, without malice; and may be either

[1] Fost. 288.   [m] 4. Bl. Com. 188.   [n] Fost. 276.   [o] 4. Bl. Com. 183.
[p] Fost. 275.   [q] Fost. 275. 277. 4. Bl. Com. 185.   [r] 4. Bl. Com. 188.

voluntarily, upon a sudden heat or provocation; or involuntarily, but in the commission of some unlawful act. When manslaughter is voluntary, it is distinguished from excusable homicide by this criterion — that, in the latter case, the killing is through necessity, and to avoid immediate death; whereas, in the former, there is no necessity at all; it being a sudden act of revenge. When manslaughter is involuntary, it is distinguished from homicide by misfortune by this criterion — that the latter always happens in consequence of a lawful, the former, in consequence of an unlawful act. Manslaughter, both voluntary and involuntary, is distinguished from malicious homicide by this criterion — that the latter is with, the former without, malice.

In England, manslaughter is punished by burning in the hand, and by the forfeiture of goods and chattels.[s] In the United States, it is punished by a fine not exceeding one thousand dollars, and by imprisonment not exceeding three years.[t] In Pennsylvania,[u] it is punished by a fine at the discretion of the court, and by imprisonment not exceeding two years; and the offender shall find security for his good behaviour during life.[v]

VI. To malicious homicide the term *murder* is appropriated by the law. This name was, in ancient times, applied only to the *secret* killing of another; for which the vill or hundred where it was committed was heavily amerced. This amercement was called *murdrum*. This expression is now applied to the crime; and the crime is now considered in a very different, and much more extensive point of view, without regarding whether the person killed was killed openly or secretly.[w]

Murder is the unlawful killing of another with malice aforethought, express or implied.[x] The distinction, you observe, which is strongly marked between manslaughter and murder is, that the former is committed without, the latter with malice aforethought. It is essential, therefore, to know, clearly and accurately, the true and legal import of this characteristick distinction.

There is a very great difference between that sense which is conveyed

---

[s] 4. Bl. Com. 193.   [t] Laws U.S. 1. cong. 2. sess. c. 9. s. 7.
[u] 1. Laws. Penn. 846.
[v] The punishment of *voluntary* manslaughter, by the act of 22d April, 1794 (3. Laws. Penn. 601. s. 7.), is, for the first offence, imprisonment at hard labour, not less than two, nor more than ten years; and the offender shall be sentenced likewise to give security for his good behaviour during life, or for any less time, according to the nature and enormity of the offence. For the second offence, he shall be imprisoned as aforesaid not less than six, nor more than fourteen years. In cases of *involuntary* manslaughter, the prosecutor for the commonwealth may, with the leave of the court, wave the felony, and charge the person with a misdemeanor; who, on conviction, shall be fined and imprisoned as in cases of misdemeanor; or the prosecutor may charge both offences in the indictment; and the jury may in such case acquit the party of one, and find him guilty of the other charge. 3. Laws. Penn. 601. s. 8. *Ed.*   [w] 4. Bl. Com. 195.   [x] 3. Ins. 47.

by the expression *malice* in common language, and that to which the term is appropriated by the law. In common language, it is most frequently used to denote a sentiment or passion of strong malevolence to a particular person; or a settled anger and desire of revenge in one person against another. In law, it means the dictate of a wicked and malignant heart; of a depraved, perverse, and incorrigible disposition. Agreeably to this last meaning, many of the cases, which are arranged under the head of implied malice, will be found to turn upon this single point, that the fact has been attended with such circumstances — particularly the circumstances of deliberation and cruelty concurring — as betray the plain indications and genuine symptoms of a mind grievously depraved, and acting from motives highly criminal; of a heart regardless of social duty, and deliberately bent upon mischief. This is the true notion of malice, in the legal sense of the word. The mischievous and vindictive spirit denoted by it, must always be collected and inferred from the circumstances of the transaction. On the circumstances of the transaction, the closest attention should, for this reason, be bestowed. Every circumstance may weigh something in the scale of justice.

In England, in the United States, in Pennsylvania, and almost universally throughout the world, the crime of wilful and premeditated murder is and has been punished with death. Indeed it seems agreed by all, that, if a capital punishment ought to be inflicted for any crimes, this is unquestionably a crime for which it ought to be inflicted. Those who think that a capital punishment is enjoined against this crime by the law which is divine, will not imitate the conduct of that Polish monarch, who remitted to the nobility the penalties of murder, in a charter of pardon beginning arrogantly thus[y] — "Nos divini juris rigorem moderantes, &c."[z]

VII. Treasonable homicide is committed by a servant who kills his master, and a wife, who kills her husband. Petit treason is the name appropriated, by the law, to this crime. It arises from the relation which subsists between the person killing and the person killed. The crime which, committed by another, would be murder, is petit treason when committed by the wife, or by a servant.

[y] 4. Bl. Com. 194. [We, moderating the rigor of divine law . . .]
[z] Murder, by the act of 22d April, 1794, is distinguished into two degrees. Murder of the first degree alone is punished with death, and is the only capital crime now known to the laws of Pennsylvania. Murder perpetrated by means of poison, or by lying in wait, or by any other kind of wilful, deliberate, and premeditated killing, or committed in the perpetration, or attempt to perpetrate, any arson, rape, robbery, or burglary, is deemed murder of the first degree. All other kinds of murder are deemed murder in the second degree. The punishment of this is imprisonment at hard labour, for a period not less than five, nor more than eighteen years. 3. Laws. Penn. 599. 600. s. 1. 2. 4. *Ed.*

The punishment of this crime, in England, is, that the man is drawn and hanged; and the woman is drawn and burned.[a] By a law[b] still in force in Pennsylvania, persons convicted of this crime, or of murder, shall suffer as the laws of Great Britain now do or hereafter shall direct and require in such cases respectively.[c]

[a] 4. Bl. Com. 204.   [b] 1. Laws. Penn. 135.
[c] "Every person liable to be prosecuted for petit treason shall in future be indicted, proceeded against, and punished, as is directed in other kinds of murder." Act of 22d April, 1794. s. 3. 3. Laws Penn. 600. *Ed.*

V

OF CRIMES, IMMEDIATELY AGAINST
THE COMMUNITY

I HAVE hitherto considered crimes, which wound the community through the sides of individuals: I now come to consider one which directly and immediately aims a stab at the vitals of the community herself. I mean treason against the United States, and against the state of Pennsylvania.

Treason is unquestionably a crime most dangerous to the society, and most repugnant to the first principles of the social compact. It must, however, be observed, that as the crime itself is dangerous and hostile to the state, so the imputation of it has been and may be dangerous and oppressive to the citizens. To the freest governments this observation is by no means inapplicable; as might be shown at large by a deduction, historical and political, which would be both interesting and instructive. But, at present, we have not time for it.

To secure the state, and at the same time to secure the citizens — and, according to our principles, the last is the end, and the first is the means — the law of treason should possess the two following qualities. 1. It should be determinate. 2. It should be stable.

It is the observation of the celebrated Montesquieu,[a] that if the crime of treason be indeterminate, this alone is sufficient to make any government degenerate into arbitrary power. In monarchies, and in republicks, it furnishes an opportunity to unprincipled courtiers, and to demagogues equally unprincipled, to harass the independent citizen, and the faithful subject, by treasons, and by prosecutions for treasons, constructive, capricious, and oppressive.

In point of precision and accuracy with regard to this crime, the common law, it must be owned, was grossly deficient. Its description was uncertain and ambiguous; and its denomination and penalties were wastefully communicated to offences of a different and inferiour kind. To lop off these numerous and dangerous excrescences, and to reduce the law on this important subject to a designated and convenient form, the famous statute of treasons was made in the reign of Edward the third, on the

[a] Sp. L. b. 12. c. 7.

application of the lords and commons. This statute has been in England, except during times remarkably tyrannical or turbulent, the governing rule with regard to treasons ever since. Like a rock, strong by nature, and fortified, as successive occasions required, by the able and the honest assistance of art, it has been impregnable by all the rude and boistrous assaults, which have been made upon it, at different quarters, by ministers and by judges; and as an object of national security, as well as of national pride, it may well be styled the legal Gibraltar of England.

Little of this statute, however, demands our minute attention now; as the great changes in our constitutions have superceded all its monarchical parts. One clause of it, indeed, merits our strictest investigation; because it is transcribed into the constitution of the United States. Another clause in it merits our strongest regard; because it contains and holds forth a principle and an example, worthy of our observance and imitation.

After having enumerated and declared all the different species of treason, which it was thought proper to establish, the statute proceeds in this manner: "and because many other cases of like treason may happen in time to come, which, at present, a man cannot think or declare; it is assented, that if any other case, supposed treason, which is not specified above, happen before any judges, they shall not go to judgment in such case; but shall tarry, till it be shown and declared before the king and his parliament, whether it ought to be judged treason or other felony."

The great and the good Lord Hale observes[b] upon this clause, "the great wisdom and care of the parliament, to keep judges within the bounds and express limits of this statute, and not to suffer them to run out, upon their own opinions, into constructive treasons, though in cases which seem to have a parity of reason" — cases of like treason — "but reserves them to the decision of parliament. This," he justly says, "is a great security as well as direction to judges; and a great safeguard even to this sacred act itself."

It is so. And it was all the safeguard which the parliament, by the constitution, as it is called, of England, could give. It was a safeguard from the arbitrary constructions of courts: it was a shelter from judicial storms: but is was no security against legislative tempests. No parliament, however omnipotent, could bind its successours, possessed of equal omnipotence; and no power, higher than the power of parliament, was then or is yet recognised in the juridical system of England. What was the consequence? In the very next reign, the fluctuating and capricious one of Richard the second, the parliaments were profuse, even to ridicule — if, in such a serious subject, ridicule could find a place — in enacting new, tyrannical, and even contradictory treasons. This they did to such

[b] 1. Hale. P. C. 259.

an abominable degree, that, as we are told by the first parliament which met under his successour, "there was no man who knew how he ought to behave himself, to do, speak, or say, for doubt of the pains of such treasons." [e]

In the furious and sanguinary reign of Henry the eighth, the malignant spirit of inventing treasons revived, and was carried to such a height of mad extravagance, that, as we have seen on another occasion, the learned as well as the unlearned, the cautious as well as the unwary, the honest as well as the vicious, were entrapped in the snares. How impotent, as well as cruel and inconsistent, is tyranny in the extreme! His savage rage recoiled, at some times, upon those who were most near to him; at other times, with more justice, upon himself. The beautiful and amiable Boleyn became the victim of that very law, which her husband, in his fit of lustful passion — for the monster was callous to *love* — made for her security. When the enormities of his life and reign were drawing towards their end, his physicians saw their tyrant in their patient; and they refused to apprize him of his situation, because he had made it treason to predict his death.

Admonished by the history of such times and transactions as these, when legislators are tyrants or tools of tyrants; establishing, under their own control, a power superiour to that of the legislature; and availing themselves of that power, more permanent as well as superiour; the people of the United States have wisely and humanely ordained, that "treason against the United States shall consist only in levying war against them, or in adhering to their enemies, giving them aid and comfort." [d]

In this manner, the citizens of the Union are secured effectually from even legislative tyranny: and in this instance, as in many others, the happiest and most approved example of other times has not only been imitated, but excelled. This single sentence comprehends our whole of national treason; and, as I mentioned before, is transcribed from a part of the statute of Edward the third. By those who proposed the national constitution, this was done, that, in a subject so essentially interesting to each and to all, not a single expression should be introduced, but such as could show in its favour, that it was recommended by the mature experience, and ascertained by the legal interpretation, of numerous revolving centuries.

To the examination, and construction, and well designated force of those expressions, I now solicit your strict attention.

"Treason consists in levying war against the United States." In order to understand this proposition accurately and in all its parts, it may be necessary to give a full and precise answer to all the following questions.

[e] St. 1. Hen. 4. c. 10.   [d] Con. U.S. art. 3. s. 3.

1. What is meant by the expression "levying war?" 2. By whom may the war be levied? 3. Against whom must it be levied?

To each of these questions I mean to give an answer — if possible, a satisfactory answer; but not in the order, in which they are proposed. I begin with the second — by whom may the war spoken of be levied? It is such a war as constitutes treason. The answer then is this: the war must be levied by those who, while they levy it, are at the same time guilty of treason. This throws us back necessarily upon another question — who may commit treason against the United States? To this the answer is — those who owe obedience to their authority. But still another question rises before us — who are they that owe obedience to that authority? I answer — those who receive protection from it. In the monarchy of Great Britain, protection and allegiance are universally acknowledged to be rights and duties reciprocal. The same principle reigns in governments of every kind. I use here the expression *obedience* instead of the expression *allegiance;* because, in England, allegiance is considered as due to the natural,[e] as well as to the moral person of the king; to the man, as well as to the represented authority of the nation. In the United States, the authority of the nation is the sole object on one side. An object strictly corresponding to that, should be the only one required on the other side. The object strictly corresponding to authority is, obedience to that authority. I speak, therefore, with propriety and accuracy unexceptional, when I say, that those who owe obedience to the authority, are such as receive the protection, of the United States.

This close series of investigation has led us to a standard, which is plain and easy, as well as proper and accurate — a standard, which every one can, without the possibility of a mistake, discover by his experience, as well as by his understanding — by what he enjoys, as well as by what he sees. Every one has a monitor within him, which can tell whether he feels protection from the authority of the United States: if he does, to that authority he owes obedience. On the political, as well as on the natural globe, every point must have its antipode. Of obedience the antipode is treason.

I have now shown, by whom the war may be levied. On this subject, a great deal of learning, historical, legal, and political, might be displayed; and changes might easily be rung on the doctrines of natural, and local, and temporary, and perpetual allegiance. I purposely avoid them. The reason is, that so much false is blended with so little genuine intelligence, as to render any discovery you would make an inadequate compensation for your trouble in searching for it. The rights and duties of protection and obedience may, I think, in a much more plain and direct road, be brought home to the bosom and the business of every one.

[e] 1. Bl. Com. 371.

I now proceed to another question — what is meant by the expression "levying war?" From what has been said in answer to the former question, an answer to this is so far prepared as to inform us, that the term *war* cannot, in this place, mean such a one as is carried on between independent powers. The parties on one side are those who owe obedience. All the curious and extensive learning, therefore, concerning the laws of war as carried on between separate nations, must be thrown out of this question. This is such a war as is levied by those who owe obedience — by citizens; and therefore must be such a war, as, in the nature of things, citizens can levy.

The indictments for this treason generally describe the persons indicted as "arrayed in a warlike manner." As where people are assembled in great numbers, armed with offensive weapons, or weapons of war, if they march thus armed in a body, if they have chosen commanders or officers, if they march with banners displayed, or with drums or trumpets: whether the greatness of their numbers and their continuance together doing these acts may not amount to being arrayed in a warlike manner,[f] deserves consideration. If they have no military arms, nor march or continue together in the posture of war; they may be great rioters, but their conduct does not always amount to a levying of war.[g]

If one, with force and weapons invasive or defensive, hold and defend a castle or fort against the publick power; this is to levy war. So an actual insurrection or rebellion is a levying of war, and by that name must be expressed in the indictment.[h]

But this question will receive a farther illustration from the answer to the third question; because the fact of levying war is often evinced more clearly from the purpose for which, than from the manner in which, the parties assemble. I therefore proceed to examine the last question — against whom must the war be levied? It must be levied against the United States.

The words of the statute of treasons are, "if any one levy war against the king." I have before observed that, in England, allegiance is considered as due to the natural, as well as to the moral person of the king. This part of the statue of treasons has been always understood as extending to a violation of allegiance in both those points of view — to the levying of war not only against his person, but also against his authority or laws.[i] The levying of war against the United States can, for the reasons already suggested, be considered only in the latter view.

The question now arising is the following — Is such or such a war levied against the United States? This question, as was already intimated, will be best answered by considering the intention with which it was

[f] 1. Hale. P. C. 131. 150.   [g] Id. 131.   [h] 3. Ins. 10.
[i] 1. Haw. 37. 4. Bl. Com. 81. Fost. 211.

levied.[j] If it is levied on account of some *private* quarrel, or to take revenge of particular persons, it is not a war levied against the United States.[k] A rising to maintain a *private* claim of right; to break prisons for the release of *particular* persons, without any other circumstance of aggravation; or to remove nuisances which affect, or are thought to affect, in point of interest, the parties who assemble — this is not a levying of war against the United States.[l] Insurrections in order to throw down *all* inclosures, to open *all* prisons, to enhance the price of *all* labour, to expel foreigners in general, or those from any single nation living under the protection of government, to alter the established law, or to render it ineffectual — insurrections to accomplish these ends, by numbers and an open and armed force, are a levying of war against the United States.[m]

The line of division between this species of treason and an aggravated riot is sometimes very fine and difficult to be distinguished. In such instances, it is safest and most prudent to consider the case in question as lying on the side of the inferiour crime.[n]

Treason consists in "adhering to the enemies of the United States, giving them aid and comfort." By enemies, are here understood the citizens or subjects of foreign princes or states, with whom the United States are at open war. But the subjects or citizens of such states or princes, in actual hostility, though no war be solemnly declared, are such enemies.[o] The expressions "giving them aid and comfort" are explanatory of what is meant by adherence. To give intelligence to enemies, to send provisions to them, to sell arms to them, treacherously to surrender a fort to them, to cruise in a ship with them against the United States — these are acts of adherence, aid, and comfort.[p]

To join with rebels in a rebellion, or with enemies in acts of hostility, is treason in a citizen, by adhering to those enemies, or levying war with those rebels. But if this be done from apprehension of death, and while the party is under actual force, and he take the first opportunity which offers to make his escape; this fear and compulsion will excuse him.[q]

In England, the punishment of treason is terrible indeed. The criminal is drawn to the gallows, and is not suffered to walk or be carried; though usually a hurdle is allowed to preserve him from the torment of being dragged on the ground. He is hanged by the neck, and is then cut down alive. His entrails are taken out and burned, while he is yet alive. His head is cut off. His body is divided into four parts. His head and quarters are at the disposal of the king.[r]

---

[j] Fost. 208.   [k] Fost. 209.   [l] Id. 210.   [m] Id. 211. 213.
[n] 1. Hale. P. C. 146.   [o] Fost. 219.   [p] Fost. 217. 1. Haw. 38. 4. Bl. Com. 82.
[q] Fost. 216.   [r] 4. Bl. Com. 92.

In the United States and in Pennsylvania,[s] treason is punished in the same manner as other capital crimes.

A traitor is hostile to his country: a pirate is the enemy of mankind — *hostis humani generis.*

Piracy is robbery and depredation on the high seas; and is a crime against the universal law of society. By declaring war against the whole human race, the pirate has laid the whole human race under the necessity of declaring war against him. He has renounced the benefits of society and government: he has abandoned himself to the most savage state of nature. The consequence is, that, by the laws of self defence, every community has a right to inflict upon him that punishment, which, in a state of nature, every individual would be entitled to inflict for any invasion of his person or his personal property.[t]

"If any person," says a law of the United States, "shall commit, upon the high seas, or in any river, haven, basin, or bay, out of the jurisdiction of any particular state, murder or robbery, or any other offence, which, if committed within the body of a county, would, by the laws of the United States, be punished with death; every such offender shall be deemed, taken and adjudged to be a pirate and felon, and being thereof convicted shall suffer death." [u]

By the ancient common law, piracy committed by a subject was deemed a species of treason.[v] According to that law, it consists of such acts of robbery and depredation upon the high seas, as, committed on the land, would amount to a felony there.[w] The law of general society, as well as the law of nations, is a part of the common law.[x]

[s] Treason against the state is now punished by imprisonment at hard labour, for a period not less than six, nor more than twelve years. 3. Laws Penn. 600. For the description of treason against the state, see 1. Laws Penn. 726. 2. Laws Penn. 83. *Ed.*
[t] 4. Bl. Com. 71. [u] Laws U.S. 1. cong. 1. sess. c. 9. s. 8. [v] 4. Bl. Com. 71.
[w] 4. Bl. Com. 72. [x] Id. 73.

VI

OF CRIMES, AFFECTING SEVERAL OF THE NATURAL RIGHTS OF INDIVIDUALS

THOSE crimes and offences of which I have already treated, attack some *one* of the natural rights of man or of society: there are other crimes and offences, which attack *several* of those natural rights. Of these, nuisances are the most extensive and diversified.

A nuisance denotes any thing, which produces mischief, injury, or inconvenience. It is divided into two kinds — common and private.[a] The latter will be treated under the second division of my system: it is a damage to property. Common nuisances are a collection of personal injuries, which annoy the citizens generally and indiscriminately — so generally and indiscriminately, that it would be difficult to assign to each citizen his just proportion of redress; and yet, on the whole, so "noisome," that publick peace, and order, and tranquillity, and safety require them to be punished or abated.

On this subject, and, I believe, on this subject alone, the common law makes no distinction between a person and a thing. The exquisite propriety, with which the distinction is lost in this subject, proves strongly the importance of preserving it in every other. The exception establishes the rule.

How degraded are persons when they deserve to be classed with things! We have seen, on a former occasion,[b] that — 1. The duellists and the promoters of duels are ranked with the offals of the shambles. The station is, indeed, a most humiliating one. Let no station, however, yield to absolute despair. From the very lowest depression, as well as from the very highest exaltation, there is a return in a contrary course. In pure compassion for the degraded hero, let us give him at least one grade of promotion. Perhaps, by vigorous exertion, he may become qualified for his advanced dignity. The quarreller or promoter of quarrels of one sex, may behave so as to reflect no great disgrace on the common scold of the other. She, too, is a common nuisance.

2. A common scold, says the law, is a publick nuisance to her neighbourhood: as such she may be indicted, and, if convicted, shall be placed

[a] 3. Bl. Com. 216. 4. Bl. Com. 166.   [b] Ante. p. 654.

in a certain engine of correction, called the trebucket, castigatory, or *cucking* stool; which, in the Saxon language, signifies the scolding stool; though now it is frequently corrupted into *ducking* stool; because the residue of the sentence against her is, that when she is thus placed, she shall be plunged in the water[c] — for the purpose of prevention, it is presumed, as well as of punishment.

Our modern man of gallantry would not surely decline the honour of her company. I therefore propose humbly, that, in future, the cucking stools shall be made to hold double.

3. Eaves droppers too, another set of honourable associates — such as listen under walls, or windows, or eaves of a house, in order to hear the discourse of the family, and from that discourse to frame tales, mischievous and slanderous — these are common nuisances: they may be indicted as such; and as such may be punished by fine and finding sureties for their good behaviour.[d]

It is whispered to me, that the expression "eaves droppers" must refer to a very early and a very simple state of society, when people lived in cabins or huts: because when people live in three story houses, it would be rather awkward to listen at their eaves in order to learn the secrets of families. It is therefore suggested, that, as the common law is remarkable for its adroitness in accommodating itself to the successive manners of succeeding ages, a small alteration should be made in the description of this nuisance, in order to suit it to the present times; and that the tea table should be substituted in the place of the eaves of the house. I declare I have not the remotest objection to the proposal; provided the wine tables, whenever they merit it, be of the party.

4. To keep hogs in any city or market town is a common nuisance.[e]

5. Disorderly houses are publick nuisances; and, upon indictment, may be suppressed and fined.[f]

6. Every thing offensive and injurious to the health of a neighbourhood is a common nuisance; is liable to a publick prosecution; and may be punished by fine according to the quantity of the misdemeanor.[g]

7. Annoyances in highways, bridges, and publick rivers are likewise common nuisances.[h] Other kinds might be enumerated.

Indecency, publick and grossly scandalous, may well be considered as a species of common nuisance: it is certainly an offence, which may be indicted and punished at the common law.[i]

Profaneness and blasphemy are offences, punishable by fine and by imprisonment. Christianity is a part of the common law.[j]

[e] 4. Bl. Com. 169.   [d] Id. ibid.   [e] 4. Bl. Com. 167.   [f] Id. ibid.
[g] Id. ibid.   [h] Id. ibid.   [i] 1. Haw. 7. 1. Sid. 168. Wood. Ins. 412.
[j] 2. Str. 834. 4. Bl. Com. 59.

VII

OF CRIMES AGAINST THE RIGHTS OF
INDIVIDUALS ACQUIRED UNDER
CIVIL GOVERNMENT

UNDER civil government, one is entitled not only to those rights which are natural; he is entitled to others which are acquired. He is entitled to the honest administration of the government in general: he is entitled, in particular, to the impartial administration of justice. Those rights may be infringed: the infringements of them are crimes. These we next consider.

1. Extortion is the taking of money by any officer, by colour of his office, either where none is due, or where less is due, or before it is due. At common law, this crime may be severely punished by fine and imprisonment, and by a removal from the office, in the execution of which it was committed.[a]

2. Oppression under colour of office is a crime of still more extensive and of still more malignant import. Tyrannical partiality is generally its infamous associate. These, at the common law, may be punished with fine, with imprisonment, with forfeiture of office, and with other discretionary censure regulated by the nature and the aggravations of the crimes.[b]

By a law of the United States, it is enacted, that if any supervisor or other officer of inspection of the excise shall be convicted of extortion or oppression in the execution of his office; he shall be fined not exceeding five hundred dollars, or imprisoned not exceeding six months, or both, at the discretion of the court; and shall also forfeit his office.[c]

3. Even negligence in publick offices, if gross, will expose the negligent officers to a fine; and, in very notorious cases, to a forfeiture of office.[d]

4. Embracery is an attempt to influence a jury corruptly, by promises, persuasions, entreaties, money, or entertainments. The person embracing is punished by fine and imprisonment. The yielding juror is distinguished by superiour punishment.[e]

---

[a] 1. Haw. 170. 171.   [b] 4. Bl. Com. 140.
[c] Laws U.S. 1. cong. 3. sess. c. 15. s. 39.   [d] 1. Haw. 168.   [e] 4. Bl. Com. 140.

5. Bribery is, when a judge, or other person employed in the administration of justice, takes any undue reward to influence his behaviour in office. At common law, bribery, in him who offers, in him who gives, and in him who takes the bribe, is punished with fine and imprisonment. In high offices, the punishment has deservedly been higher still.[f]

Bribery also signifies sometimes the taking or the giving of a reward for an office of a publick nature. Nothing, indeed, can be more palpably pernicious to the publick, than that places of high power and high trust should be filled, not by those who are wise and good enough to execute them, but by those who are unprincipled and rich enough to purchase them.[g]

By a law of the United States, if any person shall give a bribe to a judge for his judgment in a cause depending before him; both shall be fined and imprisoned at the discretion of the court; and shall for ever be disqualified to hold any office of honour, trust, or profit under the United States.[h]

6. Perjury is a crime committed, when a lawful oath is administered in some judicial proceeding, by one who has authority, to a person who swears absolutely and falsely, in a matter material to the issue or cause in question.[i]

An oath, says my Lord Coke, is so sacred, and so deeply concerns the consciences of men, that it cannot be administered to any one, unless it be allowed by the common law, or by act of parliament; nor by any one, who has not authority by common law, or by act of parliament: neither can any oath allowed by the common law, or by act of parliament, be altered, unless by act of parliament.[j] For these reasons, it is much to be doubted whether any magistrate is justifiable in administering voluntary affidavits, unsupported by the authority of law. It is more than possible, that, by such idle oaths, a man may frequently incur the guilt, though he evade the temporal penalties of perjury.

It is a part of the foregoing definition of perjury, that it must be when the person swears *absolutely*. In addition to this, it has been said, that the oath must be direct, and not as the deponent thinks, or remembers, or believes.[k] This doctrine has, however, been lately questioned; and, it seems, on solid principles. When a man swears, that he believes what, in truth, he does not believe, he pronounces a falsehood as much, as when he swears absolutely that a thing is true, which he knows not to be true. My Lord Chief Justice De Grey, in a late case, said, that it was a mistake, which mankind had fallen into, that a person could not be convicted of perjury for deposing on oath according to his belief.[l] It is certainly true,

[f] 4. Bl. Com. 139.   [g] 1. Haw. 168.   [h] Laws U.S. 1. cong. 2. sess. c. 9. s. 21.
[i] 3. Ins. 164.   [j] 3. Ins. 165.   [k] Id. 166. 1. Haw. 175.
[l] Leach. 304.

says my Lord Mansfield, that a man may be indicted for perjury, in swearing that he believes a fact to be true, which he must know to be false.[m]

At common law, the punishment of perjury has been very various. Anciently it was punished with death; afterwards with banishment, or cutting out the tongue; afterwards by forfeiture; now by fine and imprisonment, and incapacity to give testimony.[n] To these last mentioned punishments, that of the pillory is added by a law of the[o] United States.[p]

7. Subornation of perjury is the crime of procuring another to take such a false oath as constitutes perjury. It is punished as perjury.[q]

8. Conspiracy is a crime of deep malignity against the administration of justice. Not only those, who falsely and maliciously cause an innocent man to be indicted and tried, are properly conspirators; but those also are such, who *conspire* to indict a man falsely and maliciously, whether they do or do not any act in the prosecution of the conspiracy.[r] From the description of this crime it is obvious, that at least two persons are necessary to constitute it.[s]

He who is convicted of a conspiracy to accuse another of a crime which may touch his life, shall have the following judgment pronounced against him: that he shall lose *liberam legem,* the freedom and franchise of the law, by which he is disqualified to be a juror or a witness, or even to appear in a court of justice: that his houses and lands and goods shall be forfeited during his life: that his trees shall be rooted up, his lands shall be wasted, his houses shall be rased, and his body shall be imprisoned. This is commonly called the villainous judgment: and is given by the common law.[t] By that law, all confederacies whatever wrongfully to prejudice a third person are highly criminal.[u]

9. Common barratry is another offence against the administration of justice. A common barrator is a common mover, or exciter, or maintainer of suits or quarrels, either in courts, or in the country. One act only will not constitute a barrator. He must be charged as a common barrator.[v] He is the common nuisance of society under a civil government.

A common barrator is to be fined, imprisoned, and bound to his good behaviour: if he be of the profession of the law, he is also to be further punished by being disabled, in future, to practise.[w]

---

[m] Leach. 304.   [n] 4. Bl. Com. 137.   [o] 1. Cong. 2. sess. c. 9. s. 18.

[p] By a late act of assembly in Pennsylvania (6. Laws Penn. 513.) it is provided, that persons convicted of perjury, or subornation of perjury, shall forfeit and pay any sum not exceeding five hundred dollars, and suffer imprisonment and be kept at hard labour during any term not exceeding seven years; and further, shall thereafter be disqualified from holding any office of honour, trust, or profit in the commonwealth, and from being admitted as a legal witness in any cause. *Ed.*

[q] 4. Bl. Com. 137.   [r] 1. Haw. 189.   [s] Id. 192.   [t] 1. Haw. 193.

[u] Id. 190.   [v] Id. 243.   [w] Id. 244.

10. At common law, the embezzling, defacing, or altering of any record, without due authority, was a crime highly punishable by fine and imprisonment.[x]

By a law of the United States, if any person shall feloniously steal, take away, alter, falsify, or otherwise avoid any record, writ, process, or other proceedings in any of the courts of the United States, by means of which any judgment shall be reversed, made void, or not take effect; such person shall be fined not exceeding five thousand dollars, or imprisoned not exceeding seven years, and whipped not exceeding thirty nine stripes.[y]

11. To obstruct the execution of lawful process, is a crime of a very high and presumptuous nature: to obstruct an arrest upon criminal process, is more particularly so. It has been holden, that the party opposing such an arrest becomes a partner in the crime — an accessory in felony, and a principal in treason.[z]

By a law of the United States, if any person shall knowingly and wilfully obstruct, resist, or oppose any officer of the United States in serving or attempting to serve any mesne process or warrant, or any rule or order of any of the courts of the United States, or any other legal or judicial writ or process whatsoever; or shall assault, beat, or wound any officer, or other person duly authorized, in serving or executing any such writ, rule, order, process, or warrant; he shall be imprisoned not exceeding twelve months, and fined not exceeding three hundred dollars.[a]

12. When one is arrested upon a criminal process, it is an offence even to escape from custody; and this offence may be punished by fine and imprisonment.[b] But if an officer, or a private person,[c] who has the custody of another, permits him to escape, either by negligence, or, still more, by connivance; such officer or private person is culpable in a much higher degree. He has not the natural desire of liberty to tempt — he has official obligations to prevent it. If he permits it through negligence, he may be punished by fine: if he permits it by consent or connivance, his conduct is generally agreed to amount to the same kind of crime, and to deserve the same degree of punishment, as the crime of which the prisoner is guilty, and for which he is committed; whether trespass, or felony, or treason.[d]

13. To break a prison was, at the common law, a capital crime, whatever might have been the cause, for which the person breaking it was committed. The reason assigned was — interest reipublicæ ut carceres sint in tuto.[e] Seldom is there reason to complain of the common, as of a rigorous law. In this instance, however, there is unquestionably reason for

---

[x] Id. 112.   [y] Laws U.S. 1. cong. 2 sess. c. 9. s. 15.
[z] 4. Bl. Com. 129. 2. Haw. 121.   [a] Laws U.S. 1. cong. 2. sess. c. 9. s. 22.
[b] 2. Haw. 122.   [c] 2. Haw. 138.   [d] Id. 134. 1. Hale. P. C. 590.
[e] Ins. 589. [It concerns the state that prisons be safe places of confinement.]

complaint. The Mirrour complains of it as a hard law. Its severity was moderated by a statute made in the reign of Edward the second.[f] By that statute, the breaking of a prison is not a capital crime, unless the party breaking it was committed for a capital crime. But to break prison, when lawfully committed for an inferiour offence, is a misdemeanor, and may be punished with fine and imprisonment.[g]

14. A rescue is the freeing of another, by force, from imprisonment, or from an arrest. In the person rescuing, it is generally the same crime, as a breach of prison would have been in the person breaking it. There is, however, one exception: a person, who is committed for treason and breaks the prison, is guilty of felony only: he, who rescues him, is guilty of treason.[h]

By a law of the United States,[i] if any person rescue one convicted of a capital crime, the person rescuing shall be punished capitally: if he rescue one committed, for, but not convicted of a capital crime, or one committed for, or convicted of a crime not capital; he shall be fined not exceeding five hundred dollars, and imprisoned not exceeding one year.

15. Offences against the courts, have always been considered as offences against the administration of justice. By the ancient common law before the conquest, to strike or to draw a sword in them, was a capital crime:[j] and the law still retains so much of the ancient severity, as only to exchange the loss of life for that of the offending limb.

If, while the courts in Westminster hall are sitting; or if, before justices of assize, or justices of oyer and terminer, any one shall draw a weapon upon any judge, though he strike not; or if he strike a juror or any other person, with or without a weapon; he shall lose his right hand, shall forfeit all his goods and all the profits of his lands during his life, and shall suffer perpetual imprisonment.[k]

[f] Id. ib. St. 1. Ed. 2. s. 2.   [g] 2. Haw. 128. 4. Bl. Com. 131.
[h] 2. Haw. 139. 140.   [i] 1. Cong. 2. sess. c. 9. s. 23.   [j] 3. Ins. 140.
[k] 1. Haw. 57. 3. Ins. 140.

VIII

OF THE PERSONS CAPABLE OF COMMITTING CRIMES; AND OF THE DIFFERENT DEGREES OF GUILT INCURRED IN THE COMMISSION OF THE SAME CRIME

I HAVE now enumerated the crimes and offences known to the common law; and have stated their punishments, as inflicted either by that law, or by positive statutes of the United States or of Pennsylvania.

When we come to a retrospect of this enumeration of crimes and punishments, we shall find that it is fruitful of much instruction, both of the speculative and of the practical kind. At present, let us consider who are capable and who are not capable of committing crimes. The general rule is, that all are capable of committing them. This general rule will be best illustrated and proved by ascertaining its exceptions. We have seen already, that the common law measures crimes chiefly by the intention. The intention necessarily supposes the joint operations of the understanding and the will. If the operation of either is wanting, no crime can exist. In ideots, at all times; in lunaticks, except during their lucid intervals; and in infants, till they arrive at the age of discretion, the operation of the understanding is wanting. In ministerial officers, in wives, in persons under duress, the operation of the will is frequently presumed, by the law, to be wanting. In all such cases, the law imputes not criminality of intention.

On this subject, I cannot now enter into a detail: suffice it to have mentioned the general principles, according to which the particular cases are classed and determined.

In the commission of the same crime, the law often distinguishes different degrees of guilt. One may be a principal or an accessory: a principal may be so in the first or in the second degree: an accessory may be so before or after the fact. In some crimes, there are no accessories; in others, there are none before the fact.

The part acted by a principal is coexistent with the commission of the crime: the part acted by an accessory is antecedent or subsequent to it.

A principal in the first degree, is he who personally perpetrates the crime: a principal in the second degree, is he who is present, aiding and abetting it.[a]

An accessory before the fact is he who, though absent when the crime was committed, yet procured, counselled, commanded, or abetted the commission of it:[b] an accessory after the fact is he who, knowing a crime to be committed, receives, relieves, comforts, or assists the criminal.[c]

In treason, there are no accessories either before or after the fact; for all consenters, aiders, abettors, and knowing receivers and comforters of traitors, are themselves principals. As to the course of proceeding, however, those who actually committed the treasonable fact, should be tried before those who consented or aided: for, in a contrary course of proceeding, this inconvenience might follow, that those who, in other crimes, would be principals in the second degree, might be convicted, and afterwards those who, in other crimes, would be principals in the first degree, might be acquitted. This most evidently would be absurd.[d]

In trespass, and in crimes not felonious, all those who, in felonious crimes, would be accessories before the fact, are deemed principals; and those who, in felonious crimes, would be accessories after the fact, are not considered as having committed any offence.[e]

The distinction between accessories after and accessories before the fact, and between accessories and principals, ought to be carefully and accurately preserved: for in many cases, there is a real difference between the degrees of guilt, and a proportioned difference ought to be established, where it is not already established, between the degrees of punishment.

The distinction between principals in the first and those in the second degree, though preserved in theory, and sometimes in the course of proceedings on the trial, is, nevertheless, lost universally in the scale of punishments. He who watches, at a distance, to prevent a surprise, which might defeat the execution of a concerted plan, is punished equally with him, who, in the execution of it, uses the assassinating poignard, not necessary, not generally intended, but deemed solely by him who uses it as, in some measure, contributing to the principal and the concerted purpose. In such an immense disparity of guilt, there ought to be a disparity of punishment.

These reflections receive support from considerations of utility, as well as from those of intrinsick justice. When a number confederate in a common enterprise, whose supposed advantages are to be equally participated, it is their effort to share only an equal proportion of the danger, as they are to receive only an equal proportion of the gain. This effort, instead of being countenanced by measuring the same punishment to all who act any part in the concerted enterprise, should be counterworked

[a] 1. Hale. P. C. 615.   [b] Id. ibid.   [c] 1. Hale. P. C. 618.   [d] Id. 613.
[e] Id. ibid.

by graduating the punishment according to the part which each has acted. If the principal, who personally perpetrates the crime — for there is generally a capital part to be acted by some one — is distinguished, in punishment, from those who are only present, aiding and abetting the common adventure; this will increase the difficulty of finding one, who will act this capital and conspicuous part; as his danger will become greater in proportion to the greater severity of his punishment.

Besides; where there is society in danger, there is society in exertion; for even in criminal enterprises the social nature is not lost. Let one be selected, solitary, to perpetrate a crime and to suffer a punishment, in the pain and guilt of which none are to be involved but himself; he will no longer be buoyed up on a fluid surrounding him at an equal level; and as it sinks down from him, he will sink down to it. Among associates in crimes, the law should sow the seeds of dissension.

Misprision consists in the concealment of a crime, which ought to be revealed.[f]

By a law of the United States, misprision of treason is punished with a fine not exceeding a thousand dollars, and imprisonment not exceeding seven years;[g] and misprision of felony, with imprisonment not exceeding three years, and a fine not exceeding five hundred dollars.[h]

The receiving of goods, known to be stolen, is a high misdemeanor at the common law. By a law of the United States, it is punished in the same manner as larceny.[i]

Theft-bote, or the receiving again of one's goods which have been stolen, or other amends, upon an agreement not to prosecute, was formerly held to render one an accessory to the larceny: it is now punished only with fine and imprisonment. But merely to receive the goods again is no offence, unless some favour be shown to the thief.[j]

On the subject, concerning principals and accessories, as well as on the former, concerning the incapacity of guilt, I cannot now enter into a detail: suffice it here, as it sufficed there, to mention the general principles which will govern and illustrate the particular instances.

[f] 3. Ins. 36. 4. Bl. Com. 119.   [g] Laws U.S. 1 cong. 2 sess. c. 9. s. 2.   [h] Id. s. 6.
[i] Id. s. 17.   [j] 1. Haw. 125.

IX

OF THE DIRECT MEANS USED BY THE LAW TO PREVENT OFFENCES

I SHOULD now, according to my general plan, "point out the different steps, prescribed by the law, for apprehending, detaining, trying, and punishing offenders." But it will be proper first to consider a short, though a very interesting, title of the criminal law — the direct means which it uses to prevent offences.

These are, security for the peace; security for the good behaviour; and the peaceful, but active and authoritative interposition of every citizen, much more of every publick officer of peace, to prevent the commission of threatened, or the completion of inchoate crimes.

1. Security for the peace consists in being bound, alone, or with one or more sureties, in an obligation for an ascertained sum, with a condition subjoined that the obligation shall be void, if the party shall, during the time limited, keep the peace towards all the citizens, and particularly towards him, on whose application the security is taken.[a]

Whenever a person has just cause to fear that another will kill, or beat, or imprison him, or burn his house, or will procure others to do such mischief to his person or habitation; he may, against such person, demand security for the peace; and every justice of the peace is bound to grant it, when he is satisfied, upon oath, that the party demanding it is, and has just reason to be, under such fear; and that the security is not demanded from malice, nor for vexation.[b] Upon many occasions, a justice of the peace may officially take security for the peace, though no one demand it. He may take it of those who, in his presence, shall make an affray, or shall threaten to kill or beat any person, or shall contend together with hot words, or shall go about with unusual weapons or attendants, to the terrour of the citizens.[c]

If the party to be bound is in the presence of the justice, and will not find such sureties as are required; he may be immediately committed for his disobedience, and until he find them: but if he is absent, he cannot be committed without a warrant to find sureties. This warrant should be

[a] 1. Haw. 129. 4. Bl. Com. 249.   [b] 1. Haw. 127.   [c] Id. 126.

under seal, and should mention on whose application, and for what cause, it is granted.[d]

The obligation or recognisance to keep the peace may be forfeited by any actual violence to the person of another, whether done by the party himself, or by others through his procurement: it may be forfeited by any unlawful assembly to the terrour of the citizens; and even by words tending directly to a breach of the peace, as by challenging one to fight, or, in his presence, threatening to beat him. But it is not forfeited by words merely of heat and choler; nor by a bare trespass on the lands or goods of another, unaccompanied with violence to his person.[e]

2. Security for the good behaviour includes security for the peace and more; but they are of great affinity with each other; and both may be contained in the same recognisance. It is not easy, upon this subject, to find precise rules for the direction of the magistrate: much is left to his own discretion. It seems, however, that he may be justified in demanding this security from those, whose characters he shall have just reason to suspect as scandalous, quarrelsome, or dangerous.

It has been said, that whatever is a good cause for binding a man to his good behaviour, will be a good cause likewise to forfeit his recognisance for it. But this rule is too large. One is bound, to prevent what may never happen: he is bound for giving cause of alarm; not for having done any mischief. His recognisance, however, may certainly be broken by the commission of any actual misbehaviour, for the prevention of which it was taken.[f]

3. I have mentioned the peaceful, but active and authoritative interposition of every citizen, much more of every publick officer of the peace, as a means for preventing the commission of threatened, and the completion of inchoate crimes. This subject has not received the attention, which it undoubtedly merits; nor has it been viewed in that striking light, in which it ought to be considered.

In every citizen, much more in every publick officer of peace and justice, the whole authority of the law is vested — to every citizen, much more to every publick officer of peace and justice, the whole protection of the law is extended, for the all-important purpose of preventing crimes. From every citizen, much more from every publick officer of peace and justice, the law demands the performance of that duty, in performing which they are clothed with legal authority, and shielded by legal protection.

The preservation of the peace and the security of society has, in every stage of it, been an object peculiarly favoured by the common law. To accomplish this object, we can trace, through the different periods of so-

[d] Id. 128.   [e] 1. Haw. 130. 131.   [f] Id. 129. 131.

ciety, regulations suited to its different degrees of simplicity, or of rudeness, or of refinement.

The much famed law of decennaries, by which, in small districts, all were reciprocally bound for the good behaviour of all, was well adapted to the age of the great Alfred, when commerce was little known, and the habits and rules of enlarged society were not introduced.

In times more turbulent, precautions for the security of the citizens were taken, more fitted to those turbulent times. The statute of Winchester, made in the thirteenth year of the reign of Edward the first, contains many regulations upon this subject; but they were regulations for enforcing the "ancient police" of the kingdom;[g] and their design is expressly declared to have been, to prevent the increase of crimes; or, in the language of that day, "to abate the power of felons."

For the purposes of prevention, it was directed, that, in great walled towns, the gates should be shut from the setting to the rising of the sun: that, during that time, watches, as had been *formerly* used, should, in proportion to the number of inhabitants, watch continually: that if any stranger passed by, these watches should arrest and detain him till the morning: and that if any one resisted the arrest, hue and cry should be raised; and those, who kept watch, should follow the hue and cry from town to town, till the offender was taken. Every week, or at least every fifteenth day, the bailiffs of towns were obliged to make inquiry concerning all who lodged in the suburbs; and if they found any who lodged or received persons, of whom it was suspected that they were "persons against the peace," they were to do what was right in the matter.[h]

The hue and cry was an institution of the common law: the Mirrour, speaking of the ancient laws before the conquest, makes express mention of pursuit from town to town at the hue and cry. The passage is very remarkable, and deserves, on many accounts, to be transcribed at large. It is a part of that section which has for its title — "the first constitutions ordained by the ancient kings, from King Alfred." Among others are introduced the following articles — "Every one of the age of fourteen years and upwards shall be ready to kill capital offenders in their notorious crimes, or to pursue them from town to town at hue and cry." "If they can neither kill nor apprehend them, they shall take care to have them put in the exigent, in order that they may outlaw or banish them in the following manner," &c.[i]

If a man, who is under a recognisance to keep the peace, beat or fight with one who attempts to kill *any* stranger; it is not a forfeiture of his recognisance.[j]

If, as we have seen upon a former occasion,[k] a person who interposes

[g] 1. Reev. 442.   [h] St. 13. Ed. 1. c. 4.   [i] 4. Cou. Ang. Norm. 487.
[j] 1. Haw. 131.   [k] Ante. pp. 657–658.

to part the combatants in a sudden affray, and gives notice to them of his friendly intention, be assaulted by them or either of them, and, in the struggle, should happen to kill; this will be justifiable homicide. On the other hand, if this person be killed by the combatants, or either of them, it will be murder. To preserve the publick peace, and to prevent mischief, it is the duty of every man, in such cases, to interpose.[1]

When the law enjoins a duty, it both protects and authorizes the discharge of it. Ministers of justice, it will be admitted on all hands, are, while in the execution of their offices, under the peculiar protection of the law. Without such protection, the publick peace and tranquillity could not, by any means, be preserved. But this peculiar protection of the law is not confined personally to one, who is a minister of justice: it is extended to all those who come in aid of him, and afford their assistance for the preservation of the peace. Even all those who *attend* for that purpose are under the same protection. It is immaterial whether they were or were not commanded to render their service upon the occasion. This peculiar protection of the law extends still farther. It reaches to private persons who, though no minister of justice be present, interpose for preventing mischief in the case of an affray. They are in the discharge of a duty which the law requires. The law is their warrant; and they may justly be considered as persons employed in the publick service, and in the advancement of justice.[m]

If so, in the case of an affray, in which, on each side, the same disposition is shown; much more so, in a case of premeditated, concerted, planned, prepared, riotous, felonious, and treasonable outrage, on one side — connived at, perhaps countenanced, by those in the administration of the government. In such a case, the legal duty, the legal authority, and the legal protection operate with tenfold energy and force. In such a case, the law may well be said to throw herself, without reserve, upon the arms of the citizens. In such cases, the citizens, with open arms, are bound to receive her, and to give her that protection, which, in return, she confers upon them.

The application of this important principle of preventive justice is admirably fitted to small, as well as to the greatest occasions. If it was strictly made upon all occasions, the benefits redounding to society would be immense. The petulant ill nature of the boy, the quarrelsome temper of the man, the rapacious aim of the robber, and the malignant disposition of the assassin, would be immediately checked in their operations. The principles themselves, unsupplied with fuel to inflame them, would, at last, be extinguished.

Thus much for the means, which the law employs directly for the benevolent purpose of preventing crimes.

[1] Fost. 272.   [m] Fost. 309.

X

OF THE DIFFERENT STEPS PRESCRIBED BY THE LAW, FOR APPREHENDING, DETAINING, TRYING, AND PUNISHING OFFENDERS

I NOW proceed to the different steps which the law prescribes for apprehending, detaining, trying, and punishing criminals.

A warrant is the first step usually taken for their apprehension.

A warrant is a precept from a judicial to a ministerial officer of justice, commanding him to bring the person mentioned in it, before him who issues it, or before some other officer having judicial authority in the cause.[a] This warrant should be under the hand and seal of the magistrate issuing it: it should mention the time and place of making it, and the cause for which it is granted. It may be either to bring the party generally before any magistrate, or specially to bring him before the magistrate only who grants it. It may be directed to the sheriff, constable, or to a private person; for the warrant constitutes him, for this purpose, an authorized officer.[b]

By the constitution of Pennsylvania,[c] no warrant to seize persons shall issue without describing them as nearly as may be, nor without probable cause supported by oath or affirmation. Such warrant may be granted, even by any justice of the peace, for treason, felony, or any other offence against the peace.[d]

When the warrant is received by the person to whom it is directed, he is authorized, and, if a publick officer, obliged to execute it, so far as the jurisdiction of the magistrate and himself extend.[e] A sheriff may depute others; but every other person is obliged himself to execute it; though others may lawfully assist him. A warrant directed to all constables generally can be executed by each only in his own precinct: but a warrant directed to a particular constable by name, may be executed by him any where within the jurisdiction of the magistrate.[f]

The execution of the warrant is commenced by an arrest; which is the apprehending or restraining of the person, whom it mentions or de-

[a] Wood. Ins. 81. 1. Bl. Com. 137. 4. Bl. Com. 287.   [b] 2. Haw. 85.
[c] Art. 9. s. 8.   [d] 2. Haw. 84.   [e] 4. Bl. Com. 288.   [f] 2. Haw. 86.

scribes.[g] But, besides those arrests which are made in the execution of warrants, there are others enjoined or justified by the law.

All, of age, who are present when a felony is committed, or when a dangerous wound is given, are, on pain of fine and imprisonment, bound to apprehend the person who has done the mischief.[h] If the crime has been committed out of their view, they are, upon a hue and cry, obliged to pursue with the utmost diligence, and endeavour to apprehend him who has committed it. Hue and cry is the pursuit of an offender from place to place, till he is taken: all who are present when he commits the crime, are bound to raise it against him on his flying for it. Every one is obliged to assist an officer demanding his assistance, in order to apprehend a felon, to suppress an affray, or to secure the persons of affrayers.[i] In all these cases, the doors of houses may, if necessary, be broken open for the apprehension of the offenders, if admittance is refused on signifying the cause of demanding it.[j]

It is a general rule, that, at any time, and in any place, every private person is justified in arresting a traitor or a felon; and, if a treason or a felony has been committed, he is justified in arresting even an innocent person, upon his reasonable suspicion that by such person it has been committed.[k] If one see another upon the point of committing a treason or a felony, or doing any act which would manifestly endanger the life of another; he may lay hold on him, and detain him till it may be presumed reasonably that he has altered his design.[l] In the case of a mere breach of the peace, no private person can arrest one for it after it is over.[m]

Whenever an arrest may be justified by a private person, it may *a fortiori* be justified by an officer of justice.[n] In addition to their own personal exertions, they have a right to demand the assistance of others.[o] A constable may not only arrest affrayers, but may also detain them till they find security for the peace.[p] A justice of the peace may, by parol, authorize any one to arrest another, who, in his presence, is guilty of an actual breach of the peace, or, in his absence, is engaged in a riot.[q]

Whenever a person is arrested for a crime, he ought to be brought before a justice of the peace, or other judicial magistrate. This magistrate is obliged immediately to examine into the circumstances of the crime alleged; and according to the result of this examination, the person accused should be either discharged, or bailed, or committed to prison.

If it clearly appear that no crime was committed, or, if committed, that the suspicion conceived against the prisoner is entirely unfounded; he should be restored to his liberty.[r]

To bail a person is to deliver him to his sureties, who give sufficient

[g] 4. Bl. Com. 286.   [h] 2. Haw. 74.   [i] Id. 75.   [j] Id. 86. 4. Bl. Com. 289.
[k] 2. Haw. 76.   [l] Id. 77.   [m] Id. ibid.   [n] 2. Haw. 80.   [o] Id. 81.
[p] Id. ibid.   [q] Id. 83.   [r] Id. 87.

security for his appearance: he is intrusted to their friendly custody, instead of being committed to the confinement of the gaol. At the common law, every man accused or even indicted of treason or of any felony whatever, might be bailed upon good surety: for at the common law, says my Lord Coke,[s] the gaol was his pledge, who could find no other: he could be bailed, till he was convicted.

This part of the common law, however, is, in England, greatly altered by parliamentary provisions, which restrict, in numerous instances, the power of admitting to bail. Indeed it is obvious, that between the law of capital punishments and that of commitments, the connexion must be intimate and inseparable. In capital offences, no bail can be a security equal to the actual custody of the person: for what is there, which a man may not be induced to forfeit to save his life?[t] One court in England, and only one — the court of king's bench, or, in the time of the vacation, any judge of that court — still possesses the discretionary power of bailing in any case, according to its circumstances; excepting only such persons as are committed by either house of parliament, while the session lasts, and such as are committed for contempts by any of the superiour courts of justice.[u]

To refuse or to delay bail, where it ought to be granted, is a misdemeanor at the common law,[v] and may be punished on an indictment. By the constitution of Pennsylvania,[w] it is declared, as an inviolable rule, "that excessive bail shall not be required;" and "that all prisoners shall be bailable by sufficient sureties; unless for capital offences, when the proof is evident or presumption great."

If the crime is not bailable, or if the prisoner cannot find sureties, the magistrate is under the disagreeable necessity of ordering, by a warrant under his hand and seal and containing the cause of the order, that he shall be imprisoned in the publick gaol, till he be thence delivered by the due course of law.[x] This is a commitment.

This imprisonment, it ought to be remembered, is for the purpose only of keeping, not for that of punishing the prisoner: he ought, for this reason, to be treated with every degree of tenderness, of which his safe custody will possibly admit. In particular, a gaoler is not justified, by the law, in fettering a prisoner, unless where he is unruly, or where it is absolutely necessary to prevent an escape.[y] "Solent præsides in carcere continendos damnare ut in vinculis contineantur; sed hujusmodi interdicta sunt a lege, quia carcer ad continendos, et non puniendos, haberi debeat."[z] "Custodes vero gaolarum pænam sibi commissis non augeant, nec eos tor-

---

[s] 2. Ins. 189. [t] 4. Bl. Com. 294. [u] Id. 296. [v] 2. Haw. 90.
[w] Art. 9. s. 13, 14. [x] 4. Bl. Com. 297. [y] 3. Ins. 34.
[z] Bract. 105. a. [Guards are accustomed to condemn those who are to be held in prison to being confined in chains; but things of this sort are forbidden by law, because a prison ought to be regarded as confining men, not punishing them.]

queant; sed, omni sævitia remota, pietateque adhibita, judicia in ipsos promulgata debite exequantur." [a] Such is the law of imprisonment, ancient and approved.

When the party is taken, and bailed or imprisoned; the next step in order is, to institute a prosecution against him. This may be done by four different methods — by appeal; by information; by presentment; by indictment.

1. An appeal is an accusation by one private person against another for some crime: it is a private action of the party injured, demanding punishment for the injury which he has suffered: it is also a prosecution for the state, on account of the crime committed against the publick.[b]

In ancient times there were appeals for a breach of the peace, for a battery, and for false imprisonment, as well as for more aggravated injuries and crimes; but they have been out of use, and converted into actions of trespass, for many hundred years.[c]

An appeal lies for mayhem, for larceny, for arson, for rape, for death. It is brought by the party ravished, robbed, maimed, or whose house was burned; or by the wife, or, if no wife, by the heir, of the person killed.[d] An appeal may be brought previous to an indictment; and if the defendant be acquitted, he cannot afterwards be indicted for the same crime: if he is found guilty, he shall suffer the same punishment as if he had been convicted on a prosecution by an indictment.[e] An appeal may be discharged by the concurrence of all the parties interested — by the pardon of the crown, and by the release of the appellant.[f]

The appeal can be traced to the ancient forests of Germany. "Luitur homicidium," says Tacitus,[g] "certo armentorum ac pecorum numero; recipitque satisfactionem universa domus."

On this subject there is, in our law books, an immense profusion of professional learning. As the appeal is now but little used, I decline any minute inquiry concerning it: as it is still in force, it would have been improper wholly to have omitted it.

2. A second mode of prosecuting crimes and offences is by information. Some informations are brought partly at the suit of the state, and partly at the suit of a citizen. These are a species of *qui tam*[h] actions; and will be considered when we treat concerning civil suits.

Informations in the name of the state or of the crown alone are of two

---

[a] Fleta. l. 1. c. 26. [Indeed the guards of jails should not increase the punishment for those committed to their care nor should they torture them. But, with all cruelty removed, and with piety brought to bear, they ought to execute the judgments promulgated against their prisoners.]

[b] 4. Bl. Com. 308. 2 Haw. 155. [c] 2. Haw. 157.

[d] 2. Haw. 164. 4. Bl. Com. 310. [e] 4. Bl. Com. 311. [f] 1. Hale. P. C. 9.

[g] De mor. Ger. c. 21. [Homicide is atoned for by a certain number of cattle and sheep; and the entire family receives satisfaction.]

[h] 4. Bl. Com. 303.

kinds: those which are filed *ex officio* by the publick prosecutor, and are properly at the suit of the publick; and those which are carried on in the name, indeed, of the commonwealth or crown, but, in fact, at the instance of some private person or common informer. The first have been the source of much; the second have been the source of intolerable vexation: both were the ready tools, by using which Empson and Dudley, and an arbitrary star chamber, fashioned the proceedings of the law into a thousand tyrannical forms. Neither, indeed, extended to capital crimes: but ingenious tyranny can torture in a thousand shapes, without depriving the person tortured of his life.

Restraints have, in England, been imposed upon the last species: but the first — those at the king's own suit, filed by his attorney general — are still unrestrained.[1] By the constitution of Pennsylvania, both kinds are effectually removed. By that constitution, however, informations are still suffered to live: but they are bound and gagged. They are confined to official misdemeanors; and even against those, they cannot be slipt but by leave of the court. By that constitution, "no person shall, for any indictable offence, be proceeded against criminally by information" — "unless by leave of the court, for oppression and misdemeanor in office." Military cases are also excepted.[j]

3. Presentment is a third species of prosecution. A presentment, in its most extensive signification, comprehends inquisitions of office, of which the coroner's inquest is one: it comprehends likewise regular indictments, which are preferred and found. But, in its proper sense, it is an accusation found by a grand jury, of their own motion, and from their own knowledge and observation, without any bill being laid before them by the prosecutor for the publick. This presentment is afterwards reduced into proper form by the publick prosecutor; and in this form is sent to the grand jury, in the same manner as bills which are originally preferred to them by that officer. These bills and this presentment, found in form, are indictments.

When the grand jury, after having heard the evidence adduced to support a bill, think it insufficient for this purpose, they endorse on the bill "ignoramus," and direct the foreman to sign this endorsement. By this endorsement it is meant, that though the matters charged in the bill may be true, their truth is not sufficiently evinced to the jury. If the charge in the bill appears to be supported, it is then endorsed "a true bill," and as such is signed by the foreman.

A grand jury must consist of at least twelve members, because twelve are necessary — it must not consist of more than twenty three members, because twelve are sufficient, to find an indictment; and twelve would not be a majority of a greater number.

[1] Id. 307.   [j] Art. 9. s. 10.

At the common law, a grand jury cannot find an indictment for any crime, but such as has been committed within the county or precinct, for which they are returned.[k]

A bill cannot be returned true in part, and false in part; it must be returned "a true bill" or "ignoramus" for the whole. Nor can it be returned specially or conditionally.[1]

Much might be said concerning the form of indictments generally, and also concerning the particular form of the indictment for each particular species of crimes: but this kind of learning, which, by the by, ought neither to be overlooked nor disregarded by the professional lawyer, is found in full and minute detail in the numerous books and treatises of the criminal law. To these I beg leave to refer you. To go fully into particulars would employ too great a proportion of my lectures: to go imperfectly would convey no information that could be deemed regular or satisfactory.

Suffice it to observe, as a general and important principle with regard to indictments, that as to persons, times, and places, and, above all, as to the descriptions of crimes, the most precise certainty which can be reasonably expected is indispensably required. Certainty, indeed, is a governing and a pervading quality in all good legislation, and in all good administration of law. In this very important quality, the common law, pure and unadulterated, has attained a very uncommon degree of perfection. I add, that the common law is equally remarkable for the simplicity as for the accuracy of its forms. I repeat it — they deserve the close study and attention of every lawyer by profession. Even to others, who have leisure and a taste to inspect minute as well as splendid beauties, the forms of the common law will afford entertainment and instruction.

The principles of the great institution of grand juries have been explained fully in another place.

When a person is indicted, and is not already committed or under bail, the next step in the legal arrangement is, to issue process against him, in order that he may be obliged to answer the charge, of which he stands indicted.

On an indictment for any crime under the degree of treason or felony, the process proper to be first awarded, at the common law, is a *venire facias*, which, from the very name of it, is only in the nature of a summons to require the appearance of the party.[m] If this process is not obeyed, and it is seen by the return that he has lands in the county by which he may be distrained; then a distress shall be awarded against him, from time to time, till he appear. But if the return shows that he has no lands in the county; then a writ of *capias* is awarded against him. By this writ, as is intimated from its name, the sheriff is commanded to take the

<hr />

[k] 2. Haw. 220.   [1] Id. 210.   [m] 2. Haw. 283.

body of the person accused, and have him before the court at the time and place specified in the writ itself. If he cannot be taken on the first capias, a second, and so on, shall be issued.[n] On an indictment for felony or treason, a capias is always the first process.[o]

We are told that, in the case of misdemeanors in England, it is now the usual practice for any judge of the court of king's bench, upon certificate of an indictment found, to award a writ of capias immediately against the defendant.[p]

If the party abscond, and cannot be taken; then, after the several writs have been issued against him in regular number according to the nature of the crime with which he is charged, he is, at five county courts, proclaimed and required to surrender himself; and if he does not appear at the fifth requisition, he is then adjudged to be outlawed — put out of the protection of the law.[q]

When one is outlawed on an indictment for a misdemeanor, he forfeits his goods and chattels. In felony or treason, outlawry is a conviction and an attainder of the crime charged in the indictment.[r] Any one may arrest an outlaw for those crimes, in order to bring him to execution. He was formerly said "gerere caput lupinum," and might be knocked on the head like a wolf, by every one who met him. But the law is now very justly holden to be otherwise. As to the security of his person, the greatest and the most notorious criminal is still under the protection, though liable to the punishment, of the law. It is lawful, as has been said, to apprehend him, in order to bring him to legal punishment. But to kill him wantonly, wilfully, or deliberately, merely because he is an outlaw, is murder.[s]

The proceedings necessary to an outlawry are uncommonly circumstantial, and must be exact to the minutest degree. Indeed, it is proper that they should be so. The consequence is, that an outlawry may, in most instances, be reversed on a writ of errour. When this is done, the person indicted is admitted to his defence against the indictment.

When a person indicted comes or is brought before the proper court, he is arraigned; in other words, he is called upon by his name, the indictment is read to him, and he is asked what he has to say in answer to the indictment.

At this important crisis of his fate, when his life may depend upon a word, and when, for this reason, every word should, as far as possible, be the result of perfect recollection and freedom, he must not be loaded with fetters or chains; he must not be brought to the bar in a contumelious manner; he ought to be used with all the humanity and gentleness consistent with the situation, in which he unfortunately stands; and he

---

[n] 2. Haw. 283.   [o] Id. 284.   [p] 4. Bl. Com. 314.   [q] 4. Bl. Com. 314.
[r] Id. ibid. 2. Hale. P. C. 205.   [s] 1. Hale. P. C. 497.

should suffer no uneasiness, except that which proceeds from internal causes.[t] The judge should exhort him to answer without fear; and should give him assurance that justice shall be duly administered.[u] "Cum captus coram justiciariis producendus fuerit, produci non debet ligatis manibus (quamvis aliquando compedibus propter periculum evasionis) et hoc ideo, ne videatur coactus ad aliquam purgationem suscipiendam".[v]

Is it necessary to fortify, by authority, the law of humanity? Sometimes it is. Sometimes the law of humanity, even when fortified by authority, has been pleaded in vain. The cruel violation, as well as the benign observance, of the principles of goodness and law ought to be known and marked. The last should be approved and imitated: the first should be detested and avoided. In the present enlightened century — and humanity should surely attend knowledge — a chief justice of the court of king's bench suffered a person in irons to be arraigned for treason before him, though he was informed, that they were so grievous as to prevent the prisoner's sleeping except in a single posture, and that even while he was before the court, he would be unable to stand, unless the gaoler — for the gaoler had more bowels than the judge — unless the gaoler assisted him to hold up his chains.[w]

It is usual to desire the prisoner to hold up his hand when he is arraigned. This formality is not improper, because it serves to identify the person: it is not necessary, because the person may be identified in another manner. My Lord Bacon mentions a Welshman, who put a curious construction on this ceremony. Having been at a court, where he saw the prisoners hold up their hands at the bar as they severally received their sentences, he told one of his acquaintances that the judge was an excellent fortune teller; for if he only looked upon the hand of a person, he could immediately declare what would be his fate.[x]

A person, upon being arraigned, must stand mute, or give an answer.

One is considered as standing mute, when he gives no answer at all; when he gives such an answer as cannot be received; and when he pleads not guilty, but, on being asked how he will be tried, either refuses to say any thing, or will not put himself upon the country.[y]

On standing mute, the judgment was indeed a terrible one — "that he be sent to the prison from whence he came, and put into a dark lower room, and there be laid naked upon the bare ground, upon his back, without any clothes or rushes under him, or to cover him, his legs and arms drawn and extended with cords to the four corners of the room, and

[t] 2. Haw. 308.   [u] 2. Ins. 316.
[v] Bract. 137. a. [When the prisoner is to be brought into the presence of his judges, he should not be led forth with hands tied (although sometimes with foot-fetters on account of the danger of escape) and that for this reason, lest he seem forced to undergo some ordeal.]
[w] 6. St. Tri. 231.   [x] 3. Ld. Bac. 270.   [y] 2. Hale. P. C. 316.

upon his body laid as great a weight of iron as he can bear, and more. The first day he shall have three morsels of barley bread without drink; the next day he shall have three draughts of standing water next the door of the prison, without bread; and this to be his diet till he die." [z] To the execution even of this terrible judgment some have submitted, that from forfeiture their estates might be rescued for the benefit of their children; for by standing mute, forfeiture and the corruption of blood are prevented.

The origin of the *peine fort et dure* it is exceedingly difficult to trace: it seems, however, to be no legitimate offspring of the ancient common law: by that law, the standing mute amounted to a confession of the charge.[a]

By the law of Scotland, if the pannel stands mute and will not plead, the trial shall proceed as usual; and it is left to him to manage his own defence, as he shall think proper.[b] The spirit of this law is adopted by the legislature of the United States.[c] "If a person indicted shall stand mute, the court shall proceed to his trial, as if he had pleaded not guilty, and shall render judgment accordingly." [d]

To an indictment, the prisoner may give an answer, or plead, as the law terms it, in a great variety of ways.

I. He may admit the facts, as stated in the indictment, to be true; but, at the same time, may deny that the facts, thus stated and admitted, amount in law to the crime charged in the indictment. This is a demurrer. Thus, if one is indicted for larceny committed by stealing apples growing on a tree, he may demur to this indictment; in other words, he may admit that he took the apples from the tree, but deny that the fact of taking them amounts in law to the crime of larceny; because apples, unsevered from the tree, are not personal goods; and because of personal goods only larceny can be committed. This demurrer brings regularly before the court the legal question, whether the facts stated constitute the crime charged in the indictment. When the prosecutor joins in this demurrer — when he avers that the facts stated constitute the crime charged; then an issue is said to be joined. An issue is the result of the pleadings in a single point, denied on one side and affirmed on the other. It is either an issue in law, such as has now been mentioned; or it is an issue in fact, such as will be mentioned hereafter.

It seems to be taken for granted, by many respectable writers on the criminal law, that if, on a demurrer to an indictment, the point of law is determined against the prisoner, he shall have the same judgment pronounced against him as if he had been convicted by a verdict. With

---

[z] Id. 319.   [a] 4. Bl. Com. 323.   [b] Bar. on St. 87.
[c] Laws U.S. 1. cong. 2. sess. c. 9. s. 30.
[d] A similar provision is contained in an act of assembly of Pennsylvania. 3 Laws Penn. 119. *Ed*.

regard to crimes not capital this seems to be the case: but with regard to capital crimes, no adjudication is produced in support of the opinion. My Lord Hale indeed says, in one place of his valuable history of the pleas of the crown, that if a person be indicted of felony, and demur to the indictment, and it be judged against him, he shall have judgment to be hanged; for it is a confession, and, indeed, a wilful confession of the indictment.[e] In another place, however, he takes a distinction between this kind of confession, which, though voluntary, is still extrajudicial, and that full and solemn confession, which will by and by be mentioned. An extrajudicial confession, says he, though it be in court, as where the prisoner freely discloses the fact, and demands the opinion of the court whether it be felony, will not be recorded by the court, even if, upon the fact thus disclosed, it appear to be felony; but he will still be admitted to plead *not guilty* to the indictment.[f] There seems to be a solid reason for this distinction: for though a demurrer admits the truth of the facts as stated in the indictment, yet it cannot be considered as an explicit and solemn confession of what is more material — the criminal and felonious intention, with which the facts were done. This criminal and felonious intention is the very point or *gist*, as the law calls it, of the indictment; and should be answered explicitly and directly.

II. This answer may be given by a solemn and judicial confession, not only of the fact, but of the *crime* — in the language of the law, it may be done by pleading *guilty*.

Upon this subject of confession on the part of the criminal, three very interesting questions arise with respect to capital crimes: for of those only I now speak. 1. Is a confession necessary? 2. Ought it to be made? 3. Ought it to be received as a sufficient foundation for a conviction, and judgment against life?

1. In many countries, his confession is considered as absolutely indispensable to the condemnation of the criminal. The Marquis of Beccaria conjectures that this rule has been taken from the mysterious tribunal of penitence, in which the confession of sins is a necessary part of the sacrament: thus, says he, have men abused the unerring light of revelation.[g] This confession they endeavour to obtain by the oath, and by the torture, of the person accused. He is obliged to answer interrogatories. These interrogatories — we are told; for of experience on this subject we are happily ignorant — these interrogatories are reduced to a system, captious, uncandid, and ensnaring; and terrour is frequently added to fraud.[h] The practice of demanding the oath of the accused is said, by the famous President de Lamoignon, to have derived its origin from the customs of the inquisition.[i]

[e] 2. Hale. P. C. 257. [f] 2. Hale. P. C. 225. [g] Bec. c. 16.
[h] 5. War. Bib. 321. [i] 8. War. Bib. 195.

Very opposite, upon this subject, is the genius of the Gentoo code. In that very ancient body of law, we find it expressly declared, that wherever a true testimony would deprive a man of his life; if a false testimony would be the preservation of it, such false testimony is lawful.[j]

Between those extremes the constitution of Pennsylvania[k] observes the temperate mean. "In prosecutions by indictment or information, a man cannot be compelled to give evidence against himself." This is likewise an immemorial and an established principle of the common law.

In the case of oaths, says Beccaria, which are administered to a criminal to make him speak the truth, when the contrary is his greatest interest, there is a palpable contradiction between the laws and the natural sentiments of mankind. Can a man think himself obliged to contribute to his own destruction? Why should he be reduced to the terrible alternative of doing this, or of offending against God? For the law, which, in such a case, requires an oath, leaves him only the choice of being a bad christian, or of being a martyr. Such laws, continues he, are useless as well as unnatural: they are like a dike opposed directly to the course of the torrent: it is either immediately overwhelmed, or, by a whirlpool which itself forms, it is gradually undermined and destroyed.[l]

If it is useless, unjust, and unnatural, to attempt the extracting of truth by means of the oath; what is it, to make this attempt by means of the torture? This, like the former, is happily unknown to the common law. This, like the former, can be traced to the merciless tribunals of the inquisition. This, like the former, has been a practice both general and destructive.

To the civil law, its origin has been frequently ascribed. My Lord Coke, in his third Institute, declares himself explicitly of this opinion. He says, that in the reign of Henry the sixth, the Duke of Exeter and the Duke of Suffolk intended to have brought the civil laws into England; and, for a beginning, first brought into the tower the rack or brake allowed in many cases by the civil law.[m] To systems, as well as to men, justice should be done. From the imputation of a sanguinary as well as of a tyrannical spirit, the Roman law, at least in its brighter ages, deserves to be rescued. The different periods in the history of that celebrated law should be carefully distinguished; and the redness or the blackness of one era ought not to shade or stain the purity and the splendour of another.

In the times of the republick, torture was known at Rome; and this, it must be owned, was too much to be known any where. It was confined, however, to the slaves. The whole torrent of Cicero's eloquence was poured indignant upon the infamous Verres, because he had the audacity as well as cruelty to torture a Roman citizen, with his eyes turned

---

[j] Gent. Laws. 115.   [k] Art. 9. s. 9.   [l] Bec. c. 18.   [m] 3. Ins. 35.

towards Rome. "Cædebatur virgis in medio foro Messanæ civis Romanus, judices; cum interea nullus gemitus, nulla vox alia istius miseri, inter dolorem crepitumque plagarum, audebatur, nisi hæc, civis Romanus sum." — "O nomen dulce libertatis! O jus eximium nostræ civitatis! O lex Porcia, legesque Semproniæ! O graviter desiderata, et aliquando reddita plebi Romanæ tribunicia potestas! Huccine tandem omnia reciderunt, ut civis Romanus, in provincia populi Romani, in oppido fœderatorum, ab eo qui beneficio populi Romani fasces et secures haberet, deligatus in foro virgis cæderetur? Quid, cum ignes ardentesque laminæ cæterique cruciatus admovebantur?" [n] — "Non fuit his omnibus iste contentus. Spectet, inquit, patriam: in conspectu legum libertatisque moriatur." [o]

In another place, the same exquisite judge of human nature and of law describes, in the most masterly manner, the futility of that kind of proof, which arose from the torture of slaves. "Quæstiones nobis servorum, ac tormenta accusator minitatur; in quibus quanquam nihil periculi suspicamur, tamen illa tormenta gubernat dolor, moderatur natura cujusque tum animi tum corporis; regit quæsitor, flectit libido, corrumpit spes, infirmat metus, ut in tot rerum angustiis nihil veritati loci relinquatur." [p]

About three hundred years after Cicero, the celebrated Ulpian, characterized as "the friend of the laws and of the people," [q] speaks of torture in the same strain — "Res est fragilis et periculosa, et quæ veritatem fallat. Nam plerique patientia sive duritia tormentorum ita tormenta contemnunt, ut exprimi eis veritas nullo modo possit: alii tanta sunt impatientia, ut in quovis mentiri, quam pati tormenta velint. Ita fit, ut etiam vario modo fateantur, ut non tantum se, verum etiam alios comminentur." [r]

[n] Cic. in Ver. V. 62. 63. [A Roman citizen, Judges, was scourged with whips in the middle of the forum of Messana. When all the while no other groan, no other word, was heard from that poor wretch amid the pain and noise of the lashes but this: I am a Roman citizen.

O sweet name of liberty! O most excellent law of our state! O Porcian Law and the Sempronian Laws! O power of the tribunate, urgently longed for and finally restored to the Roman People! Have then all things regressed to this point, that a Roman citizen, in a province of the Roman People and in a town of the allies, should be bound and lashed in the forum by a man who held the insignia of office by the beneficence of the Roman People? And what about when fires, burning plates, and other tortures were brought to bear?]

[o] Id. 66. [But he (i.e. Verres) was not content with all this. He will, he says, gaze upon his Fatherland; may he die in the gaze of her laws and liberty!]

[p] Cic. pro. P. Syl. c. 28. [The accuser threatens us with investigations and tortures of our slaves; although we suspect not the slightest danger to ourselves in such matters, even so those torturings are controlled by pain, moderated by the nature of the mind and body of the individual, ruled by the investigator, bent by desire, corrupted by hope, weakened by fear — so that, in short, in so many exigencies no place is left for the truth.]

[q] 1. Gib. 249.

[r] 2. War. Bib. 23. [It is a treacherous and dangerous thing, and such as to delude the truth. For many, whether through capacity to suffer or toughness, so defy the

The early christians also bore their testimony against the cruel and absurd practice. "Cum quæritur," says St. Augustine, "utrum vir sit nocens, cruciatur; et innocens luit pro incerto scelere certissimas poenas; non quia illud commisisse detegitur, sed quia non commisisse nescitur; ignorantia judicis calamitas innocentis" — "judex torquit accusatum, ne occidat, nesciens, innocentem; tortum et innocentem occidit, quem, ne innocentem occiderit, torserat." [s]

Among the moderns, says a sensible French writer, the practice of torture has been adopted and carried to the last degree of atrocity, in those countries in which human nature has been most debased and most oppressed — I mean those of the inquisition: on the contrary, it has been abolished or moderated in those, in which the human mind has reassumed her liberty — in Geneva, in England, in France under Lewis the sixteenth.[t]

From what has been observed, the inference is clear, that the confession of the criminal is not necessary to a conviction or sentence in the case of a capital crime.

2. In the case of a capital crime, ought this confession to be made? I think not. When I say this, I speak with a reference to the effect, which this confession is allowed to have by the common law. I am justified by authority in what I say. From tenderness to life, the court is usually very averse to the receiving and recording of such a confession; and will advise the prisoner to retract it, and plead another plea to the indictment.[u] If a person under the age of twenty one years make this confession, the court in justice ought not to record it, but should put him to plead *not guilty;* or, at least, ought to inquire by an inquest of office concerning the truth and circumstances of the fact.[v] A confession, refused altogether, or received with reluctance, ought not to be made.

3. Ought this confession to be received, and considered as a sufficient foundation for a conviction and judgment against life?

By the common law, as it now is and as it always has been received, such a confession is deemed a sufficient foundation for a conviction and judgment against life. This express, judicial, and direct confession is con-

---

torments of torturers that it is impossible to extort the truth from them. Others are so little able to suffer that they are willing to lie in any way to avoid undergoing torture. Thus it happens that they even confess inconsistently, so that not only do they inform against themselves, but implicate others.]

[s] Id. 22. [When one wishes to know whether a man is guilty, he is tortured; and an innocent man suffers most definite punishments for an indefinite offense; not because he is discovered to have committed that offense, but because it is not known that he did not commit it; the judge's lack of knowledge is the innocent man's misfortune.

The judge tortures the accused lest unknowingly he should kill an innocent man; he kills the tortured and innocent man whom he had tortured in order that he not kill an innocent man.]

[t] 8. War. Bib. 197. [u] 2. Hale. P. C. 225. 4. Bl. Com. 324. [v] 1. Hale. P. C. 24.

sidered as the highest possible conviction;[w] and after it is made and received, the court does and can do nothing but pronounce the judgment of the law.[x]

It now, I apprehend, appears from principle, as it appeared a little while ago from authority, that, on an indictment for a capital crime, this express, judicial, and direct confession of it ought not to be made. He who makes it undertakes to be the arbiter of his own life: for, as we now see, the judgment of death follows as a consequence, necessary and unavoidable. A decision of this very solemn kind ought to be a decision of the society, upon the principles formerly explained, and not a decision of the party himself. For such a decision he may be unqualified, sometimes on account of his understanding, sometimes on account of his disposition. He may not be apprized of every legal ingredient, which ought to form a part in the composition of the crime which he confesses: human conduct is sometimes influenced by an irresolute impatience, as well as, at other times, by an overweening fondness of life.

It is certainly true, that persons have confessed themselves guilty of crimes, of which, indeed, they were innocent. A remarkable case of this nature is mentioned in our law books. A gentleman of the name of Harrison appeared alive, many years after three persons had been hanged for his murder; one of whom confessed it.[y] Many persons accused have confessed themselves guilty of witchcraft, and of other crimes equally problematical.

By the civil law, the confession of the person accused is not sufficient to convict him of a capital crime, without other proofs: for it may so happen, that such a confession is dictated only by the inquietude or despair of a troubled mind.[z] Another reason may likewise be assigned: he may, by a mistaken as well as by a disordered understanding, acknowledge that to be a crime, which in law is not that crime.

Thus much for confession, or the plea of *guilty* to an indictment.

III. An indictment may be answered by a plea to the jurisdiction of the court, in which it is found. This plea is proper when an indictment for any particular crime is found in a court, which has no authority to hear, try, or determine that particular crime: as if a court of quarter sessions should arraign one on an indictment for treason, of which that court has no jurisdiction.[a]

IV. An indictment may be answered by a plea in abatement — in other words, a plea, the design of which is to destroy the indictment, without answering the crime which it charges. This, in some cases, may be very proper; as when one is indicted and called to answer by a wrong name. If he suffer this mistake to pass unnoticed, it is doubtful whether he may

[w] 2. Haw. 333.   [x] 4. Bl. Com. 324.   [y] Tr. per. Pais. 603.
[z] 1. Domat. 460.   [a] 2. Hale. P. C. 256.

not afterwards be indicted for the same crime by his right name. If the plea be supported, the indictment will be abated; but he may be immediately indicted anew, by the name which he has averred to be his true one. For in all pleas in abatement it is a rule, that he who would take advantage of a mistake, must show, at the same time, how that mistake may be rectified.

V. An indictment may be answered by a plea in bar. A plea in bar does not directly deny the commission of the crime charged; but it adduces and relies on some reason calculated to show, that the prisoner cannot be tried or punished for it, either on that or on any other indictment.

A former acquittal of the same charge is a plea of this kind: for it is a maxim firmly established by the common law, that no one can be brought in danger oftener than once on account of the same crime.

A former conviction of the same crime is also a plea of this kind; and depends on the same principle.

An attainder of any capital crime is a good plea in bar of an indictment for the same, or for any other crime. The reason is, that by the attainder the prisoner is dead in law; his blood is corrupted; and his estate is forfeited; so that an attempt to attaint him a second time would be altogether nugatory and superfluous.

It is natural and obvious to remark here, how the severity of punishment becomes the parent of impunity for crimes. When one is punished, or condemned to be punished, as far as he can be punished, for one crime, he may commit another, without any fear or risk of additional punishment.

In proportion as the criminal code becomes less severe, the operation of the plea of a former attainder becomes less powerful; for it is never proper, unless when a second trial could answer no purpose.

A pardon is another plea in bar of an indictment; for, by remitting the punishment of the crime, it destroys the end which is proposed by the prosecution. In England, an advantage is gained by pleading a pardon, which cannot be obtained by it after an attainder. A pardon prevents the corruption, but cannot restore the purity of blood.

If any one of these pleas in bar is successful, the party pleading it is discharged from farther prosecution; but if they should all fail, a resource is still left.

VI. An indictment may be answered by pleading *not guilty* of the crime which it charges. An issue, you recollect, is a point denied on one side and affirmed on the other. The plea of *not guilty* is called the general issue; because, on that plea, the whole charge comes regularly and fully under examination. It is averred by the indictment: it is denied by the plea. On this plea alone — such, as we have seen from the foregoing deduction, is the benignity of the common law — on this plea alone, the prisoner can receive a final judgment against him. A judgment of acquittal may be produced by many different causes: but a sentence of condemnation can be founded only on a conviction of guilt.

When the prisoner pleads that he is not guilty; he, for the trial of his plea, puts himself upon his country. The extensive and the emphatick import of this expression, neglected because it is common, was fully illustrated on another occasion.[b]

In ancient times, a variety of methods, by which crimes might be tried, was known to the common law. A trial might be had by ordeal; and this species of trial was either by fire or by water. The corsned, or morsel of execration, was another kind of trial. The trial by battle was a third kind. A fourth kind still remains and is our boast — the trial by jury. This trial, both in the United States and in this commonwealth, is a part of the constitution as well as of the law.

The history and the general principles of this institution, celebrated so long and so justly, have already been explained to you at large. I shall, therefore, confine myself at present to such remarks, chiefly of a practical nature, as will arise from the usual course of proceedings in trials for crimes.

By the constitution of Pennsylvania,[c] persons accused of crimes shall be tried by an impartial jury of the vicinage: or, in legal interpretation, of the county.[d] By the national constitution,[e] crimes committed in any state shall be tried in that state: and by a law of the United States,[f] twelve, at least, of the jurors must be summoned from the very county, in which the crime was committed.

In the court of king's bench, there is time allowed between the arraignment and the trial, for a jury to be impanelled by a writ of *venire facias* directed to the sheriff. But justices of oyer and terminer and general gaol delivery, and justices of the quarter sessions[g] of the peace, may, by a bare award and without any writ or precept, have a panel returned by that officer: for, in consequence of a general precept directed to him beforehand, he returns to the court a panel of jurors to try all persons, who may be called upon for their trial at that session. Before such justices, it is usual, for this reason, to try criminals immediately or soon after their arraignment.[h]

Jurors must be *"homines liberi et legales,"* men free and superiour to every legal exception; for every legal exception is a cause of challenge. My Lord Coke[i] enumerates four such causes — propter honoris respectum — propter defectum — propter delictum — propter affectum. The first

---

[b] Ante. p. 529. [c] Art. 9. s. 9. [d] 2. Hale. P. C. 264.
[e] Art. 3. s. 3. [f] 1. Cong. 1. sess. c. 20. s. 29. [g] Wood. Ins. 666.
[h] 4. Bl. Com. 344, 345. 2. Haw. 405. [i] 1. Ins. 156. b.

cause relates to the peerage solely: the second is an exception against aliens and minors: the third is an exception against persons convicted of infamous crimes: the fourth is an exception which arises from bias or partiality. When this bias is apparent, the challenge founded on it is a *principal* one, and takes effect immediately: when the bias is only probable, the challenge is only to *the favour;* and its validity must be decided by triers, selected by the court for this purpose, till two are sworn of the jury. These two, as they are acknowledged or found to be impartial, become the triers of all the others.

Besides these challenges for cause, which operate as frequently as they exist, the benignity of the common law allows, as we saw before, every person indicted for a capital crime to challenge peremptorily, or without cause, any number of jurors under thirty six — the number of three juries.[j] In every capital crime, except treason, this number is, by a law of the United States,[k] reduced to twenty jurors. A person who challenges more than the number allowed, is, by the same law, to be treated as one who stands mute. That treatment we have already seen. By a law of Pennsylvania, a similar deduction is made in the number of peremptory challenges: but he, who challenges more than the number allowed, shall suffer as a criminal convicted.[l] There is a great difference between the two provisions: by that of the United States, the person indicted is treated as one who must be *tried:* by that of Pennsylvania, he is treated as one, who is *already convicted.*[m]

When an alien is tried, one half of his jury should be aliens, if he require it.[n]

On this subject of challenges it is proper to observe, that it seems to have been very familiar in the Roman law, during the existence of the commonwealth. In a criminal process, before the court of the prætor, the accuser and the accused were each allowed to except against fifteen of those returned to try the cause. This exception was denominated "*rejectio judicum*" — in the phraseology of our law, the challenge of the jury. Whenever Cicero uses the expression — judices; its legal translation is — Gentlemen of the jury.

Concerning the celebrated trial of Milo, we have a number of particular facts transmitted to us, which deserve our particular notice and attention. On the first day of the trial, or, as we would say, on the return of the *venire facias,* the *judices* — we would say the jury — were produced, that they might be balloted. The next day, they balloted eighty one persons to make up the jury. But the accuser had the liberty to

---

[j] 2. Haw. 413.   [k] 1. Cong. 2. sess. c. 9. s. 30.   [l] 1. Laws. Penn. 134.
[m] The law of Pennsylvania is now similar to that of the United States. 3. Laws. Penn. 119. *Ed.*
[n] 3. Bl. Com. 360. 4 Bl. Com. 346. 2. Haw. 420. 1. Dall. 73.

challenge fifteen; and the accused could challenge as many. By these challenges on both sides, the number of those who were to give the verdict was reduced to fifty one. In another place we have a particular account of the votes given for, and of those given against, Milo: added together, they amount to the precise number of fifty one.[o]

At Rome, as we have seen on more occasions than one, prosecutions were considered as the causes of the accusers, rather than as the causes of the commonwealth. The proceedings were regulated by this supposition. Accordingly, in a criminal prosecution, the challenge extended to such persons as either party — the accuser as well as the accused — had reason, or thought he had reason, to suspect might be influenced in their verdict by favour, affection, consanguinity, malice, or any other passion, which might lead to partiality or a corrupt judgment.[p]

When a prosecution, as well as the defence of it, was viewed as the cause of an individual, it might be reasonable enough that, in this view, the power of challenging jurors should, on both sides, be equal. But when a prosecution is considered as the cause of the community, by a part of which community this very cause is to be tried; matters now assume a very different appearance. This important difference was fully explained in the account which I gave of the radical principles, as I may call them, of the trial by jury.[q] The accused stands alone on one side: on the other side stand the whole community: the jury are indeed a *selected* part; but still they are a *part* of the whole community: the power of challenging, therefore, ought not, on both sides, to be equal.

True it is, that, at the common law, the king might challenge peremptorily, as well as the prisoner. The distinction between a publick and a private prosecutor was not sufficiently regarded. From this characteristick feature, by the way, a strong intrinsick evidence appears of the lineage of juries. But equally true it is, that the distinction was perceived at an early period, was then established — I mean in the reign of Edward the first — and has been since uniformly observed.[r] In consequence of this distinction, it has been the law, for many centuries past, that the privilege of peremptory challenges, though enjoyed by the prisoner, is refused to the king.

If, on account of the number of challenges, or the non-attendance of the jurors, so many of the panel returned as are necessary to make a jury cannot be had, the court may award a *tales* — others qualified in the same manner — to be added to the panel, till twelve are sworn to try the cause.[s]

Their oath is — that they will well and truly try and true deliverance

[o] Pet. on Jur. 114. [p] Id. 180. [q] Ante. p. 508.
[r] 2. Haw. 412. [s] 4. Bl. Com. 348.

make between the — United States — and the prisoner at the bar, and a true verdict give according to their evidence. After they are sworn, the indictment is read, and the issue which they are sworn to try is stated to them: and then the publick prosecutor opens the cause, and arranges, in such order as he thinks most proper, the evidence which is to be offered in support of the prosecution.

But it is a settled rule at the common law, as it is *now* received in England, that, in a trial for a capital crime, upon the general issue, no counsel shall be allowed the prisoner, unless some point of law, proper to be debated, shall arise. By a statute, however, made in the reign of William the third, and by another made in that of George the second, an exception to this general and severe rule is introduced, for the benefit of those who are indicted or impeached for treason.[t] This practice in England is admitted to be a hard one, and not to be very consonant to the rest of the humane treatment of prisoners by the English law. Indeed the judges themselves are so sensible of this defect in their modern practice, that they generally allow a prisoner counsel to stand by him at the bar, and instruct him what questions to ask, or even to ask questions for him.

This practice of refusing counsel to those who are indicted for a capital crime, is not agreeable to the common law as it was formerly received in England. The ancient Mirrour tells us, that, in civil causes, counsel are necessary to manage and to defend them, by the rules of law and the customs of the realm. He adds, with irresistible force, that they are still more necessary to defend indictments of felony, than causes of a less important nature.[u] On this, as on many other great and interesting subjects, we have renewed the ancient common law. It is enacted by a law of the United States,[v] that persons indicted for crimes shall be allowed to make their full defence by counsel learned in the law. It is declared by the constitution of Pennsylvania,[w] that, in all criminal prosecutions, the accused has a right to be heard by himself and his counsel.

In England, it has been an ancient and commonly received practice, that, as counsel was not allowed to any prisoner accused of a capital crime, so neither should he be suffered to exculpate himself by the testimony of witnesses. This doctrine was so unreasonable and severe, that the courts became ashamed of it, and gradually introduced a practice of examining witnesses for the prisoner: but they stopped in the middle of the road to redress — they would not examine the witnesses upon their oaths. The consequence was, that juries gave less credit to

[t] 4. Bl. Com. 349, 350.   [u] Mir. c. 3.   [v] 1. Cong. 2. sess. c. 9. s. 29.
[w] Art. 9. s. 9.

witnesses produced on the part of the prisoners, than to witnesses produced on the part of the crown.[x]

This practice, however, like the last, is not agreeable to the common law, at it was in ancient times received in England. To say the truth, says my Lord Coke,[y] we never read in any act of parliament, ancient author, bookcase, or record, that in criminal cases, the party accused should not have witnesses sworn for him; and therefore there is not so much as a *scintilla juris* against it. By a statute made in the reign of Queen Anne, the ancient common law on this point is renewed in England; and witnesses for the prisoner shall be examined upon oath, in the same manner as witnesses against him.[z]

On this subject, the ancient common law, as might have been expected, is renewed in the United States and in Pennsylvania. By a law of the former[a] it is provided, that persons indicted for crimes shall be allowed to make proof in their defence by lawful witnesses; and that, to compel the appearance of their witnesses, the court shall grant the same process as is granted to compel witnesses to appear on the prosecution. By the constitution of Pennsylvania,[b] it is declared, that, in all criminal prosecutions, the accused has a right to have compulsory process for obtaining witnesses in his favour.

The compulsory process for obtaining witnesses is a subpœna *ad testificandum*, which commands them to appear at the trial. If this command is disobeyed, an attachment issues for the contempt.[c]

In honour of the Founder of Pennsylvania it ought to be observed, that, in the charter of privileges[d] which he granted to its inhabitants, he declared, "that all criminals shall have the same privileges of witnesses and counsel as their prosecutors." On this as on many other subjects, Pennsylvania preceded England in point of liberal and enlightened improvement.

The constitution of Pennsylvania[e] declares, that, in all criminal prosecutions, the accused has a right to meet the witnesses face to face. Those who know the nature and the mischiefs of secret accusations, know the importance of this provision, and the security which it produces.

By the constitution of the United States,[f] no person shall be convicted of treason, unless on the testimony of two witnesses to the same overt act, or on confession in open court. The subject of confession has been already treated.

The courts of justice, in almost every age, and in almost every country, have had recourse to oaths, or appeals to heaven, as the most universal

---

[x] 4. Bl. Com. 352.   [y] 3. Ins. 79.   [z] St. 2. An. st. 2. c. 9.
[a] 1. Cong. 2. sess. c. 9. s. 29.   [b] Art. 9. s. 9.   [c] 3. Bl. Com. 369.   [d] S. 5.
[e] Art. 9. s. 9.   [f] Art. 3. s. 3.

and the most powerful means to engage men to declare the truth. By the common law, before the testimony of a witness can be received, he is obliged to swear, that it shall be the truth, the whole truth, and nothing but the truth.

The testimony of witnesses is one species of evidence, as we formerly saw in those lectures,[g] in which the great subject of evidence was opened, and but just opened. The general principles, upon which testimony is received and believed, were then stated in a short and summary manner, as connected with some native propensities of the human mind. The important distinction between the credibility of witnesses and their competency was explained at large,[h] when I discoursed concerning the separate provinces of courts and juries. I observed, that every intelligent person, who is not infamous or interested, is a competent witness. The common law coincides, in this point, with the law of Athens: for, by that law, no man could be a witness in his own cause; and he who, by his ill behaviour, had rendered himself infamous — ἄτιμος — was deemed unworthy of credit.[i]

The Marquis of Beccaria is of opinion, that the objection against the competency of a witness should be confined altogether to his interest; and that his infamy should not exclude him. Every man of common sense, says he, every one whose ideas have some connexion with each other, and whose sensations are conformable to those of other men, may be a witness; but the credibility of his testimony will be in proportion as he is interested in declaring or concealing the truth. Hence it appears how irrational it is to exclude persons branded with infamy; for they ought to be credited when they have no interest in giving false testimony.[j]

If this subject is investigated upon principle, it will, perhaps, be found, that the practice of the law is more congenial to the native sentiments of our mind, than are the speculations of the ingenious philosopher.

Belief is the end proposed by evidence of every kind. Belief in testimony is produced by the supposed veracity of him who delivers it. The opinion of his veracity, as we saw when we examined the general principles of testimony,[k] is shaken, either when, in former instances, we have known him to deliver testimony which has been false; or when, in the present instance, we discover some strong inducement which may prevail on him to deceive. The latter part of this observation applies to interested witnesses; and the application to them is admitted to be a proper one, and to be sufficient to exclude them from testimony. But who is a person infamous in the eye of the common law? He who has been convicted of an infamous crime. What, in the eye of the common law, is an

[g] Ante. p. 382. et seq.   [h] Ante. pp. 542–545.   [i] 1. Pot. Ant. 117.
[j] Bec. c. 13.   [k] Ante. p. 386.

infamous crime? When we investigated the true meaning of the *felleus animus*, according to the common law, we found that it indicated a disposition, deceitful, false, and treacherous.[1] He who is convicted of an infamous crime, is one who has been proved guilty of some conduct, which evinced him to have been false — to have committed the *crimen falsi;* of which so many different grades — from treason to a cheat, and both included — are known to the law.

It may, however, be urged, on the principles of Beccaria, that to the conduct of which he has been convicted, he was probably drawn by a motive of interest; and that, if no such motive exists in the present instance, the inference from the past to the present is without foundation. To this it may be justly answered, that the reason why interest excludes a witness is not, because it certainly will, but because it possibly may, occasion a deviation from the truth; and because this deviation may be produced even by an involuntary and imperceptible bias, which interest will sometimes impress upon minds intentionally honest. That this last consideration has great weight in the judgment of the law, is evident from one of the modes which it adopts to discover the existence of interest — a mode, which, I believe, can be rationally accounted for only by this last consideration. A witness, who is suspected to be interested, may be examined upon his *voir dire* — in other words, he may be required to declare, upon oath, whether he is interested or not. This mode of proceeding obviously supposes him honest as well as interested. For if it supposed him dishonest, would not the conclusion be irresistible — that he who ought not to be believed when he gives his testimony *in chief*, as it is called, ought as little to be believed, when he gives his testimony on his *voir dire?* That involuntary and unavoidable bias which interest sometimes impresses on the mind, and which, of consequence, may affect the testimony of the offered witness, is deemed by the law a sufficient reason for his exclusion from testimony.

If he whose testimony may deceive, merely because he is interested, though he be honest, shall for this reason be excluded; shall we admit the testimony of one who is false, though he be disinterested? The former is rejected, because he *may be* biassed involuntarily; for the danger of even an involuntary bias is, for this purpose, sufficient: and shall one, whom interest *has* biassed voluntarily and infamously — shall such a one be received? On good grounds, therefore, are persons infamous excluded from giving testimony.

That evidence which arises from testimony is, in the law, denominated positive. There is another kind, which the law terms presumptive. When the fact itself cannot be proved by witnesses, that which comes nearest to such proof is, the proof of such circumstances, with which the fact is

[1] Ante. p. 622.

either necessarily or usually attended. This is presumptive evidence. When those circumstances are proved, with which the fact is *necessarily* attended, the presumption is said to be violent: when those circumstances only are proved with which the fact is *usually* attended, the presumption is said to be only probable.[m]

Presumptive proof, as described by the common law, coincides with that species which, in our general view of the sources of evidence, we saw rising from experience. On that occasion,[n] it was observed, that if an object is remembered to have been frequently, still more, if it is remembered to have been constantly succeeded by certain particular consequences, the conception of the object naturally associates to itself the conception of the consequences; and on the actual appearance of the object, the mind naturally anticipates the appearance of the consequences also: that if the consequences have followed the object *constantly*, and the observations of this constant connexion have been sufficiently numerous; the evidence produced by experience amounts to a moral certainty: that, if it has been *frequent*, but not entirely uniform; the evidence amounts only to probability, and is more or less probable, as the connexion has been more or less frequent. Violent presumption, as it is termed by the law, or moral certainty, as it is denominated by philosophy, amounts to full proof:[o] probability, or probable presumption, has also its due weight.[p] The coincidence between philosophy and law is a coincidence which, to the friends of both, always gives pleasure.

It ought to be observed here, that, in cases of a capital nature, all presumptive proof should be received with caution: for the law benignly holds that it is more eligible that ten guilty persons should escape, than that one innocent person should suffer a capital punishment.

After the evidence is heard, the jury are next to consider what verdict they ought to give upon it; for they are sworn, as we have seen, to give a true verdict according to their evidence. To give a verdict is the great purpose for which they are summoned and empanelled. Till they give a verdict, therefore, they cannot be discharged.[q] This verdict may either be special — in other words, it may state particularly the facts arising in the cause, and leave to the court the decision of the law resulting from those facts; or it may be general — in other words, it may determine both the facts and the law. A general verdict is either guilty or not guilty: on a verdict of not guilty, the prisoner is discharged: by a verdict of guilty, he is convicted: on a conviction the judgment and the punishment pronounced and inflicted by the law regularly follow, unless they

---

[m] 3. Bl. Com. 371.   [n] Ante. p. 389.   [o] 1. Ins. 6. b.   [p] 3. Bl. Com. 372.
[q] 4. Bl. Com. 354.

are intercepted by errour in the proceedings, by a reprieve, or by a pardon.

When a sentence of death is pronounced, the immediate and inseparable consequence, by the common law, is attainder. The law puts him out of its protection, considers him as a bane to human society, and takes no farther care of him than barely to see him executed: he is already considered as dead in law. There is, in capital cases, a great difference between a man convicted and one attainted. Till judgment is given, there is, in such cases, still a possibility of innocence in the contemplation of the law.[r]

In England the consequences of attainder are forfeiture, escheat, and corruption of blood. Concerning these subjects we have already treated fully.

I have now enumerated and described the several crimes, the several punishments, and the modes of prosecuting criminals. In doing this, I have conformed myself to the common law and to the improvements made upon it by the constitutions and laws of the United States and of Pennsylvania.

[r] 4. Bl. Com. 373.

MISCELLANEOUS PAPERS

I

ON THE HISTORY OF PROPERTY

PROPERTY is the right or lawful power, which a person has to a thing. Of this right there are three different degrees. The lowest degree of this right is a right merely to possess a thing. The next degree of this right is a right to possess and to use a thing. The next and highest degree of this right is a right to possess, to use, and to dispose of a thing.

This right, in all its different degrees, may be vested in one, or it may be vested in more than one man. When this right is vested in more than one man, it may be vested in them either as a number of individuals, or as a body politick.

Concerning the origin and true foundation of property, or the right of persons to things, many opinions have been formed and entertained. With regard to property in land, Mr. Paley declares, that the real foundation of it is municipal law.[a] Others consider property as a natural right; but as a right, which may be extended or modified by positive institutions.[b]

The general property of man in animals, in the soil, and in the productions of the soil, is the immediate gift of the bountiful Creator of all. "God created man in his own image; in the image of God created he him: male and female created he them. And God blessed them; and God said unto them, be fruitful and multiply, and replenish the earth, and subdue it: and have dominion over the fish of the sea, and over the fowl of the air, and over every living thing that moveth upon the earth." [c] Immediately after the deluge, the great charter of general property was renewed. "God blessed Noah and his sons, and said unto them, be fruitful and multiply, and replenish the earth. And the fear of you and the dread of you shall be upon every beast of the earth, and upon every fowl of the air, and upon all that moveth upon the earth, and upon all the fishes of the sea; into your hand are they delivered. Every moving thing that liveth shall be meat for you; even as the green herb have I given you all things." [d]

The information which is expressly revealed is congenial to those

---

[a] 1. Paley. 133. 138.   [b] Ins. 2. 1. 11. El. Jur. 15.   [c] Gen. i. 27. 28.
[d] Gen. ix. 1, 2, 3.

inferences, which may be drawn by sound and legitimate reasoning. Food, raiment, and shelter are necessary and useful to us. Things proper for our food, raiment, and shelter are provided around us. It is natural to conclude, that those things were provided to supply our wants and necessities. The same train of reasoning will apply to the enjoyments, as well as to the necessities of man.

While men were few, and the supplies of every thing were abundant, it is probable that many things were possessed and used in common. With regard to the possession and use of some things, however, this could never be strictly the case. In the fruit plucked or gathered by one for his subsistence; in the spot which he occupied for his shelter or repose; in the bow which he has made for ensuring his safety, or procuring his subsistence; in the skin which he has obtained by his skill and swiftness in the chace, and which covers his body from the inclemency of the weather, he gains a high degree of exclusive right; and of this right he cannot be dispossessed without a proportioned degree of injustice. "A publick theatre," says Cicero,[e] with his usual luminous propriety, "is common to all the citizens; but the seat which each occupies may, during the entertainment, be denominated his own." But, in the early period of society, concerning which we now speak, things, in general, would be viewed as belonging equally to all; in other words, to those who should first have occasion to use or possess them.

In this situation, we have reason to believe, society continued after the deluge, while "the whole earth was of one language and of one speech." [f] On the confusion of languages, and the dispersion of families, when mankind dwelt no longer in "the same plain," [g] this general society was dissolved, and no one subject of property could, in this new situation, be reasonably deemed as belonging equally to all. The different families and associations, however, who diverged from the common centre of emigration, would still consider many things, and particularly the country in which they commenced their new settlements, as common to each family or association.

The things most immediately necessary to the subsistence of life would become the first objects of exclusive property. The next objects would be such as ministered to its conveniency and comfort. Personal property, or property in movables, would become separate; while real property, or property in land, would continue common. When the association became too numerous, and the personal property of its members became too large, to subsist or live commodiously together; then a sepa-

---

[e] De fin. l. 3. c. 20.

[f] Gen. xi. 1. Erant omnia communia et indivisa omnibus, veluti unum cunctis patrimonium esset. Just. l. 43. c. 1. [To all men everything was in common and without separation, just as if they all had a single inheritance.]

[g] Gen. xi. 2.

ration of landed possessions necessarily took place. Of these remarks we have a strong and striking illustration in the history of Abram and Lot. "Abram was very rich in cattle: Lot also had flocks, and herds, and tents. And the land was not able to bear them that they might dwell together; for their substance was great. And there was a strife between the herdmen of Abram's cattle and the herdmen of Lot's cattle. And Abram said unto Lot, let there be no strife, I pray thee, between thee and me, and between my herdmen and thy herdmen; for we be brethren. Is not the whole land before thee? Separate thyself, I pray thee, from me: if thou wilt take the left hand, then will I go to the right: or if thou depart to the right hand, then I will go to the left. And Lot lifted up his eyes, and beheld all the plain of Jordan, that it was well watered every where. Then Lot chose him all the plain of Jordan: and they separated themselves the one from the other." [h]

Even after agriculture became known and was practised in some imperfect degree, still the land continued to be the common property of the association. Cecrops, who emigrated from civilized Egypt, was the first to teach the wandering hunters or shepherds of Attica to unite in villages of husbandmen. After their union, their agricultural labours were carried on in common; and the soil, together with its immediate production, corn, and wine, and oil, were regarded as a common property.[i] Agreeably to the same spirit and the same policy, we are told, that during the heroick ages of Greece, when a tribe sallied from its woods and mountains to take possession of a more fertile territory, the soldiers fought and conquered, not for their leaders, but for themselves — that the land acquired by their joint valour was their common right — and that it was cultivated by the united labour and assiduity of all the members of the tribe.[j]

In this stage of society, land was considered as the property of the community, rather than of individuals; and the inhabitants were connected with the country which they inhabited, only as members of the same association.[k] In this view of things, the famed establishment of a community of property, which Lycurgus made at Sparta, may be deemed nothing more than a renewal of their primitive institutions, of which some traces probably remained among the simple Spartans.[l]

The Scythians, it is well known, appropriated their cattle and tents, but occupied their land in common. Such, to this day, are the laws and customs of the Tartars.

Of the Suevi,[m] the largest and most powerful tribe of the ancient

[h] Gen. xiii. 2.5. — 11.   [i] 1. Gill. 8.   [j] Id. 48.   [k] Id. 68.
[l] 1. Gill. 96.
[m] Suevorum gens est longe maxima et bellicosissima Germanorum omnium — privati ac separati agri apud eos nihil est — quotannis singula millia armatorum, bellandi causa, suis ex finibus educunt: reliqui domi manent; pro se atque illis colunt. Hi

Germans, we are informed by Cæsar, that they had no private or separate property in their land; that, every year, they sent out a proportion of their warriours in order to make war; while the rest remained at home, and cultivated the ground for all; that these war-like enterprises and peaceful occupations were pursued, in alternate years, by the different divisions of the warriours; that the tribe continued only one year in the same place; that they used corn very little; but lived chiefly on milk and flesh; and were much employed in hunting. From the pen of Tacitus[n] we have nearly the same description. They change, says he, from spot to spot; and make new appropriations according to the number of hands, and to the condition and quality of each. As the plains are very spacious, the allotments are easily assigned: for though they shift their situation annually, they have still lands to spare.

In Tacitus, however, we begin to discover some appearances, among the Germans, of a private property in lands. To a certain class of their slaves, we are told, their masters assigned habitations; and from them, as from tenants, demanded in return a certain quantity of grain, or cattle, or cloth.[o] This presupposes, in the masters, a separate property in the lands let to those slaves.

In the Highlands of Scotland, we are told, common possession of the cultivated soil, as well as of the pasture grounds, is known to this day. The arable lands are divided into as many parts, as there are tenants entitled to an equal share of possession. The stock of cattle belonging to each tenant is considered as equal: the advantages accruing to the several partitions from manure are deemed also to be equivalent; yet some portion of these divisions shifts annually from one possessor to another, in

---

rursus invicim anno post in armis sunt: illi domi remanent — neque longius anno remanere uno in loco, incolendi causa, licet; neque multum frumento, sed maximann partem lacte atque pecore vivant, multumque sunt in venationibus. Cæs. l. 4. c. 1. l. 6. c. 21. [The nation of the Suevi is by far the largest and most warlike of all the Germans — among them there is no privately owned or separate farmland — each year they lead out of their own territory a thousand armed men in order to make war; the rest remain at home, cultivating the land for themselves and the others. The next year the latter serve their turn in arms and the former remain at home — and they may not stay in one place for the sake of dwelling in it for longer than a year, nor do they live on grain very much, but for the most part on milk and their herds, and they spend a great deal of time in hunting.]

[n] Agri pro numero cultorum ab universis per vices occupantur, quos mox inter se secundum dignationem partiuntur. Facilitatem partiendi camporum spatia prestant. Arva per annos mutant; et superest ager. Tac. de mor. Ger. c. 26. [Land is occupied by them as a whole through the villages in proportion to the number of cultivators; this is soon apportioned among them according to their ranks, the area of the fields making division easy. They change their fields through the years, and there is farmland left over.]

[o] Servis utuntur. Suam quisque sedem, suos penates regit. Frumenti modum dominus, aut pecoris, aut vestis, ut colono injungit. Tac. de mor. Ger. c. 25. [They have slaves, but each slave is master of his own household. The master makes him pay an amount of grain, cattle, or clothing, like a tenant.]

such a manner, that, in a certain period of years, every tenant of the village has occupied and reaped crops from all the lands belonging to the village.[p]

It is said, that, among the Indians of Peru, the territory occupied was the property of the state, and was regulated by the magistrate; and that, when individuals were permitted to possess particular spots, these, in default of male issue, returned to the community.[q] Formerly, says Mr. Adair, the Indian law obliged every town to work together in one body, in sowing or planting their crops; though their fields are divided by proper marks, and their harvest is gathered and appropriated separately.[r] The ideas and opinions of private and exclusive property are, as we have reason to believe, extending gradually among the Indians; though their uncultivated territory is still considered as the common property of the nation or tribe.

From the detail which we have given, we are justified in deducing this general remark — that in the early and rude periods of society among all nations, the same family or association enjoyed and were understood to enjoy in many things a community of property, especially of landed property; and that, as to individuals, property was conceived to extend no farther than to those degrees, which comprehend the right of possession and temporary use of the soil.

But agriculture, and the industry attendant on agriculture, introduced gradually a new scene of things, and a new train of sentiments. This first of arts was not unknown to the restorer of mankind. Noah, after the deluge, began to be a husbandman, and he planted a vineyard.[s] Before the confusion of languages, the whole human race dwelt in the plain of Shinar. In that plain and its neighbourhood, the knowledge of agriculture was never entirely lost. Among the Babylonians, it is traced to the most early periods of their history. In the fertile territories of Egypt, watered by the Nile, the soil was cultivated with much assiduity and success.[t] When a famine, in the days of Abram, was grievous in the land of Canaan, the patriarch went down into Egypt to sojourn there.[u] On a similar occasion, Jacob said to his sons, who, with unavailing anguish, beheld the distressed situation of the family — Why do ye look one upon another? I have heard that there is corn in Egypt; get ye down thither, and buy for us from thence, that we may live, and not die.[v]

From Egypt, as we have already seen, the art of agriculture was transplanted into Attica by Cecrops. Before his arrival, the inhabitants had

[p] Grant's Ess. 97.   [q] Stu. V. 158. cites Com. Per. b. 5. c. 1. 3.   [r] Id. ibid.
[s] Gen. ix. 20.
[t] Osiris, one of the kings of Egypt, is regarded as the inventor of the plough.
Primus aratra manu solerti fecit Osiris. Tibul. l. 1. Eleg. 7. v. 29. [First Osiris made ploughs with dexterous hand.]
[u] Gen. xii. 10.   [v] Gen. xlii. 1, 2.

relied on the reproductions of the uncultivated soil for their annual subsistence; but, by the example of the Egyptians, skilled in agriculture, they were induced to submit to labour, and contract habits of useful industry.[w]

It is the observation of Cicero, that the greatest part of the arts and discoveries, which are necessary or ornamental to life and society, were derived from the Athenians into the other parts of Greece, and then into foreign countries, for the general advantage and refinement of the human race.[x] Agriculture, in particular, was brought from Greece into Italy, according to the account of this matter given by the Romans themselves.[y] As the Egyptians taught the Greeks; so the Greeks communicated their knowledge to the Italians. For many ages, the Romans knew no other form of a plough, than that which, to this day, is used in some districts of the higher Egypt.[z]

The wise and virtuous Numa was the patron of agriculture. He distributed the Romans into pagi or villages, and over each placed a superintendant to prevail with them, by every motive, to improve the practice of husbandry. To inspire their industry with redoubled vigour, he frequently condescended to be their overseer himself. This wise and judicious policy had a most happy influence upon the subsequent manners and fortunes of Rome. Our consuls, says the Roman Orator,[a] were called from the plough. Those illustrious characters, who have most adorned the commonwealth, and have been best qualified to manage the reins of government with dignity and success, dedicated a part of their time and of their labour to the cultivation of their landed estates. In those glorious ages of the republick, the farmer, the judge, and the soldier were to each other a reciprocal ornament. After having finished the publick business with glory and advantage to himself and to his country, the Roman magistrate descended, with modest dignity, from the elevation of office; and reassumed, with contentment and with pleasure, the peaceful labours of a rural and independent life.

When agriculture was once introduced, and its utility was known and experienced; it became natural to search and adopt the measures necessary for distinguishing possessions permanently; that every one who laboured and who excelled in this fundamental profession, might be secured in enjoying the fruits of his labours and his improvements. Hence the

---

[w] 1. Anac. 6.   [x] 1. Pot. Ant. 138.   [y] 1. Gog. Or. Laws. 88.   [z] Id. 90.

[a] Ab aratro arcessebantur, qui consules fierent — Apud majores nostros, summi viri, clarissimique homines, qui omni tempore ad gubernacula reipublicæ sedere debebant, tamen in agris quoque colendis aliquantum operæ temporisque consumserint. Cic. pro Ros. Am. c. 18. [From the plough men were summoned to become consuls — in the days of our ancestors, those most excellent and distinguished men, who, though they should have sat at the helm of the state all the time, none the less devoted a certain amount of time and effort to cultivating their farms.]

foundation of laws, which instituted and regulated the division and stable possession of the soil. Hence, too, the origin and the importance of land marks. In the early period in which Job lived, it was part of the description of a turbulent and wicked man, that he removed the land marks, and violently took away flocks.[b] The inspired legislator of the Jews speaks of them as of an institution, which, even in his time, was anciently established in Canaan. "Thou shalt not remove thy neighbour's land mark, which they of old times have set in thy inheritance, which thou shalt inherit in the land that the Lord thy God giveth thee to possess it."[c] Numa, mild as he was, ordered those who were guilty of this crime, to suffer a capital punishment.[d]

The inference which we draw from this long detail of facts is — that agriculture gave rise to that degree of property in land, which consists in the right of exclusive and permanent possession and use.

We have seen that among the ancient Germans, this degree of property was altogether unknown. The Saxons, who emigrated into England, and made a conquest there, were a part of the ancient German nation. Their settlement in England produced, with regard to the present subject, a considerable change in their sentiments and habits. After they settled in England, instead of continuing to be hunters, they became husbandmen. In pursuing this occupation, they ceased to wander annually from spot to spot; they became habituated and attached to a fixed residence; they acquired a permanent and an exclusive degree of property in land. This degree, among them, as among other nations, proceeded from their improvement in agriculture.[e]

We have good reason for believing, that, for some time after the settlement of the Saxons in England, the landed estates acquired by individuals were, in general, but of a small extent. Inexpert in agriculture when they first arrived, their progress in the separate appropriation of land was, therefore, slow. This slow appropriation met, besides, with obstructions and interruptions from the vigorous opposition of the Britons, who, for centuries, disputed every inch of ground with the invaders of their country. Conformably to this opinion, we find that, from the beginning of the Saxon government, the land was divided into hides. A hide comprehended as much as could be cultivated by a single plough. The general estimation of real property, by this small and inaccurate measure, points, with sufficient clearness, to the leading circumstance, which originally marked and regulated the greatest number of landed estates.[f]

But we have also good reason for believing, that, among the Saxons,

<hr />

[b] Job xxiv. 2.   [c] Deut. xix. 14.   [d] 1. Gog. Or. Laws. 32.   [e] Millar, 50,
[f] Id, 85. 144. 181.

the smallness of their landed property was compensated by its independence. They were freemen; and their law of property was, that they might challenge a power to do what they pleased with their own.[g] But this degree and quality of property will be considered afterwards.

Having traced property, and especially property in land, from its general to its separate and exclusive state, it will now be proper to consider the advantages, which the latter state possesses over the former.

This superiority of separate over common property has not been always admitted: it has not been always admitted even in America. In the early settlement of this country, we find two experiments on the operation and effects of a community of goods. The issue of each, however, was very uncomfortable.

The first was made in Virginia. An instruction was given to the colonists, that during five years next after their landing, they should trade jointly; that the produce of their joint industry should be deposited in a common magazine; and that, from this common magazine, every one should be supplied under the direction of the council. What were the consequences? I relate them in the words of the Historian of Virginia. "And now the English began to find the mistake of forbidding and preventing private property; for whilst they all laboured jointly together, and were fed out of the common store, happy was he that could slip from his labour, or slubber over his work in any manner. Neither had they any concern about the increase; presuming, however the crop prospered, that the publick store must maintain them. Even the most honest and industrious would scarcely take so much pains in a week, as they would have done for themselves in a day."[h]

The second experiment was made in the colony of New Plymouth. During seven years, all commerce was carried on in one joint stock. All things were common to all; and the necessaries of life were daily distributed to every one from the publick store. But these regulations soon furnished abundant reasons for complaint, and proved most fertile sources of common calamity. The colonists were sometimes in danger of starving; and severe whipping, which was often administered to promote labour, was only productive of constant and general discontent. This absurd policy became, at last, apparent to every one; and the introduction of exclusive property immediately produced the most comfortable change in the colony, by engaging the affections and invigorating the pursuits of its inhabitants.[i]

The right of separate property seems to be founded in the nature of men and things; and when societies become numerous, the establishment of that right is highly important to the existence, to the tranquillity, to

[g] Bac. on. Gov. 123.   [h] Stith. 39.   [i] Chal. 89. 90.

the elegancies, to the refinements, and to some of the virtues of civilized life.

Man is intended for action. Useful and skilful industry is the soul of an active life. But industry should have her just reward. That reward is property; for of useful and active industry, property is the natural result.

Exclusive property multiplies the productions of the earth, and the means of subsistence. Who would cultivate the soil, and sow the grain, if he had no peculiar interests in the harvest? Who would rear and tend flocks and herds, if they were to be taken from him by the first person who should come to demand them?

By exclusive property, the productions of the earth and the means of subsistence are secured and preserved, as well as multiplied. What belongs to no one is wasted by every one. What belongs to one man in particular is the object of his economy and care.

Exclusive property prevents disorder, and promotes peace. Without its establishment, the tranquillity of society would be perpetually disturbed by fierce and ungovernable competitions for the possession and enjoyment of things, insufficient to satisfy all, and by no rules of adjustment distributed to each.

The conveniencies of life depend much on an exclusive property. The full effects of industry cannot be obtained without distinct professions and the division of labour. But labour cannot be divided, nor can distinct professions be pursued, unless the productions of one profession and of one kind of labour can be exchanged for those of another. This exchange implies a separate property in those who make it.

The observations concerning the conveniencies of life, may be applied with equal justness to its elegancies and its refinements.

On property some of the virtues depend for their more free and enlarged exercise. Would the same room be left for the benign indulgence of generosity and beneficence — would the same room be left for the becoming returns of esteem and gratitude — would the same room be left for the endearing interchange of good offices, in the various institutions and relations of social life, if the goods of fortune lay in a mass, confused and unappropriated?

For these reasons, the establishment of exclusive property may justly be considered as essential to the interests of civilized society. With regard to land, in particular, a separate and exclusive property in it is a principal source of attachment to the country, in which one resides. A person becomes very unwilling to relinquish those well known fields of his own; which it has been the great object of his industry, and, perhaps, of his pride, to cultivate and adorn. This attachment to private landed property has, in some parts of the globe, covered barren heaths and inhospitable mountains with fair cities and populous villages; while, in other parts, the most inviting climates and soils remain destitute of inhabitants, because the rights of private property in land are not established or regarded.[1]

[1] The foregoing observations were intended to compose a part of those lectures, in which the Author designed "to trace the history of property from its lowest rude beginnings to its highest artificial refinements" (p. 94). It will be perceived that the piece is indeed but a fragment; as, however, the history of property is so far completed as to trace it from its general to its separate and exclusive state, it is thought worthy of insertion. *Ed.*

II

CONSIDERATIONS ON THE NATURE AND EXTENT OF THE LEGISLATIVE AUTHORITY OF THE BRITISH PARLIAMENT

PUBLISHED IN THE YEAR MDCCLXXIV

ADVERTISEMENT

The following sheets were written during the late non-importation agreement: but that agreement being dissolved before they were ready for the press, it was then judged unseasonable to publish them. Many will, perhaps, be surprised to see the legislative authority of the British parliament over the colonies denied *in every instance*. Those the writer informs, that, when he began this piece, he would probably have been surprised at such an opinion himself; for that it was the *result*, and not the *occasion*, of his disquisitions. He entered upon them with a view and expectation of being able to trace some constitutional line between those cases in which we ought, and those in which we ought not, to acknowledge the power of parliament over us. In the prosecution of his inquiries, he became fully convinced that such a line does not exist; and that there can be no medium between acknowledging and denying that power in *all* cases. Which of these two alternatives is most consistent with law, with the principles of liberty, and with the happiness of the colonies, let the publick determine. To them the writer submits his sentiments, with that respectful deference to their judgment, which, in all questions affecting them, every individual should pay.

August 17th, 1774.

No question can be more important to Great Britain, and to the colonies, than this — does the legislative authority of the British parliament extend over them?

On the resolution of this question, and on the measures which a resolution of it will direct, it will depend, whether the parent country, like a happy mother, shall behold her children flourishing around her, and receive the most grateful returns for her protection and love; or whether, like a step dame, rendered miserable by her own unkind conduct, she shall see their affections alienated, and herself deprived of those advantages which a milder treatment would have ensured to her.

The British nation are generous: they love to enjoy freedom: they love to behold it: slavery is their greatest abhorrence. Is it possible, then, that they would wish themselves the authors of it? No. Oppression is not a plant of the British soil; and the late severe proceedings against the colonies must have arisen from the detestable schemes of interested ministers, who have misinformed and misled the people. A regard for that nation, from whom we have sprung, and from whom we boast to have derived the spirit which prompts us to oppose their unfriendly measures, must lead us to put this construction on what we have lately seen and experienced. When, therefore, they shall know and consider the justice of our claim — that we insist only upon being treated as freemen, and as the descendants of those British ancestors, whose memory we will not dishonour by our degeneracy, it is reasonable to hope, that they will approve of our conduct, and bestow their loudest applauses on our congenial ardour for liberty.

But if these reasonable and joyful hopes should fatally be disappointed, it will afford us at least some satisfaction to know, that the principles on which we have founded our opposition to the late acts of parliament, are the principles of justice and freedom, and of the British constitution. If our righteous struggle shall be attended with misfortunes, we will reflect with exultation on the noble cause of them; and while suffering unmerited distress, think ourselves superiour to the proudest slaves. On the contrary, if we shall be reinstated in the enjoyment of those rights, to which we are entitled by the supreme and uncontrollable laws of nature, and the fundamental principles of the British constitution, we shall reap the glorious fruit of our labours; and we shall, at the same time, give to the world and to posterity an instructive example, that the cause of liberty ought not to be despaired of, and that a generous contention in that cause is not always unattended with success.

The foregoing considerations have induced me to publish a few re-marks on the important question, with which I introduced this essay.

Those who allege that the parliament of Great Britain have power to make laws binding the American colonies, reason in the following manner. "That there is and must be in every state a supreme, irresistible, absolute, uncontrolled authority, in which the *jura summi imperii*, or the rights of sovereignty, reside:" [a] "That this supreme power is, by the constitution of Great Britain, vested in the king, lords, and commons:" [b] "That, therefore, the acts of the king, lords, and commons, or, in other words, acts of parliament, have, by the British constitution, a binding force on the American colonies, they composing a part of the British empire."

I admit that the principle, on which this argument is founded, is of great importance: its importance, however, is derived from its tendency to promote the ultimate end of all government. But if the application of it would, in any instance, destroy, instead of promoting, that end, it ought, in that instance, to be rejected: for to admit it, would be to sacrifice the end to the means; which are valuable only so far as they advance it.

All men are, by nature, equal and free: no one has a right to any authority over another without his consent: all lawful government is founded on the consent of those who are subject to it: such consent was given with a view to ensure and to increase the happiness of the governed, above what they could enjoy in an independent and unconnected state of nature. The consequence is, that the happiness of the society is the *first* law of every government.[c]

This rule is founded on the law of nature: it must control every political maxim: it must regulate the legislature itself.[d] The people have a right to insist that this rule be observed; and are entitled to demand a moral security that the legislature will observe it. If they have not the first, they are slaves; if they have not the second, they are, every moment, exposed to slavery. For "civil liberty it nothing else but natural liberty, devested of that part which constituted the independence of individuals, by the authority which it confers on sovereigns, attended with a right of insisting upon their making a good use of their authority, and with a moral security that this right will have its effect." [e]

Let me now be permitted to ask — Will it ensure and increase the

<hr/>

[a] 4. Bl. Com. 48. 49.   [b] Id. 50. 51.

[c] The right of sovereignty is that of commanding finally — but in order to procure real felicity; for if this end is not obtained, sovereignty ceases to be a legitimate authority. 2. Burl. 32, 33.

[d] The law of nature is superiour in obligation to any other. 1. Bl. Com. 41.

[e] 2. Burl. 19.

happiness of the American colonies, that the parliament of Great Britain should possess a supreme, irresistible, uncontrolled authority over them? Is such an authority consistent with their liberty? Have they any security that it will be employed only for their good? Such a security is absolutely necessary. Parliaments are not infallible: they are not always just. The members, of whom they are composed, are human; and, therefore, they may err; they are influenced by interest; and, therefore, they may deviate from their duty. The acts of the body must depend upon the opinions and dispositions of the members: the acts of the body may, then, be the result of errour and of vice. It is no breach of decency to suppose all this: the British constitution supposes it: "it supposes that parliaments may betray their trust, and provides, as far as human wisdom can provide, that they may not be able to do so long, without a sufficient control." [f] Without provisions for this purpose, the temple of British liberty, like a structure of ice, would instantly dissolve before the fire of oppression and despotick sway.

It will be very material to consider the several securities, which the inhabitants of Great Britain have, that their liberty will not be destroyed by the legislature, in whose hands it is intrusted. If it shall appear, that the same securities are not enjoyed by the colonists; the undeniable consequence will be, that the colonists are not under the same obligations to intrust their liberties into the hands of the same legislature: for the colonists are entitled to all [g] the privileges of Britons. We have committed no crimes to forfeit them: we have too much spirit to resign them. We will leave our posterity as free as our ancestors left us.

To give to any thing that passes in parliament the force of a law, the consent of the king, of the lords, and of the commons[h] is absolutely necessary.[i] If, then, the inhabitants of Great Britain possess a sufficient restraint upon any of these branches of the legislature, their liberty is secure, provided they be not wanting to themselves. Let us take a view of the restraints, which they have upon the house of commons.

They elect the members of that house. "Magistrates," says Montesquieu,[j] "are properly theirs, who have the nomination of them." The members of the house of commons, therefore, elected by the people, are the magistrates of the people; and are bound by the ties of gratitude for the honour and confidence conferred upon them, to consult the interest of their constituents.

---

[f] Bol. Diss. on Part. l. 11. 12. p. 167. 179.

[g] As the law is the birthright of every subject, so wheresoever they go, they carry their laws with them. 2. P. Wms. 75.

[h] 4. Ins. 25.

[i] The commons of England have a great and considerable right in the government; and a share in the legislature without whom no law passes. 2. Ld. Ray. 950.

[j] Sp. L. b. 2. c. 2.

The power of elections has ever been regarded as a point of the last consequence to all [k] free governments. The independent exercise of that power is justly deemed the strongest bulwark of the British liberties.[1] As such, it has always been an object of great attention to the legislature; and is expressly stipulated with the prince in the bill of rights. All those are excluded from voting, whose poverty is such, that they cannot live independent, and must therefore be subject to the undue influence of their superiours. Such are supposed to have no will of their own: and it is judged improper that they should vote in the representation of a free state. What can exhibit in a more striking point of view, the peculiar care which has been taken, in order to render the election of members of parliament entirely free? It was deemed an insult upon the independent commons of England, that their uninfluenced suffrages should be adulterated by those who were not at liberty to speak as they thought, though their interests and inclinations were the same. British liberty, it was thought, could not be effectually secured, unless those who made the laws were freely, and without influence, elected by those for whom they were made. Upon this principle is reasonably founded the maxim in law — that every one, who is capable of exercising his will, is party, and presumed to consent, to an act of parliament.

For the same reason that persons, who live dependent upon the will of others, are not admitted to vote in elections, those who are under age, and therefore incapable of judging; those who are convicted of perjury or subornation of perjury, and therefore unworthy of judging; and those who obtain their freeholds by fraudulent conveyances, and would therefore vote to serve infamous purposes, are all likewise excluded from the enjoyment of this great privilege. Corruption at elections is guarded against by the strictest precautions, and most severe penalties. Every elector, before he polls, must, if demanded by a candidate or by two electors, take the oath against bribery, as prescribed by 2. Geo. 2. c. 24. Officers of the excise, of the customs, and of the post offices, officers concerned in the duties upon leather, soap, paper, striped linens imported, hackney coaches, cards and dice, are restrained from interfering in elections, under the penalty of one hundred pounds, and of being incapable of ever exercising any office of trust under the king.

Thus is the freedom of elections secured from the servility, the ignorance, and the corruption of the electors; and from the interposition of

[k] The Athenians, justly jealous of this important privilege, punished, with death, every stranger who presumed to interfere in the assemblies of the people.
[1] The English freedom will be at an end whenever the court invades the free election of parliament. Rapin.
A right that man has to give his vote at the election of a person to represent him in parliament, there to concur to the making of laws, which are to bind his liberty and property, is a most transcendant thing and of a high nature. 2. Ld. Ray. 953.

officers depending immediately upon the crown. But this is not all. Provisions, equally salutary, have been made concerning the qualifications of those who shall be elected. All imaginable care has been taken, that the commons of Great Britain may be neither awed, nor allured, nor deceived into any nomination inconsistent with their liberties.

It has been adopted as a general maxim, that the crown will take advantage of every opportunity of extending its prerogative, in opposition to the privileges of the people; that it is the interest of those who have pensions or offices at will from the crown, to concur in all its measures; that mankind in general will prefer their private interest to the good of their country; and that, consequently, those who enjoy such pensions or offices are unfit to represent a free nation, and to have the care of their liberties committed to their hands.[m] All such officers or pensioners are declared incapable of being elected members of the house of commons.

But these are not the only checks which the commons of Great Britain have, upon the conduct of those whom they elect to represent them in parliament. The interest of the representatives is the same with that of their constituents. Every measure, that is prejudicial to the nation, must be prejudicial to them and their posterity. They cannot betray their electors, without, at the same time, injuring themselves. They must join in bearing the burthen of every oppressive act; and participate in the happy effects of every wise and good law. Influenced by these considerations, they will seriously and with attention examine every measure proposed to them; they will behold it in every light, and extend their views to its most distant consequences. If, after the most mature deliberation, they find it will be conducive to the welfare of their country, they will support it with ardour: if, on the contrary, it appears to be of a dangerous and destructive nature, they will oppose it with firmness.

Every social and generous affection concurs with their interest, in animating the representatives of the commons of Great Britain to an honest and faithful discharge of their important trust. In each patriotick effort, the heartfelt satisfaction of having acted a worthy part vibrates in delightful unison with the applause of their countrymen, who never fail to express their warmest acknowledgements to the friends and benefactors of their country. How pleasing are those rewards! How much to be preferred to that paltry wealth, which is sometimes procured by meanness and treachery! I say sometimes; for meanness and treachery do not always obtain that pitiful reward. The most useful ministers to the crown, and therefore the most likely to be employed, especially in great emergencies, are those who are best beloved by the people; and those only are beloved by the people, who act steadily and uniformly in support of their liberties. Patriots, therefore, have frequently, and especially upon

---

[m] There are a few exceptions in the case of officers at will.

important occasions, the best chance of being advanced to offices of profit and power. An abject compliance with the will of an imperious prince, and a ready disposition to sacrifice every duty to his pleasure, are sometimes, I confess, the steps, by which only men can expect to rise to wealth and titles. Let us suppose that, in this manner, they are successful in attaining them. Is the despicable prize a sufficient recompense, for submitting to the infamous means by which it was procured, and for the torturing remorse with which the possession of it must be accompanied? Will it compensate for the merited curses of the nation and of posterity?

These must be very strong checks upon the conduct of every man, who is not utterly lost to all sense of praise and blame. Few will expose themselves to the just abhorrence of those among whom they live, and to the excruciating sensations which such abhorrence must produce.

But lest all these motives, powerful as they are, should be insufficient to animate the representatives of the nation to a vigorous and upright discharge of their duty, and to restrain them from yielding to any temptation that would incite them to betray their trust; their constituents have still a farther security for their liberties in the frequent election of parliaments. At the expiration of every parliament, the people can make a distinction between those who have served them well, and those who have neglected or betrayed their interest: they can bestow, unasked, their suffrages upon the former in the new election; and can mark the latter with disgrace, by a mortifying refusal. The constitution is thus frequently renewed, and drawn back, as it were, to its first principles; which is the most effectual method of perpetuating the liberties of a state. The people have numerous opportunities of displaying their just importance, and of exercising, in person, these natural rights. Then representatives are reminded whose creatures they are; and to whom they are accountable for the use of that power, which is delegated unto them. The first maxims of jurisprudence are ever kept in view — that all power is derived from the people — that their happiness is the end of government.

Frequent new parliaments are a part of the British constitution: by them only, the king can know the immediate sense of the nation. Every supply, which they grant, is justly to be considered as a testimony of the loyalty and affection, which the nation bear to their sovereign; and by this means, a mutual confidence is created between the king and his subjects. How pleasing must such an intercourse of benefits be! How must a father of his people rejoice in such dutiful returns for his paternal care! With what ardour must his people embrace every opportunity of giving such convincing proofs, that they are not insensible of his wise and indulgent rule!

Long parliaments have always been prejudicial to the prince, who summoned them, or to the people, who elected them. In that called by

King Charles I, in the year 1640, the commons proceeded at first, with vigour and a true patriotick spirit, to rescue the kingdom from the oppression under which it then groaned — to retrieve the liberties of the people, and establish them on the surest foundations — and to remove or prevent the pernicious consequences, which had arisen, or which, they dreaded, might arise from the tyrannical exercise of prerogative. They abolished the courts of the star chamber and high commission: they reduced the forests to their ancient bounds: they repealed the oppressive statutes concerning knighthood: they declared the tax of ship money to be illegal: they presented the petition of rights, and obtained a ratification of it from the crown. But when the king unadvisedly passed an act to continue them till such time as they should please to dissolve themselves, how soon — how fatally did their conduct change! In what misery did they involve their country! Those very men, who, while they had only a constitutional power, seemed to have no other aim but to secure and improve the liberty and felicity of their constituents, and to render their sovereign the glorious ruler of a free and happy people — those very men, after they became independent of the king and of their electors, sacrificed both to that inordinate power which had been given them. A regard for the publick was now no longer the spring of their actions: their only view was to aggrandize themselves, and to establish their grandeur on the ruins of their country. Their views unhappily were accomplished. They overturned the constitution from its very foundation; and converted into rods of oppression those instruments of power, which had been put into their hands for the welfare of the state; but which those, who had formerly given them, could not now reassume. What an instructive example is this! How alarming to those, who have no influence over their legislators — who have no security but that the power, which was originally derived from the people, and was delegated for their preservation, may be abused for their destruction! Kings are not the only tyrants: the conduct of the long parliament will justify me in adding, that kings are not the severest tyrants.

At the restoration, care was taken to reduce the house of commons to a proper dependence on the king; but immediately after their election, they lost all dependence upon their constituents, because they continued during the pleasure of the crown. The effects soon dreadfully appeared in the long parliament under Charles the second. They seemed disposed ingloriously to surrender those liberties, for which their ancestors had planned, and fought, and bled: and it was owing to the wisdom and integrity of two[n] virtuous ministers of the crown, that the commons of England were not reduced to a state of slavery and wretchedness by the treachery of their own representatives, whom they had indeed elected,

[n] The Earls of Clarendon and Southampton.

but whom they could not remove. Secure of their seats, while they gratified the crown, the members bartered the liberties of the nation for places and pensions; and threw into the scale of prerogative all that weight, which they derived from the people in order to counterbalance it.

It was not till some years after the revolution, that the people could rely on the faithfulness of their representatives, or punish their perfidy. By the statute 6. W. & M. c. 2. it was enacted, that parliaments should not continue longer than three years. The insecure situation of the first prince of the Hanoverian line, surrounded with rivals and with enemies, induced the parliament, soon after his accession to the throne, to prolong this term to that of seven years. Attempts have, since that time, been frequently made to reduce the continuance of parliaments to the former term: and such attempts have always been well received by the nation. Undoubtedly they deserve such reception: for long parliaments will naturally forget their dependence on the people: when this dependence is forgotten, they will become corrupt: "Whenever they become corrupt, the constitution of England will lose its liberty — it will perish." °

Such is the provision made by the laws of Great Britain, that the commons should be faithfully represented: provision is also made, that faithful representatives should not labour for their constituents in vain. The constitution is formed in such a manner, that the house of commons are able as well as willing to protect and defend the liberties intrusted to their care.

The constitution of Great Britain is that of a limited monarchy; and in all limited monarchies, the power of preserving the limitations must be placed somewhere. During the reigns of the first Norman princes, this power seems to have resided in the clergy and in the barons by turns. But it was lodged very improperly. The clergy, zealous only for the dignity and preeminence of the church, neglected and despised the people, whom, with the soil they tilled, they would willingly have considered as the patrimony of St. Peter. Attached to a foreign jurisdiction, and aspiring at an entire independence of the civil powers, they looked upon the prerogatives of the crown as so many obstacles in the way of their favourite scheme of supreme ecclesiastical dominion; and therefore seized, with eagerness, every occasion of sacrificing the interests of their sover-

° Mont. Sp. L. b. 11. c. 6. If the legislative body were perpetual; or might last for the life of the prince who convened them, as formerly; and were so to be supplied, by occasionally filling the vacancies with new representatives; in these cases, if it were once corrupted, the evil would be past remedy: but when different bodies succeed each other, if the people see cause to disapprove of the present, they may rectify its faults in the next. A legislative assembly also, which is sure to be separated again, will think themselves bound, in interest as well as duty, to make only such laws as are good. 1. Bl. Com. 189.

eign to those of the pope. Enemies alike to their king and to their country, their sole and unvaried aim was to reduce both to the most abject state of submission and slavery. The means employed by them to accomplish their pernicious purposes were, sometimes, to work upon the superstition of the people, and direct it against the power of the prince; and, at other times, to work upon the superstition of the prince, and direct it against the liberties of the people.

The power of preserving the limitations of monarchy, for the purposes of liberty, was not more properly placed in the barons. Domineering and turbulent, they oppressed their vassals, and treated them as slaves; they opposed their prince, and were impatient of every legal restraint. Capricious and inconstant, they sometimes abetted the king in his projects of tyranny; and, at other times, excited the people to insurrections and tumults. For these reasons, the constitution was ever fluctuating from one extreme to another; now despotism — now anarchy prevailed.

But after the representatives of the commons began to sit in a separate house; to be considered as a distinct branch of the legislature; and, as such, to be invested with separate and independent powers and privileges; then the constitution assumed a very different appearance. Having no interest contrary to that of the people, from among whom they were chosen, and with whom, after the session, they were again to mix, they had no views inconsistent with the liberty of their constituents, and therefore could have no motives to betray it. Sensible that prerogative, or a discretionary power of acting where the laws are silent, is absolutely necessary, and that this prerogative is most properly intrusted to the executor of the laws, they did not oppose the exercise of it, while it was directed towards the accomplishment of its original end: but sensible likewise, that the good of the state was this original end, they resisted, with vigour, every arbitrary measure, repugnant to law, and unsupported by maxims of publick freedom or utility.

The checks, which they possessed over prerogative, were calm and gentle — operating with a secret, but effectual force — unlike the impetous resistance of factious barons, or the boisterous fulminations of ambitious prelates.

One of the most ancient maxims of the English law is, that no freeman can be taxed at pleasure.[p] But taxes on freemen were absolutely necessary to defray the extraordinary charges of government. The consent of the freemen was, therefore, of necessity to be obtained. Numerous as they were, they could not assemble to give their consent in their proper persons; and for this reason, it was directed by the constitution, that they should give it by their representatives, chosen by and out of themselves.

[p] 1. Bac. 568.

Hence the indisputable and peculiar privilege of the house of commons to grant taxes.[q]

This is the source of that mild but powerful influence, which the commons of Great Britain possess over the crown. In this consists their security, that prerogative, intended for their benefit, will never be exerted for their ruin. By calmly and constitutionally refusing supplies, or by granting them only on certain conditions, they have corrected the extravagancies of some princes, and have tempered the headstrong nature of others; they have checked the progress of arbitrary power, and have supported, with honour to themselves, and with advantage to the nation, the character of grand inquisitors of the realm. The proudest ministers of the proudest monarchs have trembled at their censures; and have appeared at the bar of the house, to give an account of their conduct, and ask pardon for their faults. Those princes, who have favoured liberty, and thrown themselves upon the affections of their people, have ever found that liberty which they favoured, and those affections which they cultivated, the firmest foundations of their throne, and the most solid support of their power. The purses of their people have been ever open to supply their exigencies: their swords have been ever ready to vindicate their honour. On the contrary, those princes, who, insensible to the glory and advantage of ruling a free people, have preferred to a willing obedience the abject submission of slaves, have ever experienced, that all endeavours to render themselves absolute were but so many steps to their own downfall.

Such is the admirable temperament of the British constitution! such the glorious fabrick of Britain's liberty — the pride of her citizens — the envy of her neighbours — planned by her legislators — erected by her patriots — maintained entire by numerous generations past! may it be maintained entire by numerous generations to come!

Can the Americans, who are descended from British ancestors, and inherit all their rights, be blamed — can they be blamed *by their brethren in Britain* — for claiming still to enjoy those rights? But can they enjoy them, if they are bound by the acts of a British parliament? Upon what principle does the British parliament found their power? Is it founded on the prerogative of the king? His prerogative does not extend to make laws to bind any of his subjects. Does it reside in the house of lords? The peers are a collective, and not a representative body. If it resides any where, then, it must reside in the house of commons.

Should any one object here, that it does not reside in the house of

[q] Note. It is said in divers records, "per communitatem Angliæ nobis concess." Because all grants of subsidies or aids by parliament do begin in the house of commons, and first granted by them: also because in effect the whole profit which the king reapeth, doth come from the commons. 4. Ins. 29.

commons *only*, because that house cannot make laws without the consent of the king and of the lords; the answer is easy. Though the concurrence of all the branches of the legislature is necessary to every law; yet the same laws bind different persons for different reasons, and on different principles. The king is bound, because he assented to them. The lords are bound, because they voted for them. The representatives of the commons, for the same reason, bind themselves, and those whom they represent.

If the Americans are bound neither by the assent of the king, nor by the votes of the lords, to obey acts of the British parliament, the *sole* reason why they are bound is, because the representatives of the commons of Great Britain have given their suffrages in favour of those acts.[r] But are the representatives of the commons of Great Britain the representatives of the Americans? Are they elected by the Americans? Are they such as the Americans, if they had the power of election, would probably elect? Do they know the interest of the Americans? Does their own interest prompt them to pursue the interest of the Americans? If they do not pursue it, have the Americans power to punish them? Can the Americans remove unfaithful members at every new election? Can members, whom the Americans do not elect; with whom the Americans are not connected in interest; whom the Americans cannot remove; over whom the Americans have no influence — can such members be styled, with any propriety, the magistrates of the Americans? Have those, who are bound by the laws of magistrates not their own, any security for the enjoyment of their absolute rights — those rights, "which every man is entitled to enjoy, whether in society or out of it?"[s] Is it probable that those rights will be maintained? Is it "the primary end of government to maintain them?"[t] Shall this primary end be frustrated by a political maxim intended to promote it?

But from what source does this mighty, this uncontrolled authority of the house of commons flow? From the collective body of the commons of Great Britain. This authority must, therefore, originally reside in them: for whatever they convey to their representatives, must ultimately be in themselves.[u] And have those, whom we have hitherto been accustomed to consider as our fellow subjects, an absolute and unlimited power over us? Have they a natural right to make laws, by which we may be deprived of our properties, of our liberties, of our lives? By what title do

---

[r] This is allowed even by the advocates for parliamentary power; who account for its extension over the colonies, upon the very absurd principle of their being *virtually* represented in the house of commons.

[s] 1. Bl. Com. 123.   [t] 1. Bl. Com. 124.

[u] It is selfevident that the power, with relation to the part we bear in the legislation, is absolutely, is solely in the electors. We have no legislative authority but what we derive from them. Debates of the Commons, vol. 6. p. 75.

they claim to be our masters? What act of ours has rendered us subject to those, to whom we were formerly equal? Is British freedom denominated from the *soil*, or from the *people* of Britain? If from the latter, do they lose it by quitting the soil? Do those, who embark, freemen, in Great Britain, disembark, slaves, in America? Are those, who fled from the oppression of regal and ministerial tyranny, now reduced to a state of vassalage to those, who, then, equally felt the same oppression? Whence proceeds this fatal change? Is this the return made us for leaving our friends and our country — for braving the danger of the deep — for planting a wilderness, inhabited only by savage men and savage beasts — for extending the dominions of the British crown — for increasing the trade of the British merchants — for augmenting the rents of the British landlords — for heightening the wages of the British artificers? Britons should blush to make such a claim: Americans would blush to own it.

It is not, however, the ignominy only, but the danger also, with which we are threatened, that affects us. The many and careful provisions which are made by the British constitution, that the electors of members of parliament may be prevented from choosing representatives, who would betray them; and that the representatives may be prevented from betraying their constituents with impunity, sufficiently evince, that such precautions have been deemed absolutely necessary for securing and maintaining the system of British liberty.

How would the commons of Great Britain startle at a proposal, to deprive them of their share in the legislature, by rendering the house of commons independent of them! With what indignation would they hear it! What resentment would they feel and discover against the authors of it! Yet the commons of Great Britain would suffer less inconvenience from the execution of such a proposal, than the Americans will suffer from the extension of the legislative authority of parliament over them.

The members of parliament, their families, their friends, their posterity must be subject, as well as others, to the laws. Their interests, and that of their families, friends, and posterity, cannot be different from the interest of the rest of the nation. A regard to the former will, therefore, direct to such measures as must promote the latter. But is this the case with respect to America? Are the legislators of Great Britain subject to the laws which are made for the colonies? Is their interest the same with that of the colonies? If we consider it in a large and comprehensive view, we shall discern it to be undoubtedly the same; but few will take the trouble to consider it in that view; and of those who do, few will be influenced by the consideration. Mankind are usually more affected with a near though inferiour interest, than with one that is superiour, but placed at a greater distance. As the conduct is regulated by the passions, it is not to be wondered at, if they secure the former, by measures which will forfeit the latter. Nay, the latter will frequently be regarded in the same manner as if it were prejudicial to them. It is with regret that I produce some late regulations of parliament as proofs of what I have advanced. We have experienced what an easy matter it is for a minister, with an ordinary share of art, to persuade the parliament and the people, that taxes laid on the colonies will ease the burthens of the mother country; which, if the matter is considered in a proper light, is, in fact, to persuade them, that the stream of national riches will be increased by closing up the fountain, from which they flow.

As the Americans cannot avail themselves of that check, which interest puts upon the members of parliament, and which would operate in favour of the commons of Great Britain, though they possessed no power over the legislature; so the love of reputation, which is a powerful incitement to the legislators to promote the welfare, and obtain the approbation, of those among whom they live, and whose praises or censures will reach and affect them, may have a contrary operation with regard to the colonies. It may become popular and reputable at home to oppress us. A candidate may recommend himself at his election by recounting the many successful instances, in which he has sacrificed the interests of America to those of Great Britain. A member of the house of commons may plume himself upon his ingenuity in inventing schemes to serve the mother country at the expense of the colonies; and may boast of their impotent resentment against him on that account.

Let us pause here a little. — Does neither the love of gain, the love of praise, nor the love of honour influence the members of the British parliament in favour of the Americans? On what principles, then — on what motives of action, can we depend for the security of our liberties, of our properties, of every thing dear to us in life, of life itself? Shall we depend on their veneration for the dictates of natural justice? A very little share of experience in the world — a very little degree of knowledge in the history of men, will sufficiently convince us, that a regard to justice is by no means the ruling principle in human nature. He would discover himself to be a very sorry statesman, who would erect a system of jurisprudence upon that slender foundation. "He would make," as my Lord Bacon says, "imaginary laws for imaginary commonwealths; and his discourses, like the stars, would give little light, because they are so high." [v]

But this is not the worst that can justly be said concerning the situation of the colonies, if they are bound by the acts of the British legislature. So far are those powerful springs of action, which we have mentioned, from interesting the members of that legislature in our favour, that, as has been already observed, we have the greatest reason to dread

[v] 2. Ld. Bac. 537.

their operation against us. While the happy commons of Great Britain congratulate themselves upon the liberty which they enjoy, and upon the provisions — infallible, as far as they can be rendered so by human wisdom — which are made for perpetuating it to their latest posterity; the unhappy Americans have reason to bewail the dangerous situation to which they are reduced; and to look forward, with dismal apprehension, to those future scenes of woe, which, in all probability, will open upon their descendants.

What has been already advanced will suffice to show, that it is repugnant to the essential maxims of jurisprudence, to the ultimate end of all governments, to the genius of the British constitution, and to the liberty and happiness of the colonies, that they should be bound by the legislative authority of the parliament of Great Britain. Such a doctrine is not less repugnant to the voice of her laws. In order to evince this, I shall appeal to some authorities from the books of the law, which show expressly, or by a necessary implication, that the colonies are not bound by the acts of the British parliament; because they have no share in the British legislature.

The first case I shall mention was adjudged in the second year of Richard the third. It was a solemn determination of all the judges of England, met in the exchequer chamber, to consider whether the people in Ireland were bound by an act of parliament made in England. They resolved, "that they were not, as to such things as were done in Ireland; but that what they did out of Ireland must be conformable to the laws of England, because they were the subjects of England. Ireland," said they, "has a parliament, who make laws; and our statutes do not bind them; *because they do not send knights to parliament:* but their persons are the subjects of the king, in the same manner as the inhabitants of Calais, Gascoigne, and Guienne." [w]

This is the first case which we find in the books upon this subject; and it deserves to be examined with the most minute attention.

1. It appears, that the matter under consideration was deemed, at that time, to be of the greatest importance: for ordinary causes are never adjourned into the exchequer chamber; only such are adjourned there as are of uncommon weight, or of uncommon difficulty. "Into the exchequer chamber," says my Lord Coke,[x] "all cases of difficulty in the king's bench, or common pleas, &c. are, and of ancient time have been, adjourned, and there debated, argued, and resolved, by all the judges of England and barons of the exchequer." This court proceeds with the greatest deliberation, and upon the most mature reflection. The case is

[w] 4. Mod. 225. 7. Rep. 22. b. Calvin's case.
[x] 4. Ins. 110.

first argued on both sides by learned counsel; and then openly on several days, by all the judges. Resolutions made with so much caution, and founded on so much legal knowledge, may be relied on as the surest evidences of what is law.

2. It is to be observed, that the extent of the legislative authority of parliament is the very *point* of the adjudication. The decision was not incidental or indigested: it was not a sudden opinion, unsupported by reason and argument: it was an express and deliberate resolution of that very doubt, which they assembled to resolve.

3. It is very observable, that the reason, which those reverend sages of the law gave, why the people in Ireland were not bound by an act of parliament made in England, was the same with that, on which the Americans have found their opposition to the late statutes made concerning them. The Irish did not send members to parliament; and, therefore, they were not bound by its acts. From hence it undeniably appears, that parliamentary authority is derived *solely* from representation — that those, who are bound by acts of parliament, are bound for this only reason, because they are represented in it. If it were not the *only* reason, parliamentary authority might subsist independent of it. But as parliamentary authority fails wherever this reason does not operate, parliamentary authority can be founded on no other principle. The law never ceases, but when the reason of it ceases also.

4. It deserves to be remarked, that no exception is made of any statutes, which bind those who are not represented by the makers of them. The resolution of the judges extends to *every* statute: they say, without limitation — "our statutes do not bind them." And indeed the resolution ought to extend to every statute; because the reason, on which it is founded, extends to every one. If a person is bound only because he is represented, it must certainly follow that wherever he is not represented he is not bound. No sound argument can be offered, why one statute should be obligatory in such circumstances, and not another. If we cannot be deprived of our property by those, whom we do not commission for that purpose; can we, without any such commission, be deprived, by them, of our lives? Have those a right to imprison and gibbet us, who have not a right to tax us?

5. From this authority it follows, that it is by no means a rule, that the authority of parliament extends to all the subjects of the crown. The inhabitants of Ireland were the subjects of the king as of his crown of England; but it is expressly resolved, in the most solemn manner, that the inhabitants of Ireland are not bound by the statutes of England. Allegiance to the king and obedience to the parliament are founded on very different principles. The former is founded on protection: the latter, on

representation. An inattention to this difference has produced, I apprehend, much uncertainty and confusion in our ideas concerning the connexion, which ought to subsist between Great Britain and the American colonies.

6. The last observation which I shall make on this case is, that if the inhabitants of Ireland are not bound by acts of parliament made in England, *a fortiori*, the inhabitants of the American colonies are not bound by them. There are marks of the subordination of Ireland to Great Britain, which cannot be traced in the colonies. A writ of errour lies from the king's bench in Ireland,[y] to the king's bench, and consequently to the house of lords, in England; by which means the former kingdom is subject to the control of the courts of justice of the latter kingdom. But a writ of errour does not lie in the king's bench, nor before the house of lords, in England, from the colonies of America. The proceedings in their courts of justice can be reviewed and controlled only on an appeal to the king in council.[z]

The foregoing important decision, favourable to the liberty of all the dominions of the British crown that are not represented in the British Parliament, has been corroborated by subsequent adjudications. I shall mention one that was given in the king's bench, in the fifth year of King William and Queen Mary, between Blankard and Galdy.[a]

The plaintiff was provost marshal of Jamaica, and by articles, granted a deputation of that office to the defendant, under a yearly rent. The defendant gave his bond for the performance of the agreement; and an action of debt was brought upon that bond. In bar of the action, the defendant pleaded the statute of 5. Ed. 6. made against buying and selling of offices that concern the administration of justice, and averred that this office concerned the administration of justice in Jamaica, and that, by virtue of that statute, both the bond and articles were void. To this plea the plaintiff replied, that Jamaica was an island inhabited formerly by the Spaniards, "that it was conquered by the subjects of the kingdom of England, commissioned by legal and sufficient authority for that purpose; and that since that conquest its inhabitants were regulated and governed by their own proper laws and statutes, and not by acts of parliament or the statutes of the kingdom of England." The defendant, in his rejoinder, admits that, before the conquest of Jamaica by the English, the inhabitants were governed by their own laws, but alleges that "since the conquest it was part of the kingdom of England, and governed by the laws and statutes of the kingdom of England, and not by laws and statutes peculiar to the island." To this rejoinder the plaintiff demurred, and the defendant joined in demurrer.

[y] 4. Ins. 356.   [z] 1. Bl. Com. 108. 231.   [a] 4. Mod. 215. Salk. 411.

Here was a cause to be determined judicially upon this single question in law — Were the acts of parliament or statutes of England in force in Jamaica? It was argued on the opposite sides by lawyers of the greatest eminence, before Lord Chief Justice Holt (a name renowned in the law) and his brethren, the justices of the king's bench. They unanimously gave judgment for the plaintiff; and, by that judgment, expressly determined — That the acts of parliament or statutes of England were not in force in Jamaica. This decision is explicit in favour of America; for whatever was resolved concerning Jamaica is equally applicable to every American colony.

Some years after the adjudication of this case, another was determined in the king's bench, relating to Virginia; in which Lord Chief Justice Holt held, that the laws of England did not extend to Virginia.[b]

I must not be so uncandid as to conceal, that in Calvin's case, where the above mentioned decision of the judges in the exchequer chamber, concerning Ireland, is quoted, it is added, by way of explanation of that authority, — "which is to be understood, unless it (Ireland) be especially named." Nor will I conceal that the same exception[c] is taken notice of, and seems to be allowed, by the judges in the other cases relating to America. To any objection that may, hence, be formed against my doctrine, I answer, in the words of the very accurate Mr. Justice Foster, that "general rules thrown out in argument, and carried farther than the true state of the case then in judgment requireth, have, I confess, no great weight with me."[d]

The question before the judges in the cases I have reasoned from, was not how far the naming of persons in an act of parliament would affect them; though, unless named, they would not be bound by it: the question was, whether the legislative authority of parliament extended over the inhabitants of Ireland or Jamaica or Virginia. To the resolution of the latter question the resolution of the former was by no means necessary, and was, therefore, wholly impertinent to the point of the adjudication.

But farther, the reason assigned for the resolution of the latter question is solid and convincing: the American colonies are not bound by the acts of the British parliament, because they are not represented in it. But what reason can be assigned why they should be bound by those acts, in which they are specially named? Does naming them give those, who do them that honour, a right to rule over them? Is this the source of the supreme, the absolute, the irresistible, the uncontrolled authority of parliament?

[b] Salk. 666.
[c] This exception does not seem to be taken in the case of 2d. Richard III. which was the foundation of all the subsequent cases.
[d] Fost. 313.

These positions are too absurd to be alleged; and a thousand judicial determinations in their favour would never induce one man of sense to subscribe his assent to them.[e]

The obligatory force of the British statutes upon the colonies, when named in them, must be accounted for, by the advocates of that power, upon some other principle. In my Lord Coke's Reports, it is said, "that albeit Ireland be a distinct dominion, yet, *the title thereof being by conquest*, the same, by judgment of law, may be, by express words, bound by the parliaments of England." In this instance, the obligatory authority of the parliament is plainly referred to a title by conquest, as its foundation and original. In the instances relating to the colonies, this authority seems to be referred to the same source: for any one, who compares what is said of Ireland, and other conquered countries, in Calvin's case, with what is said of America, in the adjudications concerning it, will find that the judges, in determining the latter, have grounded their opinions on the resolutions given in the former.[f] It is foreign to my purpose to inquire into the reasonableness of founding the authority of the British parliament over Ireland, upon the title of conquest, though I believe it would be somewhat difficult to deduce it satisfactorily in this manner. It will be sufficient for me to show, that it is unreasonable, and injurious to the colonies, to extend that title to them. How came the colonists to be a con-

[e] Where a decision is manifestly absurd and unjust, such a sentence is not law. 1. Bl. Com. 70.

The legality of the opinion "that the people in Ireland were bound by the statutes of England, when particularly named by them," seems afterwards to have been doubted of by Lord Coke himself, in another place of his works. After having mentioned the resolution in the exchequer chamber in the time of Richard the third, and having taken notice that question is made of it in some of the books, and particularly in Calvin's case, he says, "that the question concerning the binding force of English statutes over Ireland is now by common experience and opinion without any scruple resolved; that the acts of parliament made in England, since the act of the 10th H. 7. (he makes no exceptions) do not bind them in Ireland; but all acts made in England before 10. H. 7. *by the said act made in Ireland An.* 10. *H. 7. c.* 22, do bind them in Ireland." 12. Rep. 111.

[f] It is plain that Blackstone understood the opinion of the judges — that the colonies are bound by acts of the British parliament, if named in them — to be founded on the principle of conquest. It will not be improper to insert his commentary upon the resolutions respecting America. "Besides these adjacent islands, (Jersey, &c.) our more distant plantations in America and elsewhere are also, in some respects, subject to the English laws. Plantations, or colonies in distant countries, are either such where the lands are claimed in right of occupancy only, by finding them desart and uncultivated, and peopling them from the mother country; or where, when, already cultivated, they have been either gained by conquest, or ceded to us by treaties. Our American plantations are principally of this latter sort; being obtained in the last century, either *by right of conquest*, and driving out the natives (with what natural justice I shall not at present inquire) or by treaties." 1. Bl. Com. 106. 107.

Lord Chief Justice Holt, in a case above cited, calls Virginia a conquered country. Salk. 666.

quered people? By whom was the conquest over them obtained? By the house of commons? By the constituents of that house? If the idea of conquest must be taken into consideration when we examine into the title by which America is held, that idea, so far as it can operate, will operate in favour of the colonists, and not against them. Permitted and commissioned by the crown, they undertook, at their own expense, expeditions to this distant country, took possession of it, planted it, and cultivated it. Secure under the protection of their king, they grew and multiplied, and diffused British freedom and British spirit, wherever they came. Happy in the enjoyment of liberty, and in reaping the fruits of their toils; but still more happy in the joyful prospect of transmitting their liberty and their fortunes to the latest posterity, they inculcated to their children the warmest sentiments of loyalty to their sovereign, under whose auspices they enjoyed so many blessings, and of affection and esteem for the inhabitants of the mother country, with whom they gloried in being intimately connected. Lessons of loyalty to parliament, indeed, they never gave: they never suspected that such unheard of loyalty would be required. They never suspected that their descendants would be considered and treated as a conquered people; and therefore they never taught them the submission and abject behaviour suited to that character.

I am sufficiently aware of an objection, that will be made to what I have said concerning the legislative authority of the British parliament. It will be alleged, that I throw off all dependence on Great Britain. This objection will be held forth, in its most specious colours, by those, who, from servility of soul, or from mercenary considerations, would meanly bow their necks to every exertion of arbitrary power: it may likewise alarm some, who entertain the most favourable opinion of the connexion between Great Britain and her colonies; but who are not sufficiently acquainted with the nature of that connexion, which is so dear to them. Those of the first class, I hope, are few; I am sure they are contemptible, and deserve to have very little regard paid to them: but for the sake of those of the second class, who may be more numerous, and whose laudable principles atone for their mistakes, I shall take some pains to obviate the objection, and to show that a denial of the legislative authority of the British parliament over America is by no means inconsistent with that connexion, which ought to subsist between the mother country and her colonies, and which, at the first settlement of those colonies, it was intended to maintain between them: but that, on the contrary, that connexion would be entirely destroyed by the extension of the power of parliament over the American plantations.

Let us examine what is meant by a *dependence* on Great Britain: for it is always of importance clearly to define the terms that we use. Blackstone, who, speaking of the colonies, tells us, that "they are no part of the mother country, but distinct (though dependent) dominions," [g] explains dependence in this manner. "Dependence is very little else, but an obligation to conform to the will or law of that superiour person or state, upon which the inferiour depends. The original and true ground of this superiority, in the case of Ireland, is what we usually call, though somewhat improperly, the right of conquest; a right allowed by the law of nations, if not by that of nature; but which, in reason and civil policy, can mean nothing more, than that, in order to put an end to hostilities, a compact is either expressly or tacitly made between the conqueror and the conquered, that if they will acknowledge the victor for their master, he will treat them for the future as subjects, and not as enemies." [h]

The original and true ground of the superiority of Great Britain over the American colonies is not shown in any book of the law, unless, as I have already observed, it be derived from the right of conquest. But I have proved, and I hope satisfactorily, that this right is altogether inapplicable to the colonists. The original of the superiority of Great Britain over the colonies is, then, unaccounted for; and when we consider the ingenuity and pains which have lately been employed at home on this subject, we may justly conclude, that the only reason why it is not accounted for, is, that it cannot be accounted for. The superiority of Great Britain over the colonies ought, therefore, to be rejected; and the dependence of the colonies upon her, if it is to be construed into "an obligation to conform to the will or law of the superiour state," ought, in *this* sense, to be rejected also.

My sentiments concerning this matter are not singular. They coincide with the declarations and remonstrances of the colonies against the statutes imposing taxes on them. It was their unanimous opinion, that the parliament have no right to exact obedience to those statutes; and, consequently, that the colonies are under no obligation to obey them. The dependence of the colonies on Great Britain was denied, in those instances; but a denial of it in those instances is, in effect, a denial of it in all other instances. For, if dependence is an obligation to conform to the will or law of the superiour state, any exceptions to that obligation must destroy the dependence. If, therefore, by a dependence of the colonies on Great Britain, it is meant, that they are obliged to obey the laws of Great Britain, reason, as well as the unanimous voice of the Americans, teaches us to disown it. Such a dependence was never thought of by those who left Britain, in order to settle in America; nor by their sovereigns, who gave them commissions for that purpose. Such an obligation has no correspondent right: for the commons of Great Britain have no dominion over their equals and fellow subjects in America: they can confer no right to their delegates to bind those equals and fellow subjects by laws.

[g] 1. Bl. Com. 107.   [h] Id. 103.

There is another, and a much more reasonable meaning, which may be intended by the dependence of the colonies on Great Britain. The phrase may be used to denote the obedience and loyalty, which the colonists owe to the *kings* of Great Britain. If it should be alleged, that this cannot be the meaning of the expression, because it is applied to the kingdom, and not to the king, I give the same answer that my Lord Bacon gave to those who said that allegiance related to the kingdom and not to the king; because in the statutes there are these words — "born within the allegiance of England" — and again — "born without the allegiance of England." "There is no trope of speech more familiar," says he, "than to use the place of addition for the person. So we say commonly, the line of York, or the line of Lancaster, for the lines of the duke of York, or the duke of Lancaster. So we say the possessions of Somerset or Warwick, intending the possessions of the dukes of Somerset, or earls of Warwick. And in the very same manner, the statute speaks, allegiance of England, for allegiance of the king of England." [1]

Dependence on the mother country seems to have been understood in this sense, both by the first planters of the colonies, and also by the most eminent lawyers, at that time, in England.

Those who launched into the unknown deep, in quest of new countries and habitations, still considered themselves as subjects of the English monarchs, and behaved suitably to that character; but it no where appears, that they still considered themselves as represented in an English parliament, or that they thought the authority of the English parliament extended over them. They took possession of the country in the *king's* name: they treated, or made war with the Indians by *his* authority: they held the lands under *his* grants, and paid *him* the rents reserved upon them: they established governments under the sanction of *his* prerogative, or by virtue of *his* charters: — no application for those purposes was made to the parliament: no ratification of the charters or letters patent was solicited from that assembly, as is usual in England with regard to grants and franchises of much less importance.

My Lord Bacon's sentiments on this subject ought to have great weight with us. His immense genius, his universal learning, his deep insight into the laws and constitution of England, are well known and much admired. Besides, he lived at that time when settling and improving the American plantations began seriously to be attended to, and successfully to be carried into execution.[j] Plans for the government and regulation of the colonies were then forming: and it is only from the first

[1] 4. Ld. Bac. 192. 193. Case of the postnati of Scotland.
[j] During the reign of Queen Elizabeth, America was chiefly valued on account of its mines. It was not till the reign of James 1. that any vigorous attempts were made to clear and improve the soil.

general idea of these plans, that we can unfold, with precision and accuracy, all the more minute and intricate parts, of which they now consist. "The settlement of colonies," says he, "must proceed from the option of those who will settle them, else it sounds like an exile: they must be raised by the *leave*, and not by the *command* of the *king*. At their setting out, they must have their commission, or letters patent, from the *king*, that so they may acknowledge their *dependency upon the crown* of England, and under his protection." In another place he says, "that they still must be subjects of the realm." [k] "In order to regulate all the inconveniences, which will insensibly grow upon them," he proposes, "that the king should erect a subordinate council in England, whose care and charge shall be, to advise, and put in execution, all things which shall be found fit for the good of those new plantations; who, upon all occasions, shall give an account of their proceedings to the king or the council board, and from *them* receive such directions, as may best agree with the government of that place." [1] It is evident, from these quotations, that my Lord Bacon had no conception that the parliament would or ought to interpose,[m] either in the settlement or the government of the colonies. The only relation, in which he says the colonists must still continue, is that of subjects: the only dependency, which they ought to acknowledge, is a dependency on the crown.

This is a dependence, which they have acknowledged hitherto; which they acknowledge now; and which, if it is reasonable to judge of the future by the past and the present, they will continue to acknowledge hereafter. It is not a dependence, like that contended for on parliament, slavish and unaccountable, or accounted for only by principles that are false and inapplicable: it is a dependence founded upon the principles of reason, of liberty, and of law. Let us investigate its sources.

The colonists ought to be dependent on the king, because they have hitherto enjoyed, and still continue to enjoy, his protection. Allegiance is the faith and obedience, which every subject owes to his prince. This obedience is founded on the protection derived from government: for protection and allegiance are the reciprocal bonds, which connect the prince and his subjects.[n] Every subject, so soon as he is born, is under the

---

[k] The parliament have no subjects. My Lord Bacon gives, in this expression, an instance of the trope of speech before mentioned. He says, the subjects of the *realm*, when he means the subjects of the *king* of the realm.

[1] 1. Ld. Bac. 725, 726.

[m] It was chiefly during the confusions of the republick, when the king was in exile, and unable to assert his rights, that the house of commons began to interfere in colony matters.

[n] Between the sovereign and subject there is duplex et reciprocum ligamen; quia sicut subditus regi tenetur ad obedientiam; ita rex subdito tenetur ad protectionem: merito igitur ligeantia dicitur a ligando, quia continet in se duplex ligamen. [. . . a double and reciprocal bond. Because just as the subject is bound to

royal protection, and is entitled to all the advantages arising from it. He therefore owes obedience to that royal power, from which the protection, which he enjoys, is derived. But while he continues in infancy and nonage, he cannot perform the duties which his allegiance requires. The performance of them must be respited till he arrive at the years of discretion and maturity. When he arrives at those years, he owes obedience, not only for the protection which he now enjoys, but also for that which, from his birth, he has enjoyed; and to which his tender age has hitherto prevented him from making a suitable return. Allegiance now becomes a duty founded upon principles of gratitude, as well as on principles of interest: it becomes a debt, which nothing but the loyalty of a whole life will discharge.[o] As neither climate, nor soil, nor time entitle a person to the benefits of a subject; so an alteration of climate, of soil, or of time cannot release him from the duties of one. An Englishman, who removes to foreign countries, however distant from England, owes the same allegiance to his king there which he owed him at home; and will owe it twenty years hence as much as he owes it now. Wherever he is, he is still liable to the punishment annexed by law to crimes against his allegiance; and still entitled to the advantages promised by law to the duties of it: it is not cancelled; and it is not forfeited. "Hence all children born in any part of the world, if they be of English parents continuing at that time as liege subjects to the king, and having done no act to forfeit the benefit of their allegiance, are *ipso facto* naturalized: and if they have issue, and their descendants intermarry among themselves, such descendants are naturalized to all generations." [p]

Thus we see, that the subjects of the king, though they reside in foreign countries, still owe the duties of allegiance, and are still entitled to the advantages of it. They transmit to their posterity the privilege of naturalization, and all the other privileges which are the consequences of it.[q]

Now we have explained the dependence of the Americans. They are the subjects of the king of Great Britain. They owe him allegiance. They

---

obey the king, so the king is bound to protect the subject. Rightly therefore are kings called "Lieges" from "ligo, to bind or tie" because this double tie holds them in it.] 7. Rep. 5a. Calvin's case.

[o] The king is protector of all his subjects: in virtue of his high trust, he is more particularly to take care of those who are not able to take care of themselves, consequently of infants, who, by reason of their nonage, are under incapacities; from hence natural allegiance arises, as a debt of gratitude, which can never be cancelled, though the subject owing it goes out of the kingdom, or swears allegiance to another prince. 2. P. Wms. 123. 124.

[p] 4. Ld. Bac. 192. Case of the postnati of Scotland.

[q] Natural born subjects have a great variety of rights, which they acquire by being born in the king's ligeance, and can never forfeit by any distance of place or time, but only by their own misbehaviour; the explanation of which rights is the principal subject of the law. 1. Bl. Com. 371.

have a right to the benefits which arise from preserving that allegiance inviolate. They are liable to the punishments which await those who break it. This is a dependence, which they have always boasted of. The principles of loyalty are deeply rooted in their hearts; and there they will grow and bring forth fruit, while a drop of vital blood remains to nourish them. Their history is not stained with rebellious and treasonable machinations: an inviolable attachment to their sovereign, and the warmest zeal for his glory, shine in every page.

From this dependence, abstracted from every other source, arises a strict connexion between the inhabitants of Great Britain and those of America. They are fellow subjects; they are under allegiance to the same prince; and this union of allegiance naturally produces a union of hearts. It is also productive of a union of measures through the whole British dominions. To the king is intrusted the direction and management of the great machine of government. He therefore is fittest to adjust the different wheels, and to regulate their motions in such a manner as to cooperate in the same general designs. He makes war: he concludes peace: he forms alliances: he regulates domestick trade by his prerogative, and directs foreign commerce by his treaties with those nations, with whom it is carried on. He names the officers of government; so that he can check every jarring movement in the administration. He has a negative on the different legislatures throughout his dominions, so that he can prevent any repugnancy in their different laws.

The connexion and harmony between Great Britain and us, which it is her interest and ours mutually to cultivate, and on which her prosperity, as well as ours, so materially depends, will be better preserved by the operation of the legal prerogatives of the crown, than by the exertion of an unlimited authority by parliament.[r]

[r] After considering, with all the attention of which I am capable, the foregoing opinion — that all the different members of the British empire are distinct states, independent of each other, but connected together under the same sovereign in right of the same crown — I discover only one objection that can be offered against it. But this objection will, by many, be deemed a fatal one. "How, it will be urged, can the trade of the British empire be carried on, without some power, extending over the whole, to regulate it? The legislative authority of each part, according to your doctrine, is confined within the local bounds of that part: how, then, can so many interfering interests and claims, as must necessarily meet and contend in the commerce of the whole, be decided and adjusted?"

Permit me to answer these questions by proposing some others in my turn. How has the trade of Europe — how has the trade of the whole globe, been carried on? Have those widely extended plans been formed by one superintending power? Have they been carried into execution by one superintending power? Have they been formed — have they been carried into execution, with less conformity to the rules of justice and equality, than if they had been under the direction of one superintending power?

It has been the opinion of some politicians, of no inferiour note, that all regulations of trade are useless; that the greatest part of them are hurtful; and that the stream of commerce never flows with so much beauty and advantage, as when it is not diverted from its natural channels. Whether this opinion is well founded or not, let others determine. Thus much may certainly be said, that commerce is not so properly the object of laws, as of treaties and compacts. In this manner, it has been always directed among the several nations of Europe.

But if the commerce of the British empire must be regulated by a general super-intending power, capable of exerting its influence over every part of it, why may not this power be intrusted to the king, as a part of the royal prerogative? By making treaties, which it is his prerogative to make, he directs the trade of Great Britain with the other states of Europe: and his treaties with those states have, when considered with regard to his subjects, all the binding force of laws upon them. (1. Bl. Com. 252.) Where is the absurdity in supposing him vested with the same right to regulate the commerce of the distinct parts of his dominions with one another, which he has to regulate their commerce with foreign states? If the history of the British constitution, relating to this subject, be carefully traced, I apprehend we shall discover, that a prerogative in the crown, to regulate trade, is perfectly consistent with the principles of law. We find many authorities that the king cannot lay impositions on traffick; and that he cannot restrain it *altogether*, nor confine it to monopolists: but none of the authorities, that I have had an opportunity of consulting, go any farther. Indeed many of them seem to imply a power in the crown to regulate trade, where that power is exerted for the great end of all prerogative — the publick good.

If the power of regulating trade be, as I am apt to believe it to be, vested, by the principles of the constitution, in the crown, this good effect will flow from the doctrine: a perpetual distinction will be kept up between that power, and a power of laying impositions on trade. The prerogative will extend to the former: it can, under no pretence, extend to the latter: as it is given, so it is limited, by the law.

III

SPEECH DELIVERED IN THE CONVENTION
FOR THE PROVINCE OF PENNSYLVANIA

HELD AT PHILADELPHIA, IN JANUARY, 1775

WHENCE, Sir, proceeds all the invidious and ill-grounded clamour against the colonists of America? Why are they stigmatized, in Britain, as licentious and ungovernable? Why is their virtuous opposition to the illegal attempts of their governours represented under the falsest colours, and placed in the most ungracious point of view? This opposition, when exhibited in its true light, and when viewed, with unjaundiced eyes, from a proper situation, and at a proper distance, stands confessed the lovely offspring of freedom. It breathes the spirit of its parent. Of this ethereal spirit, the whole conduct, and particularly the late conduct, of the colonists has shown them eminently possessed. It has animated and regulated every part of their proceedings. It has been recognised to be genuine, by all those symptoms and effects, by which it has been distinguished in other ages and other countries. It has been calm and regular: it has not acted without occasion: it has not acted disproportionably to the occasion. As the attempts, open or secret, to undermine or to destroy it, have been repeated or enforced; in a just degree, its vigilance and its vigour have been exerted to defeat or to disappoint them. As its exertions have been sufficient for those purposes hitherto, let us hence draw a joyful prognostick, that they will continue sufficient for those purposes hereafter. It is not yet exhausted; it will still operate irresistibly whenever a necessary occasion shall call forth its strength.

Permit me, sir, by appealing, in a few instances, to the spirit and conduct of the colonists, to evince, that what I have said of them is just. Did they disclose any uneasiness at the proceedings and claims of the British parliament, before those claims and proceedings afforded a reasonable cause for it? Did they even disclose any uneasiness, when a reasonable cause for it was *first* given? Our rights were invaded by their regulations of our internal policy. We submitted to them: we were unwilling to oppose them. The spirit of liberty was slow to act. When those invasions were renewed; when the efficacy and malignancy of them were attempted to be redoubled by the stamp act; when chains were formed for us; and preparations were made for rivetting them on our limbs — what measures did we pursue? The spirit of liberty found it necessary now to act: but she acted with the calmness and decent dignity suited to her character. Were we rash or seditious? Did we discover want of loyalty to our sovereign? Did we betray want of affection to our brethren in Britain? Let our dutiful and reverential petitions to the throne — let our respectful, though firm, remonstrances to the parliament — let our warm and affectionate addresses to our brethren, and (we will still call them) our friends in Great Britain — let all those, transmitted from every part of the continent, testify the truth. By their testimony let our conduct be tried.

As our proceedings during the existence and operation of the stamp act prove fully and incontestably the painful sensations that tortured our breasts from the prospect of disunion with Britain; the peals of joy, which burst forth universally, upon the repeal of that odious statute, loudly proclaim the heartfelt delight produced in us by a reconciliation with her. Unsuspicious, because undesigning, we buried our complaints, and the causes of them, in oblivion, and returned, with eagerness, to our former unreserved confidence. Our connexion with our parent country, and the reciprocal blessings resulting from it to her and to us, were the favourite and pleasing topicks of our publick discourses and our private conversations. Lulled into delightful security, we dreamt of nothing but increasing fondness and friendship, cemented and strengthened by a kind and perpetual communication of good offices. Soon, however, too soon, were we awakened from the soothing dreams! Our enemies renewed their designs against us, not with less malice, but with more art. Under the plausible presence of regulating our trade, and, at the same time, of making provision for the administration of justice, and the support of government, in some of the colonies, they pursued their scheme of depriving us of our property without our consent. As the attempts to distress us, and to degrade us to a rank inferiour to that of freemen, appeared now to be reduced into a regular system, it became proper, on our part, to form a regular system for counteracting them. We ceased to import goods from Great Britain. Was this measure dictated by selfishness or by licentiousness? Did it not injure ourselves, while it injured the British merchants and manufacturers? Was it inconsistent with the peaceful demeanour of subjects to abstain from making purchases, when our freedom and our safety rendered it necessary for us to abstain from them? A regard for our freedom and our safety was our only motive; for no sooner had the parliament, by repealing part of the revenue laws, inspired us with the flattering hopes that they had departed from their intentions of oppressing and of taxing us, than we forsook our plan for defeating those intentions, and began to import as formerly. Far from being peevish or captious, we took no publick notice even of their declaratory law of dominion over us: our candour led us to consider it as a decent expedient of retreating from the actual exercise of that dominion.

But, alas! the root of bitterness still remained. The duty on tea was reserved to furnish occasion to the ministry for a new effort to enslave and to ruin us; and the East India Company were chosen, and consented, to be the detested instruments of ministerial despotism and cruelty. A cargo of their tea arrived at Boston. By a low artifice of the governour, and by the wicked activity of the tools of government, it was rendered impossible to store it up, or to send it back; as was done at other places. A number of persons unknown destroyed it.

Let us here make a concession to our enemies: let us suppose that the transaction deserves all the dark and hideous colours, in which they have painted it: let us even suppose — for our cause admits of an excess of candour — that all their exaggerated accounts of it were confined strictly to the truth: what will follow? Will it follow, that every British colony in America, or even the colony of Massachusetts Bay, or even the town of Boston in that colony, merits the imputation of being factious and seditious? Let the frequent mobs and riots that have happened in Great Britain upon much more trivial occasions shame our calumniators into silence. Will it follow, because the rules of order and regular government were, in that instance, violated by the offenders, that, for this reason, the principles of the constitution, and the maxims of justice, must be violated by their punishment? Will it follow, because those who were guilty could not be known, that, therefore, those who were known not to be guilty must suffer? Will it follow, that even the guilty should be condemned without being heard? — That they should be condemned upon partial testimony, upon the representations of their avowed and embittered enemies? Why were they not tried in courts of justice known to their constitution, and by juries of their neighbourhood? Their courts and their juries were not, in the case of Captain Preston, transported beyond the bounds of justice by their resentment: why, then, should it be presumed, that, in the case of those offenders, they would be prevented from doing justice by their affection? But the colonists, it seems, must be stript of their judicial, as well as of their legislative powers. They must be bound by a legislature, they must be tried by a jurisdiction, not their own. Their constitutions must be changed: their liberties must be abridged: and those, who shall be most infamously active in changing their constitutions and abridging their liberties, must, by an express provision, be exempted from punishment.

I do not exaggerate the matter, sir, when I extend these observations to all the colonists. The parliament meant to extend the effects of their proceedings to all the colonists. The plan, on which their proceedings are formed, extends to them all. From an incident, of no very uncommon or atrocious nature, which happened in one colony, in one town in that colony, and in which only a few of the inhabitants of that town took a part, an occasion has been taken by those, who probably intended it, and who certainly prepared the way for it, to impose upon that colony, and to lay a foundation and a precedent for imposing upon all the rest, a system of statutes, arbitrary, unconstitutional, oppressive, in every view and in every degree subversive of the rights, and inconsistent with even the name of freemen.

Were the colonists so blind as not to discern the consequences of these measures? Were they so supinely inactive as to take no steps for guarding against them? They were not. They ought not to have been so. We saw a breach made in those barriers, which our ancestors, British and American, with so much care, with so much danger, with so much treasure, and with so much blood, had erected, cemented, and established for the security of their liberties and — with filial piety let us mention it — of ours: we saw the attack actually begun upon one part: ought we to have folded our hands in indolence, to have lulled our eyes in slumbers, till the attack was carried on, so as to become irresistible, in every part? Sir, I presume to think not. We were roused; we were alarmed, as we had reason to be. But still our measures have been such as the spirit of liberty and of loyalty directed; not such as a spirit of sedition or of disaffection would pursue. Our counsels have been conducted without rashness and faction: our resolutions have been taken without phrensy or fury.

That the sentiments of every individual concerning that important object, his liberty, might be known and regarded, meetings have been held, and deliberations carried on in every particular district. That the sentiments of all those individuals might gradually and regularly be collected into a single point, and the conduct of each inspired and directed by the result of the whole united, county committees — provincial conventions — a continental congress have been appointed, have met and resolved. By this means, a chain — more inestimable, and, while the necessity for it continues, we hope, more indissoluble than one of gold — a chain of freedom has been formed, of which every individual in these colonies, who is willing to preserve the greatest of human blessings, his liberty, has the pleasure of beholding himself a link.

Are these measures, sir, the brats of disloyalty, of disaffection? There are miscreants among us — wasps that suck poison from the most salubrious flowers — who tell us they are. They tell us that all those assemblies are unlawful, and unauthorized by our constitutions; and that all their deliberations and resolutions are so many transgressions of the duty of subjects. The utmost malice brooding over the utmost baseness, and nothing but such a hated commixture, must have hatched this calumny. Do not those men know — would they have others not to know — that it was impossible for the inhabitants of the same province, and for the legislatures of the different provinces, to communicate their sentiments to one another in the modes appointed for such purposes, by their different constitutions? Do not they know — would they have others not to know — that all this was rendered impossible by those very persons, who now, or whose minions now, urge this objection against us? Do not they know — would they have others not to know — that the different assemblies, who could be dissolved by the governours, were, in consequence of ministerial mandates, dissolved by them, whenever they attempted to turn their attention to the greatest objects, which, as guardians of the liberty of their constituents, could be presented to their view? The arch enemy of the human race torments them only for those actions, to which he has tempted, but to which he has not necessarily obliged them. Those men refine even upon infernal malice: they accuse, they threaten us (superlative impudence!) for taking those very steps, which we were laid under the disagreeable necessity of taking by themselves, or by those in whose hateful service they are enlisted. But let them know, that our counsels, our deliberations, our resolutions, if not authorized by the forms, because that was rendered impossible by our enemies, are nevertheless authorized by that which weighs much more in the scale of reason — by the spirit of our constitutions. Was the convention of the barons at Running Meade, where the tyranny of John was checked, and magna charta was signed, authorized by the forms of the constitution? Was the convention parliament, that recalled Charles the second, and restored the monarchy, authorized by the forms of the constitution? Was the convention of lords and commons, that placed King William on the throne, and secured the monarchy and liberty likewise, authorized by the forms of the constitution? I cannot conceal my emotions of pleasure, when I observe, that the objections of our adversaries cannot be urged against us, but in common with those venerable assemblies, whose proceedings formed such an accession to British liberty and British renown.

The resolutions entered into, and the recommendations given, by the continental congress, have stamped, in the plainest characters, the genuine and enlightened spirit of liberty upon the conduct observed, and the measures pursued, in consequence of them. As the invasions of our rights have become more and more formidable, our opposition to them has increased in firmness and vigour, in a just, and in no more than a just, proportion. We will not import goods from Great Britain or Ireland: in a little time we will suspend our exportations to them: and, if the same illiberal and destructive system of policy be still carried on against us, in a little time more we will not consume their manufactures. In that colony where the attacks have been most open, immediate, and direct, some farther steps have been taken, and those steps have met with the deserved approbation of the other provinces.

Is this scheme of conduct allied to rebellion? Can any symptoms of disloyalty to his majesty, of disinclination to his illustrious family, or of disregard to his authority be traced in it? Those, who would blend, and whose crimes have made it necessary for them to blend, the tyrannick acts of administration with the lawful measures of government, and to veil every flagitious procedure of the ministry under the venerable mantle of majesty, pretend to discover, and employ their emissaries to publish the pretended discovery of such symptoms. We are not, however, to be imposed upon by such shallow artifices. We know, that we have not violated the laws or the constitution; and that, therefore, we are safe as long as the laws retain their force and the constitution its vigour; and that, whatever our demeanour be, we cannot be safe much longer. But another object demands our attention.

We behold — sir, with the deepest anguish we behold — that our opposition has not been as effectual as it has been constitutional. The hearts of our oppressors have not relented: our complaints have not been heard: our grievances have not been redressed: our rights are still invaded: and have we no cause to dread, that the invasions of them will be enforced in a manner, against which all reason and argument, and all opposition of every peaceful kind, will be vain? Our opposition has hitherto increased with our oppression: shall it, in the most desperate of all contingencies, observe the same proportion?

Let us pause, sir, before we give an answer to this question: the fate of us; the fate of millions now alive; the fate of millions yet unborn depends upon the answer. Let it be the result of calmness and of intrepidity: let it be dictated by the principles of loyalty, and the principles of liberty. Let it be such, as never, in the worst events, to give us reason to reproach ourselves, or others reason to reproach us for having done too much or too little.

Perhaps the following resolution may be found not altogether unbefitting our present situation. With the greatest deference I submit it to the mature consideration of this assembly.

"That the act of the British parliament for altering the charter and constitution of the colony of Massachusetts Bay, and those 'for the impartial administration of justice' in that colony, for shutting the port of Boston, and for quartering soldiers on the inhabitants of the colonies, are unconstitutional and void; and can confer no authority upon those who act under colour of them. That the crown cannot, by its prerogative, alter the charter or constitution of that colony: that all attempts to alter the said charter or constitution, unless by the authority of the legislature of that colony, are manifest violations of the rights of that colony, and illegal: that all force employed to carry such unjust and illegal attempts into execution is force without authority: that it is the right of British subjects to resist such force: that this right is founded both upon the letter and the spirit of the British constitution."

To prove, at this time, that those acts are unconstitutional and void is, I apprehend, altogether unnecessary. The doctrine has been proved fully, on other occasions, and has received the concurring assent of British America. It rests upon plain and indubitable truths. We do not send members to the British parliament: we have parliaments (it is immaterial what name they go by) of our own.

That a void act can confer no authority upon those, who proceed under colour of it, is a selfevident proposition.

Before I proceed to the other clauses, I think it useful to recur to some of the fundamental maxims of the British constitution; upon which, as upon a rock, our wise ancestors erected that stable fabrick, against which the gates of hell have not hitherto prevailed. Those maxims I shall apply fairly, and, I flatter myself, satisfactorily to evince every particular contained in the resolution.

The government of Britain, sir, was never an arbitrary government: our ancestors were never inconsiderate enough to trust those rights, which God and nature had given them, unreservedly into the hands of their princes. However difficult it may be, in other states, to prove an original contract subsisting in any other manner, and on any other conditions, than are naturally and necessarily implied in the very idea of the first institution of a state; it is the easiest thing imaginable, since the revolution of 1688, to prove it in our constitution, and to ascertain some of the material articles, of which it consists. It has been often appealed to: it has been often broken, at least on one part: it has been often renewed: it has been often confirmed: it still subsists in its full force: "it binds the king as much as the meanest subject." [a] The measures of his power, and the limits, beyond which he cannot extend it, are circumscribed and regulated by the same authority, and with the same precision, as the measures of the subject's obedience, and the limits, beyond which he is under no obligation to practise it, are fixed and ascertained. Liberty is, by the constitution, of equal stability, of equal antiquity, and of equal authority with prerogative. The duties of the king and those of the subject are plainly reciprocal: they can be violated on neither side, un-

[a] Bol. Pat. King. 122.

less they be performed on the other.[b] The law is the common standard, by which the excesses of prerogative as well as the excesses of liberty are to be regulated and reformed.

Of this great compact between the king and his people, one essential article to be performed on his part is — that, in those cases where provision is expressly made and limitations set by the laws, his government shall be conducted according to those provisions, and restrained according to those limitations — that, in those cases, which are not expressly provided for by the laws, it shall be conducted by the best rules of discretion, agreeably to the general spirit of the laws, and subserviently to their ultimate end — the interest and happiness of his subjects — that, in no case, it shall be conducted contrary to the express, or to the implied principles of the constitution.

These general maxims, which we may justly consider as fundamentals of our government, will, by a plain and obvious application of them to the parts of the resolution remaining to be proved, demonstrate them to be strictly agreeable to the laws and constitution.

We can be at no loss in resolving, that the king cannot, by his prerogative, alter the charter or constitution of the colony of Massachusetts Bay. Upon what principle could such an exertion of prerogative be justified? On the acts of parliament? They are already proved to be void. On the discretionary power which the king has of acting where the laws are silent? That power must be subservient to the interest and happiness of those, concerning whom it operates. But I go farther. Instead of being supported by law, or the principles of prerogative, such an alteration is totally and absolutely repugnant to both. It is contrary to express law. The charter and constitution we speak of are confirmed by the only legislative power capable of confirming them: and no other power, but that which can ratify, can destroy. If it is contrary to express law, the consequence is necessary, that it is contrary to the principles of prerogative: for prerogative can operate only when the law is silent.

In no view can this alteration be justified, or so much as excused. It cannot be justified or excused by the acts of parliament; because the authority of parliament does not extend to it: it cannot be justified or excused by the operation of prerogative; because this is none of the cases, in which prerogative can operate: it cannot be justified or excused by the legislative authority of the colony: because that authority never has been, and, I presume, never will be given for any such purpose.

If I have proceeded hitherto, as I am persuaded I have, upon safe and sure ground, I can, with great confidence, advance a step farther, and say, that all attempts to alter the charter or constitution of that colony, unless

---

[b] Bol. Tracts. 293. The compact between the king and people is mutual, and the parties are mutually bound. 11. Parl. Deb. 455. (Ld. Chesterfield.)

by the authority of its own legislature, are violations of its rights, and illegal.

If those attempts are illegal, must not all force, employed to carry them into execution, be force employed against law, and without authority? The conclusion is unavoidable.

Have not British subjects, then, a right to resist such force — force acting without authority — force employed contrary to law — force employed to destroy the very existence of law and of liberty? They have, sir, and this right is secured to them both by the letter and the spirit of the British constitution, by which the measures and the conditions of their obedience are appointed. The British liberties, sir, and the means and the right of defending them, are not the grants of princes; and of what our princes never granted they surely can never deprive us.

I beg leave, here, to mention and to obviate some plausible but ill founded objections, that have been, and will be, held forth by our adversaries, against the principles of the resolution now before us. It will be observed, that those employed for bringing about the proposed alteration in the charter and constitution of the colony of Massachusetts Bay act by virtue of a commission for that purpose from his majesty: that all resistance of forces commissioned by his majesty, is resistance of his majesty's authority and government, contrary to the duty of allegiance, and treasonable. These objections will be displayed in their most specious colours: every artifice of chicanery and sophistry will be put in practice to establish them: law authorities, perhaps, will be quoted and tortured to prove them. Those principles of our constitution, which were designed to preserve and to secure the liberty of the people, and, for the sake of that, the tranquility of government, will be perverted on this, as they have been on many other occasions, from their true intention; and will be made use of for the contrary purpose of endangering the latter, and destroying the former. The names of the most exalted virtues, on one hand, and of the most atrocious crimes, on the other, will be employed in direct contradiction to the nature of those virtues, and of those crimes: and, in this manner, those who cannot look beyond names, will be deceived; and those, whose aim it is to deceive by names, will have an opportunity of accomplishing it. But, sir, this disguise will not impose upon us. We will look to things as well as to names: and, by doing so, we shall be fully satisfied, that all those objections rest upon mere verbal sophistry, and have not even the remotest alliance with the principles of reason or of law.

In the first place, then, I say, that the persons who allege, that those, employed to alter the charter and constitution of Massachusetts Bay, act by virtue of a commission from his majesty for that purpose, speak improperly, and contrary to the truth of the case. I say, they act by virtue of no such commission: I say, it is impossible they can act by virtue of such a commission. What is called a commission either contains particular directions for the purpose mentioned; or it contains no such particular directions. In neither case can those, who act for that purpose, act by virtue of a commission. In one case, what is called a commission is void; it has no legal existence; it can communicate no authority. In the other case, it extends not to the purpose mentioned. The latter point is too plain to be insisted on — I prove the former.

"Id rex potest," says the law, "quod de jure potest." [c] The king's power is a power according to law. His commands, if the authority of Lord Chief Justice Hale[d] may be depended upon, are under the directive power of the law; and consequently invalid, if unlawful. Commissions, says my Lord Coke,[e] are legal; and are like the king's writs; and none are lawful, but such as are allowed by the common law, or warranted by some act of parliament.

Let us examine any commission expressly directing those to whom it is given, to use military force for carrying into execution the alterations proposed to be made in the charter and constitution of Massachusetts Bay, by the foregoing maxims and authorities; and what we have said concerning it will appear obvious and conclusive. It is not warranted by any act of parliament; because, as has been mentioned on this, and has been proved on other occasions, any such act is void. It is not warranted, and I believe it will not be pretended that it is warranted, by the common law. It is not warranted by the royal prerogative; because, as has already been fully shown, it is diametrically opposite to the principles and the ends of prerogative. Upon what foundation, then, can it lean and be supported? Upon none. Like an enchanted castle, it may terrify those, whose eyes are affected by the magick influence of the sorcerers, despotism and slavery: but so soon as the charm is dissolved, and the genuine rays of liberty and of the constitution dart in upon us, the formidable appearance vanishes, and we discover that it was the baseless fabrick of a vision, that never had any real existence.

I have dwelt the longer upon this part of the objections urged against us by our adversaries; because this part is the foundation of all the others. We have now removed it; and they must fall of course. For if the force, acting for the purposes we have mentioned, does not act, and cannot act, by virtue of any commission from his majesty, the consequence is undeniable, that it acts without his majesty's authority; that the resistance of

[c] 9. Rep. 123.
[d] 1. Hale. P. C. 43. 44. Vide on this head. 4. Bac. 149. 9. Parl. Hist. 168, 170, 179, 180. Vent. 63, 169. 3. Ins. 237, 238, 240.
[e] 3. Ins. 165.

it is no resistance of his majesty's authority; nor incompatible with the duties of allegiance.

And now, sir, let me appeal to the impartial tribunal of reason and truth — let me appeal to every unprejudiced and judicious observer of the laws of Britain, and of the constitution of the British government — let me appeal, I say, whether the principles on which I argue, or the principles on which alone my arguments can be opposed, are those which ought to be adhered to and acted upon — which of them are most consonant to our laws and liberties — which of them have the strongest, and are likely to have the most effectual, tendency to establish and secure the royal power and dignity.

Are we deficient in loyalty to his majesty? Let our conduct convict, for it will fully convict, the insinuation, that we are, of falsehood. Our loyalty has always appeared in the true form of loyalty — in obeying our sovereign according to law:[f] let those, who would require it in any other form, know, that we call the persons who execute his commands, when contrary to law, disloyal and traitors. Are we enemies to the power of the crown? No, sir: we are its best friends: this friendship prompts us to wish, that the power of the crown may be firmly established on the most solid basis: but we know, that the constitution alone will perpetuate the former, and securely uphold the latter. Are our principles irreverent to majesty? They are quite the reverse: we ascribe to it perfection, almost divine. We say, that the king can do no wrong: we say, that to do wrong is the property, not of power, but of weakness. We feel oppression; and will oppose it; but we know — for our constitution tells us — that oppression can never spring from the throne. We must, therefore, search elsewhere for its source: our infallible guide will direct us to it. Our constitution tells us, that all oppression springs from the ministers of the throne. The attributes of perfection, ascribed to the king, are, neither by the constitution, nor in fact, communicable to his ministers. They may do wrong: they have often done wrong: they have been often punished for doing wrong.

Here we may discern the true cause of all the impudent clamour and unsupported accusations of the ministers and of their minions, that have been raised and made against the conduct of the Americans. Those ministers and minions are sensible, that the opposition is directed, not against his majesty, but against them: because they have abused his majesty's confidence, brought discredit upon his government, and dero-

---

[f] Rebellion being an opposition, not to persons, but authority, which is founded only in the constitution and laws of the government, those, whoever they be, who by force break through, and by force justify the violation of them, are truly and properly rebels. Puffend. 720. 721. notes.

gated from his justice. They see the publick vengeance collected in dark clouds around them: their consciences tell them, that it should be hurled, like a thunder bolt, at their guilty heads. Appalled with guilt and fear, they skulk behind the throne. Is it disrespectful to drag them into publick view, and make a distinction between them and his majesty, under whose venerable name they daringly attempt to shelter their crimes? Nothing can more effectually contribute to establish his majesty on the throne, and to secure to him the affections of his people, than this distinction. By it we are taught to consider all the blessings of government as flowing from the throne; and to consider every instance of oppression as proceeding, which in truth is oftenest the case, from the ministers.

If, now, it is true, that all force employed for the purposes so often mentioned, is force unwarranted by any act of parliament; unsupported by any principle of the common law; unauthorized by any commission from the crown — that, instead of being employed for the support of the constitution and his majesty's government, it must be employed for the support of oppression and ministerial tyranny — if all this is true — and I flatter myself it appears to be true — can any one hesitate to say, that to resist such force is lawful: and that both the letter and the spirit of the British constitution justify such resistance?

Resistance, both by the letter and the spirit of the British constitution, may be carried farther, when necessity requires it, than I have carried it. Many examples in the English history might be adduced, and many authorities of the greatest weight might be brought, to show, that when the king, forgetting his character and his dignity, has stepped forth, and openly avowed and taken a part in such iniquitous conduct as has been described; in such cases, indeed, the distinction above mentioned, wisely made by the constitution for the security of the crown, could not be applied; because the crown had unconstitutionally rendered the application of it impossible. What has been the consequence? The distinction between him and his ministers has been lost: but they have not been raised to his situation: he has sunk to theirs.

IV

SPEECH DELIVERED ON 26th NOVEMBER, 1787, IN THE CONVENTION OF PENNSYLVANIA

ASSEMBLED TO TAKE INTO CONSIDERATION THE CONSTITUTION FRAMED, BY THE FEDERAL CONVENTION, FOR THE UNITED STATES

THE system proposed, by the late convention, for the government of the United States, is now before you. Of that convention I had the honour to be a member. As I am the only member of that body who have the honour to be also a member of this, it may be expected that I should prepare the way for the deliberations of this assembly, by unfolding the difficulties which the late convention were obliged to encounter; by pointing out the end which they proposed to accomplish; and by tracing the general principles which they have adopted for the accomplishment of that end.

To form a good system of government for a single city or state, however limited as to territory, or inconsiderable as to numbers, has been thought to require the strongest efforts of human genius. With what conscious diffidence, then, must the members of the convention have revolved in their minds the immense undertaking which was before them. Their views could not be confined to a small or a single community, but were expanded to a great number of states; several of which contain an extent of territory, and resources of population, equal to those of some of the most respectable kingdoms on the other side of the Atlantick. Nor were even these the only objects to be comprehended within their deliberations. Numerous states yet unformed, myriads of the human race, who will inhabit regions hitherto uncultivated, were to be affected by the result of their proceedings. It was necessary, therefore, to form their calculations on a scale commensurate to a large portion of the globe.

For my own part, I have been often lost in astonishment at the vastness of the prospect before us. To open the navigation of a single river was lately thought, in Europe, an enterprise adequate to imperial glory. But could the commercial scenes of the Scheldt be compared with those that, under a good government, will be exhibited on the Hudson, the Delaware, the Potowmack, and the numerous other rivers, that water and are intended to enrich the dominions of the United States?

The difficulty of the business was equal to its magnitude. No small share of wisdom and address is requisite to combine and reconcile the jarring interests, that prevail, or seem to prevail, in a single community. The United States contain already thirteen governments mutually independent. Those governments present to the Atlantick a front of fifteen hundred miles in extent. Their soil, their climates, their productions, their dimensions, their numbers are different. In many instances a difference and even an opposition subsists among their interests; and a difference and even an opposition is imagined to subsist in many more. An apparent interest produces the same attachment as a real one; and is often pursued with no less perseverance and vigour. When all these circumstances are seen and attentively considered, will any member of this honourable body be surprised, that such a diversity of things produced a proportioned diversity of sentiment? will he be surprised that such a diversity of sentiment rendered a spirit of mutual forbearance and conciliation indispensably necessary to the success of the great work? and will he be surprised that mutual concessions and sacrifices were the consequences of mutual forbearance and conciliation? When the springs of opposition were so numerous and strong, and poured forth their waters in courses so varying, need we be surprised that the stream formed by their conjunction was impelled in a direction somewhat different from that, which each of them would have taken separately?

I have reason to think that a difficulty arose in the minds of some members of the convention from another consideration — their ideas of the temper and disposition of the people, for whom the constitution is proposed. The citizens of the United States, however different in some other respects, are well known to agree in one strongly marked feature of their character — a warm and keen sense of freedom and independence. This sense has been heightened by the glorious result of their late struggle against all the efforts of one of the most powerful nations of Europe. It was apprehended, I believe, by some, that a people so high spirited would ill brook the restraints of an efficient government. I confess that this consideration did not influence my conduct. I knew my constituents to be high spirited; but I knew them also to possess sound sense. I knew that, in the event, they would be best pleased with that system of government, which would best promote their freedom and happiness. I have often revolved this subject in my mind. I have supposed one of my constituents to ask me, why I gave such a vote on a particular question? I have always thought it would be a satisfactory answer to say — because I judged, upon the best consideration I could give, that such a vote was right. I have thought that it would be but a very poor compliment to my constituents to say, that, in my opinion, such a vote would have been proper, but that I supposed a contrary one would be more agreeable to those who sent me to the convention. I could not, even in idea, expose myself to such a retort as, upon the last answer, might have been justly made to me. Pray, sir, what reasons have you for supposing that a right vote would displease your constituents? Is this the proper return for the high confidence they have placed in you? If they have given cause for such a surmise, it was by choosing a representative, who could entertain such an opinion of them. I was under no apprehension, that the good people of this state would behold with displeasure the brightness of the rays of delegated power, when it only proved the superiour splendour of the luminary, of which those rays were only the reflection.

A very important difficulty arose from comparing the extent of the country to be governed, with the kind of government which it would be proper to establish in it. It has been an opinion, countenanced by high authority, "that the natural property of small states is, to be governed as a republick; of middling ones, to be subject to a monarch; and of large empires, to be swayed by a despotick prince; and that the consequence is, that, in order to preserve the principles of the established government, the state must be supported in the extent it has acquired; and that the spirit of the state will alter in proportion as it extends or contracts its limits." [a] This opinion seems to be supported, rather than contradicted, by the history of the governments in the old world. Here then the difficulty appeared in full view. On one hand, the United States contain an immense extent of territory, and, according to the foregoing opinion, a despotick government is best adapted to that extent. On the other hand, it was well known, that, however the citizens of the United States might, with pleasure, submit to the legitimate restraints of a republican constitution, they would reject, with indignation, the fetters of despotism. What then was to be done? The idea of a confederate republick presented itself. This kind of constitution has been thought to have "all the internal advantages of a republican, together with the external force of a monarchical government." [b] Its description is, "a convention, by which several states agree to become members of a larger one, which they intend to establish. It is a kind of assemblage of societies, that constitute a new one, capable of increasing by means of farther association." [c] The expanding quality of such a government is peculiarly fitted for the United States, the greatest part of whose territory is yet uncultivated.

But while this form of government enabled us to surmount the difficulty last mentioned, it conducted us to another, of which I am now to take notice. It left us almost without precedent or guide; and conse-

[a] Mont. Sp. L. b. 8. c. 20.   [b] Id. b. 9. c. 1. 1. Paley, 199–202.
[c] Mont. Sp. L. b. 9. c. 1.

quently, without the benefit of that instruction, which, in many cases, may be derived from the constitution, and history, and experience of other nations. Several associations have frequently been called by the name of confederate states, which have not, in propriety of language, deserved it. The Swiss cantons are connected only by alliances. The United Netherlands are indeed an assemblage of societies; but this assemblage constitutes no *new one;* and, therefore, it does not correspond with the full definition of a confederate republick. The Germanick body is composed of such disproportioned and discordant materials, and its structure is so intricate and complex, that little useful knowledge can be drawn from it. Ancient history discloses, and barely discloses to our view, some confederate republicks — the Achæan league, the Lycian confederacy, and the Amphyctionick council. But the facts recorded concerning their constitutions are so few and general, and their histories are so unmarked and defective, that no satisfactory information can be collected from them concerning many particular circumstances, from an accurate discernment and comparison of which alone, legitimate and practical inferences can be made from one constitution to another. Besides, the situation and dimensions of those confederacies, and the state of society, manners, and habits in them, were so different from those of the United States, that the most correct descriptions could have supplied but a very small fund of applicable remark. Thus, in forming this system, we were deprived of many advantages, which the history and experience of other ages and other countries would, in other cases, have afforded us.

Permit me to add, in this place, that the science even of government itself seems yet to be almost in its state of infancy. Governments, in general, have been the result of force, of fraud, and of accident. After a period of six thousand years has elapsed since the creation, the United States exhibit to the world the first instance, as far as we can learn, of a nation, unattacked by external force, unconvulsed by domestick insurrections, assembling voluntarily, deliberating fully, and deciding calmly, concerning that system of government, under which they would wish that they and their posterity should live. The ancients, so enlightened on other subjects, were very uninformed with regard to this. They seem scarcely to have had any idea of any other kinds of governments, than the three simple forms designated by the epithets, monarchical, aristocratical, and democratical. I know that much and pleasing ingenuity has been exerted, in modern times, in drawing entertaining parallels between some of the ancient constitutions and some of the mixed governments that have since existed in Europe. But I much suspect that, on strict examination, the instances of resemblance will be found to be few and weak; to be suggested by the improvements, which, in subsequent ages, have been made in government, and not to be drawn immediately from the ancient constitutions themselves, as they were intended and understood by those who framed them. To illustrate this, a similar observation may be made on another subject. Admiring criticks have fancied, that they have discovered in their favourite Homer the seeds of all the improvements in philosophy, and in the sciences, made since his time. What induces me to be of this opinion is, that Tacitus, the profound politician Tacitus, who lived towards the latter end of those ages which are now denominated ancient, who undoubtedly had studied the constitutions of all the states and kingdoms known before and in his time, and who certainly was qualified, in an uncommon degree, for understanding the full force and operation of each of them, considers, after all he had known and read, a mixed government, composed of the three simple forms, as a thing rather to be wished than expected: and he thinks, that if such a government could even be instituted, its duration could not be long. One thing is very certain, that the doctrine of representation in government was altogether unknown to the ancients. Now the knowledge and practice of this doctrine is, in my opinion, essential to every system, that can possess the qualities of freedom, wisdom, and energy.

It is worthy of remark, and the remark may, perhaps, excite some surprise, that representation of the people is not, even at this day, the sole principle of any government in Europe. Great Britain boasts, and she may well boast, of the improvement she has made in politicks, by the admission of representation: for the improvement is important as far as it goes; but it by no means goes far enough. Is the executive power of Great Britain founded on representation? This is not pretended. Before the revolution, many of the kings claimed to reign by divine right, and others by hereditary right; and even at the revolution, nothing farther was effected or attempted, than the recognition of certain parts of an original contract,[a] supposed at some remote period to have been made between the king and the people. A contract seems to exclude, rather than to imply, delegated power. The judges of Great Britain are appointed by the crown. The judicial authority, therefore, does not depend upon representation, even in its most remote degree. Does representation prevail in the legislative department of the British government? Even here it does not predominate; though it may serve as a check. The legislature consists of three branches, the king, the lords, and the commons. Of these, only the latter are supposed by the constitution to represent the authority of the people. This short analysis clearly shows, to what a narrow corner of the British constitution the principle of representation is confined. I believe it does not extend farther, if so far, in any other government in Europe. For the American States were reserved the glory and the happiness of diffusing this vital principle through all the constituent parts of government. Rep-

[a] 1. Bl. Com. 233.

resentation is the chain of communication between the people, and those to whom they have committed the exercise of the powers of government. This chain may consist of one or more links; but in all cases it should be sufficiently strong and discernible.

To be left without guide or precedent was not the only difficulty, in which the convention were involved, by proposing to their constituents a plan of a confederate republick. They found themselves embarrassed with another of peculiar delicacy and importance; I mean that of drawing a proper line between the national government and the governments of the several states. It was easy to discover a proper and satisfactory principle on the subject. Whatever object of government is confined in its operation and effects within the bounds of a particular state, should be considered as belonging to the government of that state; whatever object of government extends in its operation or effects beyond the bounds of a particular state, should be considered as belonging to the government of the United States. But though this principle be sound and satisfactory, its application to particular cases would be accompanied with much difficulty; because, in its application, room must be allowed for great discretionary latitude of construction of the principle. In order to lessen or remove the difficulty arising from discretionary construction on this subject, an enumeration of particular instances, in which the application of the principle ought to take place, has been attempted with much industry and care. It is only in mathematical science, that a line can be described with mathematical precision. But I flatter myself that, upon the strictest investigation, the enumeration will be found to be safe and unexceptionable; and accurate too, in as great a degree as accuracy can be expected in a subject of this nature. Particulars under this head will be more properly explained, when we descend to the minute view of the enumeration which is made in the proposed constitution.

After all, it will be necessary, that, on a subject so peculiarly delicate as this, much prudence, much candour, much moderation, and much liberality should be exercised and displayed, both by the federal government and by the governments of the several states. It is to be hoped, that those virtues in government will be exercised and displayed, when we consider, that the powers of the federal government and those of the state governments are drawn from sources equally pure. If a difference can be discovered between them, it is in favour of the federal government; because that government is founded on a representation of the whole union; whereas the government of any particular state is founded only on the representation of a part, inconsiderable when compared with the whole. Is it not more reasonable to suppose, that the counsels of the whole will embrace the interest of every part, than that the counsels of any part will embrace the interests of the whole?

I intend not, sir, by this description of the difficulties with which the convention were surrounded, to magnify their skill or their merit in surmounting them, or to insinuate that any predicament, in which the convention stood, should prevent the closest and most cautious scrutiny into the performance, which they have exhibited to their constituents and to the world. My intention is of far other and higher aim — to evince by the conflicts and difficulties which must arise from the many and powerful causes which I have enumerated, that it is hopeless and impracticable to form a constitution, which will, in every part, be acceptable to every citizen, or even to every government in the United States; and that all which can be expected is, to form such a constitution as, upon the whole, is the best that can possibly be obtained. Man and perfection! — a state and perfection! — an assemblage of states and perfection! Can we reasonably expect, however ardently we may wish, to behold the glorious union?

I can well recollect, though I believe I cannot convey to others, the impression, which, on many occasions, was made by the difficulties which surrounded and pressed the convention. The great undertaking, at some times, seemed to be at a stand; at other times, its motions seemed to be retrograde. At the conclusion, however, of our work, many of the members expressed their astonishment at the success with which it terminated.

Having enumerated some of the difficulties which the convention were obliged to encounter in the course of their proceedings, I shall next point out the end which they proposed to accomplish. Our wants, our talents, our affections, our passions, all tell us that we were made for a state of society. But a state of society could not be supported long or happily without some civil restraint. It is true that, in a state of nature, any one individual may act uncontrolled by others; but it is equally true, that, in such a state, every other individual may act uncontrolled by him. Amidst this universal independence, the dissensions and animosities between interfering members of the society would be numerous and ungovernable. The consequence would be, that each member, in such a natural state, would enjoy less liberty, and suffer more interruption, than he would in a regulated society. Hence the universal introduction of governments of some kind or other into the social state. The liberty of every member is increased by this introduction, for each gains more by the limitation of the freedom of every other member, than he loses by the limitation of his own. The result is, that civil government is necessary to the perfection and happiness of man. In forming this government, and carrying it into execution, it is essential that the interest and authority of the whole community should be binding on every part of it.

The foregoing principles and conclusions are generally admitted to be just and sound with regard to the nature and formation of single governments, and the duty of submission to them. In some cases they will apply, with much propriety and force, to states already formed. The advantages and necessity of civil government among individuals in society are not greater or stronger than, in some situations and circumstances, are the advantages and necessity of a federal government among states. A natural and a very important question now presents itself. Is such the situation — are such the circumstances of the United States? A proper answer to this question will unfold some very interesting truths.

The United States may adopt any one of four different systems. They may become consolidated into one government, in which the separate existence of the states shall be entirely absorbed. They may reject any plan of union or association, and act as separate and unconnected states. They may form two or more confederacies. They may unite in one federal republick. Which of these systems ought to have been proposed by the convention? — To support with vigour, a single government over the whole extent of the United States, would demand a system of the most unqualified and the most unremitted despotism. Such a number of separate states, contiguous in situation, unconnected and disunited in government, would be, at one time, the prey of foreign force, foreign influence, and foreign intrigue; at another, the victim of mutual rage, rancour, and revenge. Neither of these systems found advocates in the late convention: I presume they will not find advocates in this. Would it be proper to divide the United States into two or more confederacies? It will not be unadvisable to take a more minute survey of this subject. Some aspects, under which it may be viewed, are far from being, at first sight, uninviting. Two or more confederacies would be each more compact and more manageable, than a single one extending over the same territory. By dividing the United States into two or more confederacies, the great collision of interests, apparently or really different and contrary, in the whole extent of their dominion, would be broken, and in a great measure disappear in the several parts. But these advantages, which are discovered from certain points of view, are greatly overbalanced by inconveniences that will appear on a more accurate examination. Animosities, and perhaps wars, would arise from assigning the extent, the limits, and the rights of the different confederacies. The expenses of governing would be multiplied by the number of federal governments. The danger resulting from foreign influence and mutual dissensions would not, perhaps, be less great and alarming in the instance of different confederacies, than in the instance of different though more numerous unassociated states. These observations, and many others that might be made on the subject, will be sufficient to evince, that a division of the United States into a number of separate confederacies would probably be an unsatisfactory and an unsuccessful experiment. The remaining system which the American States may adopt is, a union of them under one confederate republick. It will not be necessary to employ much time or many arguments to show, that this is the most eligible system that can be proposed. By adopting this system, the vigour and decision of a wide spreading monarchy may be joined to the freedom and beneficence of a contracted republick. The extent of territory, the diversity of climate and soil, the number, and greatness, and connexion of lakes and rivers, with which the United States are intersected and almost surrounded, all indicate an enlarged government to be fit and advantageous for them. The principles and dispositions of their citizens indicate, that in this government liberty shall reign triumphant. Such indeed have been the general opinions and wishes entertained since the era of our independence. If those opinions and wishes are as well founded as they have been general, the late convention were justified in proposing to their constituents one confederate republick, as the best system of a national government for the United States.

In forming this system, it was proper to give minute attention to the interest of all the parts; but there was a duty of still higher import — to feel and to show a predominating regard to the superiour interests of the whole. If this great principle had not prevailed, the plan before us would never have made its appearance. The same principle that was so necessary in forming it, is equally necessary in our deliberations, whether we should reject or ratify it.

I make these observations with a design to prove and illustrate this great and important truth — that in our decisions on the work of the late convention, we should not limit our views and regards to the state of Pennsylvania. The aim of the convention was, to form a system of good and efficient government on the more extensive scale of the United States. In this, as in every other instance, the work should be judged with the same spirit with which it was performed. A principle of duty as well as of candour demands this.

We have remarked, that civil government is necessary to the perfection of society: we now remark, that civil liberty is necessary to the perfection of civil government. Civil liberty is natural liberty itself, devested only of that part, which, placed in the government, produces more good and happiness to the community, than if it had remained in the individual. Hence it follows, that civil liberty, while it resigns a part of natural liberty, retains the free and generous exercise of all the human faculties, so far as it is compatible with the publick welfare.

In considering and developing the nature and end of the system before us, it is necessary to mention another kind of liberty, which has not yet, as far as I know, received a name. I shall distinguish it by the appellation of *federal liberty*. When a single government is instituted, the individuals of which it is composed surrender to it a part of their natural inde-

pendence, which they before enjoyed as men. When a confederate republick is instituted, the communities of which it is composed surrender to it
a part of their political independence, which they before enjoyed as states.
The principles which directed, in the former case, what part of the natural liberty of the man ought to be given up, and what part ought to
be retained, will give similar directions in the latter case. The states should
resign to the national government that part, and that part only, of their
political liberty, which, placed in that government, will produce more
good to the whole, than if it had remained in the several states. While
they resign this part of their political liberty, they retain the free and
generous exercise of all their other faculties as states, so far as it is compatible with the welfare of the general and superintending confederacy.

Since states as well as citizens are represented in the constitution before us, and form the objects on which that constitution is proposed to
operate, it was necessary to notice and define federal as well as civil liberty.

These general reflections have been made in order to introduce, with
more propriety and advantage, a practical illustration of the end proposed
to be accomplished by the late convention.

It has been too well known — it has been too severely felt — that the
present confederation is inadequate to the government and to the exigencies of the United States. The great struggle for liberty in this country, should it be unsuccessful, will probably be the last one which she
will have for her existence and prosperity, in any part of the globe. And
it must be confessed, that this struggle has, in some of the stages of its
progress, been attended with symptoms that foreboded no fortunate issue.
To the iron hand of tyranny, which was lifted up against her, she manifested, indeed, an intrepid superiority. She broke in pieces the fetters
which were forged for her, and showed that she was unassailable by force.
But she was environed by dangers of another kind, and springing from
a very different source. While she kept her eye steadily fixed on the efforts of oppression, licentiousness was secretly undermining the rock on
which she stood.

Need I call to your remembrance the contrasted scenes, of which we
have been witnesses? On the glorious conclusion of our conflict with
Britain, what high expectations were formed concerning us by others!
What high expectations did we form concerning ourselves! Have those
expectations been realized? No. What has been the cause? Did our citizens
lose their perseverance and magnanimity? No. Did they become insensible of resentment and indignation at any high handed attempt, that might
have been made to injure or enslave them? No. What then has been the
cause? The truth is, we dreaded danger only on one side: this we man-
fully repelled. But on another side, danger, not less formidable, but more

insidious, stole in upon us; and our unsuspicious tempers were not sufficiently attentive, either to its approach or to its operations. Those, whom
foreign strength could not overpower, have well nigh become the victims of internal anarchy.

If we become a little more particular, we shall find that the foregoing
representation is by no means exaggerated. When we had baffled all the
menaces of foreign power, we neglected to establish among ourselves
a government, that would ensure domestick vigour and stability. What
was the consequence? The commencement of peace was the commencement of every disgrace and distress, that could befal a people in a peaceful state. Devoid of national power, we could not prohibit the extravagance of our importations, nor could we derive a revenue from their
excess. Devoid of national importance, we could not procure for our ex-
ports a tolerable sale at foreign markets. Devoid of national credit, we saw
our publick securities melt in the hands of the holders, like snow before
the sun. Devoid of national dignity, we could not, in some instances,
perform our treaties on our parts; and, in other instances, we could
neither obtain nor compel the performance of them on the part of others.
Devoid of national energy, we could not carry into execution our own
resolutions, decisions, or laws.

Shall I become more particular still? The tedious detail would disgust
me: nor is it now necessary. The years of languor are past. We have felt
the dishonour, with which we have been covered: we have seen the
destruction with which we have been threatened. We have penetrated to
the causes of both, and when we have once discovered them, we have
begun to search for the means of removing them. For the confirmation
of these remarks, I need not appeal to an enumeration of facts. The proceedings of congress, and of the several states, are replete with them.
They all point out the weakness and insufficiency of the present confederation as the cause, and an efficient general government as the only
cure of our political distempers.

Under these impressions, and with these views, was the late convention
appointed; and under these impressions, and with these views, the late
convention met.

We now see the great end which they proposed to accomplish. It was
to frame, for the consideration of their constituents, one federal and national constitution — a constitution that would produce the advantages of
good, and prevent the inconveniences of bad government — a constitution, whose beneficence and energy would pervade the whole union, and
bind and embrace the interests of every part — a constitution that would
ensure peace, freedom, and happiness, to the states and people of America.

We are now naturally led to examine the means, by which they proposed to accomplish this end. This opens more particularly to our view the important discussion before us. But previously to our entering upon it, it will not be improper to state some general and leading principles of government, which will receive particular applications in the course of our investigations.

There necessarily exists in every government a power, from which there is no appeal; and which, for that reason, may be termed supreme, absolute, and uncontrollable. Where does this power reside? To this question, writers on different governments will give different answers. Sir William Blackstone will tell you, that in Britain, the power is lodged in the British parliament; that the parliament may alter the form of the government; and that its power is absolute and without control. The idea of a constitution, limiting and superintending the operations of legislative authority, seems not to have been accurately understood in Britain. There are, at least, no traces of practice, conformable to such a principle. The British constitution is just what the British parliament pleases. When the parliament transferred legislative authority to Henry the eighth, the act transferring it could not, in the strict acceptation of the term, be called unconstitutional.

To control the power and conduct of the legislature by an overruling constitution, was an improvement in the science and practice of government reserved to the American States.

Perhaps some politician, who has not considered, with sufficient accuracy, our political systems, would answer, that, in our governments, the supreme power was vested in the constitutions. This opinion approaches a step nearer to the truth, but does not reach it. The truth is, that, in our governments, the supreme, absolute, and uncontrollable power remains in the people. As our constitutions are superiour to our legislatures; so the people are superiour to our constitutions. Indeed the superiority, in this last instance, is much greater; for the people possess, over our constitutions, control in act, as well as in right.

The consequence is, that the people may change the constitutions, whenever and however they please. This is a right, of which no positive institution can ever deprive them.

These important truths, sir, are far from being merely speculative: we, at this moment, speak and deliberate under their immediate and benign influence. To the operation of these truths, we are to ascribe the scene, hitherto unparallelled, which America now exhibits to the world — a gentle, a peaceful, a voluntary, and a deliberate transition from one constitution of government to another. In other parts of the world, the idea of revolutions in government is, by a mournful and indissoluble association, connected with the idea of wars, and all the calamities attendant on wars. But happy experience teaches us to view such revolutions in a very different light — to consider them only as progressive steps in improving the knowledge of government, and increasing the happiness of society and mankind.

Oft have I viewed with silent pleasure and admiration the force and prevalence, through the United States, of this principle — that the supreme power resides in the people; and that they never part with it. It may be called the *panacea* in politicks. There can be no disorder in the community but may here receive a radical cure. If the errour be in the legislature, it may be corrected by the constitution; if in the constitution, it may be corrected by the people. There is a remedy, therefore, for every distemper in government, if the people are not wanting to themselves. For a people wanting to themselves, there is no remedy: from their power, as we have seen, there is no appeal: to their errour, there is no superiour principle of correction.

There are three simple species of government — monarchy, where the supreme power is in a single person — aristocracy, where the supreme power is in a select assembly, the members of which either fill up, by election, the vacancies in their own body, or succeed to their places in it by inheritance, property, or in respect of some personal right or qualification — a republick or democracy, where the people at large retain the supreme power, and act either collectively or by representation.

Each of these species of government has its advantages and disadvantages.

The advantages of a monarchy are, strength, despatch, secrecy, unity of counsel. Its disadvantages are, tyranny, expense, ignorance of the situation and wants of the people, insecurity, unnecessary wars, evils attending elections or successions.

The advantages of aristocracy are, wisdom, arising from experience and education. Its disadvantages are, dissensions among themselves, oppression to the lower orders.

The advantages of democracy are, liberty, equal, cautious, and salutary laws, publick spirit, frugality, peace, opportunities of exciting and producing abilities of the best citizens. Its disadvantages are, dissensions, the delay and disclosure of public counsels, the imbecility of publick measures retarded by the necessity of a numerous consent.

A government may be composed of two or more of the simple forms abovementioned. Such is the British government. It would be an improper government for the United States; because it is inadequate to such an extent of territory; and because it is suited to an establishment of different orders of men. A more minute comparison between some parts of the British constitution, and some parts of the plan before us, may, perhaps, find a proper place in a subsequent period of our business.

What is the nature and kind of that government, which has been proposed for the United States, by the late convention? In its principle, it is purely democratical: but that principle is applied in different forms, in order to obtain the advantages, and exclude the inconveniences of the simple modes of government.

If we take an extended and accurate view of it, we shall find the streams of power running in different directions, in different dimensions, and at different heights, watering, adorning, and fertilizing the fields and meadows, through which their courses are led; but if we trace them, we shall discover, that they all originally flow from one abundant fountain. In this constitution, all authority is derived from THE PEOPLE.

Fit occasions will hereafter offer for particular remarks on the different parts of the plan. I have now to ask pardon of the house for detaining them so long.

V

ORATION DELIVERED ON THE FOURTH OF JULY 1788, AT THE PROCESSION FORMED AT PHILADELPHIA

TO CELEBRATE THE ADOPTION OF THE CONSTITUTION OF THE UNITED STATES

M Y friends and fellow citizens, your candid and generous indulgence I may well bespeak, for many reasons. I shall mention but one. While I express it, I feel it in all its force. My abilities are unequal — abilities far superiour to mine would be unequal — to the occasion on which I have the honour of being called to address you.

A people free and enlightened, establishing and ratifying a system of government, which they have previously considered, examined, and approved! This is the spectacle, which we are assembled to celebrate; and it is the most dignified one that has yet appeared on our globe. Numerous and splendid have been the triumphs of conquerors. But from what causes have they originated? — Of what consequences have they been productive? They have generally begun in ambition: they have generally ended in tyranny. But nothing tyrannical can participate of dignity: and to freedom's eye, Sesostris himself appears contemptible, even when he treads on the necks of kings.

The senators of Rome, seated on their curule chairs, and surrounded with all their official lustre, were an object much more respectable: and we view, without displeasure, the admiration of those untutored savages, who considered them as so many gods upon earth. But who were those senators? They were only a part of a society: they were vested only with inferiour powers.

What is the object exhibited to our contemplation? A whole people exercising its first and greatest power — performing an act of sovereignty, original and unlimited!

The scene before us is unexampled as well as magnificent. The greatest part of governments have been the deformed offspring of force and fear. With these we deign not comparison. But there have been others which have formed bold pretensions to higher regard. You have heard of Sparta, of Athens, and of Rome; you have heard of their admired constitutions, and of their high-prized freedom. In fancied right of these, they conceived themselves to be elevated above the rest of the human race, whom they marked with the degrading title of barbarians. But did they, in all their pomp and pride of liberty, ever furnish, to the astonished world, an exhibition similar to that which we now contemplate? Were their constitutions framed by those, who were appointed for that purpose, by the people? After they were framed, were they submitted to the consideration of the people? Had the people an opportunity of expressing their sentiments concerning them? Were they to stand or fall by the people's approving or rejecting vote? To all these questions, attentive and impartial history obliges us to answer in the negative. The people were either unfit to be trusted, or their lawgivers were too ambitious to trust them.

The far-famed establishment of Lycurgus was introduced by deception and fraud. Under the specious pretence of consulting the oracle concerning his laws, he prevailed on the Spartans to make a temporary experiment of them during his absence, and to swear that they would suffer no alteration of them till his return. Taking a disingenuous advantage of their scrupulous regard for their oaths, he prevented his return by a voluntary death, and, in this manner, endeavoured to secure a proud immortality to his system.

Even Solon — the mild and moderating Solon — far from considering himself as employed only to *propose* such regulations as he should think best calculated for promoting the happiness of the commonwealth, made and promulgated his laws with all the haughty airs of absolute power. On more occasions than one, we find him boasting, with much selfcomplacency, of his extreme forbearance and condescension, because he did not establish a despotism in his own favour, and because he did not reduce his equals to the humiliating condition of his slaves.

Did Numa submit his institutions to the good sense and free investigation of Rome? They were received in precious communications from the goddess Egeria, with whose presence and regard he was supremely favoured; and they were imposed on the easy faith of the citizens, as the dictates of an inspiration that was divine.

Such, my fellow citizens, was the origin of the most splendid establishments that have been hitherto known; and such were the arts, to which they owed their introduction and success.

What a flattering contrast arises from a retrospect of the scenes which we now commemorate? Delegates were appointed to deliberate and propose. They met and performed their delegated trust. The result of their deliberations was laid before the people. It was discussed and scrutinized in the fullest, freest, and severest manner — by speaking, by writing, and by printing — by individuals and by publick bodies — by its friends and by its enemies. What was the issue? Most favourable and most glorious to the system. In state after state, at time after time, it was ratified — in some states unanimously — on the whole, by a large and very respectable majority.

It would be improper now to examine its qualities. A decent respect for those who have accepted it, will lead us to presume that it is worthy of their acceptance. The deliberate ratifications, which have taken place, at once recommend the system, and the people by whom it has been ratified.

But why, methinks I hear some one say — why is so much exultation displayed in celebrating this event? We are prepared to give the reasons of our joy. We rejoice, because, under this constitution, we hope to see just government, and to enjoy the blessings that walk in its train.

Let us begin with Peace — the mild and modest harbinger of felicity! How seldom does the amiable wanderer choose, for her permanent residence, the habitations of men! In their systems, she sees too many arrangements, civil and ecclesiastical, inconsistent with the calmness and benignity of her temper. In the old world, how many millions of men do we behold, unprofitable to society, burthensome to industry, the props of establishments that deserve not to be supported, the causes of distrust in the times of peace, and the instruments of destruction in the times of war? Why are they not employed in cultivating useful arts, and in forwarding publick improvements? Let us indulge the pleasing expectation, that such will be the operation of government in the United States. Why may we not hope, that, disentangled from the intrigues and jealousies of European politicks, and unmolested with the alarm and solicitude to which these intrigues and jealousies give birth, our counsels will be directed to the encouragement, and our strength will be exerted in the cultivation, of all the arts of peace?

Of these, the first is agriculture. This is true in all countries: in the United States, its truth is of peculiar importance. The subsistence of man, the materials of manufactures, the articles of commerce — all spring originally from the soil. On agriculture, therefore, the wealth of nations is founded. Whether we consult the observations that reason will suggest, or attend to the information that history will give, we shall, in each case, be satisfied of the influence of government, good or bad, upon the state of agriculture. In a government, whose maxims are those of oppression, property is insecure. It is given, it is taken away, by caprice. Where there is no security for property, there is no encouragement for industry. Without industry, the richer the soil, the more it abounds with weeds. The evidence of history warrants the truth of these general remarks. Attend to Greece; and compare her agriculture in ancient and in modern times. Then, smiling harvests bore testimony to the bountiful boons of liberty. Now, the very earth languishes under oppression. View the Campania of Rome. How melancholy the prospect! Whichever way you turn your afflicted eyes, scenes of desolation crowd before them. Waste and barrenness appear around you in all their hideous forms. What is the reason? With double tyranny the land is cursed. Open the classick page: you trace, in chaste description, the beautiful reverse of every thing you have seen. Whence proceeds the difference? When that description was made, the force of liberty pervaded the soil.

But is agriculture the only art, which feels the influence of government? Over manufactures and commerce its power is equally prevalent. There the same causes operate — and there they produce the same effects. The industrious village, the busy city, the crowded port — all these are the gifts of liberty; and without a good government, liberty cannot exist.

These are advantages, but these are not all the advantages, that result from a system of good government. — Agriculture, manufactures, and commerce will ensure to us plenty, convenience, and elegance. But is there not something still wanting to finish the man? Are internal virtues and accomplishments less estimable, or less attracting than external arts and ornaments? Is the operation of government less powerful upon the former than upon the latter? By no means. Upon this as upon a preceding topick, reason and history will concur in their information and advice. In a serene mind, the sciences and the virtues love to dwell. But can the mind of a man be serene, when the property, liberty, subsistence of himself, and of those for whom he feels more than he feels for himself, depend on a tyrant's nod. If the dispirited subject of oppression can, with difficulty, exert his enfeebled faculties, so far as to provide, on the incessant demands of nature, food just enough to lengthen out his wretched existence, can it be expected that, in such a state, he will experience those fine and vigorous movements of the soul, without the full and free exercise of which, science and virtue will never flourish? Look around you to the nations that now exist. View, in historick retrospect, the nations that have heretofore existed. The collected result will be, an entire conviction of these all-interesting truths — where tyranny reigns, there is the country of ignorance and vice — where good government prevails, there is the country of science and virtue. Under a good government, therefore, we must look for the accomplished man.

But shall we confine our views even here? While we wish to be accomplished men and citizens, shall we wish to be nothing more? While we perform our duty, and promote our happiness in this world, shall we bestow no regards upon the next? Does no connexion subsist between the two? From this connexion flows the most important of all the blessings of good government. But here let us pause — unassisted reason can guide us no farther — she directs us to that heaven-descended science, by which life and immortality have been brought to light.

May we not now say, that we have reason for our joy? But while we cherish the delightful emotion, let us remember those things, which are requisite to give it permanence and stability. Shall we lie supine, and look in listless languor, for those blessings and enjoyments, to which exertion is inseparably attached? If we would be happy, we must be active. The constitution and our manners must mutually support and be supported. Even on this festivity, it will not be disagreeable or incongruous to review the virtues and manners that both justify and adorn it.

Frugality and temperance first attract our attention. These simple but powerful virtues are the sole foundation, on which a good government can rest with security. They were the virtues, which nursed and educated infant Rome, and prepared her for all her greatness. But in the giddy hour of her prosperity, she spurned from her the obscure instruments, by which it was procured; and, in their place, substituted luxury and dissipation. The consequence was such as might have been expected. She preserved, for some time, a gay and flourishing appearance; but the internal health and soundness of her constitution were gone. At last, she fell a victim to the poisonous draughts, which were administered by her perfidious favourites. The fate of Rome, both in her rising and in her falling state, will be the fate of every other nation that shall follow both parts of her example.

Industry appears next among the virtues of a good citizen. Idleness is the nurse of villains. The industrious alone constitute a nation's strength. I will not expatiate on this fruitful subject. Let one animating reflection suffice. In a well constituted commonwealth, the industry of every citizen extends beyond himself. A common interest pervades the society. Each gains from all, and all gain from each. It has often been observed, that the sciences flourish all together: the remark applies equally to the arts.

Your patriotick feelings attest the truth of what I say, when, among the virtues necessary to merit and preserve the advantages of a good government, I number a warm and uniform attachment to liberty, and to the constitution. The enemies of liberty are artful and insidious. A counterfeit steals her dress, imitates her manner, forges her signature, assumes her name. But the real name of the deceiver is licentiousness. Such is her effrontery, that she will charge liberty to her face with imposture: and she will, with shameless front, insist that herself alone is the genuine character, and that herself alone is entitled to the respect, which the genuine character deserves. With the giddy and undiscerning, on whom a deeper impression is made by dauntless impudence than by modest merit, her pretensions are often successful. She receives the honours of liberty, and liberty herself is treated as a traitor and a usurper. Generally, however, this bold impostor acts only a secondary part. Though she alone appear upon the stage, her motions are regulated by dark ambition, who sits concealed behind the curtain, and who knows that despotism, his other favourite, can always follow the success of licentiousness. Against these enemies of liberty, who act in concert, though they appear on opposite sides, the patriot citizen will keep a watchful guard.

A good constitution is the greatest blessing, which a society can enjoy. Need I infer, that it is the duty of every citizen to use his best and most unremitting endeavours for preserving it pure, healthful, and vigorous? For the accomplishment of this great purpose, the exertions of no one citizen are unimportant. Let no one, therefore, harbour, for a moment, the mean idea, that he is and can be of no value to his country: let the contrary manly impression animate his soul. Every one can, at *many* times, perform, to the state, *useful* services; and he, who steadily pursues the road of patriotism, has the most inviting prospect of being able, at *some* times, to perform *eminent* ones. Allow me to direct your attention, in a very particular manner, to a momentous part, which, by this constitution, every citizen will frequently be called to act. All those in places of power and trust will be elected either immediately by the people, or in such a manner that their appointment will depend ultimately on such immediate election. All the derivative movements of government must spring from the original movement of the people at large. If to this they give a sufficient force and a just direction, all the others will be governed by its controlling power. To speak without a metaphor, if the people, at their elections, take care to choose none but representatives that are wise and good, their representatives will take care, in their turn, to choose or appoint none but such as are wise and good also. The remark applies to every succeeding election and appointment. Thus the characters proper for publick officers will be diffused from the immediate elections of the people over the remotest parts of administration. Of what immense consequence is it, then, that this primary duty should be faithfully and skilfully discharged! On the faithful and skilful discharge of it, the publick happiness or infelicity, under this and every other constitution, must, in a very great measure, depend. For, believe me, no government, even the best, can be happily administered by ignorant or vicious men. You will forgive me, I am sure, for endeavouring to impress upon your minds, in the strongest manner, the importance of this great duty. It is the first concoction in politicks; and if an errour is committed here, it can never be corrected in any subsequent process: the certain consequence must be disease. Let no one say, that he is but a single citizen; and that his ticket will be but one in the box. That one ticket may turn the election. In battle, every soldier should consider the publick safety as depending on his single arm: at an election, every citizen should consider the publick happiness as depending on his single vote.

A progressive state is necessary to the happiness and perfection of man. Whatever attainments are already reached, attainments still higher should be pursued. Let us, therefore, strive with noble emulation. Let us suppose we have done nothing, while any thing yet remains to be done. Let us, with fervent zeal, press forward, and make unceasing advances in every thing that can support, improve, refine, or embellish society. To enter into particulars under each of these heads, and to dilate them according to their importance, would be improper at this time. A few remarks on the last of them will be congenial with the entertainments of this auspicious day.

If we give the slightest attention to nature, we shall discover, that with utility, she is curious to blend ornament. Can we imitate a better pattern? Publick exhibitions have been the favourite amusements of some of the wisest and most accomplished nations. Greece, in her most shining era, considered her games as far from being the least respectable among her publick establishments. The shows of the circus evince that, on this subject, the sentiments of Greece were fortified by those of Rome.

Publick procession may be so planned and executed as to join both the properties of nature's rule. They may instruct and improve, while they entertain and please. They may point out the elegance or usefulness of the sciences and the arts. They may preserve the memory, and engrave the importance of great political events. They may represent, with peculiar felicity and force, the operation and effects of great political truths. The picturesque and splendid decorations around me furnish the most beautiful and most brilliant proofs, that these remarks are far from being imaginary.

The commencement of our government has been eminently glorious: let our progress in every excellence be proportionably great. It will — it must be so. What an enrapturing prospect opens on the United States! Placid husbandry walks in front, attended by the venerable plough. Lowing herds adorn our vallies: bleating flocks spread over our hills: verdant meadows, enamelled pastures, yellow harvests, bending orchards, rise in rapid succession from east to west. Plenty, with her copious horn, sits easy smiling, and, in conscious complacency, enjoys and presides over the scenes. Commerce next advances in all her splendid and embellished forms. The rivers, and lakes, and seas, are crowded with ships. Their shores are covered with cities. The cities are filled with inhabitants. The arts, decked with elegance, yet with simplicity, appear in beautiful variety, and well adjusted arrangement. Around them are diffused, in rich abundance, the necessaries, the decencies, and the ornaments of life. With heartfelt contentment, industry beholds his honest labours flourishing and secure. Peace walks serene and unalarmed over all the unmolested regions — while liberty, virtue, and religion go hand in hand, harmoniously, protecting, enlivening, and exalting all! Happy country! May thy happiness be perpetual!

VI

SPEECH ON CHOOSING THE MEMBERS OF THE SENATE BY ELECTORS; DELIVERED ON 31st DECEMBER, 1789, IN THE CONVENTION OF PENNSYLVANIA

ASSEMBLED FOR THE PURPOSE OF REVIEWING, ALTERING, AND AMENDING THE CONSTITUTION OF THE STATE

WELL assured I am,[a] that the subject now before the convention must appear to honourable members, for whom I have much regard, under an aspect very different from that, in which it makes its approaches to me. Indeed it has not always appeared to myself in precisely the same light, in which I now view it. One reason may be, that I have not formerly been accustomed to contemplate it from the point of sight, at which I now stand, and from which it is my duty, enjoined by the strongest ties, to make the most attentive and accurate observations. I have considered it as a subject of speculative discussion. I have taken of it such a slight and general survey, as one person would take of the estate of another, without any expectation that it, or one similar to it, would ever become his own. On such a vague and superficial examination, I have not studied or investigated its inconveniences or defects.

[a] The debate, in the course of which this speech was delivered, related to the following provisions in the draft of a constitution reported to the convention by a committee appointed for the purpose.

"The citizens of the city of Philadelphia and of the several counties in this state, qualified to elect representatives, when assembled for that purpose, shall, if occasion require, at the same time, at the same places, and in the same manner, for every representative, elect two persons resident within their city or county respectively, as electors of the senator or senators of their district.

"Within   days after their election, the electors of each district shall meet together at some convenient place within the district, and elect the senator or senators for their district.

"No elector shall be chosen a senator.

"No person shall be chosen an elector, who shall not have resided in the district three years next before his election. And no person shall be chosen an elector, who is a member of the legislature, or who holds any office in the appointment of the executive department." *Ed*.

The very respectable senate of Maryland, chosen by electors, furnishes with letters of recommendation every institution, to which it bears even a distant resemblance. The moderation, the firmness, the wisdom, and the consistency, which have characterized the proceedings of that body, have been of signal benefit to the state, of whose government it forms a part; and have been the theme of just applause in her sister states. It is by no means surprising, that a favourable opinion has been entertained concerning the principles and manner of its constitution.

But now that the question relative to those points comes before us, in the discharge of our high trust, we must devest ourselves of every prepossession, which we may have hitherto indulged; and must scrutinize the subject closely, strictly, deeply, and minutely. It is incumbent upon us to weigh well, 1. Whether the qualities, that so deservedly appreciate the senate of Maryland, may not be secured to a senate, formed and organized upon very different and more eligible principles. 2. Whether the principles, upon which that senate has been formed and organized, are applicable to the plan laid before the convention.

It is admitted, on one side, that the electors should be chosen by the same persons, by whom it is contended, on the other side, that the senators should be chosen. The only question, then, is, whether an intermediate grade of persons, called electors, should be introduced between the senators and the people.

I beg leave to state to the house the light, in which this subject has appeared to me, on an examination which I may venture to style attentive; and to make some remarks, naturally resulting, in my opinion, from the views I have taken of it on different sides.

When I am called upon to appoint other persons to make laws for me, I do it because such an appointment is of absolute necessity; for the citizens of Pennsylvania can neither assemble nor deliberate together in one place. When I reflect, that the laws which are to be made may affect my own life, my own liberty, my own property, and the lives, liberties, properties, and prospects of others likewise, who are dearest to me, I consider the trust, which I place in those for whom I vote to be legislators, as the greatest that one man can, in the course of the business of life, repose in another. I know none, indeed, that can be greater, except that, with which the members of this convention are now honoured; and which happens not but once, and often not once, in the successive revolutions of numerous centuries. But I console myself, that the same trust, which is committed by me, is also committed by others, who are as deeply interested in its exercise as I am. I console myself further, that those, to whom this trust is committed, are the *immediate* choice of myself, and of those others equally interested with myself.

But, by the plan before you, I am now called upon to delegate this trust in a manner, and to transfer it to a distance, which I have never experienced before — I am called upon, not to appoint legislators of my own choice, but to impower others to appoint whomsoever they shall think proper, to be legislators over me, and over those nearest to me in the different relations of life — I am called upon to do this, not only for myself, but for thousands of my constituents, who have confided to me their interests and rights in this convention. — I am called upon to do this for my constituents, and for myself, for the avowed purpose of introducing a choice, different from that which they or I would make. I say *different;* because, if the people and the electors would choose the same senators, there cannot be even a shadow of pretence for acting by the nugatory intervention of electors. I am called upon to do this, not only for the purpose of introducing a choice of senators different from that which the people would make; but for the additional purpose of introducing a new state of things and relations hitherto unknown between the people and their legislators. On the principles of representation, as hitherto understood and practised, there was a trust, and one of the most intimate and important kind, between the people and their representatives, and a responsibility of the latter to the former. On the plan reported, that trust and that responsibility will certainly be weakened: it is doubtful whether they will not be wholly destroyed. Can a trust subsist without some mutual agreement or consent? Can responsibility, resulting from an election, operate in behalf of those who do not choose? Suppose one of the citizens, who chose an elector, who chose a senator, to expostulate with that senator concerning some part of his senatorial conduct; might not the senator retort upon him — Sir, I know not you in this business: I was not chosen a senator by you: I was chosen by ——. To them I am ready to account for what I have done. You chose them my electors: if any thing is amiss, you will please to look to them for satisfaction. For, give me leave to tell you, that I know not you nor the other people of your district in my conduct as a senator: neither you nor they chose me. The constitution, sir, supposes that neither they nor you would have chosen me, if you had been indulged with a choice; for the constitution supposes an election made by electors to be very different indeed from that which would be made by the people. — What answer could be made to this?

But if this must be styled a trust, it is certainly one of a new and of a very extraordinary nature. It may subsist not only without the will or knowledge of those from whom it originates; but, on the principles of this plan, it may subsist against their will declared in the most publick and explicit manner. Suppose a senator to behave altogether to the dissatisfaction of a district, for which he is appointed: suppose the people unanimously inclined to remove him at the next election. Can they do it? No.

Suppose them to give the most unequivocal instructions to the electors for this purpose: the electors may choose him, the instructions notwithstanding: and the senator may brave them and tell them that he will legislate for them, and make them feel all the effects of his legislative power, in spite of their unavailing efforts to the contrary.

Sir, I will consider well — I will ponder long — before I consent that legislators be introduced in a shape so very questionable. I am placed in a new situation. Permit me to view it again. I am called upon to transfer a right — the right of *immediate* representation in the legislature — a right which I have hitherto retained unalienated — a right which has never, heretofore, been transferred by the citizens of Pennsylvania. Certainly, sir, this new situation requires that I should make a solemn pause — look around me, and reflect what my constituents and I have been, and what we are likely to be.

Many honourable members of this convention are, I presume, in the same predicament with myself; both as it respects their constituents, and as it respects themselves. On every account, it is proper to weigh this subject well.

Those who advocate the plan of electors must do so, either to avoid inconveniences which cannot be avoided, or to obtain advantages which cannot be obtained, in an election by the people themselves. We are, therefore, naturally led to institute a comparison between the two modes of election; and to estimate and balance the qualities and consequences of each.

The subject is of high and extensive importance in the theory and practice of government; and well deserves a full, a patient, and a candid investigation.

The works of human invention are progressive; and frequently are not completed, till after a slow and lengthened series of gradual improvements, remotely distant from one another both in place and in time. To the theory and practice of government this observation is applicable with peculiar justness and peculiar force. In this science, few opportunities have been given to the human mind of indulging itself in easy and unrestrained investigation: still fewer opportunities have offered of verifying and correcting investigation by experiment. An age — a succession of ages elapses, before a system of jurisprudence rises from its first rude beginnings. When we have made a little progress, and look forward, a few eminences in prospect are fondly supposed the greatest elevation we shall be obliged to ascend. But these, once gained, disclose, behind them, new and superiour degrees of excellence yet unattained. In beginning and continuing the pursuit of those arduous paths, through which this science leads us, the tracts, which we explore, point to others, which yet remain to be explored.

If the *discoveries* in government are difficult and slow; how much more arduous must it be to attain, in practice, the advantage of those discoveries, after they have been made! Of some governments, the foundation has been laid in necessity; of others, in fraud; of others, in force; of how few, in deliberate and discerning choice! If, in their commencement, they have been so unpropitious to the principles of freedom, and to the means of happiness; shall we wonder that, in their progress, they have been equally unfavourable to advances in virtue and excellence?

Let us ransack the records of history: in all our researches, how few fair instances shall we be able to find, in which a government has been formed, whose end has been the happiness of those for whom it was designed? how few fair instances shall we be able to find, in which such a government has been administered with a steady direction towards that end?

To these considerations, we must add others, which show still further the numerous and strong obstacles, that lie in the way of improvement in jurisprudence. Government founded on improper principles, and directed to improper objects, has a powerful and pernicious bias both upon those who rule, and those who are ruled. Its bias upon the first will occasion no surprise: its bias upon the second, however surprising, is not, perhaps, less efficacious, whether we consider their sentiments or their conduct. Thus the principles of despotism become the principles of a whole nation, blinded and degraded by its destructive influence. Power, splendour, influence, prejudice, fashion, habit, pride, and meanness, are all arranged to countenance and support those principles.

When we revolve, when we compare, when we combine the remarks we have been now making; when we take a slight glance of others that might be offered; we shall be at no loss to account for the slow and small progress, that, after a long lapse of ages, has been made in the science and practice of government.

This progress has been peculiarly slow and small in the discovery and improvement of the interesting doctrines and rules of election and representation. If government, with regard to other subjects, may be said, as with propriety it has been said, to be still in its infancy; we may well consider it, with regard to this subject, as only in its childhood. And yet this is the subject, which must form the basis of every government, that is, at once, efficient, respectable, and free. The pyramid of government — and a republican government may well receive that beautiful and solid form — should be raised to a dignified altitude: but its foundations must, of consequence, be broad, and strong, and deep. The authority, the interests, and the affections of the people at large are the only basis, on which a superstructure, proposed to be at once durable and magnificent, can be rationally erected.

Representation is the chain of communication between the people, and those to whom they have committed the exercise of the powers of government. If the materials, which form this chain, are sound and strong; I shall not be very anxious about the degree to which they are polished. But, in order to impart the true republican lustre to freemen, I know no means more efficacious, than to invite and admit them to the rights of suffrage, and to enhance, as much as possible, the value of that right.

I well know how shamefully this right, all-important as it is, has been neglected — I well know how often we have seen the election ground, thinly frequented, or almost deserted, bear mournful testimony to the indolence or to the indifference of the electors. I well know by what frivolous causes they have sometimes been induced to forego the enjoyment of the noblest right of men. But we will indulge the fond conjecture, that this supineness has been owing neither to defect nor degeneracy in the minds and principles of our citizens, nor to ignorance or disregard of the exalted rank, to which, as citizens of a free commonwealth, they are entitled. It has been occasioned, we flatter ourselves, by the narrow point of view, in which the right of election, before the revolution, was considered; and by the few objects, to which the exercise of it was directed. Before that event, the doctrine and the exercise of authority by representation was confined in Pennsylvania, as in England, to one branch of one of the great powers, into which we have seen government divided: and over even that branch a double negative was held suspended by two powers, neither of them professing to derive their authority from the people. Our surprise will be diminished, and our reprehension will be softened, by reflecting, that, in this dependent situation, the ardour of citizenship was probably *damped* as well as confined. Habits, once formed and become familiar, are not soon or easily laid aside. Our customs do not always or immediately vary in proportion to the variation of their causes. Indifference to elections, once less important, has continued, though their importance has been amazingly increased. But this, we hope, will not be the case long. The magnitude of the right will, we trust, secure, in future, the merited attention to the exercise of it.

What is the right of suffrage, which we now display, to be viewed, admired, and enjoyed by our constituents? Is it to go to an obscure tavern in an obscure corner of an obscure district, and to vote, admidst the fumes of spiritous liquors, for a justice of the peace? There, indeed, no lesson would probably be learned, but that of low vice; no example would probably be shown, but that of illiberal cunning. Is it even to choose the members of one part of a legislature, the patriotick counsels and efforts of which part are liable, at every moment, to be controlled and frustrated by the negatives of other powers, independent of the authority, and indifferent, perhaps unfriendly, to the interests of the people? Here, indeed, there might be room for lessons of frigid caution, and timid prudence. It might not be thought advisable to elect a representative of bold, undissembled, and inflexible virtue: he might be obnoxious to his superiours in the other line; and, instead of averting, might provoke the exercise of their overruling power.

Of much higher import — of much more improving efficacy, is that right, which is now the object of our contemplation. It is a right to choose, in large and respectable assemblies, all the legislative, and many of the executive officers of the government; it is a right to choose those, who shall be invested with the authority and with the confidence of the people, and who may employ that authority and that confidence for the noblest interests of the commonwealth, without the apprehension of disappointment or control.

This, surely, must have a powerful tendency to open, to enlighten, to enlarge, and to exalt the mind. I cannot sufficiently express my own ideas of the dignity and value of this right. In real majesty, an independent and unbiassed elector stands superiour to princes, addressed by the proudest titles, attended by the most magnificent retinues, and decorated with the most splendid regalia. His sovereignty is original: theirs is only derivative.

The benign influence flowing from the possession and exercise of this right deserves to be fully and clearly pointed out. The man who enjoys the right of suffrage on the extensive scale which we have marked, will naturally turn his attention to the contemplation of publick men and publick measures. The inquiries he will make, the information he will receive, and his own reflections on both will afford a beneficial and amusing employment to his mind. I am far from insinuating that every citizen should be an enthusiast in politicks, or that the interests of himself, his family, and those who depend on him for their comfortable situation in life, should be absorbed in Quixote speculations about the management or the reformation of the state. But there is surely a golden mean in things; and there can be no real incompatibility between the discharge of one's publick and that of his private duty. Let private industry receive the warmest encouragement; for it is the basis of publick happiness. But must the bow of honest industry be always bent? At no moment shall a little relaxation be allowed? That relaxation, if properly directed, may prove to be instructive as well as agreeable. It may consist in reading a newspaper, or in conversing with a fellow citizen. May not the newspaper convey some interesting intelligence, or contain some useful essay? For all newspapers are not dedicated to the demon of slander. May not the conversation take a pleasing and an improving turn? Many hours, I believe, are every where spent in talking about the unimportant occurrences of the day or in the neighbourhood; and, perhaps, the frailties or the involuntary imperfections of a neighbour form too often one of the sweet but poisonous ingredients of the discourse. Would it be any great detriment to society or to individuals, if other characters, and with different views, were brought upon the carpet?

At every election, a number of important appointments must be made. To do this, is, indeed, the business of a day. But it ought to be the business of much more than a day to be prepared for doing it well. When a citizen elects to office — give me leave to repeat it — he performs an act of the first political consequence. He should be employed, on every convenient occasion, in making researches after proper persons for filling the different departments of power; in discussing, with his neighbours and fellow citizens, the qualities that should be possessed by those who fill the several offices; and in acquiring information, with the spirit of manly candour, concerning the manners, and history, and characters of those, who are likely to be candidates for the publick choice. A habit of conversing and reflecting on these subjects, and of governing his actions by the result of his deliberations, will form, in the mind of the citizen, a uniform, a strong, and a lively sensibility to the interests of his country. The same causes will produce a warm and an enlightened attachment to those, who are best fitted and best disposed to support and advance those interests.

By these means, and in this manner, pure and genuine patriotism — that kind, which consists in liberal investigation and disinterested conduct — is produced, cherished, and strengthened in the mind: by these means, and in this manner, the warm and generous emotion glows and is reflected from breast to breast.

Investigations of this nature would be useful and improving not to their authors only: they would be so to their objects likewise. The love of honest and well-earned fame is deeply rooted in honest and susceptible minds. Can there be a stronger incentive to the energy of this passion, than the hope of becoming the object of wellfounded and distinguishing applause? Can there be a more complete gratification of this passion, than the satisfaction of knowing that this applause is given — that it is given upon the most honourable principles, and acquired by the most honourable pursuits? To souls truly ingenuous, indiscriminate praise, misplaced praise, flattering praise, interested praise have no bewitching charms. But when publick approbation is the result of publick discernment, it must be highly pleasing to those who give, and to those who receive it.

Let us now review a little the steps we have trod: let us reconsider the ground we have passed over, and the observations we have made. Have I painted the rights of election in colours too flattering? — Have I placed their importance in a light too strong? — Have I described their influence in language, or in sentiments, that have been exaggerated? I presume that I have not.

If, then, the remarks which I have made, and the deductions which I have drawn, will bear — and I trust they will bear — the test of strict and sober scrutiny; what is the result necessarily flowing from the whole? It is undeniably this — that the right of suffrage, properly understood, properly valued, properly cultivated, and properly exercised, is a rich mine of intelligence and patriotism — that it is an abundant source of the most rational, the most improving, and the most endearing connexion among the citizens — and that it is a most powerful, and, at the same time, a most pleasing bond of union between the citizens, and those whom they select for the different offices and departments of government.

If these things are so; why should this right, so valuable and important, the cause of so many blessings, moral, intellectual, and political, be weakened — why should it be interrupted by the interjection of electors? Reasons irresistibly cogent will certainly be urged and supported, before such a measure will be adopted by the members of this convention.

It has been already mentioned, that those who advocate the plan of electors must do so, either to avoid inconveniences which cannot be avoided, or to obtain advantages which cannot be obtained, in an election by the people. What inconveniences will be avoided?

Will the meetings of the people be less frequent, less troublesome, or less expensive in choosing electors than in choosing senators? In respect both of frequency and of trouble they will be precisely the same. In respect of expense, the inconvenience will be increased by choosing electors; for it will be but reasonable that an allowance be made to them for their time, trouble, and their services. In these respects, therefore, no inconvenience will be avoided, but an inconvenience will be incurred, by choosing electors.

Will inconveniences respecting the objects of choice attend elections by the people, and be avoided in elections by electors? What are those inconveniences?

Will the choice of the people be less valid than the choice of electors? That will not be pretended, since the electors themselves will derive *all* their authority from the people.

Will the choice of the people be less honourable than the choice of electors? In republican governments, the people are the fountain of honour as well as of power.

Will the choice of the people be less disinterested than the choice of electors? Interest will probably be consulted in both choices: but, in the first, the interests of the individuals, added together, will form precisely the aggregate interest of the whole; whereas, in the last, the interests of the electors, added together, will form but a small part of the interests of the whole; and that small part may be altogether unattached, nay, it may be altogether repugnant, to the remainder.

Will the choice of the people be less impartial than the choice of electors? The answer to this question is determined by the answer to the last. An impartial choice, in the case before us, is a choice that embraces the interests of the whole; a partial choice is that which embraces the interests only of a part. A choice by the people is most likely to suit the first description: a choice by electors is most likely to suit the last.

Will the choice of the people be made with less solicitude and fewer precautions for their common advantage than the choice of electors? If every individual among the people attends to his own advantage; the common advantage, which is the joint result of the whole, will be provided for. But every elector may be very attentive to his own advantage; and yet the common advantage may be left wholly unprovided for.

Will the choice of the people be less wise than the choice of electors? We have already seen that it will not be less valid, nor less honourable, nor less disinterested, nor less impartial, nor less for the common advantage: having seen all this, we may pronounce the presumption to be violent, that it will not be less wise. Upon this presumption we shall leave the matter for the present.

Permit me to observe, in the mean time, that inconveniences unavoidable in elections by the people, but altogether foreign from elections by electors, ought to be shown clearly and undeniably on the other side.

The next inquiry is — what advantages can be obtained in elections by electors, that are unattainable in elections by the people.

This side of the inquiry is, in my view, very much anticipated by the discussion of the other side: indeed it appears to me wholly unproductive. To those who think and speak in favour of electors, it may disclose sources of abundant fertility: to their investigations and discoveries I cheerfully leave it; observing, under this head, that the advantages to be gained, as well as the inconveniences to be avoided, ought to be shown clearly and undeniably on the other side. For if, upon the whole, the balance shall hang in equilibrio; the predilection, for the strong reason already mentioned, will certainly be in favour of a choice by the people themselves, and not by electors.

This predilection ought to operate for another reason, which has not yet been mentioned. It will be cheerfully admitted, that all power is originally in the people: the consequence, unavoidable, is, that power ought to be exercised personally by the people, when this can be done without inconvenience and without disadvantage. In some of the small republicks of Greece, and in the first ages of the commonwealth of Rome, the people voted, even on the passing of laws, in their aggregate capacity. Among the ancient Germans this was also done upon great occasions. "De minoribus consultant principes," says Tacitus, in his masterly account of

Germany, "de majoribus omnes." * And from the practices of the ancient Germans, some of the finest maxims of modern government are drawn. If, therefore, no inconvenience will be avoided, and no advantage will be obtained by the plan of electors — and this is the case, so far as we have yet seen — that plan should not be substituted in the place of a choice of senators by the people themselves.

Were we to satisfy ourselves with this partial and incomplete consideration of the subject; I apprehend we should be extremely unwilling to transfer the choice of senators from the people to electors. But if we pursue the examination a little further, we shall find still stronger reasons for this reluctance: for we shall find, I believe, that, by such a transfer, instead of avoiding inconveniences and obtaining advantages, we shall sacrifice advantages for the acquisition of inconveniences.

The political connexion between the people and those whom they distinguish by elective offices, and the reciprocal sensations and engagements resulting from that connexion, I consider as most interesting in their nature, and most momentous in their consequences. This connexion should be as intimate as possible: if possible, it should be indissoluble. Confidence — mutual and endearing confidence — between those who impart power and those to whom power is imparted, is the brightest gem in the diadem of a republick. Let us sedulously avoid every danger of its being broken or lost.

Will there be the same generous emotions of confidence in the body of citizens towards the senators? — Will there be the same warm effusions of gratitude in the senators towards the body of the citizens, if the cold breath of electors is suffered to blow between them? Can the senator say to the people — you are my constituents; for you chose me? Can the people say to the senator — you are our trustee, for you are the object of our choice? Will not these relations, equally delightful and attractive on both sides, be greatly weakened — will not their influence be greatly diminished, by the interposition of electors?

But let us contemplate this subject in a still more serious and important point of view. The great desideratum in politicks is, to form a government, that will, at the same time, deserve the seemingly opposite epithets — efficient and free. I am sanguine enough to think that this can be done. But, I think, it can be done only by forming a popular government. To render government efficient, powers must be given liberally: to render it free as well as efficient, those powers must be drawn from the people, as directly and as immediately as possible. Every degree of removal is attended with a corresponding degree of danger. I know that removals, or

---

* [On matters of lesser importance, the chieftains make decisions; on those of greater weight, the whole people decides.]

at least one removal, is, in many instances, necessary in the executive and judicial departments. But is this a reason for multiplying or lengthening them without necessity? Is it a reason for introducing them into the legislative department, the most powerful, and, if ill constituted, the most dangerous, of all? No. But it is a strong reason for excluding them wherever they can be excluded; and for shortening them as much as possible wherever they necessarily take place. Corruption and putridity are more to be dreaded from the length, than from the strength, of the streams of authority.

On this great subject, I offer my sentiments, as it is my duty to do, without reserve. I think — that all the officers in the legislative department should be the immediate choice of the people — that only one removal should take place in the officers of the executive and judicial departments — and that, in this last department, a very important share of the business should be transacted by the people themselves.

These are, in a few words, the great outlines of the government, which I would choose. I fondly flatter myself that all the parts of it might be safely, compactly, and firmly knit together; and that the qualities of goodness, wisdom, and energy might animate, sustain, and pervade the whole.

And for what should we sacrifice all the valuable connexions, principles, and advantages, which have been mentioned? For electors? — Who are those electors to be? Logicians sometimes describe the subjects of their profound lucubrations negatively as well as positively. Let us borrow a hint from them, on this occasion. Who are those electors *not* to be? 1. They will be such as the people will think not the fittest to represent them in the most numerous branch of the legislature; for no representatives can be electors. 2. They will be such as the people will think not the fittest to be senators; for no elector can be a senator; and therefore the people will not choose those to be electors, whom they would wish to see in the senate. 3. They will be such as the governour *has* thought not the fittest for any office in the executive or judicial departments; for persons holding appointments in any of those departments cannot be electors. I was going to say, in the fourth place, that they will be such as will be thought not the fittest for any office under the executive department in future. But here, I find, I am mistaken. For they may hold offices the moment after their election of senators; and I will not assert it to be impossible, that they will acquire their qualifications for those offices by their conduct in that election.

Thus far we have pursued their negative descriptions. The task of expatiating on their positive qualities, I beg leave, for the present, to assign to those who must be supposed to understand them much better. For they must certainly know well the purifying virtues of those political alembicks, through which they wish to see our senators sublimated and refined.

Among the numerous good qualities of the electors, we hope, one will be — that they will be unsusceptible of intrigue or cabal among themselves. A second, we hope, will be — that they will be inaccessible to the impressions of intrigue and cabal from others. A third, we hope, will be — that as the people, by choosing them electors, have intimated decently that they think *them* not the fittest persons to be senators, *they* will cultivate the same decent reserve with regard to their brothers, their cousins, their other relations, their friends, their dependents, and their patrons.

VII

SPEECH DELIVERED, ON *19th JANUARY, 1790,*
IN THE CONVENTION OF PENNSYLVANIA

ASSEMBLED FOR THE PURPOSE OF REVIEWING, ALTERING, AND
AMENDING THE CONSTITUTION OF THE STATE;

ON A MOTION THAT

"NO MEMBER OF CONGRESS FROM THIS STATE, NOR ANY PERSON
HOLDING OR EXERCISING ANY OFFICE OF TRUST OR PROFIT
UNDER THE UNITED STATES, SHALL, AT THE SAME TIME,
HOLD AND EXERCISE ANY OFFICE WHATEVER
IN THIS STATE."

IT has frequently been my lot to plead the cause of others; sometimes of individuals, sometimes of publick bodies, oftener than once of the commonwealth of Pennsylvania. It is now my lot to be under the hard necessity of pleading my own. That commonwealth, whose cause I have pleaded — and pleaded successfully — that commonwealth, in whose service I have laboured faithfully — I defy even my enemies to refute the assertion — though, to myself, very unprofitably — that commonwealth, which I have served in times of safety and in times of danger, through good report, and through bad report — that commonwealth, sir, if the present motion shall be adopted, is about to strip me of the most valuable rights of citizenship. And this is to be done without any offence or cause of forfeiture on my part; unless to have been highly honoured by the president and senate of the United States is, in her consideration, now become a crime, and to have accepted of the high honour is, in her eye, become a cause of forfeiture.

Well, then, may I say, that I am now to plead my own cause. All the citizen is roused within me; and I dissemble neither my feelings nor my interest: for both my interest and my feelings as a citizen of Pennsylvania assure me, in a manner which I cannot mistake, but which, at the same time, I cannot express, that this cause is personally my own. As such, therefore, I shall openly and directly consider and plead it. I am afraid, however, that I shall acquit myself but awkwardly: the task is new and unfamiliar: the path before me I have not hitherto trod. But a ray of consolation darts upon me. Though the cause is personally, it is not exclusively my own. I plead the cause likewise of some of the most distinguished citizens of Pennsylvania: I plead what will soon be the cause of others of her citizens equally distinguished: I plead what will continue, in future ages, to be the cause of her best, and those who ought to be her most favoured sons: I plead, sir, the cause of Pennsylvania herself: for Pennsylvania herself will certainly suffer, if she shall be deprived of the services of such of her citizens, as shall be best qualified for serving her. To deprive her of the services of such citizens is the evident tendency, the evident object, and the evident principle of the present motion: for such will be the citizens selected for the offices of the United States.

But here, sir, I must beg not to be misunderstood. When I speak of the principle and object and tendency of the motion, I mean not to apply those expressions to the principles, the views, or the wishes of its honourable mover. Between the first and the last there may be, and, I think, there probably is, a very considerable difference. In suggesting this, I pay not, to his principles, a compliment at the expense of his understanding; for to the most enlightened mind it is no disparagement to suppose, that, at first sight, it does not perceive all the distant bearings and relations and dependencies, which a motion, especially one so extensive as this, may, on investigation, be found to have.

The motion is in these words: "No member of congress from this state, nor any person holding or exercising any office of trust or profit under the United States, shall, at the same time, hold and exercise any office whatever in this state." It embraces all this broad and comprehensive position — every person, who is employed or trusted by the United States, ought, for that reason, to be incapacitated from being employed or trusted by the commonwealth of Pennsylvania, one of those states who compose the union. This position, your adoption of the motion will establish in its fullest force and extent. It will become a part, not merely of the law, but of the constitution of the land; and will be a binding and perpetual rule for the future conduct of this commonwealth. This, sir, and nothing short of this, is the true and necessary import of the question before you.

It is not, that some offices under the United States may, in point of propriety, or in point of policy, in the nature of their exercise, or in the place where they are exercised, be inconsistent with some offices under Pennsylvania. This, I will readily admit, may be the case under those different governments. It has been admitted to be the case in an instance already agreed to without opposition — I mean that of the governour. This may often be the case with regard to different offices even under the same government. Of this there are many examples in the system before you. They have encountered no disapprobation from me or any other member.

Again: the position, in the motion before you, is not, that it would be inconsistent or improper for the same person to hold, in any case, more offices than one. No, sir: this motion may be adopted, and yet one person may have twenty different offices accumulated upon him under this very constitution. For the position is not, "that no person, holding any one office, shall, at the same time, hold any other office, under this state:" but the position is, "that every person, holding an office under the United States, should be excluded from every office whatsoever in this state." For this reason, sir, all the numerous observations, which we heard on Saturday, from the honourable mover, concerning the profuse and improvident donations of offices, which the people, in a fit of fondness, might heap on the head of a popular favourite, however they might suit other purposes, were evidently beside the purpose of the motion. The motion, though adopted, will not prevent, nor is it calculated to prevent, such thoughtless and injudicious accumulations.

I have always flattered myself, that the constitution of the United States would be a bond of union, and not a principle of inveterate alienage, far less of hostility, between the several states; certainly and more particularly, between each of them and the United States. "A more perfect union" is declared to be one end of that constitution. That constitution, I believe, was intended to be the centre of attraction for that "more perfect union." Shall we convert that constitution, as far as it can depend on Pennsylvania — fortunately for the union, we can convert it no farther — into a principle of repulsion? If that is the design of this committee; if that is an object, for the accomplishment of which our constituents sent us here; the motion before you is well fitted for fulfilling that design; it is well fitted for accomplishing that object. Under the operation of this motion, if the government of the United States shall hereafter distinguish a citizen of Pennsylvania with an "office of profit or trust;" that government must become, however reluctantly, the repulsive agent in destroying the better half of his right of citizenship; and, consequently, of diminishing, by the better half, his political connexion with this commonwealth.

This, sir, is no inflated or exaggerated representation of the matter: the account is strictly and severely true. The right of citizenship consists in these two things: 1. A right to elect. 2. A right to be elected into office. Of the two, the last is certainly not the least valuable or important. Of the last I shall be deprived by your adoption of the motion before you. I call for the principles and reasons of deprivation. I demand, sir — for I have a right to demand — from the justice of this committee, that those principles and reasons be clearly shown and incontestably proved, before the sentence of deprivation be passed against me. I think I heard, on Saturday, an opinion mentioned as being decidedly formed. I trust that the expression was used inadvertently: I trust that the honourable members of this committee will hear, and weigh, and consider, before they decide.

Believe me, sir, the principle, more than any foreseen consequence, of disfranchisement wounds and alarms me. We are told in history, that a person, whose inclination had never led him beyond the gates of Rome, sickened and died, when Augustus, in a wanton trick of his absolute power, confined him within those very limits, beyond which he had never previously wished to go. 'Tis one thing, sir, to be without an office: 'tis a very different thing to be disqualified from holding an office, and to wander about like a person attainted and cut off from the community. The first is often the effect of choice: the last never is; it is the result of dire necessity. The idea of disqualification is a most mortifying idea, when applied by one to himself: it is a most insulting idea, when applied to him by others. And can you think, sir, that I would wish to become or continue the constant mark of mortification or insult? No, sir; I can, at least, comfort myself, that I will not be reduced to this situation. The motion of the honourable gentleman is not armed — fortunately it cannot be armed — with the sting of the edict of Augustus: it may prompt me to go; but it cannot compel me to stay. I can cross the Delaware. In New Jersey, I shall be received as a citizen — a full citizen — of the state; and, at the same time, may hold a dignified and important office under the United States. What I say concerning New Jersey, I may say concerning New Hampshire, Massachusetts, Connecticut, New York, Delaware, Maryland, North Carolina, South Carolina, and Georgia. For none of those states, so far as I know or have been informed, view honourable employments under the national government through the inverted speculum of the motion, which presents them as causes of disqualification and disfranchisement. Nay, sir, I believe I can go to Rhode Island, and be received there as more than a half citizen, if I choose it; for I have not heard, that that state, antifederal as it is, has passed an act of incapacity against the officers of the United States.

But we are told, that the commonwealth of Virginia has observed a different conduct; and has exhibited an example, which we are now solicited to imitate. I wish, sir, to know if this favourite example forms a part of the constitution of Virginia. If it does not — and I presume it does not — I wish to see the law that has produced it: I wish to examine that law: I wish to know the reason of that law: I wish to know the time when, and the occasion on which, that law was made: I wish to know the temper and the *national* principles of the legislature, which made that law. I have been informed, how correctly I will not undertake to vouch, that an antifederal leader in Virginia, foiled by the convention of that commonwealth in his opposition to the national government, introduced into the legislature, and succeeded in fixing some stigma, as far as that legislature could fix a stigma, upon the federal characters of that state. Perhaps, sir, my information is correct; and this law may be the very thing. Perhaps, sir, it may have been the production of the convulsive throes of an antifederal fit. If so — and I think the conjecture a probable one — so soon as the fit shall be over — and, I hope, it will be over soon, if it is not over already — Virginia will remove its effects by considerately repealing the law, which it had precipitately occasioned.

But shall we, sir, suffer ourselves to become infected with the transient, though violent disorder of a neighbouring state? Shall we do more, sir? — shall we inoculate this disorder to become a perpetual and incurable poison in the very vitals of our constitution? I confess I did not expect to see the symptoms of this distemper reappear so soon in Pennsylvania, after all the successful efforts that have been made to expel them from her borders.

It seems that I ought to be incapacitated from enjoying the confidence of this state, while I hold an office under the United States. And yet I may hold *one* office in this state, and not be incapacitated from holding twenty or thirty more. And yet I may hold an office under New Jersey, and not be incapacitated. I may hold an office under *any* other, and even under *every* other state in the Union, and not be incapacitated. I may hold an office under France, under any other state in Europe, under any other state in the world, and not be incapacitated. I may have held an office under Great Britain, and, under that office, may have acted against the United States and against this state, during all the late war; I may still hold that very office, and not be incapacitated. But — the position occurs again — if I hold an office under the United States, I must be incapacitated from any trust under Pennsylvania.

Whence, sir? — in the name of wonder — whence this principle of hostility — this principle of hostility, operating solely and peculiarly — between this commonwealth and the United States? Let it be explained: let us know its origin: let us know its nature: let us know its extent: let us know its effects.

If this principle exists, and ought to be provided against; it is surprising that no such provision was made or recommended against it, by the general convention, formed of members from all the states in the Union — a convention, which, I believe, understood the interests of the Union and of all its parts. If it ought to be a part of our constitution that "no person, holding any office under the United States, shall, at the same time, hold any office in this state;" it ought to have been a part of the constitution of the United States, that "no person, holding any office under Pennsylvania, or any other state in the Union, shall, at the same time, hold any office in the national government." But no such art is to be found in that constitution. We may presume — I suggest it with deference — we may presume, that the whole knew the proper connexion between itself and its parts; and provided for the preservation, the strength, and the limits of that connexion, as well as *one* of the parts can know and provide for the preservation, the strength, and the limits of its connexion with the whole. But no such provision as this is made by those, who had the whole state of the Union before them: the inference is fair, that this provision is dictated, not by a general and comprehensive, but by a partial and contracted view of the subject.

Will the principle of this motion contribute to preserve or to strengthen the political connexion between the United States and the commonwealth of Pennsylvania? Will it not, on the other hand, contribute to weaken, to interrupt, or to dissolve it? The principle of this motion, sir, is a principle of political alienage: I go farther — it contains a declaration of political hostility by this commonwealth against the United States. It declares that this commonwealth ought not to trust or employ any person, whom the United States have thought worthy of trust or employment. On what foundation can such a declaration rest? It can have no reasonable foundation, unless the interests and views of the United States are, in their nature and tendency, hostile to the interests and views of this commonwealth. Let it be shown wherein this hostility of views and interests consists.

I have already admitted, that there are many instances, in which offices under different governments are incompatible in point of propriety, or in point of policy, in the nature of their exercise, or in the place where they are exercised. I have admitted also, that an accumulation of offices may be very improper under the same government. But it has appeared, that the principle, the tendency, and the object of this motion are not to prevent any incompatibilities or improprieties of these kinds.

On the other hand, there are many instances, in which different offices, not only under the same government, but even under different governments, may be held, not only with great propriety, but even with great advantage to the publick, by the same persons. Against the enjoyment of this publick advantage, the motion before you is levelled and directed.

And yet, sir, our own experience has attested its happy effects. During the late war, we reaped solid benefits from the exertions and talents of officers — in one instance, of a very distinguished officer — in the service of France. Would we have reaped those benefits, had France adopted, against the United States, the unfriendly principle, which is now recommended to a state, hitherto one of the most federal and one of the most affectionate in the Union? Suppose the sovereign of those officers to have declared to them in the spirit of this motion — "the moment you accept any office under the United States, you shall be disqualified, by that acceptance, from holding any office in my service," — what would have been the consequence? The United States would have been deprived of their military skill and assistance. But, happily for us, the king of France was not actuated by the spirit of this motion: shall I risk the expression, that he was more federal?

On how many sudden and unforeseen emergencies may the services of a stated officer of the United States be useful, perhaps, in the opinion of the publick, necessary for this commonwealth! On how many sudden and unforeseen emergencies may the services of a stated officer of this commonwealth be useful, perhaps, in the opinion of the publick, necessary for the United States? Why, in both cases, should the door of mutual, useful, necessary, and patriotick exertion be constitutionally shut? For this motion will operate both ways. If the officers of the United States are to be considered as aliens with regard to their capacity of holding offices under this commonwealth: the officers of this commonwealth must be considered as aliens with regard to their capacity of holding offices under the United States.

When I say, sir, that, in both instances, they must be considered as aliens; I use an expression much too soft: for under both constitutions — that of the United States and that which we propose — aliens may be employed in many offices. This motion, if adopted, will, therefore, introduce, between the United States, and this state, as to offices, more than a state of alienage. I was justified in saying, that this motion contained a principle and declaration of political hostility, as to offices, between this commonwealth and the United States. Before the sentence of disfranchisement from office in Pennsylvania be passed, by the adoption of this motion, against the officers of the United States; I again demand that it be clearly shown wherein the principle of political hostility between the two governments consists.

I think it has been suggested, that unless the principle of this motion be introduced into the constitution, the government of the United States may acquire, in Pennsylvania, an influence dangerous to her counsels, dangerous to her interests, and dangerous even to her existence. That government, it was supposed, might, by appointing to its offices the officers of this state, attach them to the measures, the interests, and the counsels of the United States, in opposition to the measures, the interests, and the counsels of Pennsylvania. Like the motion, this reasoning in support of it is founded on an implied principle of hostility between the two governments. Before the committee subscribe to the reasoning, they will require that the principle of hostility be shown.

But let us, for a moment, suppose it to exist: let us suppose that the measures, and interests, and counsels of the United States are in diametrical and inveterate opposition to those of Pennsylvania: let us suppose, that, in order to promote those adverse interests, to establish those adverse counsels, and to carry into effect those adverse measures, the president and senate of the United States should call to their aid, and associate in their designs, the officers of Pennsylvania; would it be politick or wise in Pennsylvania to cooperate, in the most effectual manner, with the president and senate for the accomplishment of their plans? Could she do this more effectually by any means, than by detaching from her all the officers of the state, whom the president and senate would wish to attach to them? Could she detach them from her more effectually by any means, than by disfranchising them from their offices, and by treating them as aliens, nay, worse than aliens? Could she do this more effectually by any means, than by cutting asunder the strongest ties of political connexion and political affection between her and them?

I believe, sir, you may hear, from some states, a series of reasoning, very opposite to that before mentioned: you may hear a train of reflection to the following purpose: What! shall we part with the interests, with the affections, and with the services of our citizens, because they are called into the service of the United States? No. Let us retain their interests; for their interests will be ours: let us retain their affections; for these, at least, may remain with us: let us retain their services, as far as they shall be compatible — and, in many instances, they will be compatible — with their superiour duty to the United States.

Whether this train of reflection and reasoning be just and strong, I shall not pretend to determine. I shall only observe, that, as far as I know, the conduct of every state in the union has been consonant to it, excepting only that of the commonwealth of Virginia — and shall I, after some time, be obliged to make the cruel addition — and excepting likewise that of the commonwealth of Pennsylvania?

'Tis possible, sir, though I will not allow it to be probable, that this cruel addition must be made. 'Tis possible, though, again, I will not allow it to be probable, that Pennsylvania may become as infamous for her antifederal, as she has hitherto been renowned for her federal principles. 'Tis possible, though, still, I will not allow it to be probable, that she may hereafter be as much dishonoured by the littleness, as she has heretofore been admired for the liberality, of her politicks. Her counsels may take an inverted and diminishing turn. Those, sir, who cannot shine in a spacious sphere, will wish to draw some notice in a contracted one. Those, who cannot be distinguished by acting a part in an enlarged system, will endeavour to distinguish themselves by acting as the little but principal puppets in a narrow and separated scene. Into such hands, sir, it is possible —

though I once more enter my protest against the probability of the event, — that Pennsylvania, for her sins, may fall.

If this very improbable, but very possible event should take place; then, indeed, the cruel addition, which I have already mentioned, must be made. Yet even then, this cruel circumstance would carry with it, in some degree, its own alleviation. In such a circumstance, the pangs of separation from Pennsylvania would become less severe. Even in such a circumstance, I hope one consolation might be constitutionally allowed me. On my way to the government of the United States, I might turn and look back from the opposite shore of the Delaware; and though Pennsylvania should reject my faithful services, she might permit me, with a fluttering heart and faultering tongue, to wish her well.

But, sir, I will not pursue the consideration of an event so irreconcilable with the present genius and principles of Pennsylvania. Is *she* jealous, because her sons are received into the arms of the United States? No, sir. Was she to open her lips upon this occasion, we should hear the following, or some such as the following, accents: "Though I cheerfully resign you to the service of the Union, in which my own service is, to many important purposes, included; yet I renounce not your affections; nor do I abdicate my well founded claim to your duty. You may still be of use to me; and I retain my right to the exertions of your usefulness, whenever I shall call upon you on a proper occasion. In the mean time, employ your utmost efforts for the interest of the United States: by doing this, you will essentially promote mine; and you will be likewise better prepared, and better disposed for serving me, whenever I shall particularly require your service." Such would be the language, such would be the sentiments, of our venerable political parent. Such, sir, without personification, and without an allegory, I believe to be literally and strictly the language and sentiments of a great majority of the people of this commonwealth. This language and these sentiments are in direct contradiction to the language and principles of the motion before you. To which will this committee pay the greatest regard?

VIII

A CHARGE DELIVERED TO THE GRAND JURY IN THE CIRCUIT COURT OF THE UNITED STATES, FOR THE DISTRICT OF VIRGINIA

IN MAY, 1791

GENTLEMEN of the grand jury, to prevent crimes is the noblest end and aim of criminal jurisprudence. To punish them is one of the means necessary for the accomplishment of this noble end and aim. The The impunity of an offender encourages him to repeat his offences. The witnesses of his impunity are tempted to become his disciples in his guilt. These considerations form the strongest — some view them as the sole argument for the infliction of punishments by human laws.

There are, in punishments, three qualities, which render them the fit preventives of crimes. The first is their moderation. The second is their speediness. The third is their certainty.

We are told by some writers, that the number of crimes is unquestionably diminished by the severity of punishments. If we inspect the greatest part of the criminal codes; their unwieldy bulk and their ensanguined hue will force us to acknowledge, that this opinion may plead, in its favour, a very high antiquity, and a very extensive reception. On accurate and unbiassed examination, however, it will appear to be an opinion unfounded and pernicious, inconsistent with the principles of our nature, and, by a necessary consequence, with those of wise and good government.

So far as any sentiment of generous sympathy is suffered, by a merciless code, to remain among the citizens, their abhorrence of crimes is, by the barbarous exhibitions of human agony, sunk in their commiseration of criminals. These barbarous exhibitions are productive of another bad effect — a latent and gradual, but a powerful, because a natural, aversion to the laws. Can laws, which are a natural and a just object of aversion, receive a cheerful obedience, or secure a regular and uniform execution? The expectation is forbidden by some of the strongest principles in the human frame. Such laws, while they excite the compassion of society for those who suffer, rouse its indignation against those who are active in the steps preparatory to their sufferings.

We may easily conjecture the result of those combined emotions, operating vigorously in concert. The criminal will, probably, be dismissed without prosecution by those whom he has injured. If prosecuted and tried, the jury will probably find, or think they find, some decent ground, on which they may be justified, or at least excused, in giving a verdict of acquittal. If convicted, the judges will, with avidity, receive and support every, the nicest exception to the proceedings against him; and, if all other things should fail, will have recourse to the last expedient within their reach for exempting him from rigorous punishment — that of recommending him to the mercy of the pardoning power. In this manner, the acerbity of punishment deadens the execution of the law.

The criminal, pardoned, repeats the crime, under the expectation that the impunity also will be repeated. The habits of vice and depravity are gradually formed within him. Those habits acquire, by exercise, continued accessions of strength and inveteracy. In the progress of his career, he is led to engage in some desperate attempt. From one desperate attempt he boldly proceeds to another, till, at last, he necessarily becomes the victim of that preposterous rigour, which repeated impunity had taught him to despise, because it had persuaded him that he might always escape.

When, on the other hand, punishments are moderate and mild, every one will, from a sense of interest and of duty, take his proper part in detecting, in exposing, in trying, and in passing sentence on crimes. The consequence will be, that criminals will seldom elude the vigilance, or baffle the energy, of publick justice.

True it is, that, on some emergencies, excesses of a temporary nature may receive a sudden check from rigorous penalties: but their continuance and their frequency introduce and diffuse a hardened insensibility among the citizens; and this insensibility, in its turn, gives occasion or pretence to the farther extension and multiplication of those penalties. Thus one degree of severity opens and smooths the way for another, till, at length, under the specious appearance of necessary justice, a system of cruelty is established by law.

Such a system is calculated to eradicate all the manly sentiments of the soul, and to substitute, in their place, dispositions of the most depraved and degrading kind. It is the parent of *pusillanimity*. A nation broke to cruel punishments becomes dastardly and contemptible. For, in nations, as well as individuals, cruelty is always attended by cowardice. It is the parent of *slavery*. In every government, we find the genius of freedom depressed in proportion to the sanguinary spirit of the laws. It is hostile to the prosperity of nations, as well as to the dignity and virtue of men.

The laws, which Draco framed for Athens, are said emphatically to have been written in blood. What did they produce? An aggravation of those very calamities, which they were intended to remove. A scene of the greatest and most complicated distress was accordingly exhibited by the miserable Athenians, till they found relief in the wisdom and moderation of Solon. It is a standing observation in China — and China has enjoyed a very long experience — that in proportion as the punishments of criminals are increased, the empire approaches to a new revolution. The Porcian law provided, that no citizen of Rome should be exposed to a sentence of death. Under the Porcian law, the commonwealth grew and flourished. Severe punishments were established by the emperours. Under the emperours, Rome declined and fell.

The principles both of utility and of justice require, that the commission of a crime should be followed by a speedy infliction of its punishment.

The association of ideas has vast power over the sentiments, the passions, and the conduct of men. When a penalty marches close in the rear of the offence, against which it is denounced; an association, strong and striking, is produced between them: and they are viewed in the inseparable relation of cause and effect. When, on the contrary, the punishment is procrastinated to a remote period; this connexion is considered as weak and precarious; and the execution of the law is beheld and suffered as a detached instance of severity, warranted by no cogent reason, and springing from no laudable motive.

It is just, as well as useful, that the punishment should be inflicted soon after the commission of the crime. It should never be forgotten, that imprisonment, though often necessary for the safe custody of the person accused, is, nevertheless, in itself, a punishment — a punishment galling to some of the finest feelings of the heart — a punishment too, which, since it precedes conviction, may be as undeserved as it is distressing. But imprisonment is not the only penalty, which an accused person undergoes before his trial. He undergoes also the corroding torment of suspense — the keenest agony, perhaps, which falls to the lot of suffering humanity. This agony is by no means to be estimated by the real probability or danger of conviction: it bears a compound proportion to the delicacy of sentiment and the strength of imagination possessed by him, who is doomed to become its prey.

These observations show, that those accused of crimes should be speedily tried, and that those convicted of them should be speedily punished. But with regard to this, as with regard to almost every other subject, there is an extreme on one hand as well as on the other; and the extremes on each hand should be avoided with equal care. In some cases, at some times, and under some circumstances, a delay of the trial and of the punishment, instead of being hurtful or pernicious, may, in the highest degree, be salutary and beneficial, both to the publick, and to him who is accused or convicted.

Prejudices may naturally arise, or may be artfully fomented, against the crime, or against the man who is charged with having committed it. A delay should be allowed, that those prejudices may subside, and that neither jurors nor judges may, at the trial, act under the fascinating impression of sentiments conceived before the evidence is heard, instead of the calm influence of those which should be only its impartial and deliberate result. A sufficient time should be given to prepare the prosecution on the part of the state, and the defence of it on the part of the prisoner. This time must vary according to different persons, different crimes, and different situations.

After conviction, the punishment assigned to an inferiour offence should be inflicted with much expedition. This will strengthen the useful association between them; one appearing as the immediate and unavoidable consequence of the other. When a sentence of death is pronounced, such an interval should be permitted to elapse before its execution as will render the language of political expediency consonant to the language of religion.

Under these qualifications, the speedy punishment of crimes should form a part in every system of criminal jurisprudence.

But the certainty of punishments is that quality, which is of the greatest importance in order to constitute them fit preventives of crimes. This quality is, in its operation, most merciful as well as most powerful. When a criminal determines on the commission of a crime, he is not so much influenced by the lenity of the punishment, as by the expectation that, in some way or other, he may be fortunate enough to avoid it. This is particularly the case with him, when this expectation is cherished by examples or by experience of impunity. It was the saying of Solon, that he had completed his system of laws by the combined energy of justice and strength. By this expression he meant to denote, that laws, of themselves, would be of very little service, unless they were enforced by a faithful and an effectual execution of them. The strict execution of every *criminal* law is the dictate of humanity as well as of wisdom.

This strict execution is greatly promoted by accuracy in the publick police, by vigilance and activity in the ministerial officers of justice, by a prompt and regular communication of intelligence, and by a proper distribution of rewards for the discovery and apprehension of criminals.

Among all the plans and establishments, however, which have been devised for securing the wise and uniform execution of the criminal laws, the institution of grand juries holds the most distinguished place. This institution is, at least in the present times, the peculiar boast of the common law. The era of its commencement, and the particulars attending its gradual progress and improvement, are concealed behind the thick veil of a very remote antiquity. But one thing concerning it is certain. In the annals of the world, there is not found another institution so well adapted for avoiding all the inconveniences and abuses, which would otherwise arise from malice, from rigour, from negligence, or from partiality in the prosecution of crimes.

Among the Romans, any one of the citizens, as well as the person more immediately injured, might prosecute a publick offence. This practice produced mischiefs very great, and of very opposite kinds. Prosecutions were conducted, on some occasions, from motives of rancour and revenge. On other occasions, they were undertaken by a friend, perhaps a confederate of the criminal, with a view to ensure his impunity.

In several of the *feudal* nations, the judge himself was originally the prosecutor. The gross impropriety of such a regulation appears at the first view. The prosecutor is a party: can the same person be both a party and a judge? To remove the grievances, to which this regulation gave birth, a publick prosecutor was appointed to manage the judicial business of the crown, or of the community, before the proper tribunals.

But that crimes may be prosecuted duly and regularly, it is necessary that impartial and authentick information of their existence should be obtained. To furnish such information is the great object of the institution of grand juries.

Sometimes the grand jury bring forward accusations of their own proper motion: sometimes they proceed upon particular charges formally laid before them by the publick prosecutor. These two modes are distinguished by the well known appellations of *presentment* and *indictment*. In both, it is the right, and it is the duty of a grand jury, to inquire diligently, and to present truly.

It is your immediate business, gentlemen, to make inquiries and give official information concerning such crimes and offences as may have been committed against the constitution and laws of the United States, and are cognizable by this circuit court held for the district of Virginia in the middle circuit. To assist you in those inquiries, I shall describe to you the jurisdiction, which, in criminal matters, is vested in the circuit courts; and I shall give you a very plain and concise account of the crimes and offences known to the constitution and laws of the United States, and of the punishments denounced against those crimes and offences.

The circuit courts have *exclusive* jurisdiction of all crimes and offences, which are cognizable under the authority of the United States, except where it is or shall be provided otherwise by law. They have also *concurrent* jurisdiction with the district courts, of the crimes and offences, which are cognizable in those courts.[a] The crimes and offences, of which the district courts have jurisdiction, and of which, consequently, the circuit courts have *concurrent* jurisdiction, are all such as are cognizable under the authority of the United States, provided they be committed within the respective districts, or on the high seas; and provided they be those on which no other punishment than a fine not exceeding one hundred dollars, imprisonment not exceeding six months, or whipping not exceeding thirty stripes is to be inflicted.[b]

Treason generally occupies the first place in the long catalogue of crimes. On this subject, so interesting to the publick and to the citizens, a very important improvement has been ingrafted by the constitution of the United States.

If the description of treason be vague and indeterminate under any government; this alone will be a sufficient cause why that government should degenerate into tyranny. If the denomination and the penalties of treason be communicated to offences of a different and inferiour kind; the horrour, which would otherwise attend this complicated crime, is weakened by the association with things, to which, in truth, it has neither relation nor resemblance.

In the reign of Henry the eighth, a law was made in England by which any one, who predicted the death of the king, was declared guilty of treason. Arbitrary power, on some occasions, recoils upon those who exert it. When this capricious and tyrannical prince lay on his death bed, his physicians would not inform him of his danger, because they would not incur the penalties of his law. We are told by the English parliament itself, that, at another period, so many "pains of treason were ordained by statute, that no man knew how to behave himself, to do, speak, or say, for doubt of such pains."

Under our national government, we have not only a legal, but a constitutional security against arbitrary and constructive treasons.

1. Under that government, treason against the United States can be committed *only* by levying war against them, or by adhering to their enemies, giving them aid and comfort.[c]

2. Misprision of treason consists in knowing the commission of treason, and not disclosing it, as soon as may be, to the president or some one of the judges of the United States, or to the first executive magistrate or some one of the judges or justices of a particular state.[d]

Other crimes and offences against the United States may be comprised under the following enumeration. — 3. Wilful murder, committed in any place under the exclusive jurisdiction of the United States,[e] or upon the high

[a] Laws U.S. Cong. 1. sess. 1. c. 20. s. 11.　[b] Laws U.S. Con. 1. sess. 1. c. 20. s. 9.
[c] Con. U.S. art. 3. s. 3.　[d] Laws U.S. Con. 1. sess. 2. c. 9. s. 2.
[e] Laws U.S. con. 1. sess. 2. c. 9. s. 3.

seas, or in any river, haven, basin or bay not within the jurisdiction of any particular state.[f] 4. Manslaughter committed in any place under the exclusive jurisdiction of the United States,[g] or upon the high seas.[h] 5. Robbery committed upon the high seas, or in any river, haven or bay not within the jurisdiction of any particular state.[i] 6. The piratical and felonious running away with any vessel, or with any goods to the value of fifty dollars, or yielding up such vessel voluntarily to any pirate, by any captain or mariner of such vessel.[j] 7. The laying of violent hands, by a seaman, upon his commander, in order to hinder his fighting in defence of his ship or goods committed to his trust.[k] 8. The making of a revolt in a ship by any seaman.[l] 9. Piracy or robbery (as specified in the law) or any act of hostility against the United States or a citizen thereof, committed by any citizen upon the high seas, on pretence of authority from any person, or under colour of a commission from a foreign prince or state.[m] 10. Confederacy with pirates.[n] 11. The false making, altering, forging, or counterfeiting of any certificate, indent, or other publick security of the United States.[o] 12. The causing or procuring of any certificate, indent, or other publick security of the United States to be falsely made, altered, forged, or counterfeited.[p] 13. Acting or assisting willingly in the false making, altering, forging, or counterfeiting of any such certificate, indent, or other publick security.[q] 14. The uttering, putting off, or offering, in payment or for sale, of any such false, forged, altered, or counterfeited certificate, indent, or other publick security, with intention to defraud any person, and with knowledge that the same is false, altered, forged, or counterfeited.[r] 15. The causing of any such false, forged, altered, or counterfeited certificate, indent, or other publick security to be uttered, put off, or offered, in payment or for sale, with the knowledge and intention already mentioned.[s] 16. The setting at liberty by force, and the rescuing of any person, convicted of a capital crime, or, before conviction, committed for a capital crime, or committed for or convicted of any other offence.[t] 17. Misprision of felony, which consists in knowing the commission of wilful murder or other felony upon the high seas, or within any fort, arsenal, dock yard, magazine, or other place or district of country under the sole and exclusive jurisdiction of the United States, and not disclosing it as soon as may be to some one of the judges or other person in civil or military authority under the United States.[u] 18. The cutting off of the ear, the cutting out or disabling of the tongue, the putting out of an eye, the slitting of the nose, the cutting off of the nose or a lip, the cutting off or disabling of any limb or member of any person, unlaw-

[f] Id. s. 8.   [g] Id. s. 7.   [h] Id. s. 12.   [i] Id. s. 8.   [j] Id. ibid.
[k] Laws U.S. con. 1. sess. 2. c. 9. s. 8.   [l] Id. ibid.   [m] Id. s. 9.   [n] Id. s. 12.
[o] Id. s. 14.   [p] Id. ibid.   [q] Id. ibid.   [r] Id. ibid.   [s] Id. ibid.
[t] Id. s. 23.   [u] Laws U.S. con. 1. sess. 2. c. 9. s. 6.

fully, on purpose and of malice aforethought, and with intention, in so doing, to maim or disfigure such person: provided these crimes be committed in any place under the exclusive jurisdiction of the United States, or upon the high seas, in any vessel belonging to the United States or to any citizen of the United States.[v] 19. Perjury committed wilfully and corruptly on oath or affirmation in any suit or matter before any court, or in any deposition taken pursuant to a law, of the United States.[w] 20. The procuring of any person to commit corrupt and wilful perjury in any of the cases just mentioned.[x] 21. The giving, directly or indirectly, of any sum of money, or any other bribe, present, or reward, or any promise, contract, obligation, or security for the payment or delivery of any money, present, or reward, or any other thing, to procure the opinion, judgment, or decree of any judge of the United States in any suit or matter depending before him.[y] 22. The accepting by any judge of any such sum of money, bribe, present, reward, promise, contract, obligation, or security.[z] 23. Oppression or extortion by any supervisor or officer of inspection, in the execution of his office.[a] 24. The landing, in any place within the limits of the United States, of goods entered for exportation, with a view to draw back the duties.[b] 25. The resisting or impeding of any officer of the customs, or any person assisting him, in the execution of his duty.[c] 26. The resisting or opposing, knowingly and wilfully, of any officer of the United States in serving or attempting to serve process of any court of the United States: and the assaulting, beating, or wounding of any officer, or other person duly authorized, in serving or attempting to serve such process.[d] 27. The felonious stealing, taking away, altering, falsifying, or otherwise avoiding of any record, writ, process, or other proceeding in any court of the United States, by means whereof any judgment shall not take effect, or shall be reversed or made void.[e] 28. The acknowledging or procuring to be acknowledged, in any court of the United States, of any recognizance, bail, or judgment, in the name of any person not privy or consenting to it. There is an exception with regard to attornies duly admitted.[f] 29. Taking and carrying away, with an intent to steal or purloin the personal goods of another, upon the high seas, or in any place within the exclusive jurisdiction of the United States.[g] 30. The embezzling, purloining, or conveying away of any victuals provided for any soldiers, gunners, marines, or pioneers, or of any arms, ordnance, munition, shot, powder, or habiliments of war, belonging to the United States, by any person having the charge or custody thereof; provided such embezzling, purloining, or carrying away

---

[v] Id. s. 13.   [w] Id. s. 18.   [x] Id. ib.   [y] Id. s. 21.

[z] Laws U.S. con. 1. sess. 2. c. 9. s. 21.   [a] Id. sess. 3. c. 15. s. 39.

[b] Id. sess. 2. c. 35. s. 59.   [c] Id. sess. 2. c. 35. s. 50.   [d] Id. sess. 2. c. 9. s. 22.

[e] Id. sess. 2. c. 9. s. 15.   [f] Id. ibid.   [g] Id. sess. 2. c. 9. s. 16.

be for lucre, or willingly, advisedly and of purpose to impede the service of the United States.[h] 31. The suing forth, or prosecuting, or executing of any writ or process, by which the person of any publick foreign minister, received as such by the president of the United States, or any domestick or domestick servant of any such minister, may be arrested or imprisoned, or his goods seized.[i] 32. The violation of any safe conduct or passport duly obtained under the authority of the United States.[j] 33. The assaulting, striking, wounding, imprisoning, or, in any other manner, infracting the laws of nations by offering violence to the person of a publick minister.[k]

In the foregoing catalogue, murder, manslaughter, robbery, piracy, forgery, perjury, bribery, and extortion are mentioned as crimes and offences; but they are neither defined nor described. For this reason, we must refer to some *preexisting* law for their definition or description. To what preexisting law should this reference be made?

This is a question of immense importance and extent. It must receive an answer; but I cannot, in this address, assign my reasons for the answer which I am to give — The reference should be made to the *common law*.

To the common law, then, let us resort for the definition or description of the crimes and offences, which, in the laws of the United States, have been named, but have not been described or defined. You will, in this manner, gentlemen, be furnished with a legal standard, by the judicious application of which you may ascertain, with precision, the true nature and qualities of such facts and transactions as shall become the objects of your consideration and research.

In our law books, murder is thus described: it is when a person, of sound memory and of the age of discretion, unlawfully killeth any reasonable creature with malice aforethought, express or implied. Manslaughter is described as — the unlawful killing of another, without malice, either express or implied. The distinction strongly marked between murder and manslaughter is, that the former is committed with, the latter, without malice aforethought. It is essential, therefore, to know clearly and accurately the true and legal import of this characteristick distinction.

There is a very considerable difference between that sense, which is conveyed by the expression, malice, in common language, and that, to which the term is appropriated by the law. In common language, it is most frequently used to denote a sentiment or passion of strong malevolence to a particular person; or a settled anger and desire of revenge in one person against another. In law, it means the dictate of a wicked and

[h] Laws U.S. con. 1. sess. 2. c. 9. s. 16. [i] Id. s. 25. 26. [j] Id. s. 28.
[k] Id. ibid.

malignant heart; of a depraved, perverse, and incorrigible disposition. Agreeably to this last meaning, many of the cases, which are arranged under the head of implied malice, will be found to turn upon this single point; that the fact has been attended with such circumstances — particularly the circumstances of deliberation and cruelty concurring — as betray the plain indications and genuine symptoms of a mind grievously depraved, and acting from motives highly criminal; of a heart regardless of social duty, and fatally bent upon mischief. This is the true notion, of *malice* in the *legal* sense of the word. The mischievous and vindictive spirit denoted by it must always be collected and inferred from the circumstances of the transaction. On the circumstances of the transaction, the closest attention should, for this reason, be bestowed. Every circumstance may weigh something in the scale of justice.

Robbery is a felonious and violent taking, from the person of another, of money or goods to any value, putting him in fear. From this definition it appears, that to constitute a robbery, the three following ingredients are indispensable. 1. A felonious intention, or *animus furandi.* 2. Some degree of violence and putting in fear. 3. A taking from the *person* of another. Upon each of these three points there is much learned disquisition in the books of the law.

Piracy is robbery and depredation upon the high seas. The word *pirate*, says my Lord Coke,[1] in Latin *pirata*, is derived from the Greek word πειρατης, which is again fetched from πειραι *a transeundo mari*, or roving upon the sea; and, therefore, in English, a pirate is called a *rover* or *robber* upon the sea.

Piracy is a crime against the universal law of society: a pirate is *hostis humani generis*, an enemy of the whole human race. By declaring war against all mankind, he has laid all mankind under the necessity of declaring war against him. He has renounced the benefits and protection of government and society: he has abandoned himself to a savage state of nature. The consequence is, that, by the laws of selfdefence, every community has a right to inflict upon him that punishment, which, in a state of nature, every individual would be entitled to inflict for any invasion of his person or personal property.

"If any *person*," says a law of the United States, "shall commit, upon the high seas, or in any river, haven, basin, or bay, out of the jurisdiction of any particular state, *murder*, or *robbery*, or *any other* offence, which, if committed within the *body of a county*, would, by the laws of the United States, be punishable with death; every such offender shall be deemed, taken, and adjudged to be a *pirate and felon*, and being thereof convicted, shall suffer death." [m]

[1] 3. Ins. 113.   [m] Laws U.S. 1. con. 2. sess. c. 9. s. 8.

Placed in the high and responsible office of a judge of the United States, I feel myself under an official obligation to state some doubts, which arise in my mind upon this part of the law. Impressed, as I ought to be, both as a citizen and a judge, with the strongest regard for the legislative authority of the United States, I propose those doubts most respectfully, and with the greatest degree of diffidence.

Piracy, as we have seen, is a crime against the universal law of society. By that law, it may be punished by every community. But the description of piracy, according to *that* law, is a *robbery* and *depredation* on the high seas. Is a *murder*, committed upon the high seas, a *piracy* within the description of that law? "If a pirate, at sea,[n] assault a ship, but, by force, is prevented entering her; and, in the *attempt*, the pirate *kill* a person in the other ship; they are all principals in such a *murder*, if the common law have jurisdiction of the offence; but by the law *maritime*, if the parties be known, they *only* who gave the wound shall be *principals*, and the rest, *accessories*." From this authority and the foregoing description of piracy, taken jointly into our consideration, we might, perhaps, be naturally led to infer, 1. That a murder perpetrated in the *attempt* to commit a piracy, is not a piracy. 2. That *this* crime perpetrated in *such* an attempt, is, by the *maritime law* to be tried and punished as a *murder*, in which those, who *all* attempted the *piracy*, shall be considered as criminal in *different* degrees, according to the part, which they *severally* acted with regard to the *homicide*.

The maritime law is not the law of any particular country: it is the general law of nations. "Non erit alia lex Romæ, alia Athenis; alia nunc, alia posthac; sed et apud omnes gentes et omni tempore una eademque lex obtinebit." [o]

The law of nations has its foundation in the principles of natural law, applied to states; and in voluntary institutions, arising from custom or convention. This law is universal in its authority over the civilized part of the world; and is supported by the consideration of its general utility, as well as that of its obligatory force. This universal system has always been most liberally recognized in that country, from which we derive the boasted inheritance of the common law. According to the clear opinion declared by the great *Lord Chancellor Talbot*, the law of nations is, in *its full extent*, a part of the law of England.[p]

True it is, that, so far as the law of nations is *voluntary* or *positive*, it may be altered by the municipal legislature of any state, in cases affecting *only* its own citizens. True it is also, that, by a treaty, the voluntary or positive law of nations may be altered so far as the alteration shall affect *only* the contracting parties. But equally true it is, that

[n] Molloy. c. 4. s. 13.   [o] 2. Burr. 887 [ante, p. 279, note m].   [p] 2. Burr. 1481.

no state or states can, by treaties or municipal laws, alter or abrogate the law of nations any farther. This they can no more do, than a citizen can, by his single determination, or two citizens can, by a private contract between them, alter or abrogate the laws of the community, in which they reside.

Now the doubts, to which I have alluded, appear directly before us. Is a *person, not* a citizen of the United States, who shall commit a murder upon the high seas, liable, *under this law,* to be deemed, taken and adjudged to be a *pirate* and felon, and, as *such,* to suffer death? This question may be divided into two subordinate ones. 1. Was it the intention of the legislature, that this law should extend, in its operation, to persons not citizens of the United States? In the very next section, the phrase is altered, and instead of saying, if any *person* shall commit, it is said, if any *citizen* shall commit any piracy, &c. Shall the construction be, that the legislature mean the same thing, when they use expressions so very different? 2. On the supposition, that the law was designed to extend, in its operation, to persons not citizens of the United States; can this design be carried into effect, consistently with the predominant authority of the law of nations, and of the universal law of society?

The case may very probably happen, and come before a grand jury for their official investigation. It was proper to suggest my doubts concerning it. I hope I have suggested them in the manner which I proposed to myself.

I return to the definitions and descriptions given, by the common law, of the crimes and offences mentioned, but not described or defined, in the laws of the United States.

To forge, says my Lord Coke, is metaphorically taken from the smith, who beateth upon his anvil, and forgeth what fashion or shape he will. The offence is called *crimen falsi;* the crime of falsehood; and the offender, *falsarius,* a falsifier. And this is properly taken when the act is done in the name of another person.[q] With regard, however, to this last part of the description of forgery, it has been since adjudged repeatedly and very solemnly to be too narrow. It expresses, indeed, the most obvious meaning of the word, and comprehends that species of forgery which is most commonly practised; but there are other species, which will not come within the letter of that description. An alteration in the name or quantity of land conveyed, or in the sum of money secured, is of this kind, and comes within the legal notion of forgery.

Wilful and corrupt perjury is a crime committed, when a lawful oath is administered, in some judicial proceeding, by one who has authority, to a person who swears absolutely and falsely, in a matter material to the issue or cause in question.

---

[q] 3. Ins. 169.

"An oath," says my Lord Coke, "is so sacred, and so deeply concerns the consciences of men, that it cannot be administered *to* any one, unless it be allowed by the common law, or by act of parliament; nor *by* any one, who has not authority by common law, or by act of parliament: neither can any oath, allowed by the common law, or by act of parliament, be altered, unless by act of parliament." [r] For these reasons, it is much to be doubted whether any magistrate is justifiable in administering voluntary affidavits unsupported by the authority of law. It is more than possible, that, by such idle oaths, a man may frequently incur the guilt, though he evade the temporal penalties of perjury.

It is a part of the foregoing definition of perjury, that it must be when the person swears *absolutely*. In addition to this, it has been said, that the oath must be *direct*, and not, as the deponent thinks, or remembers, or believes.[s] This doctrine has, however, been lately questioned, and, it seems, on solid principles. When a man swears, that he believes what, in truth, he does not believe, he pronounces a falsehood as much as when he swears absolutely, that a thing is true, which he knows not to be true. My Lord Chief Justice De Grey, in a late case, said, that it was a mistake, which mankind had fallen into, that a person could not be convicted of perjury for deposing on oath, according to his belief.[t] It is certainly true, says my Lord Mansfield, that a man may be indicted for perjury, in swearing that he believes a fact to be true, which he must know to be false.[u]

Bribery is when a judge, or other person concerned in the administration of justice, takes any undue reward to influence his behaviour in office. He who offers or gives, as well as he who receives this undue reward, is guilty of an offence against the law.

Extortion, taken in a large sense, is any oppression by colour or pretence of right; but, in its proper sense, it is a great misprision, in wresting by any officer, under colour of his office, any money, either when none at all is due, or not so much is due, or when it is not yet due.

I have now enumerated, and, by references to the common law, have explained the crimes and offences known to the constitution and laws of the United States. It is next in order to consider the several punishments, which are annexed to those crimes and offences.

These punishments are of seven different kinds: disqualification for office — fine — imprisonment — whipping — pillory — incapacity to give testimony — death. To some crimes more kinds of punishment than one are assigned. To resistance of the officers of the customs is annexed a fine.[v] To the landing of goods entered for exportation imprisonment is

---

[r] 3. Ins. 165.   [s] Id. 166. 1. Haw. 175.   [t] Leach. 304.   [u] Ibid.
[v] Laws U.S. con. 1. sess. 2. c. 35. s. 50.

the punishment allotted.[w] To bribery[x] and extortion[y] the punishments of disqualification, fine, and imprisonment are assigned. To misprision of treason,[z] manslaughter,[a] misprision of felony,[b] atrocious maiming,[c] a confederacy with pirates,[d] resistance against process,[e] a rescue of persons not convicted of any capital crime,[f] serving process for arresting a publick minister,[g] the violation of a safe conduct, and violence to the person of a publick minister,[h] are assigned the punishments of fine and imprisonment. Stealing or falsifying records, and fraudulently acknowledging bail, are punished with fine, imprisonment, and whipping.[i] Fine and whipping are the punishments annexed to larceny.[j] To perjury and subornation of perjury are allotted the punishments of fine, imprisonment, the pillory, and incapacity to give testimony.[k]

It deserves to be remarked, that, in every instance of punishment by fine, imprisonment, or whipping, limits are fixed on the side of severity; none, on the side of mercy.

Against forging,[l] against procuring or assisting to forge publick securities,[m] against uttering or causing to be uttered securities, which are forged,[n] against the rescue of persons convicted of capital crimes,[o] against piracy,[p] against robbery,[q] against acts of hostility as specified in the law,[r] against making a revolt in a ship, against violently hindering the captain of a vessel to fight in its defence, against piratically running away with any vessel,[s] against murder,[t] and against treason,[u] the punishment of death is denounced.

Accessories before[v] the fact of murder, robbery, or other piracy upon the seas shall suffer death. Accessories after[w] the fact shall be fined and imprisoned. Receivers of stolen goods[x] shall be liable to like punishments as in the case of larceny.

It is proper to point out to a grand jury the kinds and the grades of *punishments;* because the respect due to the legislature will lead us to conclude, that there are similar kinds and well adjusted grades of *crimes;* because the probability of a crime is in the inverse proportion to its atrociousness; and because, of consequence, a grand jury will require a degree of evidence adequate to the criminality of every charge, which comes under their consideration.

No person shall be prosecuted for any capital crime, wilful murder or forgery excepted, unless the indictment for it shall be found within three years after its commission: nor shall any person be prosecuted for an

[w] Id. s. 59.   [x] Id. sess. 2. c. 9. s. 21.   [y] Id. sess. 3. c. 15. s. 39.
[z] Id. sess. 2. c. 9. s. 2.   [a] Id. s. 7. 12.   [b] Id. s. 6.   [c] Id. s. 13.
[d] Id. s. 12.   [e] Id. s. 22.   [f] Id. s. 23.   [g] Id. s. 26.   [h] Id. s. 28.
[i] Id. s. 15.   [j] Id. s. 16.   [k] Id. s. 18.
[l] Laws U.S. con. 1. sess. 2. c. 9. s. 14.   [m] Id. ibid.   [n] Id. ibid.
[o] Id. s. 23.   [p] Id. s. 8.   [q] Id. ibid.   [r] Id. s. 9.   [s] Id. s. 8.
[t] Id. s. 3.   [u] Id. s. 1.   [v] Id. s. 10.   [w] Id. s. 11.   [x] Id. s. 17.

offence not capital, or for a crime or forfeiture under a penal law, unless the indictment or information for it shall be found or instituted within two years after the commission of the offence, or after the fine or forfeiture has incurred. But these provisions shall not operate in favour of such as flee from justice.[y]

One, who is indicted of treason, shall have, at least three days before his trial, a copy of the indictment, and a list, containing the names and places of abode, of the jurors and of the witnesses to be produced on the trial. A person indicted for any other capital crime shall have, at least two entire days before his trial, such a list of the jury, and a copy of the indictment.[z]

The trial of all crimes shall be by jury.[a]

Every one indicted shall be allowed to make his full defence by counsel learned in the law. The court, or a judge of the court, before whom he is to be tried, shall, on his request, assign him counsel, such as he shall desire, but not exceeding two; and his counsel shall have free access to him at all seasonable hours. He shall also be admitted to make, in his defence, any proof, which he can produce by witnesses: to compel the attendance of his witnesses at his trial he shall have legal process, similar to that, which is granted to compel witnesses to appear on the prosecution against him.[b]

No person shall be convicted of treason, unless on the testimony of two witnesses to the same overt act, or on confession in open court.[c]

The benefit of clergy shall not be used or allowed, upon the conviction of any crime, for which, by any statute of the United States, the punishment is or shall be declared to be death.[d]

The manner of inflicting the punishment of death shall be by hanging the person convicted, by the neck, until dead.[e]

No conviction or judgment for any offence, yet punishable by the laws of the United States, shall work corruption of blood, or any forfeiture of estate.[f]

I have now, gentlemen, given you an account, plain and concise, and yet, I hope, not altogether imperfect, of the criminal code of the United States. It will be interesting and instructive to compare this code, in some of its most remarkable regulations, with that of some other country. For this comparison, I select the criminal code of England. I select it, because, in other parts of Europe, it has been proposed as a model, on account of its mildness; and because, contrasted with many systems of criminal law, it is, indeed, comparatively mild. "That the English system of jurisprudence has its abuses, I will readily agree," says a writer of a nation

[y] Laws U.S. con. 1. sess. 2. c. 9. s. 32. [z] Id. s. 29.   [a] Con. U.S. art. 2. s. 2.
[b] Laws U.S. con. 1. sess. 2. c. 9. s. 29. [c] Con. U.S. art. 3. s. 3.
[d] Laws U.S. con. 1. sess. 2. c. 9. s. 31. [e] Id. s. 33.   [f] Id. s. 24.

long the rival of England; "but that it has fewer abuses than the system of any other civilized country, is what I am able to prove." [g]

It is the opinion of some writers, highly respected for their good sense, as well as for their humanity, that capital punishments are, in no case, necessary. It is an opinion, which I am certainly well warranted in offering — that nothing but the most absolute necessity can authorize them. Another opinion I am equally warranted in offering — that they should not be aggravated by any sufferings, except those which are inseparably attached to a violent death.[h] It was worthy only of a tyrant[i] — and of a tyrant it was truly characteristick — to give standing instructions to his executioners, that they should protract the expiring moments of the tortured criminal; and should manage the butchering business with such studied and slow barbarity, as that his powers of painful sensation should continue to the very last — *ut mori se sentiat.*[*]

Hear from the mouth of a celebrated lawyer — celebrated, however, for his learning, more than for his humanity — the sentence pronounced against treason by the law of England: hear this sentence, full of horrours, represented as flowing from admirable clemency and moderation.

At the trial of the conspirators in the gun powder plot, Sir Edward Coke concluded the part which he acted as attorney general, in the following very remarkable manner. "The conclusion shall be drawn from the admirable clemency and moderation of the king, in that, howsoever these traitors have exceeded all others their predecessors in mischief, yet neither will the king exceed the *usual* punishment of the law, nor invent any *new* torture or torment for them; but is graciously pleased to afford them as well an ordinary course of trial, as an *ordinary punishment*, much *inferiour to their offence.* And surely, worthy of observation is the punishment provided and appointed for high treason. For first, after a traitor hath had his just trial, and is convicted and attainted, he shall have his judgment to be *drawn* to the place of execution from his prison, as being not worthy any more to tread upon the face of the earth whereof he is made: also for that he hath been retrograde to nature, therefore he is to be drawn backward at a horse tail. And whereas God hath made the head of man his highest and most supreme part, as being his chief grace and ornament; he must be drawn with his head declining downward, and lying so near the ground as may be, being thought unfit to take the benefit of the common air. For which cause also he shall be strangled, being hanged up by the neck, between heaven and earth, as

[g] War. The. L. Crim. 18.   [h] — See they suffer death,
                        But in their deaths remember they are men.   *Cato.*
[i] Caligula.
[*] [So that he may feel himself die.]

deemed unworthy of both, or either; as likewise that the eyes of men may behold, and their hearts contemn him. Then he is to be cut down alive: his bowels and inlayed parts taken out and burnt, who inwardly had conceived and harboured in his heart such horrible treason. After, to have his head cut off, which had imagined the mischief. And, lastly, his body to be quartered, and the quarters set up in some high and eminent place, to the view and detestation of men, and to become a prey for the fowls of the air. And this is a reward due to traitors."[j]

I relieve your feelings by a custom which was observed among the Jews. They gave wine mingled with myrrh to a criminal at the time of his execution, in order to produce a stupor, and deaden the sensibility of the pain.

By the *constitution* of the United States, no attainder of *treason* shall work corruption of blood, or forfeiture, except during the life of the person attainted. By the *law* of the United States, as it now stands, no judgment for *any* offence shall work corruption of blood or forfeiture of *any* estate.

In England, the forfeiture of a criminal's personal estate accrues immediately upon his *conviction* of treason or felony. On his *attainder* for *treason*, he forfeits to the king all his lands of inheritance, and all his rights of entry to lands and tenements. On his attainder for *felony*, he forfeits his lands in fee simple to the crown for a year and a day; and the king may, within that time, commit what waste he pleases, by cutting timber, by ploughing meadows, by extirpating gardens, and by pulling down houses.

This uncivilized regulation, hostile to the genius of publick prosperity and improvement, is not, however, attended with any additional misfortune to the children of the prisoner. Their ruin is already completed by the corruption of their parent's blood. This unnatural principle — I call it unnatural, because it dissolves, as far as human laws can dissolve, the closest and the dearest ties of nature — this unnatural principle effectually intercepts from them the descent of his lands of inheritance, which, after the king's temporary right of forfeiture is satisfied, escheat to the lord of the fee.

Corruption of blood extends both upwards and downwards. A person attainted cannot inherit lands from his ancestors: he cannot transmit them to any heir: he even obstructs all descents to his posterity, whenever they must, through him, deduce their right from a more remote ancestor.

It has been alleged, in favour of forfeiture, that, since its effects extend to the family of the criminal as well as to himself, it will have a powerful operation to restrain a person from attempts against the state, not only

---

[j] 1. St. Tri. 243

by the fear of personal punishment, but also by his strongest natural affections. On a farther and closer investigation, however, it may, perhaps, be found, that this policy, as certainly it is not of the most generous, so neither is it of the most enlarged kind; since forfeitures, far from preventing, may have a tendency to multiply and to perpetuate offences and crimes.

When the law says, that the children of him, who has been guilty of crimes, shall be bereaved of all their hopes and all their rights of succession; that they shall languish in perpetual indigence and distress; that their whole life shall be one dark scene of unintermitted and unabating punishment; and that death alone shall provide for them a refuge from their misery — when such is the language, or such is the effect of the law; with what sentiments must it naturally inspire those, who are doomed to become its unfortunate, though unoffending objects? With sentiments of a deadly feud against the state, which has adopted, and which enforces it. To a law of this kind we may, with peculiar propriety, apply the maxim — une loi rigoureuse produit des crimes.

In the United States, a period is assigned, beyond which crimes and offences, two excepted, cannot be prosecuted. This regulation is well calculated to establish and to preserve the security of individuals, and the tranquillity of the state. "Si post intervallum accusare (accusator) velit," says Bracton, "non erit de jure audiendus, nisi docere poterit se fuisse justis rationibus impeditum." [k]

The advantages of a copy of the indictment, of counsel at the trial, and of process to compel the appearance of the prisoner's witnesses are enjoyed, in England, only in prosecutions for treason, but not in prosecutions for other crimes.

The greatness of those advantages may be easily estimated by contemplating the helpless, the forlorn and the anxious situation of a person, who is deprived of them in a trial for his life.

When the bill for regulating trials in cases of high treason was, in the reign of William the third, brought into parliament; that part of it, which allows counsel to the prisoner, was viewed, by the friends of freedom, as a matter of the last importance. The Lord Ashley, afterwards earl of Shaftesbury and author of the celebrated Characteristicks, was then a member of the house of commons. Actuated by that zeal for the principles of liberty, which accompanied him through life, he composed, as he was well qualified to compose, an excellent speech in support of that important provision. When he rose to deliver it, the great and respectable audience, before which he appeared, intimidated him to such a degree,

---

[k] Brac. 118 b. [If an accuser tries to bring an accusation after a period of time, he is not lawfully to be heard unless he can show he was previously hindered for just reasons.]

that he lost his powers of recollection, and was incapable of pronouncing what he had previously prepared. The house, eager to hear him, waited with solicitude till he should recover from his embarrassment, and, after some time, called loudly upon him to proceed. He proceeded in this manner: "If I, sir," — addressing himself to the speaker — "If I, sir, who rise only to give my opinion on the bill now depending, am so confounded, that I am unable to express the least of what I proposed to say; what must the condition of that man be, who, without any assistance, is pleading for his life?" [1] What must his condition be! Unacquainted with the nature and with the forms of the whole proceedings against him, unassisted by counsel, "baited by crown lawyers," distracted by uncertainty and suspense, he finds a desperate but an eligible refuge in the awful verdict of conviction, which determines his fate.

Let us turn our eyes to a more pleasing prospect. How few are the crimes — how few are the capital crimes, known to the laws of the United States, compared with those known to the laws of England! Allowance, we own, should be made for the difference between the nature of the two governments; the objects of one being *general;* those of the other, *enumerated.* But after every allowance is made for this consideration, still we may justly say — how few are the crimes — how few are the capital crimes, known to the laws of the United States, compared with those known to the laws of England! When Sir William Blackstone wrote, no fewer than one hundred and sixty actions, which men are daily liable to commit, crowded the dismal list of felonies without benefit of clergy; in other words, felonies declared to be worthy of immediate death. Actions, almost innumerable, are doomed, by the same system, to severe, though inferiour penalties.

The co-acervation of sanguinary laws is a political distemper of the most inveterate and the most dangerous kind. By such laws the people are corrupted; and when corruption arises from laws the evil may well be pronounced to be incurable; for it proceeds from the very source, from which the remedy should flow.

This comparison between the criminal laws of England and those of the United States might be carried much farther. The contrast would become still more and more striking; and, of course, the result would become still more and more satisfactory.

"How happy would mankind be," says the eloquent and benevolent Beccaria,[m] "if laws were now to be first formed!" The United States enjoy this singular happiness. Their laws are now first formed. They are formed by the legitimate representatives of free citizens and free states. Among those citizens and those states they now begin to be diffused. To

[1] Gen. Dict. vol. 9. p. 179.   [m] Chap. 28.

those citizens and those states they are objects of the greatest and most extensive importance. I speak particularly concerning the *criminal laws*. It is on the excellence of the criminal laws, says the celebrated Montesquieu,[n] that the liberty of the citizens principally depends. The knowledge, continues he, which has been already acquired in some countries, and that which may be hereafter acquired in others, with regard to the surest rules which can be observed in criminal judgments, is more interesting to the human kind, than any thing else in the universe. It is only, adds he, on the practice of this knowledge that liberty can be founded.

With regard to an individual, every one knows how much his fortunes and his character, his infelicity or his happiness depend on his education. What education is to the individual, the laws are to the community. "Good laws," says my lord Bacon, whose sentences are discourses, "make a whole nation to be as a well ordered college." [o] With what earnestness should every nation — with what peculiar earnestness should that nation, which boasts of liberty as the principle of her constitution — with what peculiar earnestness should she endeavour, that her laws, especially her criminal laws, should be improved to a degree of perfection as high as human policy and human virtue can carry them!

We have already seen, that the noblest end and aim of criminal jurisprudence is to prevent crimes: and we have already seen that punishments, mild, speedy, and certain, are means calculated for preventing them. But these are not the only means. Crimes may be prevented by the genius as well as by the execution of the criminal laws. Let them be few: let them be clear: let them be simple: let them be concise: let them be consummately accurate. Let the punishment be proportioned — let it be analogous — to the crime. Let the reformation as well as the punishment of offenders be kept constantly and steadily in view: and, while the dignity of the nation is vindicated, let reparation be made to those, who have received injury. Above all, let the wisdom, the purity, and the benignity of the civil code supersede, for they are well calculated to supersede, the severity of criminal legislation. Let the law diffuse peace and happiness; and innocence will walk in their train.

I offer no apology, gentlemen, for the nature or the length of this address. A sense of duty has drawn it from me. Every member of society should have it in his power to know when he is criminal and when he is innocent. His criminality and his innocence should be designated by the laws. The code of criminal laws, therefore, should, as far as possible, be in the hands of every citizen. In the situation, in which I have the honour to be placed, I deem it my duty to embrace every proper opportunity of disseminating the knowledge of them far and speedily. Can this be done with more propriety than in an address to a grand jury — to a

---

[n] Sp. L. b. 12. c. 2.   [o] 4. Ld. Bac. 9.

grand jury summoned and returned for the body of an extensive district — a district so extensive and important as that of Virginia? These considerations induced me to lay before you an enumeration of the crimes and the punishments known to our constitution and laws. This I have endeavoured to do with the utmost conciseness.

But, if the laws deserve it, they should be the objects of *affection* as well as of *knowledge*. Thinking, as I think, concerning the high degree of regard, to which the criminal code of the United States has an undoubted claim, I am justified in expressing, I am *obliged* to express the principles, on which I conceive that claim to be founded. This I have likewise endeavoured to do with the utmost conciseness.

I mean not, however, to recommend to you an implicit and an undistinguishing approbation of the laws of your country. Admire; but admire with reason on your side.

If, for instance, you think, that the laws respecting the publick securities are more severe than is absolutely necessary for supporting their value and their credit; it will be no crime to express your thoughts decently and properly to your representatives in congress.

Permit me to suggest another method, by which our valuable code of criminal laws may be still increased in its value. Inform and practically convince every one within your respective spheres of action and intercourse, that, as excellent laws improve the virtue of the citizens, so the virtue of the citizens has a reciprocal and benign energy in heightening the excellence of the law.

How happy are the people, by whom the laws are known and rationally beloved! The rational love of the laws generates the enlightened love of our country. The enlightened love of our country is propitious to every virtue, which can adorn and exalt the citizen and the man.

IX

CONSIDERATIONS ON THE BANK
OF NORTH AMERICA

PUBLISHED IN THE YEAR 1785

An attack is made on the credit and institution of the Bank of North America. Whether this attack is justified by the principles of law and sound policy, is a natural subject of inquiry. The inquiry is as necessary and interesting, as it is natural: for, though some people represent the bank as injurious and dangerous, while others consider it as salutary and beneficial to the community, all view it as an object of high importance; deserving and demanding the publick attention.

In the investigation of this subject,[a] it will be requisite to discuss some great and leading questions concerning the constitution of the United States, and the relation which subsists between them and each particular state in the Union. Perhaps it is to be wished that this discussion had not been rendered necessary; and that those questions had rested some time longer among the *arcana imperii:* but they are now presented to the publick; and the publick should view them with firmness, with impartiality, and with all the solicitude befitting such a momentous occasion.

A gentleman,[b] who had the best opportunities of observing, and who possesses the best talents for judging on the subject, informs his fellow citizens officially, that "it may be not only asserted, but demonstrated, that, without the establishment of the national bank, the business of the department of finance could not have been performed" in the late war.

The millennium is not yet come. War, with all the horrours and miseries in his train, may revisit us. The finances may again be deranged: "publick credit may, again, be at an end: no means may be afforded adequate to the publick expenses." Is it wise or politick to deprive our country, in such a situation, of a resource, which happy experience has

---

[a] The publication of these considerations was occasioned by a bill, introduced into the legislature of Pennsylvania, to repeal an act of assembly passed in the year 1782, by which a charter of incorporation had been granted to the Bank of North America. The bill was passed into a law, in September, 1785. *Ed.*

[b] Vide the preface to the statement of the accounts of the United States.

shown to be of such essential importance? Will the citizens of the United States be encouraged to embark their fortunes on a similar bottom in a future war, by seeing the vessel, which carried us so successfully through the last, thrown aside, like a useless hulk, upon the return of peace?

It will not be improper to recal to our remembrance the origin, the establishment, and the proceedings of the Bank of North America.

In May, 1781, the superintendant of finance laid before congress a plan of a bank. On the 26th of that month, congress passed the following resolution concerning it.

"Resolved, That congress do approve of the plan for establishing a national bank in these United States, submitted to their consideration by Mr. Robert Morris, the 17th May, 1781, and that they will promote and support the same by such ways and means, from time to time, as may appear necessary for the institution, and consistent with the publick good.

"That the subscribers to the said bank shall be incorporated, agreeably to the principles and terms of the plan, under the name of "The President, Directors, and Company of the Bank of North America," so soon as the subscription shall be filled, the directors and president chosen, and application made to congress for that purpose, by the president and directors elected.

"Resolved, That it be recommended to the several States, by proper laws for that purpose, to provide that no other bank or bankers shall be established or permitted within the said states respectively during the war.

"Resolved, That the notes hereafter to be issued by the said bank, payable on demand, shall be receivable in payment of all taxes, duties, and debts, due or that may become due or payable to the United States.

"Resolved, that congress will recommend to the several legislatures to pass laws, making it felony without benefit of clergy, for any person to counterfeit bank notes, or to pass such notes, knowing them to be counterfeit; also making it felony without benefit of clergy, for any president, inspector, director, officer, or servant of the bank, to convert any of the property, money, or credit of the said bank to his own use, or in any other way to be guilty of fraud or embezzlement, as officers or servants of the bank."

Under these resolutions a subscription was opened for the national bank: this subscription was not confined to Pennsylvania: the citizens of other States trusted their property to the publick faith; and before the end of December, 1781, the subscription was filled, "from an expectation of a charter of incorporation from congress." Application was made to congress by the president and directors, then chosen, for an act of incorporation. "The exigencies of the United States rendered it indispensably necessary that such an act should be immediately passed." [e] Congress, at the same time that they passed the act of incorporation, recommended to the legislature of each state, to pass such laws as they might judge necessary for giving its ordinance its full operation, agreeably to the true intent and meaning thereof, and according to the recommendations contained in the resolution of the 26th day of May preceding.

The bank immediately commenced its operations. Its seeds were small, but they were vigorous. The sums paid in by individuals upon their subscriptions did not amount in the whole to seventy thousand dillars. The sum invested by the United States, in bank stock, amounted to something more than two hundred and fifty thousand dollars: but this sum may be said to have been paid in with one hand and borrowed with the other; and before the end of the first three months, farther sums were advanced to the United States, and an advance was made to this state.[d] Besides, numerous accommodations were afforded to individuals. Little was it then imagined that the bank would ever be represented as unfriendly to circulation. It was viewed as the source and as the support of credit, both private and publick: as such, it was hated and dreaded by the enemies of the United States: as such, it was loved and fostered by their friends.

Pennsylvania, distinguished on numerous occasions by her faithful and affectionate attachment to federal principles, embraced, in the first session of her legislature after the establishment of the bank, the opportunity of testifying her approbation of an act, which had been found to be indispensably necessary. Harmonizing with the sentiments and recommendations of the United States, the assembly passed an act,[e] "for preventing and punishing the counterfeiting of the common seal, bank bills, and bank notes, of the president, directors, and company of the Bank of North America." In the preamble to this act, which, according to the constitution of this state, expresses the reasons and motives for passing it, the "necessity" of taking "effectual measures for preventing and punishing frauds and cheats which may be put upon the president, directors, and company of the Bank of North America," is explicitly declared by the legislature.

The sentiments and conduct of other states, respecting the establishment of the national bank by congress, were similar to those of Pennsylvania. The general assembly of Rhode Island and Providence Plantations[f] made it felony, without benefit of clergy, "to counterfeit any note or notes issued, or to be issued, from the Bank of North America, as approved and *established* by the United States in Congress assembled."

---

[e] See the act in the appendix.
[d] See in the appendix the different sums advanced to this state.
[e] 18th of March, 1782.   [f] January Sessions, 1782.

The state of Connecticut enacted,[g] that a tax should be laid, payable in money, or "notes issued by the directors of the national bank, *established* by an ordinance of the United States in congress assembled." By a law of Massachussetts, the subscribers to the national bank, approved of by the United States, were "incorporated, on the behalf of that commonwealth, by the name of the president, directors and company of the Bank of North America, according to the terms of the ordinance to incorporate the said subscribers, passed by the United States in congress assembled on the thirty first day of December, 1781." The same law further enacts, "that all notes or bills, which have been or shall be issued by, for, or in the name of the said president, directors, and company, and payable on demand, shall be receivable in the payment of all taxes, debts and duties, due or that may become due, or payable to, or for account of, the said United States." In the preamble of this law, the legislature declares that "a national bank is of great service, as well to the publick as to individuals."

The president and directors of the bank had a delicate and a difficult part to act. On one hand, they were obliged to guard against the malice and exertions of their enemies: on the other, it was incumbent on them to sooth the timidity of some of their friends. The credit of a bank, as well as all other credit, depends on opinion. Opinion, whether well or ill founded, produces, in each case, the same effects upon conduct. Some thought that an act of incorporation from the legislature of this state would be beneficial; none apprehended that it could ever be hurtful to the national bank. Prudence, therefore, and a disposition, very natural in that season of doubt and diffidence, to gratify the sentiments, and even the prejudices, of such as might become subscribers or customers to the bank, directed an application to the assembly for "a charter, similar to that granted by the United States in congress assembled." But though the directors were willing to avail themselves of encouragement from every quarter, they meant not to relinquish any of their rights, or to change the foundation on which they rested. They made their application in their *corporate* character.[h] They expressly mentioned to the assembly, that the United States in congress assembled had granted to the bank a charter of incorporation, and that the institution was to be carried on under their immediate auspices. The legislature thought that it was proper and reasonable to grant[i] the request of the *president and directors of the Bank of North America;* and assigned, as a reason for the act, "that the United States in congress assembled, from a conviction of the support

[g] 10th January, 1782.
[h] Their letter to the president of the supreme executive council, on this occasion, is in the appendix.
[i] 1st. of April, 1782.

which the finances of the United States would receive from the establishment of a *national bank,* passed an ordinance to incorporate the subscribers for this purpose, by the name and style of the president, directors, and company of the Bank of North America."

The first clause of the law enacts, that "those who are, and those who shall become subscribers to the said bank, be, and forever hereafter shall be, a corporation and body politick, to all intents and purposes."

It is further enacted, that "the said corporation be, and shall be forever hereafter, able and capable in law to do and execute all and singular matters and things, that to them shall or may appertain to do."

To show, in the most striking light, the kind sentiments of the legislature towards the institution, it is further enacted, that "this act shall be construed and taken most favourably and beneficially for the said corporation."

On these facts and proceedings, two questions of much national importance present themselves to our view and examination.

I. Is the Bank of North America legally and constitutionally instituted and organized, by the charter of incorporation granted by the United States in congress assembled?

II. Would it be wise or politick in the legislature of Pennsylvania, to revoke the charter which it has granted to the institution?

The discussion of these two questions will naturally lead us to the proper conclusions concerning the validity and the utility of the bank.

I. Had the United States in congress assembled a legal and constitutional power to institute and organize the Bank of North America, by a charter of incorporation?

The objection, under this head, will be — that the articles of confederation express all the powers of congress, that in those articles no power is delegated to that body to grant charters of incorporation, and that, therefore, congress possess no such power.

It is true, that, by the second article of the confederation, "each state retains its sovereignty, freedom and independence, and every power, jurisdiction, and right, which is not, by the confederation, *expressly* delegated to the United States in congress assembled."

If, then, any or each of the states possessed, previous to the confederation, a power, jurisdiction, or right, to institute and organize, by a charter of incorporation, a bank for North America; in other words — commensurate to the United States; such power, jurisdiction, and right, unless expressly delegated to congress, cannot be legally or constitutionally exercised by that body.

But, we presume, it will not be contended, that any or each of the states could exercise any power or act of sovereignty extending over all the other states, or any of them; or, in other words, incorporate a bank, commensurate to the United States.

The consequence is, that this is not an act of sovereignty, or a power, jurisdiction, or right, which, by the second article of the confederation, must be expressly delegated to congress, in order to be possessed by that body.

If, however, any person shall contend that any or each of the states can exercise such an extensive power or act of sovereignty as that above mentioned; to such person we give this answer — The state of Massachussetts has exercised such power and act: it has incorporated the Bank of North America. But to pursue my argument.

Though the United States in congress assembled derive *from the particular states* no power, jurisdiction, or right, which is not expressly delegated by the confederation, it does not thence follow, that the United States in congress have *no other* powers, jurisdiction, or rights, than those delegated by the particular states.

The United States have general rights, general powers, and general obligations, not derived from any particular states, nor from all the particular states, taken separately; but resulting from the union of the whole: and, therefore, it is provided, in the fifth article of the confederation, "that for the more convenient management of the *general interests* of the United States, delegates shall be annually appointed to meet in congress."

To many purposes, the United States are to be considered as one undivided, independent nation; and as possessed of all the rights, and powers, and properties, by the law of nations incident to such.

Whenever an object occurs, to the direction of which no particular state is competent, the management of it must, of necessity, belong to the United States in congress assembled. There are many objects of this extended nature. The purchase, the sale, the defence, and the government of lands and countries, not within any state, are all included under this description. An institution for circulating paper, and establishing its credit over the whole United States, is naturally ranged in the same class.

The act of independence was made before the articles of confederation. This act declares, that *"these United colonies,"* (not enumerating them separately) "are free and independent states; and that, as free and independent states, *they* have full power to do *all* acts and things which independent states may, of right, do."

The confederation was not intended to weaken or abridge the powers and rights, to which the United States were previously entitled. It was not intended to transfer any of those powers or rights to the particular states, or any of them. If, therefore, the power now in question was vested in the United States before the confederation; it continues vested in them still. The confederation clothed the United States with many though, perhaps, not with sufficient powers: but of none did it disrobe them.

It is no new position, that rights may be vested in a political body, which did not previously reside in any or in all the members of that body. They may be derived solely from the union of those members.[j] "The case," says the celebrated Burlamaqui, "is here very near the same as in that of several voices collected together, which, by their union, produce a harmony, that was not to be found separately in each."

A number of unconnected inhabitants are settled on each side of a navigable river; it belongs to none of them; it belongs not to them all, for they have nothing in common: let them unite; the river is the property of the united body.

The arguments drawn from the political associations of individuals into a state will apply, with equal force and propriety, to a number of states united by a confederacy.

New states must be formed and established: their extent and boundaries must be regulated and ascertained. How can this be done, unless by the United States in congress assembled?

States are corporations or bodies politick of the most important and dignified kind.

Let us now concentre the foregoing observations, and apply them to the incorporation of the Bank of North America by congress.

By the civil law, corporations seem to have been created by the mere and voluntary association of their members, provided such convention was not contrary to law.[k]

By the common law, something more is necessary — all the methods whereby corporations exist are, for the most part, reducible to that of the king's letters patent, or charter of incorporation.[l]

From this it will appear that the creation of a corporation is, by the common law, considered as the act of the executive rather than of the legislative powers of government.

Before the revolution, charters of incorporation were granted by the proprietaries of Pennsylvania, under a derivative authority from the crown, and those charters have been recognised by the constitution and laws of the commonwealth since the revolution.

From analogy, therefore, we may justly infer, that the United States in congress assembled, possessing the executive powers of the union, may, in virtue of such powers, grant charters of incorporation for accomplishing objects that comprehend the general interests of the United States.

But the United States in congress assembled possess, in many instances, and to many purposes, the legislative as well as the executive powers of

[j] 2. Burl. 42.   [k] 1. Bl. Com. 472.   [l] Bl. Com. 472. 473.

the union; and therefore, whether we consider the incorporation of the bank as a law, or as a charter, it will be equally within the powers of congress: for the object of this institution could not be reached without the exertion of the combined sovereignty of the union.

I have asked — how can new states, which are bodies politick, be formed, unless by the United States in congress assembled? Fact, as well as argument, justifies my sentiments on this subject. The conduct of congress has been similar on similar occasions. The same principles have directed the exercise of the same powers.

In the month of April, 1784, congress resolved, that part of the western territory "should be divided into distinct states."

They further resolved, that the settlers should, "either on their own petition, or on the order of congress, receive authority from *them* to meet together, for the purpose of establishing a temporary government, to adopt the constitution and laws of any one of the original states."

"When any such state shall have acquired twenty thousand free inhabitants, on giving due proof thereof to congress, they shall receive from *them* authority to call a convention of representatives, to establish a permanent constitution and government for themselves."

"The preceding articles," among others, "shall be formed into a charter of compact; shall be duly executed by the president of the United States in congress assembled, under his hand and the seal of the United States; shall be promulgated; and shall stand as fundamental constitutions between the thirteen original states, and each of the several states now newly described, unalterable from and after the sale of any part of the territory of such state, but by the joint consent of the United States in congress assembled, and of the particular state within which such alteration is proposed to be made."

It will be difficult, I believe, to urge against the power of congress to grant a charter to the Bank of North America, any argument, which may not, with equal strength and fitness, be urged against the power of that body to form, execute, and promulgate a charter of compact for the new states.

The sentiments of the representatives of the United States, as to their power of incorporating the bank, ought to have much weight with us. Their sentiments are strongly marked by their conduct, in their first resolutions respecting the bank. These resolutions are made at the same time, and on the same subject: but there is a striking difference in their manner. It was thought proper "that no other bank should be permitted within any of the states, during the war." Congress "*recommended* to the several states to make provision, for that purpose, by proper laws." It was thought prudent that the bank should be protected, by penal laws, from fraud, embezzlement, and forgery. Congress *recommended* it to the several legislatures to pass such laws. It was deemed expedient that bank notes should be received in payment of sums payable to the United States: congress *resolve*, that the notes "shall be receivable" in such payments. It was judged necessary that the bank should have a charter of incorporation: congress *resolve*, that the bank "shall be incorporated," on application made *"to congress"* for that purpose. The line of distinction between those things in which congress could only recommend, and those in which they could act, is drawn in the clearest manner. The incorporation of the national bank is ranked among those things, in which they could act.

This act of congress has, either expressly, or by implication, received the approbation of every state in the union. It was officially announced to every state by the superintendant of finance.[m] Had any one state considered it as an exercise of usurped power, would not that state have remonstrated against it? But there is no such remonstrance.

This act of congress has been most explicitly recognised by the legislature of Pennsylvania. The law for preventing and punishing frauds and cheats upon the bank was passed on the 18th of March, 1782, and before the bank had obtained a charter from this state. By that law it is made felony without benefit of clergy, to forge the common seal of the president, directors, and company of the Bank of North America. Who were the president, directors, and company of the Bank of North America? Those whom congress had made "a corporation and body politick, to all intents and purposes, by that name and style." How came that body by a "common seal?" The act of congress ordained that that body "should have full power and authority to make, have and use a common seal." In the act to incorporate the subscribers to the Bank of North America, the legislature, after reciting that the United States in congress assembled had "passed an ordinance to incorporate them," say, "the president and directors of the said bank have applied to this house for a similar act of incorporation, which request it is proper and reasonable to grant."

When the foregoing facts and arguments are considered, compared, and weighed, they will, it is hoped, evince and establish, *satisfactorily* to all, and *conclusively* on the legislature of Pennsylvania, the truth of this position —— That the Bank of North America was legally and constitutionally instituted and organized, by the charter of incorporation granted by the United States in congress assembled.

II. Would it, then, be wise or politick in the legislature of Pennsylvania, to revoke the charter which it has granted to this institution? It would not be wise or politick ——

[m] See his letter in the appendix.

1st. Because the proceeding would be nugatory. The recal of the charter of Pennsylvania would not repeal that of the United States, by which we have proved the bank to be legally and constitutionally instituted and organized.

2d. Because, though the legislature may destroy the legislative *operation*, yet it cannot undo the legislative *acknowledgment* of its own act. Though a statute be repealed, yet it shows the sense and opinion of the legislature concerning the subject of it, in the same manner as if it continued in force.[n] The legislature declared, in the law, that it was proper and reasonable to grant the request of the president and directors of the bank, for an act of incorporation similar to the ordinance of congress: no repeal of the law can weaken the force of that declaration.

3d. Because such a proceeding would wound that confidence in the engagements of government, which it is so much the interest and duty of every state to encourage and reward. The act in question formed a charter of compact between the legislature of this state, and the president, directors, and company of the Bank of North America. The latter asked for nothing but what was proper and reasonable: the former granted nothing but what was proper and reasonable: the terms of the compact were, therefore, fair and honest: while these terms are observed on one side, the compact cannot, consistently with the rules of good faith, be departed from on the other.

It may be asked — Has not the state power over her own laws? — May she not alter, amend, extend, restrain, and repeal them at her pleasure?

I am far from opposing the legislative authority of the state: but it must be observed, that, according to the practice of the legislature, publick acts of very different kinds are drawn and promulgated under the same form. A law to vest or confirm an estate in an individual — a law to incorporate a congregation or other society — a law respecting the rights and properties of all the citizens of the state — are all passed in the same manner; are all clothed in the same dress of legislative formality; and are all equally acts of the representatives of the freemen of the commonwealth. But surely it will not be pretended, that, after laws of those different kinds are passed, the legislature possesses over each the same discretionary power of repeal. In a law respecting the rights and properties of all the citizens of the state, this power may be safely exercised by the legislature. Why? Because, in this case, the interest of those who make the law (the members of assembly and their constituents) and the interest of those who are to be affected by the law (the members of assembly and their constituents) is the same. It is a common cause, and may, there-

[n] Foster, 394.

fore, be safely trusted to the representatives of the community. None can hurt another, without, at the same time, hurting himself. Very different is the case with regard to a law, by which the state grants privileges to a congregation or other society. Here two parties are instituted, and two distinct interests subsist. Rules of justice, of faith, and of honour must, therefore, be established between them: for, if interest alone is to be viewed, the congregation or society must always lie at the mercy of the community. Still more different is the case with regard to a law, by which an estate is vested or confirmed in an individual: if, in this case, the legislature may, at discretion, and without any reason assigned, devest or destroy his estate, then a person seized of an estate in fee simple, under legislative sanction, is, in truth, nothing more than a solemn tenant at will.

For these reasons, whenever the objects and makers of an instrument, passed under the form of a law, are not the same, it is to be considered as a compact, and to be interpreted according to the rules and maxims, by which compacts are governed. A foreigner is naturalized by law: is he a citizen only during pleasure? He is no more, if, without any cause of forfeiture assigned and established, the law, by which he is naturalized, may at pleasure be repealed. To receive the legislative stamp of stability and permanency, acts of incorporation are applied for from the legislature. If these acts may be repealed without notice, without accusation, without hearing, without proof, without forfeiture; where is the stamp of their stability? Their motto should be, "Levity." If the act for incorporating the subscribers to the Bank of North America shall be repealed in this manner, a precedent will be established for repealing, in the same manner, every other legislative charter in Pennsylvania. A pretence, as specious as any that can be alleged on this occasion, will never be wanting on any future occasion. Those acts of the state, which have hitherto been considered as the sure anchors of privilege and of property, will become the sport of every varying gust of politicks, and will float wildly backwards and forwards on the irregular and impetuous tides of party and faction.

4th. It would not be wise or politick to repeal the charter granted by this state to the Bank of North America, because such a measure would operate, as far as it would have any operation, against the credit of the United States, on which the interest of this commonwealth and her citizens so essentially depends. This institution originated under the auspices of the United States: the subscription to the national bank was opened under the recommendations and the engagements of congress: citizens of this state, and of the other states, and foreigners have become stockholders, on the publick faith: the United States have pledged themselves "to promote and support the institution by such ways and means, from time to time, as may appear necessary for it, and consistent with the publick good." ° They have recommended to the legislature of each state, "to pass such laws as they might judge necessary for giving the ordinance incorporating the bank its full operation." Pennsylvania has entered fully into the views, the recommendations, and the measures of congress respecting the bank. She has declared in the strongest manner her sense of their propriety, their reasonableness, and their necessity: she has passed laws for giving them their full operation. Will it redound to the credit of the United States to adopt and pursue a contrary system of conduct? The acts and recommendations of congress subsist still in all their original force: will it not have a tendency to shake all confidence in the councils and proceedings of the United States, if those acts and recommendations are now disregarded, without any reason shown for disregarding them? What influence will such a proceeding have upon the opinions and sentiments of the citizens of the United States and of foreigners? In one year they see measures respecting an object of confessed publick importance adopted and recommended with ardour by congress; and the views and wishes of that body zealously pursued by Pennsylvania: in another year they see those very measures, without any apparent reason for the change, warmly reprobated by that state: they must conclude one of two things: — that congress adopted and recommended those measures hastily and without consideration; or that Pennsylvania has reprobated them undutifully and disrespectfully. The former conclusion will give rise to very unfavourable reflections concerning the discernment both of the state and of the United States: the latter will suggest very inauspicious sentiments concerning the federal disposition and character of this commonwealth. The result of the conclusion will be — that the United States do not deserve, or that they will not receive, support in their system of finance. — These deductions and inferences will have particular weight, as they will be grounded on the conduct of Pennsylvania, hitherto one of the most federal, active, and affectionate states in the Union.

5th. It would not be wise or politick in the legislature to repeal their charter to the bank; because the tendency of such a step would be to deprive this state and the United States of all the advantages, publick and private, which would flow from the institution, in times of war, and in times of peace.

Let us turn our attention to some of the most material advantages resulting from a bank.

1st. It increases circulation, and invigorates industry. "It is not," says Dr. Smith, in his Treatise on the Wealth of Nations,ᵖ "by augmenting the capital of the country, but by rendering a greater part of that capital

° 26th May, 1781.   ᵖ Vol. 1. p. 483, 484.

active and productive than would otherwise be so, that the most judicious operations of banking can increase the industry of the country. The part of his capital which a dealer is obliged to keep by him unemployed, and in ready money, for answering occasional demands, is so much dead stock, which, so long as it remains in this situation, produces nothing either to him or to his country. The judicious operations of banking enable him to convert this dead stock into active and productive stock: into materials to work upon, into tools to work with, and into provisions and subsistence to work for; into stock which produces something both to himself and to his country. The gold and silver money which circulates in any country, and by means of which the produce of its land and labour is annually circulated and distributed to the proper consumers, is, in the same manner as the ready money of the dealer, all dead stock. It is a very valuable part of the capital of the country, which produces nothing to the country. The judicious operations of banking, by substituting paper in the room of a great part of this gold and silver, enables the country to convert a great part of this dead stock into active and productive stock; into stock which produces something to the country. The gold and silver money which circulates in any country may very properly be compared to a highway, which, while it circulates and carries to market all the grass and corn of the country, produces, itself, not a single pile of either. The judicious operations of banking, by providing, if I may be allowed so violent a metaphor, a sort of wagon-way through the air, enable the country to convert, as it were, a great part of its highways into good pasture and corn fields, and thereby to increase very considerably the annual produce of its land and labour."

The same sensible writer informs us, in another place, that "the[q] substitution of paper in the room of gold and silver money, replaces a very expensive instrument of commerce with one much less costly, and sometimes equally convenient. Circulation comes to be carried on by a new wheel, which it costs less both to erect and to maintain than the old one. — There are several sorts of paper money; but the circulating notes of banks and bankers is the species which is best known, and which seems best adapted for this purpose." — "These notes come to have the same currency as gold and silver money, from the confidence that such money can at any time be had for them."

Sir James Stewart calls banking "the great engine,[r] by which domestick circulation is carried on."

To have a free, easy, and equable instrument of circulation is of much importance in all countries: it is of peculiar importance in young and flourishing countries, in which the demands for credit, and the rewards

[q] Vol. 1. p. 434, 435.   [r] 2. Pol. Ec. 350.

of industry, are greater than in any other. When we view the extent and situation of the United States, we shall be satisfied that their inhabitants may, for a long time to come, employ profitably, in the improvement of their lands, a greater stock than they will be able easily to procure. In such a situation, it will always be of great service to them to save as much as possible the expense of so costly an instrument of commerce as gold and silver, to substitute in its place one cheaper, and, for many purposes, not less convenient; and to convert the value of the gold and silver into the labour and the materials necessary for improving and extending their settlements and plantations.

"To the banks of Scotland," says Sir James Stewart,[s] "the improvement of that country is entirely owing; and until they are generally established in other countries of Europe, where trade and industry are little known, it will be very difficult to set those great engines to work."

2d. The influence of a bank on credit is no less salutary than its influence on circulation. This position is, indeed, little more than a corollary from the former. Credit is confidence; and, before we can place confidence in a payment, we must be convinced that he who is to make it will be both able and willing to do so at the time stipulated. However unexceptionable his character and fortune may be, this conviction can never take place, unless in a country where solid property can be, at any time, turned into a circulating medium.

3d. Trade, as well as circulation and credit, derives great support and assistance from a bank. Credit and circulation produce punctuality; and punctuality is the soul of commerce. Let us appeal to experience as well as reason.

Dr. Smith says,[t] he has heard it asserted, that the trade of the city of Glasgow doubled in about fifteen years after the first erection of the banks there; and that the trade of Scotland has more than quadrupled since the first erection of the two publick banks at Edinburgh, of which one was established in 1695, and the other in 1727. Whether the increase has been in so great a proportion, the author pretends not to know. But that the trade of Scotland has increased very considerably during this period, and that the banks have contributed a good deal to this increase, cannot, he says, be doubted.

These observations, and observations similar to these, have induced Sir James Stewart to conclude, — that "Banking,[u] in the age we live, is that branch of credit which best deserves the attention of a statesman. Upon the right establishment of banks depends the prosperity of trade, and the equable course of circulation. By them solid property may be melted down. By the means of banks, money may be constantly kept at a due

---

[s] 2. Pol. Ec. 356.   [t] Vol. 1. p. 442.   [u] 2. Pol. Ec. 358.

proportion to alienation. If alienation increases, more property may be melted down. If it diminishes, the quantity of money stagnating will be absorbed by the bank, and part of the property formerly melted down in the securities granted to them will be, as it were, consolidated anew. These must pay, for the country, the balance of their trade with foreign nations: these keep the mints at work: and it is by these means, principally, that private, mercantile, and publick credit is supported."

I make no apology for the number and length of the quotations here used. They are from writers of great information, profound judgment, and unquestioned candour. They appear strictly and strongly applicable to my subject: and being so, should carry with them the greatest weight and influence; for the sentiments, which they contain and inculcate, must be considered as resulting from general principles and facts, and not as calculated for any partial purpose in this commonwealth.

But, here, it will probably be asked — Has your reasoning been verified by experience in this country? What advantages have resulted from the bank to commerce, circulation, and credit? Was our trade ever on such an undesirable footing? Is not the country distressed by the want of a circulating medium? Is not credit almost totally destroyed?

I answer — There is, unfortunately, too much truth in the representation: but if events are properly distinguished, and traced to their causes, it will be found — that none of the inconveniences abovementioned have arisen from the bank — that some of them have proceeded, at least in part, from the opposition which has been given to it — and that, as to others, its energy has not been sufficient to counteract or control them.

The disagreeable state of our commerce has been the effect of extravagant and injudicious importation. During the war, our ports were in a great measure blocked up. Imported articles were scarce and dear; and we felt the disadvantages of a stagnation in business. Extremes frequently introduce one another. When hostilities ceased, the floodgates of commerce were opened; and an inundation of foreign manufacturers overflowed the United States: we seemed to have forgot, that to pay was as necessary in trade as to purchase; and we observed no proportion between our imports, and our produce and other natural means of remittance. What was the consequence? Those who made any payments made them chiefly in specie; and in that way diminished our circulation. Others made no remittances at all, and thereby injured our credit. This account of what happened between the European merchants and our importers, corresponds exactly with what happened between our importers and the retailers spread over the different parts of the United States. The retailers, if they paid at all, paid in specie: and thus every operation, foreign and domestick, had an injurious effect on our credit, our circulation, and our commerce. But are any of these disadvantages to be ascribed to the bank? No. Is it to be accounted a fault or defect in the bank, that it did not prevent or remedy those disadvantages? By no means. Because one is not able to stem a torrent, is he therefore to be charged with augmenting its strength? The bank has had many difficulties to encounter. The experiment was a new one in this country: it was therefore necessary that it should be conducted with caution. While the war continued, the demands of the publick were great, and the stock of the bank was but inconsiderable; it had its active enemies, and its timid friends. Soon after the peace was concluded, its operations were restrained and embarrassed by an attempt to establish a new bank. A year had not elapsed after this, when the measure, which has occasioned these considerations, was introduced into the legislature, and caused, for some time, a total stagnation in the business of the institution. When all these circumstances are recollected and attended to, it will be matter of surprise that the bank has done so much, and not that it has done no more. Let it be deemed, as it ought to be, the object of publick confidence, and not of publick jealousy: let it be encouraged, instead of being opposed, by the counsels and proceedings of the state: then will the genuine effects of the institution appear; then will they spread their auspicious influence over agriculture, manufactures, and commerce.

4th. Another advantage to be expected from the Bank of North America is, the establishment of an undepreciating paper currency through the United States. This is an object of great consequence, whether it be considered in a political, or in a commercial view. It will be found to have a happy effect on the collection, the distribution, and the management of the publick revenue: it will remove the inconveniences and fluctuation attending exchange and remittances between the different states. "It is the interest of every trading state to have a sufficient quantity of paper, well secured, to circulate through it, so as to facilitate payments every where, and to cut off inland exchanges, which are a great clog upon trade, and are attended with the risk of receiving the paper of people, whose credit is but doubtful." [v]

Such are the advantages which may be expected to flow from a national bank, in times of peace. In times of war, the institution may be considered as essential. We have seen that, without it, the business of the department of finance could not have been carried on in the late war. It will be of use to recollect the situation of the United States with regard to this subject. The two or three first years of the war were sufficient to convince the British government, and the British armies, that they could not subdue the United States by military force. Their hopes of success rested on the failure of our finances. This was the source of our fears, as well as of the hopes of our enemies. By this thread our fate was suspended.

[v] 2. Pol. Ec. 415.

We watched it with anxiety: we saw it stretched and weakened every hour: the deathful instrument was ready to fall upon our heads: on our heads it must have fallen, had not publick credit, in the moment when it was about to break asunder, been entwined and supported by the credit of the bank. Congress, to speak without metaphors, had not money or credit to hire an express, or purchase a cord of wood. General Washington, on one occasion, and probably more than one, saw his army literally unable to march. Our distress was such, that it would have been destruction to have divulged it: but it ought to be known now; and when known, ought to have its proper influence on the publick mind and the publick conduct.

The expenses of a war must be defrayed, either —— 1st, by treasures previously accumulated —— or 2dly, by supplies levied and collected within the year, as they are called for —— or 3dly, by the anticipation of the publick revenues. No one will venture to refer us to the first mode. To the second the United States, as well as every state in Europe, are rendered incompetent by the modern system of war, which, in the military operations of one year, concentres the revenue of many. While our enemies adhere to this system, we must adopt it. The anticipation of revenue, then, is the only mode, by which the expenses of a future war can be defrayed. How the revenues of the United States can be anticipated without the operations of a national bank, I leave to those who attack the Bank of North America to show. They ought to be well prepared to show it; for they must know, that to be incapable of supporting a war is but a single step from being involved in one.

The result of the whole, under this head, is, — that in times of peace, the national bank will be highly advantageous; that in times of war, it will be essentially necessary, to the United States.

I flatter myself, that I have evinced the validity and the utility of the institution.

It has been surmised, that the design of the legislature is not to destroy, but to modify, the charter of the bank; and that if the directors would assent to reasonable amendments, the charter, modified, might continue in force. If this is the case, surely to repeal the law incorporating the bank is not the proper mode of doing the business. The bank was established and organized under the authority and auspices of congress. The directors have a trust and duty to discharge to the United States, and to all the particular states, each of which has an equal interest in the bank. They could not have received, from this state, a charter, unless it had been *similar* to that granted by congress. Without the approbation of congress, where all the states are represented, the directors would not be justified in agreeing to any alteration of the institution. If alterations are necessary; they should be made through the channel of the United States in congress assembled.

APPENDIX TO THE PRECEDING
CONSIDERATIONS

An Ordinance, to Incorporate the Subscribers
to the Bank of North America.

WHEREAS congress, on the twenty sixth day of May last, did, from a conviction of the support which the finances of the United States would receive from the establishment of a national bank, approve a plan for such an institution, submitted to their consideration by Robert Morris, Esq. and now lodged among the archives of congress, and did engage to promote the same by the most effectual means: and whereas the subscription thereto is now filled, from an expectation of a charter of incorporation from congress, the directors and president are chosen, and application hath been made to congress, by the said president and directors, for an act of incorporation: and whereas the exigencies of the United States render it indispensably necessary that such an act be immediately passed:

Be it therefore ordained, and it is hereby ordained by the United States in congress assembled, That those who are, and those who shall become subscribers to the said bank, be, and for ever after shall be, a corporation and body politick, to all intents and purposes, by the name and style of The President, Directors and Company of the Bank of North America.

And be it further ordained, That the said corporation are hereby declared and made able, and capable in law to have, purchase, receive, possess, enjoy and retain lands, rents, tenements, hereditaments, goods, chattels, and effects, of what kind, nature or quality soever, to the amount of ten millions of Spanish silver milled dollars, and no more, and also to sell, grant, demise, alien or dispose of the same lands, rents, tenements, hereditaments, goods, chattels and effects.

And be it further ordained, That the said corporation be, and shall be for ever hereafter, able and capable in law to sue and be sued, plead and be impleaded, answer and be answered unto, defend and be defended, in courts of record, or any other place whatsoever, and to do and execute all and singular other matters and things, that to them shall or may appertain to do.

And be it further ordained, That for the well governing of the said corporation, and the ordering of their affairs, they shall have such officers as they shall hereafter direct or appoint: provided nevertheless, that twelve directors, one of whom shall be the president of the corporation, be of the number of their officers.

And be it further ordained, That Thomas Willing be the present president; and that the said Thomas Willing and Thomas Fitzsimons, John Maxwell Nesbitt, James Wilson, Henry Hill, Samuel Osgood, Cadwallader Morris, Andrew Caldwell, Samuel Ingles, Samuel Meredith, William Bingham, Timothy Matlack, be the present directors of the said corporation, and shall so continue until another president and other directors shall be chosen, according to the laws and regulations of the said corporation.

And be it further ordained, That the president and directors of the said corporation shall be capable of exercising such power, for the well governing and ordering of the affairs of the said corporation, and of holding such occasional meetings for that purpose, as shall be described, fixed and determined by the laws, regulations and ordinances of the said corporation.

And be it further ordained, That the said corporation may make, ordain, establish and put in execution, such laws, ordinances and regulations, as shall seem necessary and convenient to the government of the said corporation: provided always, that nothing herein before contained shall be construed to authorize the said corporation to exercise any powers in any of the United States, repugnant to the laws or constitution of such state. And be it further ordained, That the said corporation shall have full power and authority to make, have, and use a common seal, with such device and inscription as they shall think proper, and the same to break, alter and renew, at their pleasure.

And be it further ordained, That this ordinance shall be construed and taken most favourably and beneficially for the said corporation.

Done by the United States in congress assembled, the thirty first day of December, in the year of our Lord one thousand seven hundred and eighty one, and in the sixth year of our independence.

JOHN HANSON, President.

Attest. CHARLES THOMSON, *Secretary.*

Office of Finance, January 8, 1782.

Sir,

I have the honour to transmit herewith an ordinance, passed by the United States in congress assembled the 31st day of December, 1781, incorporating the subscribers to the Bank of North America, together with sundry resolutions, recommending to the several states to pass such laws as they may judge necessary for giving the said ordinance its full operation. The resolutions of the 26th of May last speak so clearly to the points necessary to be established by those laws, that I need not enlarge on them. Should any thing more be found necessary upon experience, the president and directors will no doubt make suitable applications to congress, or to the states respectively, as the case may require. It affords me great satisfaction to inform your excellency, that this bank commenced its operations yesterday; and I am confident, that with proper management it will answer the most sanguine expectations of those who befriend the institution. It will facilitate the management of the finances of the United States: the several states may, when their respective necessities require, and the abilities of the bank will permit, derive occasional advantage and accommodations from it: it will afford to the individuals of all the states, a medium for their intercourse with each other, and for the payment of taxes, more convenient than the precious metals, and equally safe: it will have a tendency to increase both the internal and external commerce of North America, and undoubtedly will be infinitely useful to all the traders of every state in the Union: provided, as I have already said, it is conducted on the principles of equity, justice, prudence and economy. The present directors bear characters that cannot fail to inspire confidence; and as the corporation is amenable to the laws, power can neither sanctify any improper conduct, nor protect the guilty. Under a full conviction of these things, I flatter myself that I shall stand excused for recommending, in the strongest manner, this well meant plan, to all the encouragement and protection which your state can give, consistently with wisdom and justice. I have the honour to be, with great respect,

Your Excellency's most obedient, and most humble servant,

ROBERT MORRIS.

Circular to the Governours of each state.

An act for preventing and punishing the counterfeiting of the common seal, bank bills and bank notes of the president, directors and company of the Bank of North America, and for other purposes therein mentioned.

Sect. I. Whereas it is necessary to take effectual measures for preventing and punishing frauds and cheats, which may be put upon the president, directors and company of the Bank of North America, by altering, forging or counterfeiting the common seal, and the bank bills and bank notes of the said president, directors and company:

Sect. II. Be it therefore enacted, and it is hereby enacted by the representatives of the freemen of the commonwealth of Pennsylvania, in general assembly met, and by the authority of the same, That if any person or persons shall forge, counterfeit or alter the common seal of the said president, directors and company, or any bank bill or bank note, made or given out, or to be made or given out, for the payment of any sum of money by or for the said president, directors and company, or shall tender in payment, utter, vend, exchange or barter any such forged, counterfeit or altered bill or note, or shall demand to have the same exchanged for ready money by the said president, directors and company, or any other person or persons (knowing such bill or note so tendered, uttered, vended, exchanged or bartered, or demanded to be so exchanged, to be forged, counterfeit or altered) with intent to defraud the said president, directors, and company, or any other person or persons, bodies politick or corporate, then every such person or persons so offending, and being thereof convicted in due form of law, shall be deemed guilty of felony, and shall suffer death as a felon, without benefit of clergy.

Sect. III. And be it further enacted by the authority aforesaid, That if any president, director, or any officer or servant of the said president, directors, and company, being intrusted with any such bill or note, or any bond, deed, money or other effects, belonging to the said president, directors, and company, or having any such bill or note, or any bond, deed, money, or other effects, lodged or deposited with the said president, directors, and company, or with such officer or servant, as an officer or servant of the said president, directors and company, shall secrete, embezzle, or run away with any such bill, note, bond, deed, money or other effects, or any part of them, every president, director, officer or servant, so offending, and being thereof convicted, in due form of law, shall be deemed guilty of felony, and shall suffer death as a felon, without benefit of clergy.

Signed, by order of the House,
FREDERICK A. MUHLENBERG, Speaker.

Enacted into a Law, at Philadelphia, on Monday, the eighteenth day of March, in the year of our Lord one thousand seven hundred eighty and two.

PETER Z. LLOYD,
Clerk of the General Assembly.

Philadelphia, February 9, 1782.

Sir,

The president, directors and company of the Bank of North America, incorporated by the United States of America in congress assembled, have thought it proper to petition the General Assembly of Pennsylvania for a similar charter, and such further support from the legislature of the state, as may render the bank capable of yielding those advantages to the general cause of America, which are intended thereby: and this institution being encouraged and supported by citizens of other states, as well as that in which it happens to be established, the most respectful and proper mode of presenting the petition to that honourable house appearing to be through the supreme executive council of the state, we have enclosed the same to you, and request that you will please to lay it before the general assembly as soon as they shall meet. I have the honour to be,

Your excellency's most obedient servant,
THOMAS WILLING, *President.*

His excellency WILLIAM MOORE, *Esq. President.*

An Act to incorporate the Subscribers to the Bank of North America.

Sect. I. Whereas the United States in congress assembled, from a conviction of the support which the finances of the United States would receive from the establishment of a national bank, passed an ordinance to incorporate the subscribers for this purpose, by the name and style of "The President, Directors, and Company of the Bank of North America:"

And whereas the president and directors of the said bank have applied to this house for a similar act of incorporation, which request it is proper and reasonable to grant:

Sect. II. Be it therefore enacted, and it is hereby enacted by the representatives of the freemen of the commonwealth of Pennsylvania, in general assembly met, and by the authority of the same, That those who are, and those who shall become subscribers to the said bank, be and for ever hereafter shall be a corporation and body politick, to all intents and purposes, by the name and style of "The President, Directors and Company of the Bank of North America."

Sect. III. And be it further enacted by the authority aforesaid, That the said corporation are hereby declared and made able and capable in law, to have, purchase, receive, possess, enjoy and retain lands, rents, tenements, hereditaments, goods, chattels and effects, of what kind, nature or quality soever, to the amount of ten millions of Spanish silver milled dollars, and no more. And also to sell, grant, devise, alien, or dispose of the same lands, rents, tenements, hereditaments, goods, chattels and effects.

Sect. IV. And be it further enacted by the authority aforesaid, That the said corporation be, and shall be for ever hereafter, able and capable in law to sue and be sued, plead and be impleaded, answer and be answered unto, defend and be defended, in courts of record, or any other place whatsoever, and to do and execute all and singular other matters and things, that to them shall or may appertain to do.

Sect. V. And be it further enacted by the authority aforesaid, That for the well governing of the said corporation, and the ordering of their affairs, they shall have such officers as they shall hereafter direct or appoint. Provided nevertheless, That twelve directors, one of whom shall be the president of the corporation, be of the number of their officers.

Sect. VI. And be it further enacted by the authority aforesaid, That Thomas Willing be the present president, and that the said Thomas Willing, and Thomas Fitzsimons, John Maxwell Nesbitt, James Wilson, Henry Hill, Samuel Osgood, Cadwallader Morris, Samuel Engles, Samuel Meredith, William Bingham, Timothy Matlack and Andrew Caldwell, be the present directors of the said corporation, and shall so continue until another president and other directors shall be chosen, according to the laws and regulations of the said corporation.

Sect. VII. And be it further enacted by the authority aforesaid, That the president and directors of the said corporation shall be capable of exercising such powers, for the well governing and ordering of the affairs of the said corporation, and of holding such occasional meetings for that purpose, as shall be described, fixed and determined by the laws, regulations and ordinances of the said corporation.

Sect. VIII. And be it further enacted by the authority aforesaid, That the said corporation may make, ordain, establish and put in execution such laws, ordinances and regulations, as shall seem necessary and convenient for the government of the said corporation.

Sect. IX. Provided always, That nothing herein before contained shall be construed to authorize the said corporation to exercise any powers in this state, repugnant to the laws or constitution thereof.

Sect. X. And be it further enacted by the authority aforesaid, That the said corporation shall have full power and authority to make, have and use a common seal, with such devices and inscription as they shall think proper, and the same to break, alter and renew, at their pleasure.

Sect. XI. And be it further enacted by the authority aforesaid, That this act shall be construed and taken most favourably and beneficially for the said corporation.

Signed, by order of the House,
FREDERICK A. MUHLENBERG, *Speaker.*

Enacted into a Law, at Philadelphia, on Monday, the first day of April, in the year of our Lord one thousand seven hundred eighty and two.

PETER Z. LLOYD,
Clerk of the General Assembly.

ON the 16th day of February, 1782, advanced to the United States, on behalf of Pennsylvania, 80,000 dollars.

At different times in 1782, advanced to the commissioners for defence of the river and bay of Delaware, the sum of about 22,500 dollars.

On the 17th day of September, 1782, advanced to the state treasurer, for defence of the western frontiers, upon application of the house of assembly, 13,333 1-3 dollars, in part of a larger sum agreed to be lent, as the necessity of the state might require; but upon advice from the British commander in chief, that the Indians were called off our frontiers, this requisition stopped, and no further sum was taken out of the bank.

On the 18th day of April, 1784, paid the speaker's draft on the treasurer, accepted by him, in favour of James Mease, 16,000 dollars.

On the 6th of January, 1785, lent the managers of the house of employment, 4,000 dollars.

On the 26th of January, 1785, lent the city wardens the sum of 2,400 dollars.

Bibliographical Glossary

The purpose of this glossary is to identify the works Wilson referred to. The editions listed are not necessarily the particular ones Wilson used. In general, where multiple editions existed, I have cited an early edition, usually the first. In a few cases this did not seem advisable (e.g. Hooker's *Ecclesiastical Polity*, which was first published in embryonic form many years before the cited full-length edition which Wilson probably used), and I have then cited the earliest available full-length edition. Except for such completely self-explanatory references as those to the Bible, the United States Constitution, and national statutes, I have identified them all, even at some risk of explaining the obvious. A reader of these volumes is not likely to wonder what "Bl. Com." refers to, but "Ld. Ray." might slow him down a little, and the simplest course was to gloss everything. This has the additional advantage, as I said in the Introduction, of providing us with a compendious list of Wilson's scholarly sources.

In his classical citations, Wilson consistently uses the abbreviations l. for liber (book) and c. for capitulum (chapter).

(Addison) Tatler: Sir Richard Steele, Joseph Addison and others, *The Tatler*. London, 1709–1710.

Anac.: Jean Jacques Barthélemy, *Travels of Anacharsis the Younger in Greece* . . . First published in English in London, 1790–1791.

Anal. Rev.: *The Analytical Review*. London, 1788–1799.

Atk.: John Tracy Atkyns, *Reports of Cases Argued and Determined in the High Court of Chancery in the Time of Lord Chancellor Hardwicke.* 3 vols. London, 1765–1768.

Bac. on Gov.: See (Bacon) Discourses on Government.

(Bacon) Discourses on Government: Nathaniel Bacon, *An Historical and Political Discourse of the Laws and Government of England* . . . London, 1682.

Bar. on St.: Daines Barrington, *Observations on the More Ancient Statutes* . . . London, 1746.

(Barbeyrac) Pref. to Puff.: See Puff.

(Beccaria) C.: Cesare Beccaria, *An Essay on Crimes and Punishments. With a Commentary Attributed to Voltaire.* London, 1767.

Bever: Thomas Bever, *The History of the Legal Polity of the Roman State; and of the Rise, Progress, and Extent of the Roman Laws.* London, 1781.

Bl. Com.: Sir William Blackstone, *Commentaries on the Laws of England.* 4 vols. Oxford, 1765–1769.

Boh. Ins. Leg.: William Bohun, *Institutio Legalis; or, Introduction to the Study and Practice of the Laws of England* . . . London, 1708–1709.

Bol. Rem.: Henry St. John, Viscount Bolingbroke, *Remarks on the History of England*. London, 1743.

(Bolingbroke) Diss. on Part.: Henry St. John, Viscount Bolingbroke, *A Dissertation upon Parties* . . . London, 1735.

(Bolingbroke) Patriot King: Henry St. John, Viscount Bolingbroke, *Letters on the Spirit of Patriotism, on the Idea of a Patriotic King* . . . London, 1749.

Bol. Tracts: Henry St. John, Viscount Bolingbroke, *A Collection of Political Tracts*. London, 1748.

Bouch. The. Com.: Mathieu Antoine Bouchaud, *Théories des traites de commerce entre des nations* . . . Paris, 1777.

Bracton: Henry de Bracton, *De Legibus*. London, 1569.

Burgh Pol. Dis.: James Burgh, *Political Disquisitions; or, An Enquiry into Public Errors, Defects, and Abuses*. 3 vols. London, 1774–1775.

Burke, Reflections on French Rev.: Edmund Burke, *Reflections on the Revolution in France*. London, 1790.

Burl.: Jean Jacques Burlamaqui, *The Principles of Natural and Political Law* . . . 2 vols. London, 1763.

Burn's Ecc. Law: Richard Burn, *Ecclesiastical Law*. 2 vols. London, 1763.

Burr.: Sir James Burrow, *Reports of Cases Adjudged in the Court of King's Bench* . . . 5 vols. [London] 1766–1780.

Caes.: Caesar, *Commentarii Belli Gallici*.

(Caesar) de Bel. Gal.: Caesar, *Commentarii Belli Gallici*.

Chal.: George Chalmers, *Political Annals of the Present United Colonies*. London, 1780.

Cic. de Amic.: Cicero, *Laelius de Amicitia*.

Cic. de clar. orat.: Cicero, *Brutus*.

Cic. de fin.: Cicero, *De Finibus Bonorum et Malorum*.

Cic. de leg.: Cicero, *De Legibus*.

Cic. de leg. agr.: Cicero, *De Lege Agraria Oratio*.

Cic. de Nat. Deo.: Cicero, *De Natura Deorum*.

Cic. de off.: Cicero, *De Officiis*.

Cic. de orat.: Cicero, *De Oratore*.

Cic. Ep. ad Brut.: Cicero, *Epistulae ad Brutum*.

Cic. pro. Balb.: Cicero, *Pro Balbo*.

Cic. pro. Caec.: Cicero, *Pro A. Caecina*.

Cic. pro Cluent.: Cicero, *Pro Cluentio*.

Cic. pro dom.: Cicero, *De Domo Sua ad Pontifices Oratio*.

Cic. pro Mil.: Cicero, *Pro Milone*.

Cic. pro P. Syl.: Cicero, *Pro Publio Sulla*.

Cic. pro Rosc. Am.: Cicero, *Pro Sexto Roscio Amerino*.

Cic. Somn. Scip.: Cicero, *Somnium Scipionis* (in *De Re Publica* 6, 13).

Cic. Ver. V.: Cicero, *Actionis Secundae in C. Verrem Liber V*.

(Cicero) De Rep.: Cicero, *De Re Publica*.

(Cicero) Frag. de rep.: Cicero, *De Re Publica*. (Except for the *Somnium Scipionis*, this work was known in Wilson's time only in fragments quoted by other authors.)

(Coke) Ins.: Sir Edward Coke, *The Institutes of the Laws of England.* 4 parts. London, 1628–1644.

(Coke) Rep.: Sir Edward Coke, *The Reports of Sir Edward Coke . . . of Divers Resolutions and Judgements . . . of Cases in Law . . .* First Published in its entirety in English in London, 1658.

Col. Jur.: Frances Hargrave, *Collectanea Juridica . . .* 2 vols. London, 1791–1792.

Com. Per.: See Stu. V.

Cou. Ang. Norm.: David Houard, *Traités sur les coutumes anglo-normandes.* 4 vols. Paris, 1776.

Cro. Car.: Sir George Croke, *Reports, King's Bench and Common Bench* (1582–1641). Written in French; revised and published in English by Sir Harbottle Grimston. London, 1661–1667.

D.: See Dig.

Dag.: Henry Dagge, *Considerations on Criminal Law . . .* 3 vols. London, 1774.

Daws. Orig. Laws: George Dawson, *Origo Legum.* London, 1694.

de Bel. Gal.: See (Caesar) de Bel. Gal.

de leg.: See Cic. de leg.

De orat.: See Cic. de orat.

De Rep.: See (Cicero) De Rep.

Dig.: Corpus Juris Civilis. *Digesta.*

Domat: Jean Domat, *The Civil Law in Its Natural Order . . .* Translated by William Strahan. 2 vols. London, 1727.

Eden: William Eden, Baron Auckland, *Principles of Penal Law.* London, 1771.

Edin. Phil. Trans.: Royal Society of Edinburgh, *Transactions.* Vol. 1. Edinburgh, 1788.

El. Jur.: Richard Wooddeson, *Elements of Jurisprudence . . .* London, 1783.

Elem. Crit.: Henry Home, Lord Kames, *Elements of Criticism.* 3 vols. Edinburgh, 1762.

Encyc. Tit. Jurisprudence: *Encyclopédie méthodique: Jurisprudence.* 8 vols. Paris and Liège, 1782–1789.

F. N. B.: Sir Anthony Fitzherbert, *The New Natural Brevium . . .* (Translated into English) London, 1704.

Finch: Sir Henry Finch, *Laws, or a Discourse Thereof.* London, 1627.

Fleta: A treatise subtitled *seu Commentarius juris Anglicani,* written by an unknown author in about 1290. Wilson probably knew it only through Selden (q.v.).

(Fortescue) De Laud.: Sir John Fortescue, *De Laudibus . . .* London, 1616.

Fost.: Sir Michael Foster, *A Report of Some Proceedings . . . and of Other Cases . . .* Oxford, 1762.

Fr. Rev.: John Talbot Dillon, *Historical and Critical Memoirs of the General Revolution in France . . .* London, 1790.

Frag. de rep.: See (Cicero) Frag. de rep.

(Frederic of Prussia) K. Prus. works.: *Posthumous Works of Frederic II . . .* 13 vols. London, 1789.

Gen. Dict.: Pierre Bayle, *A General Dictionary . . . in which a New and*

Accurate Translation of that of Mr. Bayle is included . . . by John Peter Bernard . . . and Other Hands . . . 10 vols. London, 1734–1741.

Gent. Laws: Nathaniel Brassey Halhed, tr., *A Code of Gentoo Laws . . . Written in the Shanscrit Language.* London, 1776.

Gib.: See Gibbon.

Gibbon: Edward Gibbon, *The History of the Decline and Fall of the Roman Empire.* 12 vols. London, 1783–1790.

Gil.: See Gill.

Gil. Lys. and Isoc.: John Gillies, *Orations of Lysias and Isocrates.* London, 1778.

Gilb. Ev.: Sir Geoffrey Gilbert, *Law of Evidence.* Dublin, 1754.

Gill.: John Gillies, *The History of Ancient Greece, Its Colonies and Conquests.* 2 vols. London, 1786.

Gog. Or. Laws: Antoine Yves Goguet, *The Origin of Laws, Arts, and Sciences . . .* 3 vols. Edinburgh, 1761.

Grant's Ess.: James Grant, *Essays on the Origin of Society, Language, Property . . .* London, 1785.

Gro.: Hugo Grotius. *Of the Law of Warre and Peace.* London, 1654.

Guth.: William Guthrie, *A General History of England . . .* 4 vols. London, 1744–1751.

Hale P. C.: Sir Matthew Hale, *Historia Placitorum Coronae.* 2 vols. London, 1736.

Hale's Hist.: Sir Matthew Hale, *History and Analysis of the Common Law of England . . .* London, 1713.

Hardw.: Thomas Lee, *Cases Argued and Adjudged in the Court of King's Bench . . . ; During Which Time the Late Lord Chief Justice Hardwicke Presided in That Court* [1733–1738]. 2nd ed. London, 1815. (Wilson, of course, must have used the first edition, but the pagination seems to have been identical. The standard modern citation for this work is Cas. T. Hard.)

Haw.: William Hawkins, *A Treatise of Pleas of the Crown.* 2 vols. in one. London, 1716–1721.

Hein.: Johann Gottlieb Heineccius, *System of Universal Law.* 2 vols. London, 1741.

Henry: Robert Henry, *The History of Great Britain . . .* 6 vols. London, 1771–1793.

Hob.: Sir Henry Hobart, *Reports* (King's Bench, 1603–1625). London, 1641.

(Hobbes) De Cive: Thomas Hobbes, *De Cive.* [London] 1642. (It is probable that Wilson knew this work only through Pufendorf [q.v.].)

(Hobbes) Lev.: Thomas Hobbes, *Leviathan . . .* London, 1651.

Hooker: Richard Hooker, *Of the Laws of Ecclesiastical Polity.* First published in eight books with a life of the author by Isaak Walton. London, 1666.

(Hume) Ess.: David Hume, *Essays and Treatises on Several Subjects.* 2 vols. London, 1753.

(Hume) Tr. on hum. nat.: David Hume, *A Treatise of Human Nature.* London, 1739–1740.

Hutch.: Francis Hutcheson, *A System of Moral Philosophy.* 2 vols. London, 1755.

Ins.: See Just. Ins. or (Coke) Ins. depending on context.

Jenk.: David Jenkins, *Eight Centuries of Reports* . . . London, 1734.

Jour. Rep. (and) Jour. Sen.: *Annals of Congress.*

Just. Ins.: *Corpus Juris Civilis. Institutiones* (Institutes of Justinian).

Kaims, Hist. L. Tr.: Henry Home, Lord Kames, *Historical Law Tracts.* 2 vols. Edinburgh, 1758.

Kaims Pr. Eq.: Henry Home, Lord Kames, *Principles of Equity.* Edinburgh, 1760.

Kel.: Sir John Kelyng, *A Report of Divers Cases in Pleas of the Crown* . . . London, 1708. (The standard modern citation for this work is Kel. J.)

Ld. Bac.: Francis Bacon, *Works.* 4 vols. London, 1740. (Wilson may have used more than one edition of Bacon's works, but this seems the likely source for most of his citations.)

Ld. Ray.: Sir Robert Raymond, First Baron, *Reports, King's Bench and Common Pleas* [1694–1732]. 2 vols. London, 1775.

Leach: Thomas Leach, *Cases in Crown Law* . . . [1730–1789]. London, 1789.

Lel. Dem. Int. to oration de corona: Thomas Leland, translator, *The Orations of Aeschines and Demosthenes on the Crown* . . . *Volume the Third* . . . London, 1777. ("Int." refers to the translator's introduction to this volume.)

Lel. L. P. Prel.: See Lel. L. Phil. (The reference is to a "Preliminary Dissertation on the Council of Amphyctyons.")

Lel. L. Phil.: Thomas Leland, *The History of the Life and Reign of Philip, King of Macedon* . . . London, 1758.

Litt.: Sir Thomas Littleton, *Tenures in Englysshe.* London, 1544.

Liv.: Livy, *Ab Urbe Condita.*

Lock. Gov.: John Locke, *Two Treatises of Government.* London, 1690.

Locke on Hum. Und.: John Locke, *An Essay Concerning Human Understanding.* London, 1689.

M'D Ins.: Andrew MacDowell, *Institute of the Laws of Scotland* . . . 3 vols. Edinburgh, 1751–1753.

Mil.: See Millar.

Millar: John Millar, *An Historical View of the English Government, from the Settlement of the Saxons in Britain to the Accession of the House of Stewart.* London, 1787.

Milt.: John Milton, *The Works of Mr. John Milton* . . . 1697. (Wilson's reference is to this somewhat rare one-volume edition of Milton's prose, publisher unknown. The quotation in Wilson's footnote is a slight paraphrase of a sentence in *The Readie and Easie Way to Establish a Free Commonwealth.*)

Mir.: Andrew Horne, *The* . . . *Mirrour of Justices* . . . translated . . . by W. H. . . . London, 1646.

Mod.: *Modern Reports: or Select Cases, King's Bench.* 12 vols. London, 1698–1769.

Mod. Ent.: John Mallory, *Modern Entries in English* . . . 2 vols. London, 1734.

Molloy: Charles Molloy, *De Jure Maritimo et Navili; or, A Treatise of Affaires Maritime, and of Commerce.* London, 1676.

(Montesquieu) Sp. Laws: Charles Louis de Secondat, Baron de la Brède et de Montesquieu, *The Spirit of Laws*. 2 vols. London, 1750.

(Necker) Pref.: Jacques Necker, *Of the Importance of Religious Opinions*. London, 1788.

P. Wms.: William Peere Williams, *Reports of Cases, Court of Chancery . . .* (1695–1735) . . . by his son William Peere Williams. 3 vols. London, 1740–1749.

Paley: William Paley, *The Principles of Moral and Political Philosophy*. 2 vols. London, 1787.

Parl. Hist.: *The Parliamentary or Constitutional History of England . . .* 24 vols. London, 1751–1761.

Pett. (or Pet.) on Jur.: John Pettingal, *An Inquiry into the Use and Practice of Juries . . .* London, 1769.

Plin. Ep.: Pliny the Younger, *Epistulae*.

(Pope) Ess. on Man: Alexander Pope, *An Essay on Man*. London, 1733.

Pot. Ant.: John Potter, *Archaeologiae Graecae; or the Antiquities of Greece*. 2 vols. Oxford, 1697–1699.

Pri. Lect.: Joseph Priestley, *Lectures on History and General Policy . . .* London, 1788.

Pub.: *The Federalist . . .* 2 vols. New York, 1788.

Puff.: Samuel Pufendorf, *Of the Law of Nature and Nations . . .* carefully corrected, and compared with Mr. Barbeyrac's French translation, with the addition of his notes . . . Oxford, 1710.

R. O. Book. This refers to the Rolls Office books Wilson had himself compiled and which are referred to on p. 60 of the Preface.

Rapin: Paul de Rapin-Thoyras, . . . *An Historical Dissertation upon Whig and Tory . . .* London, 1717.

Reev.: John Reeves, *History of the English Law . . .* 4 vols. London, 1783–1784.

Reid Ess. Int.: Thomas Reid, *Essays on the Intellectual Powers of Man*. Edinburgh, 1785.

Reid Ess. Act.: Thomas Reid, *Essays on the Active Powers of Man*. Edinburgh, 1788.

(Reid) Inq.: Thomas Reid, *An Inquiry into the Human Mind, on the Principles of Common Sense*. Edinburgh, 1764.

Rep.: See (Coke) Rep.

Rob. Amer.: William Robertson, *The History of America*. 2 vols. London, 1777.

Rol. An. Hist.: Charles Rollin, *The Ancient History of the Egyptians, Carthaginians [etc.] . . .* 10 vols. London, 1734–1736.

Rol. R. H.: Charles Rollin, *The Roman History from the Foundation of Rome to the Battle of Actium . . .* Translated from the French. 2 vols. London, 1739.

Roll. Pref.: Perhaps Charles Rollin, *The Method of Teaching and Studying the Belles Lettres . . .* 4 vols. London, 1734.

(Rousseau) Or. Com. (and) Orig. Com.: Jean Jacques Rousseau, *The Social Contract*. (Wilson's references are to this work, probably to an English translation; but his abbreviations of the title fit no edition I have found.)

Rus. Anc. Eur.: William Russell, *The History of Ancient Europe* . . . 2 vols. London, 1793. (Manifestly Wilson could not have used this edition in 1790–91, yet it seems to be the first. This suggests that he may have made revisions of the lectures between 1791 and his death.)

Ruth.: Thomas Rutherforth, *Institutes of Natural Law*. 2 vols. Cambridge, 1754–1756.

Salk.: William Salkeld, *Reports of Cases Adjudged in the Court of King's Bench* . . . [1689–1712]. 2 vols. London, 1717.

(Saunderson) Prael.: Robert Sanderson, [probably] *De Obligatione Conscientiae* . . . London, 1660.

(Selden) Anal.: John Selden, *Analecton Anglo-Britannicon* . . . Francfurti, 1615.

(Selden) dissertation on Fleta: John Selden, *Fleta*. London, 1685.

(Selden) Table talk: John Selden, *Table Talk*. London, 1689.

Shaft.: Anthony Ashley Cooper, Earl of Shaftesbury, *Characteristicks of Men, Manners, Opinions, and Times*. 3 vols. London, 1711.

Sid.: Thomas Siderfin, *Les Reports des Divers Special Cases* . . . (1647–1670) 2 vols. in one. London, 1683–1684.

(Smith) Wealth of Nations: Adam Smith, *Wealth of Nations*. 2 vols. London and Edinburgh, 1776.

Spel. Rel.: Sir Henry Spelman, *Reliquiae Spelmannianae*. London, 1698.

St.: refers to British statutes, which were in Wilson's time usually cited as chapters of the statutes of the session of a particular regnal year; e.g. St. 13 Edw. 1 c. 24.

St. Tr.: *A Complete Collection of State-Trials* . . . 6 vols. London, 1730.

(Stewart) Pol. Ec.: Sir James Steuart, *An Inquiry into the Principles of Political Economy*. 2 vols. London, 1767.

Stith: William Stith, *The History of the First Discovery and Settlement of Virginia*. Williamsburg, 1747.

Stu. V.: Gilbert Stuart, *A View of Society in Europe* . . . Edinburgh, 1778. (The "Mr. Adair" referred to by Wilson was James Adair, author of *History of the American Indians*, London, 1775. "Com. Per." cited by Stuart refers to Garsilaso de la Vega, the Inca, *Los Comentarios Reales de los Incas*, Madrid, 1723.)

Str.: Sir John Strange, *Reports of Adjudged Cases* . . . [1713–1748]. 2 vols. London, 1755.

Sulliv.: Francis S. Sullivan, *Historical Treatise on the Feudal Law and the Constitution and Laws of England*. Dublin, 1772.

Swin.: Henry Swinburne, *Treatise of Testaments and Last Wills* . . . London, 1590.

Tac. Agric.: Tacitus, *Agricola*.

Tac. Ann.: Tacitus, *Annales*.

Tac. de mor. Germ.: Tacitus, *Germania* (the title *De Moribus Germanorum* appears in certain manuscripts).

(Taylor) Rule of Conscience: [probably] Jeremy Taylor, *The Rule and Exercises of Holy Living* . . . London, 1650.

Thom. Works: James Thomson, *The Works of Mr. Thomson*. 3 vols. London, 1738–1748.

Tibul. 1.1 Eleg.: Albius Tibullus, *Elegies*.

Tr. per Pais: Giles Duncombe, *Trials per Pais; or the Law Concerning Juries by Nisi Prius* . . . London, 1665.

Tr. on hum. nat.: David Hume, *Treatise of Human Nature*. London, 1739–1740.

Ub. Em.: Emmius Ubbo, *Graecorum Res Publicae* . . . *Lugduni Batavorum*, Ex Officina Elzeviriana, 1632.

Vat.: Emmerich de Vattel, *The Law of Nature*. Translated from the French. 2 vols. in one. London, 1759.

Vaugh.: Edward Vaughan, ed., *Reports and Arguments of* . . . *Sir John Vaughan Kt. Late Chief Justice of His Majesties Court of Common Pleas* . . . [1665–1674]. London, 1677.

Vent.: Sir Peyton Ventris, *Reports* . . . London, 1696.

War. Bib.: Jacques Pierre Brissot de Warville, *Bibliothèque philosophique du législateur, du politique, du jurisconsulte* . . . 10 vols. Berlin and Paris, 1782–1785.

War. The. L. Crim.: Jacques Pierre Brissot de Warville, *Théorie des loix criminelles*. 2 vols. Berlin, 1781.

Warv.: See War. The. L. Crim.

Whitak.: John Whitaker, *The History of Manchester*. 2 vols. London, 1771–1775.

Whitl.: Sir Bulstrode Whitelocke, *Notes Upon the King's Writ for Choosing Members of Parliament* . . . 2 vols. London, 1766.

Wils.: George Wilson, *Reports of Cases Argued and Adjudged in the King's Courts at Westminster* [1742–1774]. 2 vols. London, 1770–1775. (The standard modern citation for this work is Wils. K. B.)

Wood Ins.: Thomas Wood, *An Institute of the Laws of England*. 2 vols. London, 1720.

INDEX

Abraham, history of, 598

Abram and Lot, 713

Abstract notions and objects of nature, distinction between, 98–99

Abstraction, intellectual and moral, power of, 161–164

Accessories, before and after the fact, 677, 678, 816

Accounts, adjustment of, 492

Achaean League, 249–250, 762

Acquittal: former, 698; judgment of, 699; verdict of, 528, 531

Action, morality of an, 142

Adair, James, 715

Adams, Henry, 18n

Adams, John, 2, 13, 14, 37, 42; *Novanglus*, 3

Adams, Randolph G., 6

Addison, Joseph, 139, 593, 594

Adjournment, of legislatures, 420, 441

Aeschines, 400

Aetolian League, 250

Affray, as a common nuisance, 654, 655, 683

Age, qualifications of, 411–412

Agreements: common, 122, 179; solemn (fines) acknowledged and entered of record, 487

Agricola, Julius, 343

Agriculture, 158–159, 339, 344, 713, 715–717, 742n, 775–776

Alcoran, on mediation, 273

Alexander the Great, 84–85

Alfred the Great, 278, 347, 461, 464–465, 470, 475, 515, 527

Alienage, possible political, between U.S. and Pennsylvania, 799–801

Aliens, 359, 457, 458, 579–584, 700

Allegiance: bonds of, 243–246, 359–360, 363–364, 582; oath of, 412. *See also* American colonies, allegiance to king

Alliances, 166–167, 266

Amasis I, 580

American characteristics, 15, 37–38, 70, 72, 760–761

American colonies, 70–71, 185, 270, 359, 360–361, 459–460, 464, 742n; allegiance to king, 3, 10–11, 736–737, 742–745, 757; the case for, 721–746; common law in,

82, 360–362, 582; meaning of their dependency, 740–745; experiment in common property, 718; after the revolution, 768–769; reason for unpopularity abroad, 747–758

power of Parliament over, 3, 10–11, 112, 360, 363–368 *passim;* bound on principle of conquest, 739–741; bound by acts in which they are named, 740–745; cases proving they are not bound, 735–739

Amphictyonic Council, 247–249, 250, 258, 264, 762

Analogy, evidence arising from, 375, 390–392

Andrews, James DeWitt, 49

Anticipation and conviction, in the human mind, 384–385

Anti-Federalists, 6, 25, 26, 27

Antoninus, Marcus, 110

Antoninus Pius, 557

Appeals: of death, 613; prosecution by, 534–535, 687

Appointment to offices, 294–295, 440–441; as a power of king, 319–322

Apportionment, 1, 406, 417; of electors, 438

Apprehension, simple, a power of the mind, 229, 230

Apprentices, 584, 605–607

Arbitration, 273–274, 280, 470, 471, 492

Aristides, 447

Aristocracy, 302, 303, 771. *See also* Nobility

Aristotle, 76, 84–85, 98, 106–107, 139, 478, 573

Arraignment, 690–706 *passim*

Arrest, 420, 648–649, 676, 684–685, 810

Arson, 620–621, 644–645

Articles of Confederation, 3, 22, 23, 262–263, 828

Assault, 653–654

Assembly: unlawful, 655; of the colonies, 750–751

Assyria, 285

Athens, 105, 287–288, 340–342, 400, 406, 420n, 490, 597, 725n, 774; and aliens, 580–581; Cicero on the people of, 716; and laws of Draco, 805; impeachment

THE JOHN HARVARD LIBRARY

*The intent of
Waldron Phoenix Belknap, Jr.,
as expressed in an early will, was for
Harvard College to use the income from a
permanent trust fund he set up, for "editing and
publishing rare, inaccessible, or hitherto unpublished
source material of interest in connection with the
history, literature, art (including minor and useful
art), commerce, customs, and manners or way of
life of the Colonial and Federal Periods of the United
States . . . In all cases the emphasis shall be on the
presentation of the basic material." A later testament
broadened this statement, but Mr. Belknap's interests remained constant until his death.*

*In linking the name of the first benefactor of
Harvard College with the purpose of this later,
generous-minded believer in American culture the
John Harvard Library seeks to emphasize the importance of Mr. Belknap's purpose. The John Harvard
Library of the Belknap Press of Harvard University
Press exists to make books and documents
about the American past more readily
available to scholars and the
general reader.*